Power   **rd Edition**

Social movements have an elusive power but one that is altogether real. From the French and American Revolutions to the post-Soviet, ethnic, and terrorist movements of today, contentious politics exercises a fleeting but powerful influence on politics, society, and international relations. This study surveys the history of the modern social movements in the West and their diffusion to the global South through war and colonialism and puts forward a theory to explain their cyclical surges and declines. It offers an interpretation of the power of movements that emphasizes their effects on the lives of militants, policy reforms, political institutions, and cultural change. The book focuses on the rise and fall of social movements as part of contentious politics as the outcome of changes in political opportunities and constraints, state strategy, the new media of communication, and transnational diffusion.

Sidney G. Tarrow is Maxwell M. Upson Professor of Government and Professor of Sociology at Cornell University. His recent books include *Dynamics of Contention* (with Doug McAdam and Charles Tilly), *Contentious Europeans* (with Doug Imig), *Transnational Protest and Global Activism* (coedited with Donatella della Porta), *The New Transnational Activism*, and *Contentious Politics* (with Charles Tilly). He is currently researching war, state building, and human rights.

Cambridge Studies in Comparative Politics

General Editor
Margaret Levi   *University of Washington, Seattle*

Assistant General Editors
Kathleen Thelen   *Massachusetts Institute of Technology*
Erik Wibbels   *Duke University*

Associate Editors
Robert H. Bates   *Harvard University*
Stephen Hanson   *University of Washington, Seattle*
Torben Iversen   *Harvard University*
Stathis Kalyvas   *Yale University*
Peter Lange   *Duke University*
Helen Milner   *Princeton University*
Frances Rosenbluth   *Yale University*
Susan Stokes   *Yale University*

Other Books in the Series

Continued after the Index

Power in Movement

Social Movements and Contentious Politics

Revised and Updated Third Edition

SIDNEY G. TARROW
Cornell University

CAMBRIDGE
UNIVERSITY PRESS

CAMBRIDGE UNIVERSITY PRESS
Cambridge, New York, Melbourne, Madrid, Cape Town, Singapore,
São Paulo, Delhi, Dubai, Tokyo, Mexico City

Cambridge University Press
32 Avenue of the Americas, New York, NY 10013-2473, USA

www.cambridge.org
Information on this title: www.cambridge.org/9780521155724

First published 1994
Second edition published 1998
Revised and updated third edition 2011

Printed in the United States of America

A catalog record for this publication is available from the British Library.

Library of Congress Cataloging in Publication data

Tarrow, Sidney G.
Power in movement: social movements and contentious politics / Sidney Tarrow. – 3rd ed.
    p.   cm. – (Cambridge studies in comparative politics)
Includes bibliographical references and index.
ISBN 978-0-521-19890-5 (hardback) – ISBN 978-0-521-15572-4 (paperback)
1. Social movements – History.   2. Collective behavior – History.   3. Social change – History.
I. Title.
HM881.T37   2011
303.48′4–dc22   2010046018

ISBN 978-0-521-19890-5 Hardback
ISBN 978-0-521-15572-4 Paperback

For DEA and J LaP –
Mentors, colleagues, friends

Contents

Figures

Tables

Preface

When the second edition of *Power in Movement* appeared in 1998, it was during a period when it seemed to many that advanced industrial democracies such as America's had entered a period of social movement calm. In East Central Europe, the excitement generated by the collapse of Communism had subsided; in Western Europe, the talk was of postindustrial politics; and the United States was roiled with bitter but low-level conflicts such as that which surrounded the bedroom behavior of President Bill Clinton. In Africa, Latin America, and Southeastern Europe, festering conflicts had exploded into civil wars; to many American scholars, including this one, it seemed as if social conflict was being contained (Meyer and Tarrow, eds. 1998).

Toward the turn of the new century, changes in the "real world" and of contentious politics began to be translated into scholarly work. First, scholars questioned the airtight separation of social movement studies from other forms of contention (McAdam et al. 2001). Next, they began to ask how, if we were living in a social movement society, ordinary people were responding to the dislocations caused by global neo-liberalism. Finally, although the 1990s had been a decade of relatively contained conflict, questions were raised about the violent movements that, here and there, were already roiling the surface of society.

These questions came together in Seattle, when a coalition of domestic and transnational groups exploded onto the streets and shut down a meeting of the World Trade Organization. That protest electrified activists around the globe. In rapid succession, similar protests broke out in Genoa, Götenburg, Montreal, Prague, and Washington, DC. In that wave of contention, protesters not only attacked targets beyond the nation-state but began to experiment with a new and imaginative repertoire of contention. They combined peaceful and violent performances, face-to-face and electronic mobilization, and domestic and transnational actions, leaving many convinced of the coming decline of state sovereignty and the rise of a movement for global democracy. They also triggered a new and more aggressive repertoire of protest policing, causing the death of a protester in Genoa and the arrest of many in protests surrounding the Republican National Convention in New York in 2004.

Only a year into the new century, the massacres on 9/11/2001 unveiled a new axis of transnational conflict between insurgent Islamist movements and the United States and its allies. In the wake of those events, scholars and statesmen became aware that the era of contained contention was over. In the United States, police and federal security agencies ratcheted up surveillance of all manner of groups, whether or not they had a relationship with the Islamist threat; in Madrid and London, lethal train bombings led to fear of home-grown Islamist militants in the heart of Europe; meanwhile, in the East, a string of electoral corruption protests shook the quasi-authoritarian systems of Serbia, Ukraine, and Georgia, and the violence between Jews and Palestinians in Palestine/Israel ratcheted up with a new *Intifada*.

And that was not all: Under the government of George W. Bush, the anger, fear, and confusion of Americans at the massacres of September 11 were trans-fused into wars of reprisal and imperial expansion in Afghanistan and Iraq – the latter producing a brief but vital antiwar movement all over the planet. That movement failed to stop the rush to war, but it did give a boost to a new wave of antiwar contention. With its innovative use of the Internet to mobilize sup-porters, the movement sustained the surprising success of Governor Howard Dean in the 2004 primary elections and ultimately fed into the massive defeat of Bush's Republican Party in the elections of 2006 and 2008. The age of the Internet had entered the world of social movements.

In the meantime, global support for neo-liberalism began to erode. In Latin America, leftwing and indigenous-backed governments rose to power: first, in Venezuela and Chile; then in Brazil, Ecuador, and Bolivia. Each built on domestic sources of conflict, but all framed their domestic campaigns against global neo-liberalism. At the same time, in East Central Europe, where post-1989 governments had warmly embraced "the Washington consensus," a shift away from neo-liberal politics occurred as the costs of neo-liberalism began to sink in. And, finally, following the crisis set off by the Wall Street housing bubble, the entire edifice of the global financial system trembled, and a rhetoric of populism and class conflict spread across the world. Faced by these changes, new waves of contention began to traverse Europe and America.

Scholars were not slow to respond to these changes. The social movement canon that had been gradually constructed in the academy since the 1960s began to give way to new ideas and different perspectives. Some critics observed that scholars had focused too narrowly on Western reformist movements; oth-ers were troubled by the fact that existing models left out culture and emo-tions; still others complained that we had ignored the more violent forms of contention – civil wars, terrorist movements, and ethnic violence – that were spreading across the globe. Meanwhile, other scholars were investigating these broader expressions of contention, often with significant results, for example, in the systematic study of civil wars and guerilla insurgencies (Fearon and Laitin 2003; Collier and Sambanis, eds. 2006; Weinstein 2006).

Could these new efforts be blended with the more established tradition of social movement research? And could the latter encompass both the more violent forms of contention erupting in the global South and the dramatic increase in "nongovernmental organizations" around the planet? Some scholars – this author among them – thought the study of social movements could profit from a deliberate effort at integration with the study of other forms of contention and with newer strands of scholarship. With my collaborators, Doug McAdam and the late Charles Tilly, in a book titled *Dynamics of Contention,* we argued for an integration of social movement studies with the analysis of more violent forms of contention (McAdam, Tarrow, and Tilly 2001).

No one put this argument more pithily than the late Roger Gould, who called for a broadening of the social movement canon to encompass the study of "contentious collective action." Under this umbrella, Gould called for including in the same framework studies of "contemporary social movements along with peasant *jacqueries,* bread riots and grain seizures, slave revolts, 'rough music,' eighteenth and nineteenth century democratic societies, urban uprisings, artisanal blacklists and workshop turnouts, and revolutionary sects" (2005: 286). The second edition of *Power in Movement* already moved in this direction; this new edition has been revised and updated in the spirit of Gould's more expansive notion of contentious politics.

In 1998, when the second edition of *Power in Movement* appeared, it was still too early to integrate many of the new empirical developments and scholarly initiatives into a book already overloaded with movements, protests, campaigns, and evidence from different historical periods. That edition did include a chapter on the growing phenomenon of "transnational contention," but the book appeared before the major transnational campaigns of the new century erupted; it was too soon to take account of the growing role of the Internet as a vehicle for mobilization. And it was drafted just as its author was beginning to employ a deliberate mechanism and process approach to contentious politics. This edition attempts to fill these gaps.

This edition maintains almost the same structure as the last one. But it attempts to address four lacunae: First, it integrates new material on social movements in Europe and the United States that has appeared over the last decade. Second, the chapter on transnational contention has been expanded to take advantage of excellent new work on contention, beyond borders by Clifford Bob, Donatella della Porta, Jackie Smith, and others. Third, the book draws on new material on civil wars, terrorism, and guerilla movements, especially in the global South. And, finally, it builds on my collaboration with McAdam and Tilly, a partnership whose fruits are most evident in an almost entirely rewritten and expanded Part III.

Ithaca, New York
June 30, 2010

Acknowledgments

In revising this edition of *Power in Movement*, I have had the help of many people. Karen Beckwith's BA students at Wooster College and Bela Greskovits's graduate students at Central European University helped me to remember for whom I was writing. Particular chapters profited from the comments of Eitan Alimi, Karen Beckwith, Lance Bennett, Jennifer Earl, Ron Herring, Manuel Jiménez, Mary Fainsod Katzenstein, Doug McAdam, David S. Meyer, Debra Minkoff, Ann Mische, Jackie Smith, and Sarah Soule. Jennifer Hadden read the entire manuscript with her customary acuity and made many suggestions for improvement. Zoe Warhaft built and checked the bibliography with care and patience.

I cannot fail to recognize five people in particular. My first, and enduring, debt is still to Susan Tarrow. For more years than she may care to remember, she has awakened to the sound of computer keys clicking in the next room, a racket that followed her from New Haven and Ithaca to places as widespread as Elba, Florence, Oxford, twice to Paris, (a very wet) Quercy, Sydney, and Budapest. The computer is indifferent to her suffering, but I will be eternally grateful for her forbearance and her love.

The second is Lewis Bateman, for many years my editor at Cambridge University Press and a trusted collaborator and friend. Lew combines broad knowledge of many disciplines with a shrewd instinct for what readers will be interested in and a puckish sense of humor drawn from many years of editorial experience. His patience and his support helped me to complete this revision during an otherwise crowded period of my career.

Chuck Tilly left us before he could – as was his wont – read every word with microscopic attention. But his footprints are on every chapter, and whenever I came to a particularly difficult passage, he seemed to be looking over my shoulder. Two other individuals, the late David E. Apter and Joseph La Palombara, were my teachers before becoming colleagues and friends. The dedication of this book to them is a delayed recognition of my debt to them – alas, too late for David to read it. Each has been a model of the active, engaged scholar I have striven to emulate, and both have been more responsible than they could know for whatever success I have had.

Introduction

On May 30th, 2010, six ships left Turkey and approached the coast of Israel/ Palestine to deliver supplies to the coastal enclave of Gaza. Most of the ships were owned by a Turkish NGO called the IHH (İnsani Yardım Vakfi, or Foundation for Human Rights and Freedoms).[1] On board were over 600 peace, humanitarian, and pro-Palestinian, anti-Israel activists determined to break the blockade with which, since 2007, Israel had been strangling the economy of Gaza. Approaching the coast, the flotilla was attacked from sea and air by an Israeli commando squadron. When the attack ended, nine activists lay dead or dying, and a number of Israeli commandos were wounded, some of them seriously.

How did this happen, and what does it have to do with "contentious politics"? In 2007, the Gaza Strip, a detached part of the Palestinian territories, was taken over from the more moderate Palestinian governmental party, Fatah, in a bloody coup by the radical Hamas group. From that point on, the Israeli army began to limit access to Gaza, both for fear of arms getting into the hands of Hamas militants, who had been attacking Israeli settlements, and to isolate Hamas, an Islamist group that continued to call for Israel's destruction. Those measures were not sufficient to prevent home-made missiles from killing Israelis living in towns near the border. Under pressure from public opinion and with an election approaching, in January 2009, the Israeli Defense Forces (IDF) launched a massive land and air attack on the population of Gaza, destroying thousands of buildings, damaging a UN humanitarian center, and killing over a thousand people.

---

[1] The IHH describes itself as an Islamic charity that was formed to provide aid to Bosnia in the mid-1990s. It has been involved in aid missions in Africa and Asia and in the Palestinian territories, and it played an important role in provisioning Gaza after the Israeli blockade began in 2007. The IHH is technically an NGO, but it maintains ties with the ruling Islamist Justice and Development Party in Turkey. Its top fundraisers are Turkey's Islamist merchant class. The organization is banned in Israel. For more information, go to www.ihh.org.tr/Haber_Manset_ Ayrintilar.160±M5563920baaa.o.html (in Turkish).

After the January 2009 "operation," Israeli pressure became even greater, turning Gaza into a virtual prison for the million-and-a-half Palestinians living there. While Israel allowed in food and medicine, it controlled water and electricity supplies and blocked the entry of anything that could conceivably be used to construct weapons – including fertilizer, metal, and computer chips, as well as a list of nuisance items that included, at one time or another, light bulbs, candles, matches, books, musical instruments, crayons, clothing, coffee, tea, cookies, and shampoo.

The blockade had three major defects: First, it increased the influence of foreign humanitarian groups, including the IHH. Second, it had a devastating impact on Gaza's economy, increasing the power of Hamas through which almost all foreign aid was distributed. And third, it created a flourishing underground economy and a class of smugglers bringing in supplies through tunnels from Egypt. This led to constant Israeli attacks on the smugglers' tunnels and to rising tensions between Israel and Egypt. Cut off from the world, unable to get the supplies needed to rebuild their homes, the Gazans relied on the sympathy of fellow Arabs, the United Nations, various humanitarian groups, mainly from Western Europe, and Turkey, since 2002 under the leadership of a moderately Islamist party attempting to better its relations with fellow Muslims in the Middle East.

In January 2010, planning began for the flotilla that would leave Turkey in May to try to challenge the blockade. The IHH "brought large boats and millions of dollars of donations to a cause that had struggled to gain attention and aid the Palestinians. Particularly galling to Israel," the *New York Times* noted, "is the fact that the group comes from Turkey, an ally, but one whose relations with Israel have become increasingly strained."[2] Both directly and through its ties with the Turkish government, the Israeli government gave warnings to turn back, but the flotilla's leaders refused, and on the 31st, a squadron of Israeli warships and helicopter gunships attacked.

The flotilla was not unprepared: When Israeli commandos were lowered onto the ships on ropes from their helicopters, they were at first overwhelmed by well-trained Islamist militants. Several of the Israeli soldiers lost their weapons, which were turned on the attackers. But the numbers and the firepower of the IDF proved too much for the defenders. When the melee ended, nine militants had been killed and a number of Israeli attackers wounded, two of them seriously.

Although the IHH action was deliberately provocative,[3] seldom was there so stark a contrast between the peaceful tactics of a movement and the violent response of its target. Though an Israeli government spokesman painted the activists as "an armada of hate and violence in support of the Hamas terror

---

[2] *New York Times*, June 1, 2010.
[3] As a board member of the group said, "We became famous; we are very thankful to the Israeli authorities." *New York Times*, June 1, 2010.

organisation . . . ,"[4] the international press and progressive groups responded with outrage. Predictably, the Arab and Palestinian press were the most violent in their denunciations, but the European press was almost as vehement; the usually conservative *Economist* editorialized, "A policy of trying to imprison the Palestinians has left their jailer strangely besieged."[5] More surprising, the normally pro-Israeli *New York Times* pronounced that the Israeli blockade must end.[6]

Governments around the world were quick to respond. Denmark, France, Greece, Norway, Spain, Sweden, Egypt, and South Africa all summoned Israeli ambassadors to condemn the attack. Greece suspended joint military exercises, and Turkey withdrew its ambassador and cancelled military cooperation and joint water projects. Leftwing governments, such as Nicaragua's, suspended diplomatic relations, but even more friendly governments, such as Ireland's, cancelled an appearance of Israel's ambassador before a parliamentary committee.[7] Most important, Israel's only ally, the United States, condemned the violence and called for an end to the boycott of Gaza.

But more striking than the reactions of the press or the politicians was the overwhelming reaction of nonstate actors around the world. Civil society groups, social movements, unions, and religious groups (including some Jewish ones) condemned the attack on the flotilla and organized protests in dozens of cities. In the Arab world, 285 civil society groups signed a statement against the Israeli action; in South Africa, unions called for making every municipality an "Apartheid Israel Free Zone"; in Britain, UNITE called for a policy of divestment in Israeli companies; in Norway, the chair of the largest Norwegian union federation called for divestment by the state's pension fund; and in Sweden, the port workers' union called for a boycott of Israeli ships.[8] A number of other groups – including a coalition of European Jews – either immediately launched ships in the direction of Gaza or planned to do so in the near future.

The most widespread response was a call for a boycott.[9] And in the days after the attack, a number of well-known performance artists cancelled their

---

[4] Statement of Danny Ayalon, Deputy Foreign Minister, on May 31, 2010, quoted in www. guardian.co.uk/world/2010/may/31/q-a-gaza-freedom-flotilla. Visited on June 8, 2010.

[5] *The Economist* went on to point out that the attack on a Turkish ship and the killing of nine Turkish citizens (one of them with a U.S. passport as well) "is depriving Israel of a rare Muslim ally and mediator." *The Economist*, June 5th–11th, 2010, pp. 13–14.

[6] *The Times* criticized the Obama Administration's tepid response to the attack, urging the government to join other major powers in calling for an end of the blockade. *New York Times,* June 1, 2010. President Obama satisfied himself by characterizing the blockade as "unsustainable." Visited at www.nytimes.com/2010/06/02/opinion/02wed1.html, June 10, 2010.

[7] These selected reactions are reported in "Activism News" on its Web site at electronicintifada.net/v2/article11318.shtml. Visited June 7, 2010.

[8] These reports also come from "Activism News," cited in note no. 7.

[9] The diffusion of the boycott call was remarkable. A simple Google search for "Gaza & boycott" came up with more than one million five hundred thousand "hits." A narrower search for "Gaza & boycott & unions" produced 568,000. And what I thought would produce only a few "hits" – a search for "Gaza & boycott & *artists*" – led to 182,000 hits!

appearances in Israel. What had begun as an effort by a radical Islamist group to break a blockade ended in a global wave of negative publicity and a widespread call to boycott Israel, whose leaders refused to cooperate with an international investigation of the killings. But the combination of the brazen attempt to break the blockade, the killing of nine civilians in international waters, and the widespread condemnation of Israel's behavior did have consequences. In the United States, it began to dawn on foreign policy elites that the Israeli alliance was becoming a liability.[10] In the World Zionist Congress, a split occurred between a liberal majority that urged the Israeli government to soften its stand and a vocal minority that attempted to block the majority resolution.[11] And in Israel itself, in late June, the government bowed to international pressure and agreed to soften the blockade.[12]

WHAT WAS HAPPENING HERE?

What does the story of the Israeli attack on the Turkish-led "flotilla" tell us? We could interpret it in moral terms, either as the attempt of an intrepid band of missionaries to help their desperate co-religionists, or as the justified attempt of a besieged nation to protect its security. We could see it as an example of how small-power politics can threaten to up-end big-power relationships. We could also see it as an example of what I call "contentious politics" – what happens when collective actors join forces in confrontation with elites, authorities, and opponents around their claims or the claims of those they claim to represent.

From a contentious politics perspective, we can take away seven important lessons from the Israeli attack on the flotilla and the response to it:

First, the range of actors in the story goes well beyond the traditional subject of "social movements." Two major states, Israel and Turkey, the Islamist movement Hamas, a flotilla packed with humanitarian, peace, and pro-Palestinian NGOs, Israeli voters, European unions and governments, and global public opinion all came together in the conflict over Gaza. If we were to focus only on social movements, we would have told a rather truncated story. In this book, I will develop a relational approach to contentious politics, which focuses more

---

[10] As the usually conservative American security commentator Anthony Cordesman wrote,

> "...the depth of America's moral commitment does not justify or excuse actions by an Israeli government that unnecessarily make Israel a strategic liability when it should remain an asset."

Go to www.normanfinkelstein.com/anthony-cordesman-is-whistling-a-new-tune/. Visited June 8, 2010.

[11] For a report from a surprised liberal group that was involved in passing the resolution, go to www.jstreet.org/blog/?p-1110. Visited June 18, 2010.

[12] The Security Cabinet's decision can be found at http://www.pmo.gov.il/PMOEng/Communication/Spokesman/2010/06/spokemediniyut170610.htm. Visited June 18, 2010.

on the interactions among divergent actors than on the classical subject of social movements.

Second, the story shows how, under certain conditions, even small and temporary groups of collective actors can have explosive effects on powerful states. Without the provocation of the "freedom flotilla," it is doubtful that the world's attention would have focused on the festering sore of Gaza, or that Israel would have softened its blockade.

Third, the story illustrates the importance of spirals of *political opportunities and threats* in opening windows for contentious politics. Even in Israel, Leftist opposition groups gathered to protest the Israeli raid and were met with hostility by rightwing opponents.[13] We will give great attention to such spirals and to the "cycles of contention" that they constitute.

Fourth, the story tells us that we cannot understand episodes of contention without examining how contentious and institutional politics – including electoral politics – intersect. In the spring of 2010, Israel was governed by a weak and divided center-right coalition under a leader, Benjamin Netanyahu, who had already shown his willingness to bow to extreme xenophobic opinion. The threats to his government from the Right were important factors in the decision to attack the flotilla – an action that produced an opportunity for movement actors to mobilize. In this book, I will give particular attention to the interaction among contentious and institutional politics.

Fifth, the story shows the importance of what I will call "modular performances and repertoires" of collective action. The boycott is by now a familiar form of contention, instantly recognizable around the world. But it wasn't always so; contentious politics has to be *learned,* and once forms of contention are seen to be viable, they diffuse rapidly and become modular. So common is the boycott form that pro-Israeli groups responded to the Swedish boycott threat with a boycott threat of their own![14] An important theme of this book is the modularity of forms of contention and their diffusion.

Sixth, the story demonstrates the growing importance of transnational networking and mobilization, including mobilization through the Internet. Not only did the activists on the flotilla come from across the sea and represent several nations; an almost instant and overwhelming response to their actions came from around the world – including from the international Zionist community. We will investigate this growth of transnational contention and ask whether it is giving rise to a "global civil society."

Finally, the story shows how widespread what we will call the "social movement repertoire" has become. Some scholars have wondered whether the world is becoming "a social movement society" (Meyer and Tarrow, eds. 1998). But that term first surfaced in the 1990s, when it seemed that peaceful forms of contentious action were spreading among ordinary people. With the turn of

---

[13] Go to http://www.haaretz.com/news/national/leftist-and-rightist-israelis-clash-at-gaza-flotilla-protest-in-tel-aviv-1.294359 for a report on this clash. Visited June 8, 2010.

[14] Go to www.israelforum.com/board/showthread.php?t=10127. Visited June 7, 2010.

the new century, and especially after September 11, 2001, the phrase "social movement society" has taken on a new and more forbidding meaning. We will ask whether transgressive politics is beginning to overwhelm contained politics, and, if so, what are its implications for civil politics. But first we must clarify two key terms that will be employed in this book and their relationship to one another: social movements and contentious politics.

Social Movements in Contentious Politics

Ordinary people often try to exert power by contentious means against national states or opponents. In the last fifty years alone, the American Civil Rights movement, the peace, environmental and feminist movements, revolts against authoritarianism in both Europe and the Third World, and the rise of new Islamist movements have brought masses of people into the streets demanding change. They often succeeded, but even when they failed, their actions set in motion important political, cultural, and international changes.

Contentious politics occurs when ordinary people – often in alliance with more influential citizens and with changes in public mood – join forces in confrontation with elites, authorities, and opponents. Such confrontations go back to the dawn of history. But mounting, coordinating, and sustaining them against powerful opponents is the unique contribution of the social movement – an invention of the modern age and an accompaniment of the rise of the modern state. Contentious politics is triggered when changing political opportunities and constraints create incentives to take action for actors who lack resources on their own. People contend through known repertoires of contention and expand them by creating innovations at their margins. When backed by well-structured social networks and galvanized by culturally resonant, action-oriented symbols, contentious politics leads to sustained interaction with opponents – to social movements.

How ordinary people take advantage of incentives created by shifting opportunities and constraints; how they combine conventional and challenging repertoires of action; how they transform social networks and cultural frameworks into action – and with what outcomes; how these and other factors combine in major cycles of protest and sometimes in revolutions; how the Internet and other forms of electronic communication are changing the nature of mobilization; and how the social movement is changing in the twenty-first century – these are the main themes of this book.

These themes take on special moment given the vast spread and growing diversity of contentious politics today. Just think of the variety of social movements since the 1960s: first civil rights and student movements; ecology, feminism, and peace movements; struggles for human rights in authoritarian and semi-authoritarian systems; Islamic and Jewish religious extremism in the Middle East and Hindu militantism in India; anti-immigrant violence in Western Europe and Christian fundamentalism in the United States; ethnic nationalism in the Balkans and the former Soviet Union; and suicide bombings in Iraq,

Afghanistan, and Pakistan. Over the past five decades, a wave of new forms of contention has spread from one region of the world to another, and among different social and political actors.

Not all these events warrant the term "social movement," a term I will reserve for sequences of contentious politics based on underlying social networks, on resonant collective action frames, and on the capacity to maintain sustained challenges against powerful opponents (see Chapter 1). But all are part of the broader universe of contentious politics, which emerges, on the one hand, from within institutional politics, and can expand, on the other, into revolution. Placing the social movement and its particular dynamics historically and analytically within this universe of contentious politics is a central goal of this study.

The Approach of the Study

In this book, I will not attempt to write a history of social movements or the broader field of contentious politics. Nor will I press a particular theoretical perspective on my readers or attack others – a practice that has added more heat than light to the subject. Instead, I will offer a broad theoretical framework for understanding the place of social movements, cycles of contention, and revolutions within the more general category of contentious politics. Too often, scholars have focused on particular theories or aspects of movements to the detriment of others. One example is how the subject of revolution has been treated. It is mainly seen in comparison with other revolutions, but in isolation from ordinary politics and almost never compared with the cycles of protest that it in some ways resembles (but see Goldstone 1998). We need a broader framework with which to connect social movements to contentious politics and to politics in general.[15] This book takes up this challenge.

CONTENTIOUS COLLECTIVE ACTION

The irreducible act that lies at the base of all social movements, protests, rebellions, riots, strike waves, and revolutions is *contentious collective action*. Collective action can take many forms – brief or sustained, institutionalized or disruptive, humdrum or dramatic. Most of it occurs routinely within institutions, on the part of constituted groups acting in the name of goals that would hardly raise an eyebrow. Collective action becomes contentious when it is used by people who lack regular access to representative institutions, who act in the name of new or unaccepted claims, and who behave in ways that fundamentally challenge others or authorities.

Contentious collective action serves as the basis of social movements, not because movements are always violent or extreme, but because it is the main and often the only recourse that most ordinary people possess to demonstrate

---

[15] For this argument with illustrative syntheses, see McAdam, Tarrow, and Tilly 2001.

their claims against better-equipped opponents or powerful states. This does not mean that movements do nothing else but contend: they build organizations, elaborate ideologies, and socialize and mobilize constituencies, and their members engage in self-development and the construction of collective identities. Moreover, some movements are largely a-political, and focus on their internal lives or those of their members. But even such movements, as sociologist Craig Calhoun reminds us, encounter authorities in conflictual ways, because it is these authorities who are responsible for law and order and for setting the norms for society (1994b: 21). Organizers exploit political opportunities, respond to threats, create collective identities, and bring people together to mobilize them against more powerful opponents. Much of the history of movement/state interaction can be read as a duet of strategy and counterstrategy between movement activists and power holders.

"Collective action" is not an abstract category that is outside of history and stands apart from politics (Hardin, 1982; 1995). Contentious forms of collective action are different from market relations, lobbying, or representative politics because they bring ordinary people into confrontation with opponents, elites, or authorities. This means that the particular historical, cultural, and power conditions of their society in part determine and in part are determined by contentious politics. Ordinary people have power because they challenge power holders, produce solidarities, and have meaning to particular population groups, situations, and national cultures.

This means that we will have to embed the general formulations of collective action theory into history with the insights of sociology and political science and anthropology. In particular, we will see that bringing people together in sustained interaction with opponents requires a *social* solution – aggregating people with different demands and identities and in different locations in concerted campaigns of collective action. This involves, first, mounting collective challenges, second, drawing on social networks, common purposes, and cultural frameworks, and third, building solidarity through connective structures and collective identities to sustain collective action. These are the basic properties of social movements.

The Basic Properties of Movements

With the emergence of the social movement in the eighteenth century, as I will show in Part I, early theorists focused on the three facets of movements that they feared the most: extremism, deprivation, and violence. Both the French Revolution and early nineteenth century industrialism lent strength to this negative reaction. Led by sociologist Emile Durkheim (1951), nineteenth century observers saw social movements as the result of anomie and social disorganization – an image well captured in the phrase "the madding crowd" (see the review in McPhail 1991).

While the late nineteenth and early twentieth centuries saw the normalization of movement activism into Social Democratic and Labor Parties, the movements of the interwar period – in the form of Italian fascism, German Nazism, and Soviet Stalinism – fit the image of violence and extremism fostered earlier by the French and Industrial Revolutions. With the exacerbation of ethnic and nationalist tensions after the fall of communism in 1989–1992 and the terrorist outrages of the first decade of the twenty-first century, this negative view of social movements has been reinforced. We saw this view re-emerge in the "ancestral hatred" views of the Balkan conflicts of the 1990s, most of them uninformed by social movement theory. We saw it again in the anti-immigrant violence in Europe, which evoked the horrors of the interwar years. And we see it most dramatically in the reactions to the militantism of Al Queda and other Islamist movements since the turn of the century.

But these are extreme versions of more fundamental characteristics of social movements. Extremism is an exaggerated form of the dramatization of meaning that is found in all social movements – what I will call in Chapter 7 "movement framing"; deprivation is a particular form of the common purposes that all movements express; and violence is an exacerbation of collective challenges, often the product of public clashes with police, rather than the intention of activists. Rather than defining social movements as expressions of extremism, violence, and deprivation, they are better defined as *collective challenges, based on common purposes and social solidarities, in sustained interaction with elites, opponents, and authorities*.[16] This definition has four empirical properties: collective challenge, common purpose, social solidarity, and sustained interaction. (For a similar definition, see Tilly and Wood 2009.) Let us examine each of these briefly before turning to an outline of the book.

COLLECTIVE CHALLENGES

Collective action has many forms – from voting and interest group affiliation to bingo tournaments and football matches. But these are not the forms of action most characteristic of social movements. Movements characteristically mount *contentious* challenges through disruptive direct action against elites, authorities, other groups, or cultural codes. Most often public in nature, disruption can also take the form of coordinated personal resistance or the collective affirmation of new values (Melucci 1996).

Contentious collective challenges most often are marked by interrupting, obstructing, or rendering uncertain the activities of others. But particularly in

---

[16] Charles Tilly writes:

> Authorities and thoughtless historians commonly describe popular contention as disorderly.... But the more closely we look at that same contention, the more we discover order. We discover order created by the rooting of collective action in the routines and organization of everyday social life, and by its involvement in a continuous process of signaling, negotiation, and struggle with other parties whose interests the collective action touches.

See his *The Contentious French* (1986: 4).

authoritarian systems, where overt protest is likely to be repressed, they can also be symbolized by slogans, forms of dress or music, graffiti, or renaming of familiar objects with new or different symbols. Even in democratic states, people identify with movements by words, forms of dress or address, and private behavior that signify their collective purpose.[17]

Contention is not limited to social movements, though contention is their most characteristic way of interacting with other actors. Interest groups sometimes engage in direct challenges, as do political parties, voluntary associations, and groups of ordinary citizens who have nothing in common but a temporary coincidence of claims against others (Burstein 1998). Nor are contentious challenges the only form of action we see in movements. Movements – especially organized ones – engage in a variety of actions ranging from providing "selective incentives" to members, to building consensus among current or prospective supporters, to lobbying and negotiating with authorities, to challenging cultural codes through new religious or personal practices.

In recent decades, just as interest groups and others have increasingly engaged in contentious politics, movement leaders have become skilled at combining contention with participation in institutions. Think of the healthcare debate that roiled American politics in 2009–2010. Although it was dominated rhetorically by the debate in Congress and financially by well-heeled Washington lobbies, much of the public saw it through the lens of the so-called "Tea Parties" – in imitation of the Boston Tea Party, which helped to touch off the American Revolution – and the "town meetings" at which well-orchestrated challenges were organized against members of Congress who supported reform (see Chapter 5).

Despite their growing expertise in lobbying, legal challenges, and public relations, the most characteristic actions of social movements continue to be contentious challenges. This is not because movement leaders are psychologically prone to violence, but because they lack the stable resources – money, organization, access to the state – that interest groups and parties control. In appealing to new constituencies and asserting claims, contention may be the only resource that movements control. Movements use collective challenge to become the focal points of supporters, gain the attention of opponents and third parties, and create constituencies to represent.

COMMON PURPOSES

Many reasons have been proposed for why people affiliate with social movements, ranging from the desire of young people to flaunt authority all the way to the vicious instincts of the mob. While it is true that some movements are marked by a spirit of play and carnival and others reveal the grim frenzy of the mob, there is a more common – if more prosaic – reason why people band

---

[17] Such movements have been characterized as "discursive" by political scientist Mary Katzenstein, who studied the movement of radical Catholic women in America in her *Faithful and Fearless* (1998). I will return to the relations between discourse and collective action in Chapter 7.

together in movements: to mount common claims against opponents, authorities, or elites. Not all such conflicts arise out of class interest, but common or overlapping interests and values are at the basis of their common actions.

Both the theory of "fun and games" and that of mob frenzy ignore the considerable risks and costs involved in acting collectively against well-armed authorities. The rebel slaves who challenged the Roman Empire risked certain death when they were defeated; the dissenters who launched the Protestant Reformation against the Catholic Church took similar risks. Nor could the African American college students who sat-in at segregated lunch counters in the American South expect much fun at the hands of the thugs who awaited them with baseball bats and abuse. People do not risk their skin or sacrifice their time to engage in contentious politics unless they have good reason to do so. It takes a common purpose to spur people to run the risks and pay the costs of contentious politics.

SOCIAL SOLIDARITY

The most common denominator of social movements is thus "interest," but interest is no more than a seemingly objective category imposed by the observer. It is participants' *recognition* of their common interests that translates the potential for a movement into action. By mobilizing consensus, movement entrepreneurs play an important role in stimulating such consensus. But leaders can create a social movement only when they tap into and expand deep-rooted feelings of solidarity or identity. This is almost certainly why nationalism and ethnicity or religion have been more reliable bases of movement organization in the past than the categorical imperative of social class (Anderson 1990; C. Smith ed. 1996).[18]

Is an isolated incident of contention – for instance, a riot or a mob – a social movement? Usually not, because participants in these forms of contention typically have no more than temporary solidarity and cannot sustain their challenges against opponents. But sometimes, even riots reveal hints of a common purpose or solidarity. The ghetto riots all over America in the 1960s or in Los Angeles in 1992 were not movements in themselves, but the fact that they were triggered by police abuse indicates that they arose out of a widespread sense of injustice. Mobs, riots, and spontaneous assemblies are more an indication that a movement is in the process of formation than movements themselves.

SUSTAINING CONTENTION

Long before organized movements began, contentious politics took many forms on the scene of history – from food riots and tax rebellions to religious wars

---

[18] Some students of social movements take the criterion of common consciousness to an extreme. Rudolf Heberle, for example, thought a movement had to have a well worked-out ideology. See his *Social Movements: An Introduction to Political Sociology* (1951). But others, such as Alberto Melucci, think that movements purposefully "construct" collective identities through constant negotiation. See Melucci's "Getting Involved: Identity and Mobilization in Social Movements" (1988).

and revolutions – as we will see in Chapter 2. It is only by sustaining collective action against antagonists that a contentious episode becomes a social movement. Common purposes, collective identities, and identifiable challenges help movements to do this; but unless they can maintain their challenge, movements will evaporate into the kind of individualistic resentment that James Scott calls "resistance" (1985), will harden into intellectual or religious sects, or their members will defect from activism into isolation. Sustaining collective action in interaction with powerful opponents marks the social movement off from the earlier forms of contention that preceded it in history and accompany it today.

Yet movements are seldom under the control of a single leader or organization; how can they sustain collective challenges in the face of personal fear or egotism, social disorganization, and state repression? This is the dilemma that has animated collective action theorists and social movement scholars over the past few decades. My strongest argument will be that it is changes in public political opportunities and constraints that create the most important incentives for triggering new phases of contention for people with collective claims. These actions in turn create new opportunities both for the original insurgents and for late-comers, and eventually for opponents and power holders. The cycles of contention – and in rare cases, the revolutions – that ensue are based on the externalities that these actors enjoy and create. The outcomes of such waves of contention depend not on the justice of the cause or the persuasive power of any single movement, but on their breadth and on the reactions of elites and other groups.

I will turn to these political opportunities and constraints in Chapter 8. But here it is important to underscore what I do *not* mean by this. I do not claim that "objective" opportunities automatically trigger episodes of contentious politics or social movements, regardless of what people think or feel. Individuals need to *perceive* political opportunities and to be *emotionally engaged by their claims* if they are to be induced to participate in possibly risky and certainly costly collective actions; and they need to *perceive* constraints if they are to hesitate to take such actions. As we will see in the following chapters, individuals are often slow to appreciate that opportunities exist or that constraints have collapsed. This in turn helps to explain the important role of movement entrepreneurs in launching efforts such as the "freedom flotilla" – individuals and groups who seize opportunities, demonstrate their availability to others, and thereby trigger the cycles of contention that will be discussed in Chapter 10. It also explains why so many movements tragically fail – because their leaders perceive opportunities that are either weak or evanescent.

An Outline of the Book

In the past twenty years, and influenced by economic thought, some political scientists and sociologists began their analyses of social movements from the puzzle that collective action is often difficult to bring about. That puzzle added a lot to social movement theorizing, but it is only a puzzle – not a sociological law – because, in so many situations and against so many odds, collective action often *does* occur, on the part of people with few resources and little permanent power (Lichbach 1995).

Examining the parameters of collective action is the first task of Chapter 1. But the book will also approach three equally important problems: First, what are the dynamics of mobilization once it has begun; second, why are movement outcomes so varied; and, third, why do they so often fail to achieve their stated goals? Although Chapter 1 outlines these theories in a general way, evidence for them will be found in the movements and episodes analyzed in the remainder of the book.

In Part I, I will show how and where the national social movement developed, first in the eighteenth century West, where the resources for turning collective action into social movements could first be brought together over sustained periods and across territorial space, and then in more recent periods of history around the world. The focus of Chapter 2 is on what I will call, following the work of Charles Tilly, the modern "repertoire" of collective action. Then, in Chapter 3, I will turn to the changes in society that supported that transformation and, in Chapter 4, to the impact of capitalism and state building on the crystallization of modern contentious politics. Once the main forms of "modular collective action" were established, social movements could be diffused through Western state expansion, through print and association, and through the diffusion of these repertoires, first across the West and then across the globe. That will be the argument of Chapters 2 to 4 of the book.

But even deep-seated claims remain inert unless they can be activated. Part II will outline the four main powers that activate claims into action. In Chapter 5, I will examine the three main forms of contentious politics that movements employ – violence, disruption, and contained forms of action. In Chapter 6, I will deal with the major social and organizational bases that help to form movement organizations. In Chapter 7, I will examine how movements "make meanings," by constructing identities, mobilizing emotions, and developing collective action "frames." In Chapter 8, I will examine the kinds of political opportunities that trigger episodes of contention and the kinds of threats – especially threats from the state and the police – that limit them. These are the four main powers I see in movement.

In the third section of the book, I will turn from these analytical aspects of contentious politics and social movements to their interaction and dynamics. Contentious politics is nothing if it is not relational. Chapter 9 lays out an interactive approach to contentious politics that is based on the specification and examination of a number of key mechanisms: mechanisms such as mobilization and demobilization; campaign building and coalition formation; diffusion and scale shift; and radicalization and institutionalization.

These mechanisms are the analytical building blocks of the cycles of contention that will be studied in Chapter 10. The argument of this chapter is that once a cycle of contention is triggered, coalitions are formed, campaigns are organized, and the costs of collective action are lowered for other actors, and master frames and models of activism become more generally available. The movements that arise in such contexts do not depend as much on their internal resources as on generalized opportunities in their societies, and elites respond less to single movements than to the general context of contention that they must deal with.

Such periods of generalized disorder sometimes result in immediate repression, sometimes in reform, often in both. But in political/institutional and personal/cultural terms, the effects of cycles of contention seldom correspond to a single movement's visible goals. These effects are noted both in the changes that governments initiate and in the periods of demobilization that follow. They leave behind permanent expansions in participation, in popular culture, and in ideology, as I will argue in Chapter 11.

If the national social movement was linked to the rise of the modern national state, the central question raised by the latest wave of contention is whether we are seeing the development of a *transnational* movement culture that threatens the structure and sovereignty of the national state. The same question can be asked of the plethora of transnational "NGOs" and civil society groups that have sprung up around the globe in the last few decades. As routine and bureaucratic in their way as protests against international institutions are disruptive and erratic, these transnational NGOs play an increasing role in linking domestic social movements both to one another and to the institutions that are increasingly responsible for regulating the global economy, fighting climate change, and attempting to combat human rights abuses. These are the questions I will turn to in Chapter 12.

This will take us, in the conclusions, to the contentious politics of the current epoch and to three important new issues: "globalization," lethal conflict, and the interactions between movements and states. In the last decades of the twentieth century, a wave of democratization spread across the world, culminating in dramatic changes in southern Europe in the 1970s, in Latin America in the 1980s, and in Central and Eastern Europe after the fall of communism. But also in the 1990s, a new wave of "ugly" movements, rooted in ethnic and nationalist claims, in religious fanaticism, and in racism, broke out, bringing the world to a peak of turbulence and violence that it has not known for decades. Radical changes in electronic communication and cheap international transportation have reinforced these connections, creating the possibility of a new age of "global" social movements, but they have also given states unprecedented capacities for suppression.

Where protest and contention have become easier to mount and are largely legitimized; where police and power holders prefer to discuss tactics and issues with movements rather than repress them; where the media or the courts settle questions that once were fought over in the streets – in these conditions, will the historical form of the social movement be absorbed into ordinary politics, as were the strike and the demonstration in the last century? Or will the sheer volume of contention submerge the routine processes of electoral and interest group participation in a turbulent sea of unruly politics? The shape of the future will depend not on how violent or widespread contention has become, but on how it relates to states, capitalism, and the international system. Because all three of these are undergoing profound change, in the century that lies ahead, the world may be experiencing a new and far-reaching power in movement.

Contentious Politics and Social Movements

In this book, I will argue that contentious politics emerges in response to changes in political opportunities and threats when participants perceive and respond to a variety of incentives: material and ideological, partisan and group-based, long-standing and episodic. Building on these opportunities, and using known repertoires of action, people with limited resources can act together contentiously – if only sporadically. When their actions are based on dense social networks and effective connective structures and draw on legitimate, action-oriented cultural frames, they can sustain these actions even in contact with powerful opponents. In such cases – and *only* in such cases – we are in the presence of a social movement. When such contention spreads across an entire society – as it sometimes does – we see a cycle of contention. When such a cycle is organized around opposed or multiple sovereignties, the outcome is a revolution.

The solutions to the problem of mobilizing people into campaigns and coalitions of collective action depend on shared understandings, social networks, and connective structures and the use of culturally resonant forms of action. But above all – I shall argue – they are triggered by the ebb and flow of political struggle. In this chapter, I will lay out each of these factors as they will be used in this book to describe, analyze, and raise questions about contentious politics and social movements. Before doing so, however, it will be helpful to see how scholars – associated with four classical traditions – have conceived of the problem of collective action and its relation to grievances, resources, cultural frames, and political struggle. We will begin with the origins of social movement theory in the works of Marxist and post-Marxist scholars, before turning to the current generation of social scientific work on contentious politics.

MARX, LENIN, GRAMSCI, AND TILLY

Many sociologists trace the lineage of the field of social movements to society's negative reactions to the horrors of the French Revolution and to the outrage of the crowd.[1] Although writers such as Tarde (1989) and Le Bon (1977) make a convenient polemical starting point for theorists who reject their ideas, their work in fact was an offshoot of crowd psychology. In this book, conflict between challengers and authorities will be seen, instead, as a normal part of society and not as an aberration from it. This is why we will begin with the preeminent theorists who saw conflict inscribed in the very structure of society – Karl Marx and Friedrich Engels.

Marx and Class Conflict

It would not have occurred to the earliest theorists of social movements, Marx and Engels, to ask what makes individuals engage in collective action. Instead, they would have posed the problem as one of the readiness of society's structural development rather than one of individual choice. But although they saw collective action rooted in social structure, Marx and Engels seriously underrated the resources needed to engage in collective action, its cultural dimensions, and the importance of politics. Marx and Engels were classical structuralists who left little room for the concrete mechanisms that draw individuals into collective action. People will engage in collective action, they thought, when their social class comes into fully developed contradiction with its antagonists. In the case of the proletariat, this meant when capitalism forced it into large-scale factories, where it lost ownership of its tools but developed the resources to act collectively.

Among these resources were class consciousness and trade unions. It was the rhythm of socialized production in the factory that would pound the proletariat into a "class for itself" and give rise to the unions that gave it political form. Although there are many more elegant (and more obscure) formulations of this thesis, Marx put it most succinctly in *The Communist Manifesto*:

> The advance of industry, whose involuntary promoter is the bourgeoisie, replaces the isolation of the labourers, due to competition, by their revolutionary combination, due to association.... The real fruit of their battle lies, not in the immediate result, but in the ever-expanding union of the workers (Tucker, ed. 1978: 481 and 483).

Marx dealt summarily with a problem that has worried activists ever since: why members of a group who "should" revolt when history provides the "objective conditions" for revolt often fail to do so. Concerned with the problem that the workers' movement would not succeed unless a significant proportion of its members cooperated, he developed a theory of "false consciousness," by which he meant that if workers failed to act as "History" dictated, it was because they remained cloaked in a shroud of ignorance woven by their class enemies. The theory was unsatisfactory because no one could say whose consciousness was

---

[1] For an account of theorists who focus on civil violence as the antithesis of normal social processes, see James Rule's *Theories of Civil Violence* (1988: Chapter 3).

false and whose was real. Marx thought the problem would resolve itself when capitalism's contradictions ripened and the solidarity that came from years of toiling side by side with others like themselves would open workers' eyes to their real interests. Marx, however, died before he could test that thesis.

We now know that as capitalism developed, it produced divisions among the workers and created mechanisms that integrated them into capitalist democracies. Through nationalism and protectionism, workers often allied themselves with capitalists, suggesting that much more than class conflict was necessary to produce collective action on their behalf. A form of consciousness had to be created that would transform economic interests into revolutionary collective action. But who would create this consciousness? Marx had neither a clear concept of leadership nor a concept of working-class culture and, as a result, he seriously underspecified the political conditions that were needed to provide opportunities for revolutionary mobilization (1963b: 175).

Lenin and Resource Mobilization

The first of these problems – leadership – was the major preoccupation of Vladimir Illyich Lenin, Marx's foremost interpreter and the father of the Russian Revolution of November 1917. Learning from the Western European experience that workers on their own will act only on behalf of narrow "trade union interests," he refused to wait for objective conditions to ripen, instead proposing the creation of an elite of professional revolutionaries (1929: 52ff.). Substituting itself for Marx's proletariat, this "vanguard" would act as the self-appointed guardian of workers' "real" (i.e., revolutionary) interests. When that vanguard, in the form of the Russian Bolshevik Party, succeeded in gaining power, it transposed the equation, substituting party interest for that of the working class (and, ultimately, in its Stalinist involution, substituting the will of the leader for that of the party). In 1902, this involution was too far in the future to see. To Lenin, it seemed that organization was the solution to the collective action problem of the working class.

With the virtues of hindsight, we see that Lenin's organizational amendments to Marx's theory were a response to the particular historical conditions of Czarist Russia. In superimposing an intellectual vanguard on the young and unsophisticated Russian working class, he was adapting Marx's theory to the context of a repressive state and to the backward society it ruled – both of which retarded the development of class consciousness and inhibited collective action.[2] Nobody knows what a "mature" working class in a liberal political system would have done had it come to power independently, because after Leninism took hold in Russia, the entire international system was transformed.

---

[2] Lenin criticized the theory, then current in some socialist circles, that revolutionary leadership must *necessarily* fall mainly upon the shoulders of an extremely small intellectual force. "It is because we [in Russia] are backward." *What Is To Be Done?* (1929: 123–124).

When the theory of the vanguard was applied indiscriminately to the world Communist movement with little regard for social and political opportunities and constraints, the result was a weakening of Western social democracy and, in Italy and Central Europe, of democracy *tout court*. Some of the problems raised by Lenin's theory were addressed by one of his Western successors, Antonio Gramsci, who paid with his life for his mechanical adoption of Lenin's theory by Communist parties in the West.

Gramsci and Cultural Hegemony

When the Russian Revolution of 1917 failed to spread westward, European Marxists such as Gramsci realized that, at least in Western conditions, vanguard forms of organization would not be sufficient to raise a revolution. For Gramsci, it would be necessary to develop the workers' own consciousness, and he therefore conceived of the workers' movement as a "collective intellectual," one of whose prime tasks was to create a working-class culture. This was a subtle but important change from Leninism. Just as he had thought that Italy shared Russia's social conditions, Gramsci at first accepted Lenin's injunction that the revolutionary party had to be a vanguard. But after being clapped into Mussolini's prisons, he revised Lenin's organizational solution with two theorems: first, that a fundamental task of the party was to create a historic bloc of forces around the working class (1971: 168); and, second, that this could occur only if a cadre of "organic intellectuals" were developed from within the working class to complement the "traditional" intellectuals in the party leadership (pp. 6–23).

Both innovations turned out to hinge on a strong belief in the power of culture.[3] Gramsci's solution to the cultural hegemony of the bourgeoisie was to produce a countercultural consensus among workers, give them a capacity for taking autonomous initiatives, and build bridges between them and other social formations. The process would be a long and a slow one, requiring the party to operate within the "trenches and fortifications" of bourgeois society, while proselytizing among nonproletarian groups and learning to deal with cultural institutions such as the Church.

But Gramsci's solution – as seen in the reformist turn taken by Italian Communists, who inherited his mantle after World War II – posed a new dilemma. If the party as a collective intellectual engaged in a long-term dialogue between the working class and bourgeois society, what would prevent the

---

[3] In 1924, Gramsci wrote;

> The error of the party has been to have accorded priority in an abstract fashion to the problem of organization, which in practice has simply meant creating an apparatus of functionaries who could be depended on for their orthodoxy towards the official view.

See Antonio Gramsci, *Selections from the Prison Notebooks* (1971: LXI) i, where this passage is translated.

cultural power of the latter – what Gramsci called "the common sense of capitalist society" – from transforming the party, rather than vice versa?[4] Without a theory of political mobilization, Gramsci's solution ignored the give-and-take of politics. Gramsci did not provide a guide to how the battle within "the trenches and fortifications" of bourgeois society should be fought (1971: 229–239), nor did he differentiate between polities in which the opportunities and constraints would be strong or weak. However, he did provide a link from materialist Marxism to the constructivist turn in social movement studies of the 1980s and 1990s.

Tilly's Polity Model

Gramsci came of age during and after World War I and during the excitement of the Russian Revolution. It would take the generation that came of age after World War II to transcend the vulgar Marxist idea that politics was merely part of the "superstructure," without autonomy of its own. Charles Tilly's work can stand as one such example. Coming from under the Marxian umbrella of his great teacher, Barrington Moore Jr. (1965), Tilly was equally influenced by British Marxists such as E.P. Thompson and Eric Hobsbawm and by French social historians such as Fernand Braudel. Although Tilly's first book, *The Vendée* (1964), began from the classical Marxian premise that structural variables such as urbanization shape contention, his attention soon shifted to the importance of state structure and to state strategic imperatives (Tilly 1986; 1990). Foremost among these imperatives were the processes of war making, state building, and extraction, which led to "white-hot bargaining" between rulers and ordinary people. Early on, Tilly proposed the static "polity model" of relations among rulers, insiders, and outsiders (1978) that is reproduced in Figure 1.1. This model would guide his work for the next two decades. Later, he would substitute for it the "relational realism" that will be presented later in this book.

Summing Up

Each of these theorists – Marx, Lenin, Gramsci, and Tilly – emphasized a different element of collective action:

- Marx focused on the cleavages of capitalist society that created a mobilization potential without specifying the mechanisms that led particular workers in specific settings to revolt.
- Lenin created the movement organization that was necessary to structure this mobilization potential and prevent its dispersion into narrow trade union

---

[4] This was a special danger on the periphery of the working-class party, among the middle class and the peasantry. See Stephen Hellman, "The PCI's Alliance Strategy and the Case of the Middle Class" (1975) and Sidney Tarrow, *Peasant Communism in Southern Italy* (1967).

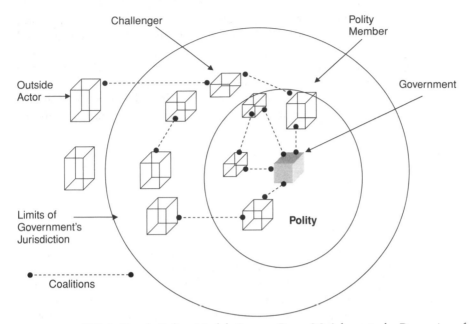

FIGURE 1.1. Tilly's Simple Polity Model. *Source:* Doug McAdam et al., *Dynamics of Contention*, p. 11. Copyright © 2001 Cambridge University Press. Reprinted with permission.

claims but lodged the mechanism of mobilization in an elite of revolutionaries.
• Gramsci centered on the need to build consensus around the party's goals but failed to specify the political conditions in which resource-poor and exploited workers could be expected to mobilize on behalf of their interests.
• The early Tilly focused on those political conditions but in a largely static way.

Contemporary social scientists – mainly sociologists and political scientists, with an assist from economists – beginning in the 1970s, have begun to propose solutions to these problems.

SOCIAL SCIENTISTS, SOCIAL MOVEMENTS,
AND COLLECTIVE ACTION

Although the parallels are seldom made explicit, these four elements in classical social movement theory are the sources of four recent traditions in the study of collective action and social movements:

• Without sharing Marx's fixation on class, *collective behavior theorists* of the 1950s and early 1960s focused on the grievances responsible for mobilization and saw them stemming from underlying structural strains.

- Without sharing Lenin's belief in an elite vanguard, *resource mobilization theorists* of the late 1960s and the 1970s concentrated on leadership and organization.
- Like Gramsci, *framing and collective identity theorists* of the 1980s and 1990s focused on the sources of consensus in a movement.
- From the 1970s on, *political process theorists* followed Tilly's lead in focusing on the political opportunities and constraints that structure contentious politics.

Let us briefly examine how these four schools of thought emerged in recent social science and what they each contribute to our understanding of contentious politics and social movements today.

Grievances and Collective Behavior Theory

Perhaps because they saw social movements from a mainly social-psychological standpoint, American sociologists took a long time to develop a politically connected view of social movements. For many years, in fact, they conceived of movements as the result of "strain," seeing them largely outside the normal institutions of society as part of a construct that came to be called "collective behavior."[5] Collective behavior theory posited that movements were little more than the most well-organized and most self-conscious part of an archipelago of "emergent" phenomena, ranging from fads and rumors, to collective enthusiasms, riots, movements, and revolutions. While political scientists focused on interest groups as "normal" parts of the political process, collective behavior theorists saw movements as exceptions to normal political processes – virtually as part of abnormal psychology.

In some versions of the theory (e.g., see Kornhauser 1959), society itself was seen to be disoriented, and mobilization resulted from the urge to recompose it. This was sometimes linked to Emile Durkheim's theory, in which individuals – unhinged from their traditional roles and identities – join social movements to escape the anomie of a "mass society" (Durkheim 1951; also see Hoffer 1951). Other versions (e.g., Gurr 1971) included no overall vision of breakdown, but individual deprivation was at the center of analysis. The most sophisticated versions of the theory linked collective behavior to a functional view of society in which societal dysfunctions produce different forms of collective behavior – some of which took the form of political movements and interest groups (Smelser 1962; Turner and Killian 1972).

Unlike Marx, who used a mechanistic class theory to predict which collectivities could be expected to mobilize at what stages of capitalism, collective behavior theorists had no preferred social subject. But like Marx, though for

---

[5] I will not attempt to summarize this school here, but refer the reader to Doug McAdam's synthesis in Chapter 1 of his *The Political Process and the Development of Black Insurgency* (1999 [1982]). For a somewhat more sympathetic account of "strain" and "breakdown" theories, see Buechler (2004).

different reasons, they tended to underspecify the mobilization process. And because they started from the assumption that collective behavior was outside the routines of everyday life, few specified its relationship to the political. This may be why few variants of collective behavior theory retained their popularity after the spectacular cycle of protest of the 1960s, which had an intimate relationship to politics (see Chapter 9).

Rational Choice and Resource Mobilization

Both in Western Europe and in the United States, the decade of the 1960s revitalized the study of social movements. All shifts in scholarly focus depend in some way on the historical conditions in which they emerge. Marx's model of class conflict was deeply marked by the emergence of capitalist enterprise in England; the interest of scholars in the collective behavior tradition with alienation and anomie was influenced by the horrors of Stalinism and fascism; in the 1960s, a new generation of scholars, many of them associated with Civil Rights or antiwar movements, saw social movements through a new, more positive lens. For former movement activists and those who studied them, Marx's theory of the proletariat producing a revolution, and the collective behavior theorists' image of "true believers" searching for roots in an atomized society, were difficult to reconcile with the determined young activists – most of them from the middle class – mobilizing in the Civil Rights and anti-Vietnam War movements (Keniston 1968).

The study of contentious politics was also affected by trends in the academy, where economics was emerging as the "master" social science. In the traces of microeconomics, for many scholars the problem for collective action came to be seen not as how classes struggle and states rule, but as how collective action is even *possible* among individuals guided by narrow economic self-interest. The most influential student of this dilemma was the American economist Mancur Olson.

For Olson and those influenced by him (DeNardo 1985), the problem of collective action was a parallel to marketing: how to attract as high a proportion of a group as possible on behalf of its collective good. Only in this way could the group convince its opponents of its own strength. In his classic book, *The Logic of Collective Action* (1965), Olson posited that, in a large group, only its most important members have a sufficient interest in its collective good to take on its leadership – not quite Lenin's "vanguard," but not far from it. The only exception to this rule is seen in small groups in which the individual good and the collective good are closely associated (pp. 43ff.).[6] The larger the group, the more people will prefer to "free ride" on the efforts of the individuals whose

---

[6] The problem of the size of the group has exercised a great fascination among scholars in both public goods and game theoretic traditions. See John Chamberlin's "Provision of Collective Goods as a Function of Group Size," Russell Hardin's *Collective Action* (1982: Chapter 3), and Gerald Marwell and Pam Oliver's *The Critical Mass in Collective Action: A*

interest in the collective good is strong enough to pursue it.[7] To overcome this problem, Olson posited that would-be leaders must either impose constraints on their members or provide them with "selective incentives" to convince them that participation is worthwhile (p. 51).

Olson's reception into the study of contentious politics was slow and uneven. This is in part because of the irony that, during a decade in which contentious politics was buzzing and blooming, he focused on why it is unlikely (Hirschman 1982). Moreover, Olson seemed to limit the motivations for collective action to material and personal incentives and lacked a theory of participation (Klandermans 2004). But what of the thousands of people who were striking, marching, rioting, and demonstrating on behalf of interests other than their own? Finally, though he named his theory "*collective* action," Olson had little to say beyond the aggregation of individuals by preexisting organizers.

How could Olson's collective action problem be reconciled with the flourishing movements of the 1960s? Two sociologists, John McCarthy and Mayer Zald, proposed an answer that focused on the resources that are increasingly available to people and groups in advanced industrial societies (1973; 1977). McCarthy and Zald agreed with Olson that the collective action problem was real, but argued that the expanded personal resources, professionalization, and external financial support available to movements in such societies provide a solution – professional movement organizations.[8]

While the earlier generation of scholars had focused on the "why" of collective action, McCarthy and Zald's theory – resource mobilization – fastened on the means available to collective actors – on its "how" (Melucci 1988). This emphasis on means was a disappointment to critics looking for deep structural explanations for the origins of movements, but it lent a refreshing concreteness to the study of movements. For McCarthy and Zald, a rational answer to Olson's paradox of the free rider lay in organization. By the early 1980s, their theory of resource mobilization by organizations had become a dominant background paradigm for sociologists studying social movements.

But McCarthy and Zald's emphasis on the "solution" of professional movement organizations seemed to ignore that many of the new movements of the 1960s and 1970s lacked formal organization when they emerged (Evans and Boyte 1992; McAdam 1999 [1982]). And in a decade in which many scholars were beginning to take what came to be called "the cultural turn," many younger scholars found a paradigmatic alternative to organization in

---

Micro-Social Theory (1993: Chapter 3), which demonstrate theoretically that the size of the group is not the critical variable that Olson thought it was.

[7] Thus, for Olson, General Motors has enough of an interest in the collective good of American auto production to take on the leadership of all domestic car producers, including those that are too small to take action on their own. If enough members of the group take a free ride, not only are the leaders' efforts to no avail – their efforts themselves will induce free riding.

[8] It is no surprise that Zald's dissertation and first book (1970) dealt with the formation, transformation, and politics of the YMCA. For an updated account of resource mobilization, see Edwards and McCarthy (2004).

culture, which began to emerge as a countermodel to resource mobilization (Williams 2004). For these critics, McCarthy and Zald took no account of emotion, focused far too much on formal organization, and left grievances out of their equation. By the 1980s, an alternative model, emphasizing movement decentralization, informal participation, and grassroots democracy, began to arise (Fantasia 1988; Rosenthal and Schwartz 1989).

Cultures of Contention

If the emphasis of the collective behavior paradigm on grievances recalled Marx, and if the focus of resource mobilization on leadership was a sequel to Lenin's organizational theory, this new turn was resonant of Gramsci's interest in culture. Just as the Italian theorist had added a cultural dimension to Lenin's concept of class hegemony, culturalist writers have tried to shift the focus of research on social movements from structural factors to the framing, the discourse, and the emotions in collective action. It is interesting to note that the earliest hint of a paradigm shift came from a Marxist – from E.P. Thompson's enculturation of the concept of class (1966).

Thompson did not want to throw class out the window, but only to substitute for the materialist version of Marxism a focus on class *self*-creation. This took him far from the factory floor – to factors like custom, grain seizures, and consumer mentalities (1971). He invented the culturally enriched concept of "the moral economy" to indicate that people do not revolt in mechanical response to grievances, but only when such grievances are empowered by a sense of injustice. This links Thompson's work to the more theoretically self-conscious "cultural turn" in recent social history (e.g., see Steinberg 1999) and to the "constructivist turn" in American political science (Finnemore and Sikkink 1998).

Thompson had used eighteenth century grain seizures to illustrate a basically Marxian theory, but the idea of a moral economy of protest had more general resonance with the cultural turn that was simultaneously percolating into social movement studies from anthropology, social psychology, and cultural history. For example, his emphasis on meaning was appropriated by an anthropologically gifted political scientist, James Scott (1976), who adapted Thompson's concept of the moral economy to study the reaction of subsistence peasants in Southeast Asia to the strains of commercialization.[9] Scott's work went well beyond the subject of social movements and resonated with the experiences of scholars and activists in the global South (Scott and Kerkvliet, eds. 1986).

Another influence came from social psychology. First from Erving Goffman's concept of framing (1974), and then from Bert Klanderman's concept of "consensus mobilization" (1988; 1997), and from William Gamson's idea

---

[9] Scott went on to apply his thinking to peasant resistance in general, in his *Weapons of the Weak* (1985), before turning to the culturalist formulation of what he called "hidden transcripts" (1990).

of "ideological packages" (1988), scholars began to examine how individuals construct their participation in movements. From assuming grievances, scholars of social movements now began to focus on how movements embed concrete grievances within emotion-laden "packages" (Gamson 1992), or in "frames" capable of convincing participants that their cause is just and important. While Goffman's work had focused on how individuals frame their actions, David Snow and his collaborators began work on the "framing" of collective action (Snow et al. 1986; Snow 2004).

A third influence came from the constructivist turn in history, with its roots in French social theory. Here the key figure was Michel Foucault, who was concerned with resistance to the overall structure of power in society. "Foucault," in Kate Nash's summary, suggested that "we begin to study power by studying resistance," by which he meant the anti-authority struggles of social movements. In particular, he thinks social movements are engaged in struggles against the imposition of identity. The construction of subjectivity by those who tell us the "truth" of who we are . . . is at the same time a subjection to the power they exercise" (Nash 2000: 3; Foucault 2000). Influenced by Foucault was the work of historical sociologist Marc Steinberg on the eighteenth century transformation of working class ideology and action (1999).

Culturally sensitive work in the 1980s and 1990s also came out of the once resolutely structuralist field of comparative revolution, first in John Foran's *Fragile Resistance: Social Transformation in Iran from 1500 to the Revolution* (1993), then in Mark Selbin's *Modern Latin American Revolutions* (1993), and finally in Jeff Goodwin's *No Other Way Out* (2001). These authors attempted to transcend the dominant structuralist trope that had dominated the study of revolution since Marx, in bold attempts to bring agency centrally into its study.[10]

To some degree, all movements construct meanings (Eyerman and Jamison 1991). But if this is the case, skeptics have asked, why do waves of movements emerge in some periods and not in others, and why are some movements more adept at manipulating cultural symbols than others (Tarrow 1992)? Without answers to these questions, culturalism might prove just as static a meta-narrative as the structuralism its proponents wished to displace. To this dilemma, political scientists and politically attuned sociologists proposed an answer: variations in political structure and in the workings of the political process.

The Political Process Model

Inspired by the rise of contentious politics in the Civil Rights movement, American scholars were first to develop a more political approach to movements, one that eventually centered on several versions of the concept that came

---

[10] When it came to the Iranian revolution, even a committed structuralist, Theda Skocpol, had to admit the importance of culture. See her essay "Rentier State and Shi'a Islam in the Iranian Revolution" in her *Social Revolutions in the Modern World* (1994).

to be known as "political opportunity structure."[11] The foundation stone in this tradition was laid by Tilly, in his 1978 classic, *From Mobilization to Revolution*.[12] In this book, Tilly elaborated a set of conditions for mobilization, foremost among which were opportunity/threat to challengers and facilitation/repression by authorities (Chapters 3, 4, 6). Just as important in the United States was the path-breaking work of Richard Cloward and Frances Fox Piven, in *Regulating the Poor* (1971) and *Poor People's Movements* (1977). They questioned the orthodox idea of Marxists such as Eric Hobsbawm that organizational leadership was the key to movement success, and they offered the clearest account of disruption in the literature on protest (1977: Chapter 1), which they considered the key to effective pressure on elites.

Tilly had argued that the development of the national social movement was concomitant, and mutually interdependent, with the rise in consolidated national states (1984b). It followed that movements could be studied only in connection with politics, and that they would vary in their strategy, structure, and success in different kinds of states. This was an insight that students of social revolution, such as Theda Skocpol (1979), were also exploring, and that comparativists in political science were quick to pick up on (Kitschelt 1986; Kriesi et al. 1995; Tarrow 1989).

Given his grounding in European social history, Tilly's model appeared resolutely structural – at least until the 1990s. But Americanists' models were more rooted in the intricacies of the political process. Political scientists such as Michael Lipsky (1968) and Peter Eisinger (1973) focused on American urban politics, with the former linking the urban movements of the 1960s to the use of protest as a political resource, and the latter correlating protest with various measures of local opportunity. In a similar vein, Piven and Cloward turned their attention to the historical relations between welfare and social protest (1993). But it was a sociologist, Doug McAdam, who synthesized these approaches into a fully fledged "political process model" of social movement mobilization by tracing the development of the American Civil Rights movement to political, organizational, and consciousness change (1999 [1982]).

While opportunity/threat and facilitation/repression were parts of the original Tillian synthesis, political process theorists tended to narrow their attention to opportunities and forget about threats. Some scholars – in Eisinger's footsteps – studied how different political structures provide greater or lesser degrees of opportunity to insurgent groups (Amenta et al. 1992; Kitschelt 1986); others looked at how particular movements exploit opportunities provided by institutions (Costain 1992); others examined how the opportunities of a particular movement change over time (Jenkins and Perrow 1977); still

---

[11] See the excellent survey in Kriesi (2004). The source of these ideas was of course Tilly's foundational work in the 1970s. The main steps in the development of this concept were provided by Eisinger (1973), Kitschelt (1986), Kriesi et al. (1995), McAdam (1999 [1982]), Piven and Cloward (1977), Tarrow (1989), and Amenta (2006).

[12] Tilly's theory of collective action has gone through several permutations since then, some of which will be outlined later in this volume. For an outline of his fundamental contributions to this field, see my review article, "Charles Tilly and the Practice of Contentious Politics" (2008).

others studied entire cycles of protest to understand how triggering of a wave of mobilization affects successor movements (Koopmans 2004; McAdam 1995; Tarrow 1989a).

As these works progressed, lacunae and ambiguities began to appear.[13] For example, political process models were almost always lodged in the democratic West. The perspective began to be systematically applied elsewhere only in the 1990s (Brockett 1991 and 1995; Boudreau 1996; O'Brien and Li 2006; O'Brien, ed. 2008), Schneider 1995). A second question – whether repression has a positive or a negative impact on movement formation – only began to be explored in the 1990s, with a series of works inspired by Donatella della Porta (1995 and 1996; della Porta et al. 1998; della Porta and Fillieule 2004). Third, while some scholars (McAdam 1996; Tarrow 1996b) worked from a limited list of dimensions of opportunity, as more and more aspects of the links between politics and movement formation emerged, the concept tended to balloon (see Gamson and Meyer's critique 1996).

Most important, the political process model was not really about the *process* of contention because most of its practitioners (including this author) failed to specify the mechanisms that connect different elements in the model to one another. Although it was refreshing to move beyond the macrostructural approach of a Marx, a Lenin, or a Gramsci, how contentious actors interacted with each other and with others remained implicit in the model, rather than explicitly specified. Concerted efforts to put the political processes of contention in motion through the specification of their component mechanisms had to await the first decade of this century (see Chapter 9).

Nevertheless, the political process/opportunities approach proposed an answer to the questions that had dogged previous approaches: *Why does contentious politics seem to develop only in particular periods of history? Why does it sometimes produce robust social movements and sometimes flicker out into sectarianism or repression? And why do movements take different forms in different political environments?* It eventually emerged that the political process model cannot claim to explain every aspect of contentious politics or social movements and is best seen not as a theory, but as a framework in which to examine the dynamics of contention. But this is possible only through synthesis with insights from other branches of social movement theory, as I will argue below.

TOWARD A SYNTHESIS

The most forceful argument of this study will be that people engage in contentious politics when patterns of political opportunities and constraints

---

[13] For a sensitive critique from the inside, see Gamson and Meyer, "Framing Political Opportunity" (1996). For a robust attack on political opportunity theory, see Jeff Goodwin and James Jasper, "Caught in a Winding, Snarling, Vine: A Critique of Political Process Theory" in their edited book, *Rethinking Social Movements* (2004), in which, to their credit, they invited responses from adherents of the approach, including the present author.

change, and then by strategically employing a repertoire of collective action, creating new opportunities, which are used by others in widening cycles of contention. When their struggles revolve around broad cleavages in society; when they bring people together around inherited cultural symbols; and when they can build on – or construct – dense social networks and connective structures, these episodes of contention result in sustained interactions with opponents in social movements. Because each of these four elements is the topic of a chapter in Part II of this book, a brief introduction should suffice here.

The Repertoire of Contention

People do not simply "act collectively." They vote, petition, assemble, strike, march, occupy premises, obstruct traffic, set fires, and attack others with intent to do bodily harm (Taylor and Van Dyke 2004). No less than in the case of religious rituals or civic celebrations, contentious politics is not born out of organizers' heads but is culturally inscribed and socially communicated. The learned conventions of contention are part of a society's public culture.[14] Social movements are repositories of knowledge of particular routines in a society's history, which helps them to overcome the deficits in resources and communication typically found among disorganized people (Kertzer 1988: 104ff.).

Because social movements seldom possess either Olson's selective incentives or constraints over followers, movement leadership has a creative function in selecting forms of collective action that people will respond to. Leaders invent, adapt, and combine various forms of contention to gain support from people who might otherwise stay at home. Economist Albert Hirschman had something like this in mind when he complained that Olson regarded collective action only as a cost – when to many it is a benefit (1982: 82–91). For people whose lives are mired in drudgery and desperation, the offer of an exciting, risky, and possibly beneficial campaign of collective action may be an incentive in itself.

Forms of contention can be common or rare, habitual or unfamiliar, solitary or part of concerted campaigns. They can be linked to themes that are inscribed in the culture or invented on the spot or – more commonly – can blend elements of convention with new frames of meaning. Protest is a resource, according to political scientist Michael Lipsky (1968). Forms of contention are themselves a collective incentive for some people under some circumstances to challenge opponents, drawing on incentives that undergird their networks of trust and solidarity (Tilly 2005b).

Particular groups have a particular history – and memory – of contention. Workers know how to strike because generations of workers struck before

---

[14] The concept first appears in Tilly's *From Mobilization to Revolution* (1978: Chapter 6), again in his "Speaking Your Mind Without Elections, Surveys or Social Movements" (1983), and then in his *The Contentious French* (1986: Chapter 1). The culmination of his research on the repertoire, published after his death in 2008, is his book *Contentious Performances*.

them; Parisians build barricades because barricades are inscribed in the history of Parisian contention; peasants seize the land carrying the symbols that their fathers and grandfathers used in the past. Political scientists Stuart Hill and Donald Rothchild put it this way:

> Based on past periods of conflict with a particular group(s) or the government, individuals construct a prototype of a protest or riot that describes what to do in particular circumstances as well as explaining a rationale for this action (1992: 192).

These are the issues that will be taken up in Chapter 5.

Networks and Mobilizing Structures

Although it is individuals who decide whether to take up collective action, it is in their face-to-face groups, their social networks, and the connective structures between them that collective action is most often activated and sustained (Diani 2004; Diani and McAdam, eds. 2004). This has been made clear through recent research both in the laboratory[15] and in the real world of movement mobilization. In the collective behavior approach, the tendency was to see isolated, deprived individuals as the main actors in collective action. But by the early 1980s, scholars were finding that it is life within groups that transforms the potential for action into social movements.[16] It is not "groupness" itself that induces mobilization but the normative pressures and solidary incentives that are encoded within networks, and out of which movements emerge and are sustained.

Institutions are particularly economical "host" settings in which movements can germinate. This was particularly true in estate societies such as

---

[15] Experimental researchers were also learning about the importance of social incentives for cooperation. In an ingenious piece of research, Gamson and his collaborators showed that a supportive group environment was essential for triggering individuals' willingness to speak out against unjust authority – authority that they might well tolerate if they faced it on their own (Gamson et al. 1982). Similarly, when Robyn Dawes and his associates carried out a series of experiments on collective choice, they found that neither egoistic motives nor internalized norms were as powerful in producing collective action as "the parochial one of contributing to one's group of fellow humans" (Dawes et al. 1988: 96). In social dilemma situations, they argue in their article "Not Me or Thee But We" as follows: "people immediately start discussing what 'we' should do, and spend a great deal of time and effort to persuade others in their own group to cooperate (or defect!), even in situations where these others' behavior is irrelevant to the speaker's own payoffs" (p. 94).

[16] For example, McAdam's work on the "Freedom Summer" campaign showed that – far more than their social background or ideologies – it was the social networks in which Freedom Summer applicants were embedded that played a key role in determining who would participate in this campaign and who would stay at home (McAdam: 1986; 1988). At the same time, European scholars such as Hanspeter Kriesi (1988) were finding that movement subcultures were the reservoirs in which collective action took shape. This dovetailed with what sociologist Alberto Melucci (1989; 1996: Chapter 4) was learning about the role of movement networks in defining the collective identity of the movements he studied in Italy.

pre-revolutionary France, where the provincial Parliaments provided institutional spaces where liberal ideas could take hold (Egret 1977). But it is also true in America today. For instance, sociologist Aldon Morris showed that the origins of the Civil Rights movement were bound up with the role of black churches (1984). And political scientist Mary Katzenstein found that the internal structures of the Catholic world were unwitting accomplices in the formation of networks of dissident religious women (1998; also see Levine 1990 and Tarrow 1988). Movements that can appropriate such institutions for their own purposes are more likely to succeed than are those that create new organizational niches (McAdam et al. 2001). The role of organizations and networks in the process of mobilization will be examined in Chapter 6.

Constructing Contention

The coordination of collective action depends on the trust and cooperation that are generated among participants by shared understandings and identities, or, to use a broader category, on the collective action frames that justify, dignify, and animate collective action. Ideology, as David Apter wrote in his classic essay in *Ideology and Discontent*, dignifies discontent, identifies a target for grievances, and forms an umbrella over the discrete grievances of overlapping groups (1964).

But "ideology" is a rather narrow way of describing the mixture of preconceptions, emotions, and interests that move people to action. In recent years, students of social movements have begun to use terms such as *cognitive frames*, *ideological packages*, and *cultural discourses* to describe the shared meanings that inspire people to collective action.[17] Whatever the terminology, rather than regarding ideology as a superimposed intellectual category, or as the automatic result of grievances, these scholars agree in seeing that movements take on passionate "framing work" (e.g., shaping grievances into broader and more resonant claims) (Snow and Benford 1988), stimulating what William Gamson calls "hot cognitions" around them (1992).

Framing relates to the generalization of a grievance and defines the "us" and "them" in a movement's structure of conflict and alliances. By drawing on inherited collective identities and shaping new ones, challengers delimit the boundaries of their prospective constituencies and define their enemies by their real or imagined attributes and evils. They do this through the images they project of both enemies and allies, as much as through the content of their ideological messages (Snow 2004). This requires paying attention to the

---

[17] Some of the main sources are collected in Bert Klandermans, Hanspeter Kriesi, and Sidney Tarrow, eds., *From Structure to Action* (1988), and in Aldon Morris and Carol Mueller, eds., *Frontiers of Social Movement Research* (1992). For an ingenious use of frame analysis to examine the ideas of ordinary American citizens, see William Gamson's *Talking Politics* (1992b).

"costumes" of collective actors as they appear on the public stage, as well as to the ideological framing of their claims. This we will attempt to do in Chapter 7.

While movement organizers actively engage in framing work, not all framing takes place under their auspices or control. In addition to building on inherited cultural understandings, they compete with the framing that goes on through the media, which transmit messages that movements must attempt to shape and influence (Gamson 2004). As sociologist Todd Gitlin found, much of the communication that helped shape the American New Left in the 1960s passed through the media, in the place of what would have had to be organizational efforts in earlier periods (1980). The new media that have exploded since the 1990s complicate but do not neutralize the influence of the media's framing capacity. Through the Internet, various forms of social networking, and personal media, individuals and groups have gained a capacity to "make the news" that far outstrips the ability of traditional print and visual media to shape collective action, as we will also see in Chapter 7.

State actors are constantly framing issues to gain support for their policies or to contest the meanings placed in public space by movements – indeed, they may take opposing sides in disputes over framing. In the struggle over meanings in which movements are constantly engaged, it is rare that they do not suffer a disadvantage in competition with states, which not only control the means of repression but have at their disposal important instruments for meaning construction. The struggle between states and movements takes place not only in the streets, but in contests over meaning (Melucci 1996; Rochon 1998).

Political Opportunities and Threats

Earlier, I argued that neither Marxist nor culturalist theorists can answer the question of why movements emerge in some periods and not in others, or why some movements prove more adept at manipulating cultural symbols than others. In the political process model sketched above, a key set of mechanisms that help to explain these variations is found in the political opportunities and threats to which movement actors respond.

- By political opportunities, I mean consistent – but not necessarily formal, permanent, or national – sets of clues that encourage people to engage in contentious politics.
- By threats, I mean those factors – repression, but also the capacity of authorities to present a solid front to insurgents – that discourage contention.

No simple formula can predict when contentious politics will emerge, both because the specification of these variables varies in different historical and political circumstances, and because different factors may vary in opposing directions. As a result, the term *political opportunity structure* should be understood not as an invariant model inevitably producing a social movement but as a set of clues for when contentious politics will emerge and will set in motion a chain of causation that may ultimately lead to sustained interaction with authorities and thence to social movements.

The concept of political opportunity emphasizes resources external to the group. Unlike money or power, these can be taken advantage of by even weak or disorganized challengers but in no way "belong" to them. In Chapter 8, I will argue that contentious politics emerges when ordinary citizens, sometimes encouraged by leaders, perceive opportunities that lower the costs of collective action, reveal potential allies, show where elites and authorities are most vulnerable, and trigger social networks and collective identities into action around common themes. Political opportunities are also shaped by features of the political system that, in turn, shape patterns of interaction between movements and political parties. And at the most general level, as I will argue in Chapter 8, opportunities and constraints are shaped by political regimes.

Similar to Hanspeter Kriesi and his collaborators (1995), I will argue that state structures and political cleavages create relatively stable opportunities (the most obvious of which are forms of access to institutions and the capacity for repression). But it is the changing opportunities and threats and the capacity of actors to take advantage of the former that provide the openings that lead them to engage in contentious politics. Whether contention ripens into social movements depends on how people act collectively; on the mobilization of consensus; and on actors' ability to create or to appropriate mobilizing structures.

To summarize what will have to be shown in greater detail in later chapters: Contentious politics is produced when threats are experienced and opportunities are perceived, when the existence of available allies is demonstrated, and when the vulnerability of opponents is exposed. Contention crystallizes challengers into a social movement when it taps into embedded social networks and connective structures and produces vivid collective action frames and supportive identities able to sustain contention against powerful opponents. By mounting familiar forms of contention, movements become focal points that transform external opportunities into resources. Repertoires of contention, social networks, and cultural frames lower the costs of bringing people into collective action, induce confidence that they are not alone, and give broader meaning to their claims. Together, these four sets of factors trigger the dynamic processes that have made social movements historically central actors in political and social change.

THE DYNAMICS OF MOVEMENT

Part III of the book will turn to the essentially *relational* nature of contentious politics. Unlike the classical political process approach, it will argue that we cannot predict the outcome of any episode of contention by focusing on what a single social movement does at a given moment in time. Challengers must be seen in relation to those they challenge and to influential allies, third parties, and the forces of order, in the context of the specific type of regime in which they operate (Tilly 2006).

Chapter 9 specifies some of the key mechanisms and processes through which challengers interact with opponents, allies, third parties, and institutions. But these interactive dynamics will be visible only through examination of more or less extended trajectories of contention, to which I turn in Chapter 10. That chapter, which ranges from relatively pacific protest cycles to fully fledged revolutions, will focus on how varied groups of people mobilize at once and on how contention diffuses through campaigns and coalitions. It will also touch on a too-little-studied process of contentious politics: how and why these same people *de*mobilize.

Chapter 11 turns from the dynamics of cycles to the outcomes of cycles of contention. In such general episodes of contention, policy elites respond not to the claims of any individual group or movement, but to the overall degree of turbulence and to the demands made by elites and opinion groups, which only partially correspond to the demands of those they claim to represent. That is why Chapter 11 has the paradoxical title "Struggling to Reform" – because individual movements almost never satisfy their largest ambitions. The important point is that, although movements usually conceive of themselves as outside of and opposed to institutions, acting collectively inserts them into complex political networks, and thus within the reach of the state.

Movements – and particularly waves of movement that are the main catalysts of social change – cannot be detached from national struggles for power. But in the last decade or so, a number of protest campaigns have clearly transcended national boundaries. What do they portend for contentious politics and, more broadly, for the shape of the future international system? Chapter 12 will employ the approach developed in the book to examine complex interactions between insiders and outsiders in the world polity.

The book closes by raising questions about three major issues in the study of contentious politics: First, how do movements interact with institutions, particularly electoral institutions; second, what about the "warring movements" that threaten the peace and stability of ordinary people; and, third, is the world becoming a "movement society," one in which the line between institutional and unruly politics is increasingly erased, or is the threat of transgressive contention producing ever more repressive states?

PART I

THE BIRTH OF THE MODERN SOCIAL MOVEMENT

2

Modular Collective Action

In the mid-1780s, as the foundations of France's old regime were crumbling, a series of scandal trials began to unfold in Paris.[1] In one of the most notorious, the Cléraux affair, a servant who had resisted the advances of her master was accused of robbing him and was hauled into court. Not only was the case decided in her favor (*pace* Dickens), but a wave of outrage against the courts and the lewd master surged across Paris. In a routine that had become familiar by the late eighteenth century, the master's house was sacked, his goods thrown into the street, and he himself barely saved from the fury of the crowd. A contemporary observer described the *émotion* in this way:

> What violences! What tumults! A furious multitude filled the streets, straining to tear down the Thibault house with an ax, then threatening to burn it; covering the family with curses and outrages; almost sacrificing them to their hatred (Lusebrink 1983: 375–376).

The affair contributed to the atmosphere of corruption that would sink the old regime in revolution, but its forms and its rhetoric were familiar from the European past.

By 1848, everything had changed. In February 1848, as a new French Revolution gathered force, Alexis de Tocqueville left his house for Parliament. Along his route, as citizens quietly watched, men were systematically putting up barricades. "These barricades," he observed,

> were skillfully constructed by a small number of men who worked industriously – not like criminals fearful of being caught *in flagrante delicto*, but like good workmen who wanted to do their job expeditiously and well. Nowhere

[1] The trials, including the one summarized here, have been most thoroughly studied by Hans-Jürgen Lusebrink in his "L'imaginaire social et ses focalisations en France et en Allemagne à la fin du XVIII siecle" (1983).

did I see the seething unrest I had witnessed in 1830, when the whole city reminded me of one vast, boiling cauldron (Tocqueville 1987: 39).

Of "seething unrest" and "boiling cauldrons" Europe would see a great deal in the months following February 1848. But at mid-century, Frenchmen were calmly building barricades, knew where to put them up, and had learned how to use them.[2] A fundamental change had occurred in the *repertoire of contention* since the attack on Master Thibault's house sixty years before. The contrast was more than one of greater scale. The tearing down of houses was a routine that had long been used against tax gatherers, brothel keepers, and grain merchants in France.[3] But this approach centered on direct sites of wrongdoing and was limited to direct attacks on its perpetrators. The barricade, in contrast, is what I call "modular." It could be mounted in a variety of sites, on behalf of a variety of goals, and against a variety of targets. Once its strategic advantages were known, the barricade could unify people with different aims and could be diffused to a variety of types of confrontation with authorities. For example, Jacques Godechot, in his inventory of the 1848 Revolutions, lists at least nine different claims for which barricades were used in France alone.[4]

Although in the 1780s, people certainly knew how to seize shipments of grain, attack tax gatherers, burn tax registers, and take revenge on wrongdoers and people who had violated community norms, they were not yet familiar with modular forms of contention such as the mass demonstration, the strike, or the urban insurrection. But by the end of the 1848 revolution, performances such as the petition, the public meeting, the demonstration, and the barricade were well-known routines of contention, which were used for a variety of purposes and by different combinations of social actors. Before examining the forms of this new repertoire and its relation to the birth of the national social movement, let us first look at the concept of the repertoire of contention and at how the repertoire developed in early modern Europe; we will then see how it spread around the world.

[2] The most sustained work on the barricades is by Marc Traugott and Roger Gould. See Traugott's "Barricades as Repertoire: Continuities and Discontinuities Across Nineteenth Century France" (1995) and his *The Insurgent Barricade* (2010). Gould's *Insurgent Identities* (1995) traces the evolution of the barricade from a weapon of neighborhood defense to a cross-neighborhood magnet for insurgents to gather around.

[3] In his "Speaking Your Mind Without Elections" (1983), Tilly describes the "sacking routine" as common in the eighteenth century, observing that it was frequently used to punish tavern or brothel keepers who cheated their customers, or public officials who had passed the bounds of legitimacy. Its use to punish a venal householder who had abused a servant seems to have been an innovation of the pre-revolutionary period. It continues to appear throughout the French Revolution, most dramatically in the Reveillon riots of May 1789. (On the latter, see Simon Schama's vivid reconstruction in *Citizens* 1989: 326–332).

[4] See Godechot's *Les Révolutions de 1848* (1971). The analysis of how the barricade diffused in 1848 is reported in Sarah Soule and Sidney Tarrow, "Acting Collectively, 1847–1849: How the Repertoire of Collective Action Changed and Where it Happened" (1991).

REPERTOIRES OF CONTENTION

In 1995, capping more than thirty years of work on collective action,[5] Charles Tilly published his major work, *Popular Contention in Great Britain, 1758–1834* (1995b). In it, Tilly defined the "repertoire of contention" as "the ways that people act together in pursuit of shared interests" (p. 41). "Looking at the history of popular movements in France from the 17th to the 20th centuries," he later wrote,

> I couldn't help noticing two related anomalies. First, although ordinary people found vigorously vital ways of making their voices heard in the midst of repressive regimes, they clung to the same few forms of collective expression and modified those forms only slowly.... Second, ordinary people never engaged in a wide variety of technically feasible ways of making collective claims that ordinary people elsewhere and in other times had readily employed (2008: xiii).

From that observation came Tilly's concept of the "repertoire of contention." The repertoire involves not only what people *do* when they are engaged in conflict with others but *what they know how to do* and what others expect them to do. Had sit-ins been tried by challengers in eighteenth century France, their targets would not have known how to respond to them, any more than the victim of a *charivari* today would know what it meant.[6] As Arthur Stinchcombe writes, "The elements of the repertoire are ... simultaneously the skills of the population members and the cultural forms of the population" (1987: 1248).

Repertoire changes depend on major fluctuations in interests, opportunities, and organizations. These, in turn, correlate roughly with changes in states and capitalism:

- Major shifts resulted from the increase in the national state's penetration of society and construction of a national administrative apparatus to make war, extract taxes, and regulate behavior.
- They also resulted from capitalism's creation of large concentrations of people with the grievances, the organization of production, and the resources to act collectively.

---

[5] Tilly's contributions to the field of collective action and social movements are so massive as to make them difficult to summarize. For a brief bibliography and critical analysis, see William Sewell Jr., "Collective Violence and Collective Loyalties in France: Why the French Revolution Made a Difference" (1990) and Sidney Tarrow, "Charles Tilly and the Practice of Contentious Politics" (2008).

[6] The *charivari* was a form of demonstration designed to poke fun at and humiliate members of a community who had broken local cultural norms, such as the widower who married a young woman, thus removing her from the marriage market. In the American West, tarring and feathering was a form of *charivari*, known in England as "rough music."

Though structurally based, these changes in repertoires will show up in the major political watersheds that I refer to in Chapter 10 as "cycles of contention."

What separated the new repertoire that Tocqueville saw on his way to Parliament from the eighteenth century forms reflected in the Cléraux affair? "If we push back into the strange terrain of western Europe and North America before the middle of the nineteenth century," writes Tilly, "we soon discover another world" of collective action (1983: 463). The traditional repertoire was parochial, segmented, and particular:

- It was *parochial* because most often the interests and interaction involved were concentrated in a single community.
- It was *segmented* because when ordinary people addressed local issues and nearby objects, they took impressively direct action to achieve their ends, but when it came to national issues and objects, they recurrently addressed their demands to a local patron or authority.
- And it was *particular* because the detailed routines of action varied greatly from group to group, from issue to issue, and from locality to locality (Tilly 1995b: 45).

Such forms of contention would often explode at public celebrations, when people took advantage of the opportunity of numerous people collected in public places, often lubricated by drink, in which high spirits and hot-headedness would combine. But these events were never entirely "spontaneous": they would draw on rich, often irreverent symbolism, religious rituals, and popular culture. Participants often converged on the residences of wrongdoers and the sites of wrongdoing, commonly appearing as members or representatives of constituted corporate groups and communities (Tilly 1983: 464).

Changes in the repertoire did not appear fully blown everywhere at once, nor did the old forms of collective action ever completely disappear. Put yourself back in western Pennsylvania at the dawn of the new American nation. Treasury Secretary Alexander Hamilton had imposed an excise tax on whiskey, a product that was important not only to lubricate the colonists' spirits but to turn grain into a product that could be shipped to market without spoiling. "Whisky," in Gordon Wood's lively account, "had become a necessary form of money for the cash-strapped Western areas" (Wood 2009: 136).

The westerners were outraged at the new tax: Had they not risen up against Britain in protest against just such fiscal impositions? And what right had the new federal government to impose taxes on the fiercely independent states? As the outrage spread, both old and new forms of contention exploded along the frontier. In Wood's words,

> While some Pennsylvanians prevented enforcement of the tax by tarring and feathering and terrorizing excise collectors, others channeled their anger into extralegal meetings of protest. They sent petitions to Congress, organized assemblies and committees of correspondence, condemned the excise tax for

being as unjust and oppressive as the Stamp Act of 1765 and ostracized everyone who favored or obeyed the excise law (p. 136).

Note the intermingling of petitions, assemblies, meetings, marches, and forming
of committees, alongside the old practices of tarring and feathering officials
and ostracizing those who cooperated with the government. Gradually, in
America – as in Europe – demonstrations, strikes, rallies, public meetings, and
similar forms of interaction came to prevail.

As compared with their predecessors, the new forms had a cosmopolitan,
modular, and autonomous character:

* They were *cosmopolitan* in often referring to interests and issues that
  spanned many localities or affected centers of power whose actions touched
  many localities.
* They were *modular* in being easily transferable from one setting or circum-
  stance to another.
* And they were *autonomous* in beginning on the claimants' own initiative
  and establishing direct contact between claimants and nationally significant
  centers of power (Tilly 1995b: 46).

The old and new repertoires are not equally general. From the sixteenth to the
eighteenth century, the forms of action used in attacks on millers and grain
merchants, tax collectors, and bakers were directly linked to the nature of
their targets and the grievances of the actors who used them. It was the lack
of generality in the older forms that impeded the rise of broader constella-
tions of interest and action. The more general nature of the new forms of
contention laid a common cultural and behavioral foundation on which social
movements could build. The question that emerges is: What is the relationship
between changes in the repertoire of contention and the birth of the social
movement? We will turn to that question after examining some traditional
forms of contention typical of early modern Europe and the British colonies of
North America.

THE TRADITIONAL REPERTOIRE

For the great French historian, Marc Bloch, collective action was a direct
reflection of social structure. In writing of peasant revolts in feudal society,
Bloch argued that "agrarian revolt seems as inseparable from the seignorial
regime as the strike from the great capitalist enterprise" (1931: 175). He saw a
general identity between the forms of collective action that people used and the
substance of their claims, which resulted from the structure of their conflicts
with others. Bloch's axiom had two main correlates: first, that the relationship
between challenger and challenged is direct; and, second, that the forms of
collective action are attached to the former's grievances and the latter's power.
But the same logic leads to constraints on who can act alongside whom and
on how widely a particular form of collective action can be used. Because if

the agrarian revolt was aimed at the landlord, it followed that peasants who participated in it would associate only with those who shared similar grievances against him in local village networks. These forms of action were rooted in the corporate structure of the feudal community. That limited the geographic reach and the scale of the episode and impeded it from developing into a generalized social movement.

Bloch was correct for the period of history he knew so well. In societies divided into orders, isolated by poor communication and lack of literacy, and organized into corporate and communal groups, the dominant forms of collective action were wedded to particular pairs of actors and to the conflicts that connected them. When Protestants built a church in a Catholic district, the Catholic community would tear it down – or burn it with the parishioners inside (Davis 1973); when millers tried to move their grain outside a hungry district to make a bigger profit, it would be seized and sold at a just price (Tilly 1975a); when authorities were responsible for the violent death of a local citizen, the funeral could turn into a funeral riot (Tamason 1980). The traditional repertoire was segmented, was aimed directly at its targets, and grew out of the corporate structure of society.

Only when they were led by people who possessed organizational or institutional resources outside of this corporate structure – for example, in the Church hierarchy – or when they coincided with opportunities presented by dynastic conflicts did these episodes become part of broader confrontations. Then they could give rise to national – or even international – conflicts, as they did in Europe's "hundred years' war." More often, they flared up like scattered sparks that were rapidly exhausted or snuffed out. For the most part, as Tilly argued, "local people and local issues, rather than nationally organized programs and parties, entered repeatedly into the day's collective confrontations" (1995a: 19).

Parochialism, direct action, and particularism combined in four of the most common types of popular revolts that fill the historical record until well into modern times. In conflicts over bread, belief, land, and death, ordinary people tried to correct immediate abuses or take revenge on those they opposed, using routines of collective action that were direct, local, and inspired by their grievances.

Demanding Bread

Probably the most common sources of contention in the course of history were the periodic food riots and grain seizures that accompanied times of dearth and increases in the price of food. In our epoch of abundance, it is easy to forget that in older periods of history, some 80 to 90 percent of a poor family's income went for food, and most of that was for bread, which was deeply vulnerable to changes in harvests, times of war, and price inflation (Kaplan 1984). Though the result of natural causes, famines almost always brought higher prices, hoarding, and speculation, providing protesters with concrete targets for their rage: merchants and middlemen, Jews, and Protestants – more rarely, nobles and princes were the targets of their desperation. As a result, providing the population with a steady and affordable source of grain was a major problem for centralizing states. Not only that, but new social actors – women – appeared in food protests so commonly that when, in 1789, hungry Parisians marched on the Palace of Versailles demanding bread, they disguised themselves as women.

For several centuries, even as national and international markets were replacing local grain sales, the forms of collective action surrounding dearth remained particularistic, direct, and dependent on inherited understandings such as the "moral economy" that Thompson wrote of. As he pointed out, "The records of the poor show . . . it is this miller, this dealer, those farmers hoarding grain, who provoke indignation and action" (1971: 98). Even during the Revolution of 1789, the forms of food seizures changed little, although they were sometimes exploited by ambitious politicians for broader ends. Remarkably, they spread rapidly, in no relationship to the degree of dearth in a region but in direct response to rumors of plots and conspiracies (Kaplan 1982).

The most ancient form of food protest was what Tilly calls the "retributive action," in which a crowd attacked a person or the property of a person accused of withholding food or profiteering (1975a: 386). Preventing a food shipment from leaving a locality was a second variant of food protest, which "acted out the belief that the locals should be fed, at a proper price, before any surplus left town" (p. 387). A third form, the price riot, was more characteristic of urban areas and became widespread with the growth of cities in the eighteenth century.

Grain seizures followed such a well-known routine that Thompson described them metaphorically as "collective bargaining by riot" (1971). They developed not so much out of raw hunger and outrage, as traditional historians thought (Beloff 1938), but, rather, were carried out by people who "believed others were unjustly depriving them of food to which they had a moral and political right" (Thompson: 389). But although often well organized, these explosions seldom gained the common purpose or the widespread solidarity needed to mount a sustained campaign. Their limitations reflected the societies in which they arose. As Tilly writes, "small in scale, leaderless, and carried on by unarmed men, women and children, the food riot rarely consolidated into a larger rebellion" (1975a: 443). Broader movements had to await the Revolution of 1789, when "ordinary complaints about the incompetence and/or immorality of the local authorities and merchants now took on a political cast" (p. 448).

Asserting Belief

Women and men in early modern Europe did not protest for bread alone. For most of known time, it has been religion and religious conflict that have produced the most savage episodes of contention. In the centuries following the first millennium after Christ, waves of heretical sects developed within and against the Catholic Church. Some of these, based on the charisma of a single leader, were easily suppressed. But others, such as the Cathars, who preached a dissident version of the Trinity, became briefly dominant in areas of southern France, where it took a crusade to root them out. Later religious groups, such as the Camisards in France or the iconoclasts in the Low Countries, already resembled social movements (Tilly 1986: 174–178).

Existing forms of church organization provided both the targets and the models for the rebellions of these sects. Collective actions mounted in the name of religion often savagely parodied their opponents' practices. In assaulting Catholics, French Protestants mimicked Catholic ritual, and Catholics responded in kind.[7] As in modern religious-based terrorism inspired by religious frenzy, the ferocity of these attacks far outstripped that of secular protests. But with hatred assuaged by blood and offending practices suppressed, no permanent new repertoires resulted. It was only when religious fervor joined with peasant revolt, dynastic ambition, or interstate conflict that rebels against religion gained access to tools that began to resemble the modern social movement.

The Protestant "saint" was the forerunner of the modern social movement militant. He not only believed deeply in his cause; he turned the mission of converting souls into a profession (Walzer 1971: Chapter 1), and he traveled from region to region and across borders as the first truly transnational movement missionary. The first "corresponding societies" were religious brotherhoods linked by couriers, secret codes, and rituals. But until then, religious movements ranged from physical attacks against Jews, Protestants, Catholics, and heretics to the sporadic local resistance of religious sects such as the Camisards or the Waldensians (Tilly 2005: Chapter 1).

Claiming Land

Almost as common in early modern history as food riots and religious conflicts were peasant revolts. Traditional peasants depended on customary rights to land, water, or forage to survive and were most easily goaded into revolt when these rights were curtailed or abused. Rights were often claimed in the name of the peasant community, whose members would accuse landlords of breaking ancient conventions and usurping contracts. Even modern "struggles for the land" in Italy and Spain frequently hearkened back to land usurpations that were more than a century old.[8]

---

[7] Natalie Davis, in her "The Rites of Violence" (1973), has given us the most vivid evocation of the brutally mimetic qualities of early modern religious conflicts in France.

[8] For examples of the re-evocation of these historical memories in peasant land seizures in southern Europe, see Eric Hobsbawm, *Primitive Rebels and Social Bandits* (1959), Julian Pitt-Rivers, *People of the Sierra* (1971), and Sidney Tarrow, *Peasant Communism in Southern Italy* (1967). For similar re-enactments in Latin America, see Hobsbawm's "Peasant Land Occupations" (1974).

The forms of land revolt often followed a ritual that took shape around the needs of the landless or the land poor. Peasants brandishing pitchforks and scythes or carrying the cross or a statue of the Virgin would assemble in the town square, march to usurped land, and "occupy" it. Such outbursts could spread from village to village like wildfire without common agents or organizations. But once the occupation was over, local groups seldom found a way to organize around broader themes and almost never made common cause with the urban poor.[9] Apparent exceptions – such as the Croquant movement of the late sixteenth century, which was organized by surprisingly modern-looking assemblies (Bercé 1990: Chapter 2) – were not based on land, but were organized against marauding bands left over from the religious wars (Bercé 1990: 72–75). Such revolts were as easy to isolate and snuff out as they had been to spark.

Mobilizing around Death

It may be surprising to think of death as a source of collective action. But it is the reaction of the *living* – especially to violent death – that is the source of protest, rather than death itself. Death has the power to trigger violent emotions and brings people together with little in common but their grief and their solidarity. It provides legitimate occasions for public gatherings, and is one of the few occasions on which officials will hesitate to charge into a crowd or ban public assemblies.

Death has always been connected to an institutionalized form of collective action – the funeral – that brings people together in ceremony and solidarity. In repressive systems, which ban public assemblies, funeral processions are often the only occasions on which protests can begin. When the death of a friend or a relative is seen as an outrage, funeral gatherings can become the site of disruption. When a public figure offends the mores of the community, he can be symbolically killed with a mock funeral. But the same reasoning tells us why death is seldom the source of a sustained social movement: Death's moment is brief, and the ritual occasion offered by a funeral is soon over. It was only in the nineteenth century, in the context of movements formed for other purposes, that funerals began to be the occasion for sustained mobilization against authorities (Tamason 1980: 15–31). In the twentieth century, in places like South Africa and Israel/Palestine, funerals provided the occasion for contentious politics and for its repression.[10]

---

[9] Focusing on the protests of agricultural laborers in England, Andrew Charlesworth in *An Atlas of Rural Protest in Britain* finds that it was only in the agrarian revolt of 1816 that "men from many different occupations over the whole of a rural area made common cause by each responding to the protests and demonstrations of their fellow workers" (1983: 146).

[10] The funeral protest became a major form of mobilization in South Africa in the 1980s. Each time the police would shoot demonstrators, a major funeral demonstration followed. During the struggle against Apartheid, the white-dominated South African government banned funeral protests, which had become sites for mobilization. The same was true of the Israeli

Demanding bread, asserting belief, claiming land, and mobilizing around
death – in all four areas of contention, collective action was violent and direct,
brief, specific, and parochial. With the exception of religious conflicts – where
trans-local institutions and common beliefs facilitated broader coalitions and
greater coordination – the actors in these forms of contention seldom moved
beyond local or sectoral interests or sustained them against authorities or elites.

It was not for lack of organization that pre–eighteenth century Europeans
failed to build sustained social movements. Indeed, when they were aroused or
had the opportunity to do so, they organized powerfully, as the religious wars
of the sixteenth and seventeenth centuries showed. Nor were food rioters or
funeral marchers "apolitical" – or even "pre-political" (Hobsbawm 1959): The
former were revolting not at famine *per se*, but against evidence that authorities
were ignoring their inherited rights, while the latter had the political shrewdness
to use a legitimate ceremony as an opportunity to air their grievances. The major
constraint on turning contention into movements was the focus of the forms
and goals of collective action on people's immediate claims, on their direct
targets, and within their local and corporate memberships (Kaplan 1982).

Of course, direct assaults on personal targets often meant violence, and this
violence triggered attempts at repression from authorities, elites, or competing
groups. The eighteenth century presents us with a particularly violent picture
of contention, not because large numbers of actors were arrayed against major
national targets, but rather, because small numbers of actors attacked nearby
targets directly with the tools at hand. When Tilly analyzed the verbs used in
newspaper accounts of contentious gatherings in the 1760s, the ones he found
most often were "attack," "control," and "move."[11] One can almost visualize
groups of farmers moving along the roads to the homes of bakers and millers
and being met by constabulary forces sent out to control them. Figure 2.1,
from Tilly's *Contentious Performances,* shows the relative frequency of these
physical action verbs in the accounts he studied from England in the 1760s.

All this would change between the eighteenth and mid-nineteenth centuries.
For this change, expansion of roads and printed communications, growth of
private associations, the coming of capitalism, and expansion of the modern
state were largely responsible. We will turn to print and association in the next
chapter, and to state expansion in Chapter 4. But first, we need to delineate
the outlines of the modern repertoire as it developed in Europe and the United
States and then spread across the globe.

authorities during the first Palestinian Intifada, a move that may have indirectly contributed
to the escalation of violence in that rebellion against Israeli occupation. On the banning of
South African funeral processions, see http://articles.latimes.com/1985–08-01/news/mn-4324-
1_south-africa-s-currency. On Palestinian use of the funeral procession as a mobilizing tool,
see Alimi (2007: 148–149).

[11] "Attack" in Figure 2.1 includes words like attack, attempt, and fight. "Control" includes
control, resist, and block. "Move" contains move, gather, proceed, enter, assemble, disperse,
and march.

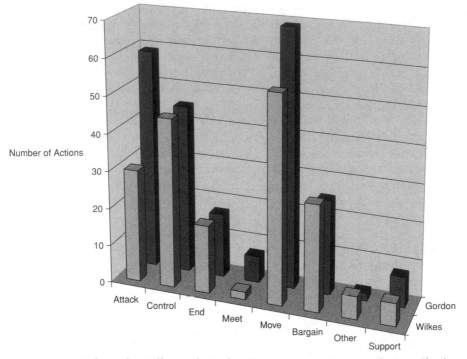

FIGURE 2.1. Verbs in the Wilkes and Gordon Campaigns, 1768–1780. *Source:* Charles Tilly, *Contentious Performances*, p. 100. Copyright © 2008 Charles Tilly. Reprinted with permission of Cambridge University Press.

THE MODERN REPERTOIRE

Bloch's axiom embedding particular forms of collective action in specific social structures, which was perfectly applicable to the estate societies he studied, does not fit nearly as well in the societies that began to emerge in Europe and North America in the eighteenth century. In these places, a new repertoire developed that was cosmopolitan rather than parochial; autonomous rather than dependent on inherited rituals or occasions; and modular rather than particular. While centering around a few key routines of confrontation, it would be adapted to different settings, and its elements combined in campaigns of collective action by coalitions of contenders. Once used and understood, the new repertoire would be diffused to other actors and employed on behalf of new challengers. The new repertoire made it possible for even scattered groups of people who did not know one another to combine in sustained challenges to authorities – in social movements.

Of course, inherited forms of the past – the *charivari*, the serenade, the illumination, the violent attack on enemies' houses – did not disappear with the invention of the new repertoire. But as new claims were constructed, and as people developed enhanced capacities for collective action, even these older forms were infused with more general meaning and were combined with newer ones. Three examples from both sides of the Atlantic in the eighteenth century will illustrate what was happening as the new repertoire came into use: boycotts; mass petitioning; and public meetings.

From Effigies to Boycotts in America

The colonists who settled on the eastern littoral of North America between the sixteenth and eighteenth centuries brought with them from Europe a repertoire of collective action. In the 1760s, as the conflict with the mother country gathered force, their first responses were traditionally European: They hung effigies from trees, burned down houses, and dumped bags of tea into Boston Harbor. It was only with increasing scale and intensified networking of colonists' actions and the ruthlessness of the British response that a sustained social movement developed.

When the British tried to impose a new and more onerous stamp duty in 1765, the instinctive response of Bostonians was to hang an effigy of the designated distributor on the future Liberty Tree. "In the evening," writes Pauline Maier, "a large crowed paraded the effigy, leveled a small building . . . reputed to be the future Stamp Office, then burned the effigy while a smaller contingent attacked the stampman's home" (1972: 54). The agitation was infectious and spread rapidly through the colonies, using forms inherited from the old country. Mock trials for stamps and stampmen were held, "funerals" were staged for liberty, and effigies were paraded in routines that strongly recalled traditional English practices (pp. 54ff.). Serious rioting was a frequent accompaniment of these proceedings. But by September, with the news that the Ministry of George Grenville had fallen in London, the wave of violence against the persons and policies of the stamp controversy subsided (p. 61; also see Tilly 2008; see Chapter 5).

But the same period saw the appearance of a more organized, more general form of action that did not involve physical contact or violence – the boycott.[12] Colonial merchants first made "nonimportation" agreements against the Sugar Act in 1764, calling for reducing the import of luxury goods from England, above all of the mourning clothes and gloves traditionally worn at funerals. "These fledgling efforts," writes Maier, "were systematized in September 1765 (with the Stamp Act controversy), and thereafter nonimportation associations were organized in other commercial centers" (1972: 74).

The boycott became a basic routine for rebellious colonists and was used over the next decade in response to virtually every effort of the British to impose stricter control. For Americans, "nonimportation could constitute an effective

---

[12] Note that the practice existed long before the term "boycott" existed, with the colonists using the term "nonimportation." The modern terminology dates only from 1880 – and in Ireland – when the practice was used against a certain Captain Boycott. It quickly spread across the West, as indicated by the French term *boycotter*.

substitute for domestic violence; opposition could retreat from the streets to the spinning wheel" (Maier, p. 75). If giving up mourning could contribute to the fall of a British minister, asked a writer in the *Boston Gazette*, "what may we not expect from a full and general Execution of this plan?" (p. 75). Thenceforth, nonimportation and boycotting became the modular weapons of the American rebellion.[13]

The effectiveness of the tactic was not lost on the British agitating against the slave trade. In 1791, the English Antislavery Association used a boycott on the importation of sugar from the West Indies to put pressure on Parliament to abolish the slave trade (Drescher 1987: 78–79). From a parochial response to new taxes from the periphery of the British empire, the boycott migrated to its core. There it combined the organized use of the press and the petition to bring about the end of the slave trade.

Mass Petitioning in England[14]

The English petition was an ancient form of action for individuals seeking redress from patrons or Parliament. As such, it was culturally acceptable, perfectly lawful, and scarcely contentious. But with growth of the economy in the eighteenth century, petitioning spread to entire trades claiming injury from expansion of the excise tax (Brewer 1989: 233). When the first great petition against slavery was circulated in 1788, a representative of the Jamaican sugar lobby was outraged: These abolitionists had not been injured by slavery, nor would they benefit personally from its end; what right had they to petition for its abolition (Drescher 1987: pp. 76–77)? By the 1790s, petitions were being launched regularly at public meetings and were accompanied by boycotts, newspaper advertisements, and lobbying in extended movement campaigns.

John Wilkes and others had used the petition for political purposes in the 1760s, and a petition had preceded the outbreak of the Gordon riots of 1780 (Tilly 2008: Chapter 4). But it was the antislavery campaign launched in bustling Manchester that effected its transformation from an individual complaint into a modular tool of contention. Manchester's industrialists first used a petition to demand repeal of the government's revenue plans in the early 1780s. They also played a leading role a few years later in the petition campaign against a customs union with Ireland (Drescher 1987: 69). These were commercial issues, but they created the modular tool that could "open

---

[13] Indeed, it was only to enforce a general boycott that was succeeding elsewhere that a coalition of Boston merchants and publicists employed the older routine of destroying imported tea. See Richard D. Brown, *Revolutionary Politics in Massachusetts* (1970).

[14] I am grateful to Seymour Drescher for his comments on an earlier version of the following section, which leans heavily on his *Capitalism and Antislavery* (1987). Also see Drescher's articles "Public Opinion and the Destruction of British Colonial Slavery" (1982) and "British Way, French Way: Opinion Building and Revolution in the Second French Slave Emancipation" (1991), as well as Leo d'Anjou's *Social Movements and Cultural Change: The First Abolitionist Campaign Revisited* (1996).

the sluices of enthusiasm" for issues with broader policy or moral content (p. 69). Self-confident and wealthy Manchester merchants extrapolated the skills developed on behalf of their business interests into a national moral campaign.

The antislavery campaign raised the numbers of petitions and the numbers of signers, who were coordinated in a single campaign by a quantum leap. More important, the men of Manchester combined the petition with the use of Britain's dense network of provincial newspapers to advertise the campaign against slavery in every major newspaper market, using the press to trigger a wave of petitions sent to Parliament from around the country (pp. 70–72). In 1792, a new antislavery campaign quintupled the number of petitions, "the largest number ever submitted to the House on a single subject or in a single session," according to Drescher (p. 80). By the 1790s, the use of mass petitions had spread: first to Radicals demanding expansion of the suffrage and protesting the curtailment of free speech by a government spooked by fear of jacobinism (Goodwin 1979); and then to advocates for electoral reform.

Public Meetings

Similar to the abolitionists, the Reform Societies of the 1820s and 1830s used the provincial press to coordinate the efforts of different local associations, linking the signing of petitions in the country with their lobbying efforts in London. But by the 1830s, the Chartists had combined the decorous presentation of mass petitions with a new form – the collective use of public space – to demonstrate the movement's claims. In presenting their "people's petitions" to Parliament, the Chartists brought thousands of people into the streets of London in April 1848.[15] From the plea of a dependent client to his patron, and from a lobby's claim of tax relief for its members, petitioning had been transformed into a public and peaceful form of collective action used to put pressure on government to demand constitutional change.

Tilly's study of the changes in contention in late eighteenth and early nineteenth century England revealed the shift from forms that had dominated in the earlier period toward public meetings. From a repertoire that was virtually dominated by verbs denoting attack and control in the 1760s' Wilkes and Gordon campaigns, the three years surrounding the first Reform Act were dominated by "meet" verbs, with a substantial minority of "move" verbs – protesters would often march to a meeting place in a combination march/demonstration that has endured to the present – and of verbs denoting "support" for the policies of one side or another in the main controversies of the period (Tilly 2008; see Chapter 4). Figure 2.2 reproduces Tilly's findings regarding the

---

[15] With revolution breaking out all over Europe and anarchy threatening in Ireland, this was too much for the government, which mobilized 150,000 "voluntary" constables to stop the presentation of the Chartists' petition on Kennington Common. See Dorothy Thompson, *The Chartists* (1984: Chapter 3), on the use of the mass petition by the Chartists. On the repressed Kennington Common demonstration, see Raymond Postgate, *The Story of a Year: 1848* (1955: 117).

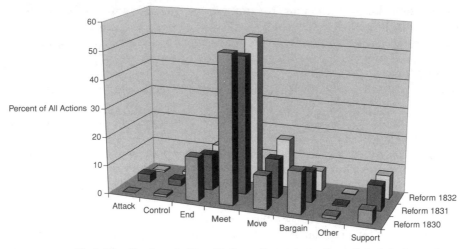

FIGURE 2.2. Verb Distributions in Two Reform Campaigns, Great Britain, 1830–1832. *Source:* Charles Tilly, *Contentious Performances*, p. 100. Copyright © 2008 Charles Tilly. Reprinted with permission of Cambridge University Press.

distribution of action verbs during the period 1830–1832 from his *Contentious Performances*.

VIOLENCE AND COUNTERVIOLENCE

Peaceful meetings, crowds of people moving cheerfully through the streets, support for the policies of one group or another – these were sure signs that the old direct action repertoire was giving way to a new national one, in which demands made on Parliament were crowding out the old local, parochial, and often violent forms. But we should not conclude that the trends were all toward pacification. Remember how elements of the old and the new repertoire intermingled in the Whiskey Rebellion in violence-prone America? Even in peaceful England, marches often incited onlookers to throw stones; public meetings often ended in a brawl; and the so-called forces of order could easily turn into police riots. This is what happened in the Peterloo massacre, where the army was called up to meet working class protesters and killed eleven people and arrested hundreds more (Tilly 2008: 134–135). Across the channel, where British-style parliamentary ascendency was not achieved until 1871, both political violence and its violent repression were far more common. There, urban insurrections employing popular forms of self-defense, such as the barricade, were more common, and police and army repression was more determined.

The Urban Insurrection in France

Even before the French Revolution, a repertoire of urban insurrection was forming in France. It was most forcefully implemented on July 14, 1789, in Paris, but the model of the urban insurrection was provincial – and not Parisian – in origin.[16] In June, 1788, angered by the Court's attempt to replace the provincial parliaments with a new system of national courts, and exacerbated by the economic distress of local craftsmen, a disturbance began in the marketplace of the Alpine city of Grenoble. What resulted was the "Day of the Tiles," probably the first fully secular urban insurrection in French history, and a foretaste of what was to come at the Bastille a year later (Sewell 1996). As in Boston, at first, the forms of action used by the Grenoblois were familiar, direct, and physical. They attacked buildings and officials at the marketplace, and when troops were sent to quell the riot, they showered them with a rain of tiles from the rooftops. But soon after, an urban leadership was formed, assembling illegally at the Chateau of Vizelle and producing a major manifesto that put pressure on the King to call the Estates General.

Although the events in Grenoble were violent and disorderly, we see there a premonition of the modern social movement. The Grenoblois employed a variety of forms of collective action in a sequence of contentious conflict with elites and authorities. Organization emerged at a meeting in Vizelle in which the claims of upper class *parlementaires*, middle class writers and clerks, artisans, glove makers, and women were merged under a broader umbrella of rights claims. In the words of some of the participants, the main demand was "the return of our magistrates, privileges and the reestablishment of the conditions which alone can make true laws" (Schama 1989: 279). The concept of rights elaborated at Vizelle went much farther than the claims of the participants. In addition to dignifying and uniting the claims of a broad coalition of social actors, it established the idea that an unauthorized assembly, acting in the name of "the laws and the people," could demand a contractual relationship with the state that went beyond parliamentary privileges or economic relief (Egret 1977: 177).

The combination of violent urban insurrection and peaceful deliberation culminated in the summer of 1789, when the violent assault on the Bastille co-occurred with the Third Estate's breakaway from the Estates General in Versailles (Sewell 1996) and gave birth to the concept of popular sovereignty. All through the French Revolution, violent *journées* co-occurred with – indeed, often triggered – shifts in power in the political elite. The same was true on a European level during the 1848 revolutions. Everywhere that barricades were built, armories invaded, and rulers, aristocrats, and Jews violently attacked, liberal assemblies came together to deliberate and fashion constitutions, often squandering their opportunities in torrents of words, while the old regimes were regrouping and getting ready to turn back the clock on reform (Godechet 1971). In many of these cities, a modular form that had developed out of old-style neighborhood protection sprang up, providing both defense against

---

[16] But see William Sewell Jr.'s persuasive argument that it was only with the taking of the Bastille in July 1789 that the urban insurrection was linked normatively to the concept of popular sovereignty in his "Historical Events as Transformation of Structures" (1996).

assaulting troops and a symbolic site for the creation of collective identity – the barricade.

The Social Construction of the Barricade

The most dramatic and most feared expression of the new repertoire in the 1800s was the barricade, which became the main instrument of armed insurrection all over Europe (Traugott 1995; 2010). Barricades had first appeared in Paris, when neighborhoods tried to protect themselves from intruders by stretching chains across the road. The term evolved after 1588, when these defenses were reinforced by filling barrels (*barriques*) with earth or paving stones.[17] At the beginning, writes Traugott, barricades "were the collaborative creations of the members of small-scale communities, often directed against the representatives of constituted authorities" (1990: 3).

By the 1830 revolution, barricades had developed into offensive strongpoints in the streets of Paris, recruiting friends and neighbors on a largely local basis. But by the February Days in the 1848 revolution, barricades were no longer local and particular modes of neighborhood defense, for they attracted "cosmopolitans" from other neighborhoods of Paris (pp. 8–9). By the time of the 1871 Paris Commune, they were vulnerable to long-distance cannon, but they still served a solidary and symbolic function (Gould 1995: 164).

One reason for the popularity of the barricade was that it helped people form new collective identities. As they faced off against hostile troops, the defenders of a barricade came to know each other as comrades and developed a division of labor among fighters, builders, and suppliers, thereby forming networks of comrades that would bring them together in future confrontations. As Traugott writes,

> ... from a vantage point atop a barricade, an entire generation of revolutionists was formed in the struggle against the Bourbon and Orleanist monarchies; matured in the struggles of the Second Republic; and saw its political aspirations crushed by the coup that ushered in the rule of Louis Napoleon (1990: 3).

France was quickly followed by its neighbors. As insurrections spread across Europe in the spring of 1848, the barricade emerged as the quintessential modular form of revolutionary activity. From February 1847 to the middle of 1849, barricades appeared as far apart as Madrid and Lisbon, Messina and Milan, and Berlin and Vienna (Godechot 1971; Soule and Tarrow 1991). In Vienna, barricades were raised to demand constitutional reform; in Sicily to

---

[17] See the discussion by Traugott in his "Barricades as Repertoire" (1995: 43–56). Also see his "Neighborhoods in Insurrection: The Parisian Quartier in the February Revolution of 1848" (1990) and his *The Insurgent Barricade* (2010). It is not clear how much use was made of barricades during the first French Revolution. Hobsbawm is of the opinion that they were never used at all (see his *The Age of Revolution: 1789–1848*, 1962:146), but Traugott disagrees in *The Insurgent Barricade*.

demand independence from Naples; in Milan and Venice to end Austrian rule; and in the smaller Po valley towns to demand unification with Piedmont. The barricades in the 1848 revolutions spread faster than a man could ride by coach from Paris to Milan. As opera composer Giuseppe Verdi, then visiting Paris, wrote, eager to take part in his country's revolution,

> Guess whether I wanted to stay in Paris when I heard the news of Milan's Revolution? I left as promptly as possible, but I arrived only in time to see those fantastic barricades![18]

Building a barricade had become a symbolic claim that you were making a revolution. Danielle Tartakowsky found evidence of the construction of thirty-one different barricades in France between 1919 and 1968 (1997). And although not all barricades resulted in successful revolutions, as late as May 1968, students in Paris were building barricades to defend their revolution (Schnapp and Vidal-Naquet 1988).

Innovation and Counterinnovation

The evolution of the barricade brings us to a strangely under-researched issue in the study of contentious politics: the relationship between innovations in the repertoire and changes in the strategies of repression. Authorities faced by contentious politics can respond by facilitation or repression or by a combination of the two. One major reason why challengers invent new forms of contention is to outwit, evade, or surprise these authorities (McAdam 1983). Police and public officials know how to respond to a strike and are guided by elaborate laws and regulations for dealing with strikers. Similarly, authorities are equipped to deal with organized violence – these days, they show up well protected and armed with tear gas and paddy wagons. Protesters who wish to avoid repression will frequently innovate in the forms of contention they employ to avoid these known deterrents, while police and public officials adapt to these changes with innovations of their own.

In Chapters 9 and 10, we will return in detail to the interaction between contention and repression. Here it is enough to note that innovation in the forms of contentious politics is a function of the relations between challengers and those whose task it is to control or repress them. Each move on the part of challengers away from expected forms of behavior might leave authorities unprepared in the short run, but eventually, the "forces of order" adapt new techniques to control them. For example, the Paris of 1848 in which Tocqueville saw men building barricades was still a city whose streets had been laid out in the Middle Ages – narrow, twisting, and often impassable. Many of them were also lined by tall buildings built higgledy-piggledy next to one another. No urban armature could have been more conducive to the building of barricades,

---

[18] From a letter of 21 April 1848 to his librettist, Piave, quoted in Open University, *Music and Revolution: Verdi* (1976: 42).

and none was less amenable to their reduction by well-armed forces of police or army. The narrow streets would not admit the cannon that the army could use to reduce barricades; approaching troops could be attacked both from behind the barricade and from projectiles hurled from roofs or windows that overhung the streets. Insurgents could easily double back behind their attackers through the rabbit warrens of backstreets. This was one of the reasons why Louis Napoleon, who came to power in a coup in 1851, ordered today's broad avenues to be cut through the center of Paris (Harvey 2006). Napoleon's cannon could quickly reduce any barricade that challengers had the temerity to erect across the Champs Elysées, turning the barricade into more of a symbolic than an actual structure of popular defense.

SMALL CHANGE AND HISTORICAL TRANSFORMATIONS

Events such as those described in this chapter are the crucibles out of which new political cultures are born (Sewell 1990; 1996). Many of the future changes in the repertoire of contention first appeared in such great events as the taking of the Bastille or the February Days in Paris. But according to Tilly, their foundations were built in the day-to-day practice of contentious politics, which in turn, depended on the development of states and capitalism. The mass petition that grew out of a prosaic business practice in Britain; the barricade that was first used to defend Parisian neighborhoods from thieves and then from soldiers; the urban insurrection that was first used to demand work in Grenoble before becoming the instrument of revolution at the Bastille – all of these grew out of incremental interactions between challengers and authorities. From the point of view of the repertoire of popular politics, great events are often no more than the culmination of changes that have been germinating unobtrusively in the body politic.

The change from the traditional repertoire to the new one was a case in point. Where the old repertoire had been parochial, direct, and segmented, the new one was national, flexible, and based on modular forms of action. With the former, grain seizures, religious conflicts, land wars, and funeral processions were segmented from one another and from elite politics. But with the latter, it was possible for workers, peasants, artisans, clerks, writers, lawyers, and aristocrats to march under the same banner and confront the same opponents. These changes facilitated coalition formation and made possible the coming of the national social movement.

This newly found power in movement had a profound impact on the structure of modern politics. For if, in the short run, people challenging authority brought down repression on their heads, over the longer run the new repertoire increased the leverage of ordinary people to challenge rulers. They eventually forced authorities to create means of social control more subtle than the cavalry charge or the cannonade. Some of these changes (e.g., the reordering of the map of Paris to combat future urban insurrections) were deliberate accretions to the vocabulary of contentious politics, but others (e.g., the parliamentarization of

British politics) were part of larger trends to which contentious actors had to adapt.

This is why short-term studies that focus on single social movement organizations will not tell us much about the relations among challengers, authorities, and third parties. Over the years, parts of the new repertoire became *tolerated* components of conventional politics. The strike became an institution of collective bargaining; the demonstration was covered by a body of law that both regulated and distinguished it from criminal activity; and the sit-in and building occupation were treated with greater leniency than ordinary delinquency. Other parts – such as the attacks on millers in times of dearth that had been tolerated earlier – were later *forbidden*. And still other parts – such as popular elections, marches, and peaceful demonstrations – were *expected* and even *required*.

How did these changes come about? And why did they begin when they did? Great national events, such as the taking of the Bastille on July 14, 1789, provided models of collective action and collective consciousness for the future. But such events were too episodic and usually were too limited to single countries to constitute universal trends; by the beginning of the nineteenth century, a new repertoire of contention was becoming internationally known and widely practiced. Though particular events left their mark on the changes we have identified, we must look beneath the surface of events for the causes of such powerful changes in popular politics. We must look, in particular, at how new forms of communication and new forms of association endowed challengers with resources, and then at how states and capitalism structured and provided new constraints on, and opportunities for, contentious politics. We turn to these structural changes in the next two chapters.

3

Print and Association

One afternoon in April, 1775, a young stable boy in Boston overheard a British army officer tell another that there would be "hell to pay tomorrow." Running to the home of a local silversmith, a certain Paul Revere, he reported what he had heard. Putting this information together with rumors he had heard of British officers gathered on Boston's long wharf, Revere and his friend Joseph Warren became convinced that the British were about to march on the town of Lexington to arrest colonial leaders John Hancock and Samuel Adams and seize stores of arms that were stocked in the town of Concord by the local militia (Gladwell 2002: 1–2). "What happened next," writes Malcolm Gladwell, "has become part of historical legend, a tale told to every American schoolchild." Revere crossed the harbor to the ferry landing at Charlestown, saddled up, and began his "midnight ride." "In every town he passed through along the way," Gladwell continues, "he knocked on doors and spread the word, telling local colonial leaders of the oncoming British, and telling them to spread the word to others":

> Church bells started ringing. Drums started beating. The news spread like a virus as those informed by Paul Revere sent out riders of their own, until alarms were going off throughout the entire region. . . . When the British finally began their march towards Lexington on the morning of the nineteenth, their foray into the countryside was met – to their utter astonishment – with organized and fierce resistance (p. 2).

Gladwell retells this familiar tale to emphasize the working of what he calls a "social epidemic." Social epidemics spread not only because of the sensational nature of the news they transmit, but also because they are carried by people with a rare gift – the gift of being a "connector" – someone who knows lots of people. "Sprinkled among every walk of life," he observes, "are a handful of people with a truly extraordinary knack of making friends and acquaintances"

(p. 41). For Gladwell – and for historian David Hackett Fischer on whose book he richly draws – Paul Revere was such a connector (Fischer 1994).

Print was another way that news of the rebellion diffused through the colonies. Bernard Bailyn reports that there were already thirty-eight American newspapers in 1775, "crowded with columns of arguments and counter-arguments appearing as letters, official documents, extracts of speeches, and sermons." Broadsides appeared everywhere, and even almanacs "carried, in odd corners and occasional columns, a considerable freight of political comment. Above all, there were pamphlets" (Bailin 1967: 1–2). But there was also association – mainly informal associations with people like Revere at their heart, but also the association of people who heard the same news, read the same pamphlets, and met in the same taverns and on the same commons. Between them, print and association produced the revolution that was launched in the wake of Revere's ride.

Social movements as we know them today began to appear in the course of the eighteenth century. They drew their underlying substance from structural changes that were associated with state building and with capitalism (see Chapter 4). The major mechanisms that the new movements drew upon were commercial print media and new models of association. These changes did not in themselves produce new grievances and conflicts, but they diffused new ways of mounting claims across territory and social strata and led ordinary people to think of themselves as part of broader collectivities. The same processes were at work in the two European societies – France and England – that were leading others on the route to the modern world through episodes of contention, as we will see in this chapter.

A REVOLUTION IN PRINT[1]

The production of printed books went back to the fifteenth century, but for a long time these were written in Latin, dealt mainly with religious subjects, and were not accessible to ordinary people. This did not mean that they were unimportant in spreading information – after all, the first political tracts were the religious books of the Protestant Reformation – but popular publications had to await the spread of literacy and lowering of the price of printed papers. Once that happened, popular newspapers and printed songs and pamphlets produced a leveling process as they diffused images of ruler and aristocrat on the same sheets as bourgeois and plebeian, mechanic and tradesman, city dweller and country notable (Anderson 1991; Habermas 1989).

---

[1] The title of this section is the same as that of the excellent collection edited by Robert Darnton and Daniel Roche on the role of the press in France before and during the revolutionary period. I am grateful to Benedict Anderson's *Imagined Communities: Reflections on the Origin and Spread of Nationalism* (1991: Chapter 3), for the origin of some of the ideas taken up and expanded in this section.

In both Europe and America, the spread of literacy was a crucial determinant of the rise of popular politics.[2] Without the capacity to read, potential insurgents would have found it harder to learn of the actions of others with similar claims, except by word of mouth. John Markoff finds that, of the forms of contention accompanying the French Revolution, tax revolts were especially characteristic of the literate countryside (1997:383). Increased demand for reading matter was part outcome and part cause of changes in the production and diffusion of commercial printing (Chartier 1991: 70ff.; Darnton 1989). While a peasant who could sign his name to a parish register might or might not have the self-confidence to claim his rights, a man who had invested in expensive publishing equipment had a commercial incentive to produce news for a larger audience, and could only find so large an audience outside the circles of the rich.

It was out of the audiences for the products of commercial print that invisible communities of discourse were formed. In places such as The Hague, Laussane, and Philadelphia, men who specialized in the production of books, newspapers, pamphlets, and cartoons found both work and profit in printing. By the middle of the eighteenth century, there began a "drive to tap new print markets, which differentiated the profit-seeking printer from the manuscript book dealer" and "worked against elitism and favoured democratic as well as heterodox trends."[3] After 1760, French booksellers began to open *cabinets de lecture* (reading rooms), which "enabled subscribers to read extensively while spending little and made prohibited titles discreetly available" (Chartier 1991: 70).

If reading increased commerce, commerce fed reading (Habermas 1989). When French booksellers asked for works of philosophy from the Société Typographique de Neuchâtel, the Swiss publisher responded: "We don't carry any, but we know where to find them and can supply them when we are asked to."[4] In America, notes Gordon Wood, "the strongest motive behind people's

---

[2] See the collection edited by Jack Goody, *Literacy in Traditional Societies* (1968), for good introductions to this subject. Lawrence Stone's "Literacy and Education in England, 1640–1900" (1969), Kenneth Lockridge's *Literacy in Colonial New England* (1974), and Roger Chartier's *The Cultural Uses of Print in Early Modern France* (1987) are good introductions to the subject. Alvin Gouldner, in his "Prologue to a Theory of Revolutionary Intellectuals," goes farthest in linking literacy to rebellion by arguing that modern radicalism is centrally rooted in written modes of discourse (1975–1976).

[3] See Elizabeth Eisenstein's "Revolution and the Printed Word" (1986). For a history of book production and reading between the sixteenth and eighteenth centuries in France, see Roger Chartier's *The Cultural Uses of Print in Early Modern France* (1987). Robert Darnton's work is required reading for understanding the importance of prohibited books and pamphlets leading up to the French Revolution. See his *The Business of Enlightenment and the Literary Underground of the Old Regime* (1979; 1982).

[4] Quoted in Darnton's "Philosophy under the Cloak," in his and Daniel Roche's *The Revolution in Print* (1989: 31). Note that the term "philosophical works" was a code name for a wide range

learning to read and write, even more than the need to understand the scrip-
tures, was the desire to do business" (1991: 313). The francophone press that
was established outside the borders of France typified the intersection of profit
and politics in the print industry. On the one hand, clandestine publications
intended for the French market allowed the small states on France's borders
to enrich their coffers; on the other, printers and publishers had a free hand
to produce books that were too subversive to be published in France. The
"neutrality" of these entrepreneurs was as subversive as capitalism, and for the
same reason – in the name of profit – they were indifferent to the claims of
religious creeds or dynastic causes (Eisenstein: 194).

Immigration by printers, publishers, and writers increased the flow of print
in early America. In 1774, a failed English excise worker named Thomas Paine
stepped off a boat in Philadelphia with a letter of introduction from Benjamin
Franklin to Robert Aiken, a well-known printer in the town. Paine's ideas
were not particularly new or even radical.[5] What made his impact on history
so great was his extraordinary talent as a publicist.[6] Paine had arrived in a
country that was literally covered in printed paper. In addition to almost forty
newspapers, there were broadsheets, speeches, extracts of sermons, and, above
all, pamphlets. It was in the form of pamphlets that the democratic implications of print really appeared. "Highly flexible, easy to manufacture, and
cheap, pamphlets were printed wherever there were printing presses, intellectual ambitions and political concerns" (Bailyn 1967: 4). By the 1790s, hundreds
of radical exiles driven from Britain and Ireland because of religious beliefs or
sympathy for the French Revolution had crossed the Atlantic; "in the several
decades following the end of the Revolutionary War," writes Gordon Wood,
"twenty-three English, Scottish and Irish radicals edited and produced no fewer
than fifty-seven American newspapers and magazines, most of which supported
the Republican cause in the politically sensitive Middle states" (Wood 2009:
253).

Communities of Print

Print was not just a one-way top-down commodity but was actually a form of
association. Editors and publishers vied to involve readers in their enterprises,

---

of censored subjects ranging from pure philosophy through political tracts to more or less pure
pornography.

[5] Paine was, as Hobsbawm notes, "the only member of the French Convention who fought openly
against the death sentence on Louis XVI." See Hobsbawm's *Labouring Men* (1964: 1–4). For an
evocative and penetrating treatment of Paine's importance, see Isaac Kramnick, *Republicanism
and Bourgeois Radicalism* (1990).

[6] Hobsbawm, *Labouring Men*, p. 2. Paine's language resembled that of the Bible much more than
that of the more learned essayists who penned political pamphlets up until his time. For example,
he used biblical parallels to convince his Bible-reading public that kingship causes wars, and that,
for the ancient Hebrews, "it was held sinful to acknowledge any being under that title but the
Lord of Hosts." *Common Sense*, Kuklick edition (1989: 8–9).

much as the first word processing producers tried to induce users to join their clubs. "By means of letters to the editor and other devices," writes Eisenstein, "the periodical press opened up a new kind of public forum," helping to create something like a public opinion well before the French Revolution (Eisenstein: 196–197). Diderot's *Encyclopédie* was only the most successful of these, linking publishers and readers, intellectuals and lay people, metropole and provinces. Such journals as the English *Present State of the Republick of Letters* and Pierre Bayle's *Nouvelles de la République des Lettres* "extended lifelines to isolated subscribers," "conveying a new sense of forward movement to their readership" (Eisenstein: 196). A new kind of social life developed around the reading and exchange of books and printed papers. In France, provincial cities such as Besançon had public libraries and reading clubs. Even residents of small towns such as Saint-Amour asked permission of the authorities "to rent a room where they could meet, read gazettes and newspapers and indulge in games of chance" (Vernus 1989: 127).

If the book was the first mass-produced commodity, newspapers were its extension – "a book sold on a colossal scale . . . a one-day bestseller," as Benedict Anderson writes (1991: 34–35). If a man could read about a great event on the same day as thousands of others he didn't know, he and they became part of the same community of readers. "Only a newspaper can put the same thought at the same time before a thousand readers," wrote Alexis de Tocqueville, astonished at the diffusion of the printed word that he found in the United States in the 1830s (1954 II: 517).

Newspapers not only diffused news widely; they were inherently subversive: If a newspaper described the actions of rulers and dignitaries in the same language it used to discuss the doings of the merchants and traders who read it, the status of rulers and readers was leveled. Rather than emanating authoritatively from above, newspapers circulated horizontally; they "spoke polyphonically," writes Anderson of a later time and place, "in a hurly-burly of editorialists, cartoonists, news agencies, columnists . . . satirists, speech-makers, and advertisers, amongst whom government order-givers had to jostle elbow to elbow" (1991: 31, 34–35).

First published in capital cities, newspapers spread to the provinces to report on doings in the metropole. In England, writes Donald Read, "such provincial newspapers helped to build up knowledge outside London of parliamentary and London politics, filling their columns not so much with local news as with news and comment copied from the London press, especially from the lively journals of the Opposition" (1964: 19). As a result, by the 1760s, provincial readers were well schooled in opposition politics, and this helps to explain why they rose up in support of Wilkes in the 1770s and responded so rapidly to antislavery a decade later.

Competing with the capital city press was not easy – even in times of revolution. In France, wrote the *Journal de Normandie* a year after the revolution began, "From the first sittings of the National Assembly," we hoped to produce our paper every day, but we found out that it isn't possible to sustain competition with newspapers from the capital" (Marseille and Margairaz 1989: 10). As a result, the provincial press became a vehicle for reporting on local news and expressing local attitudes about goings-on in the capital rather than simply reprinting news from the center.

Revolutionary episodes provided fertile ground for the creation of new journals, for not only did revolutions open opportunities to publish without fear of censorship, they also produced a public avid for news. The campaign for the Estates General in France loosed a torrent of publications, the catalogue of the Bibliothèque Nationale listing 184 periodicals published in Paris alone in 1789 and 335 in 1790 (Popkin 1989: 150). The 1848 revolution had a similar effect, but on an international scale. It spawned some 200 new journals in Paris, a wave of new newspapers in German – many as far away as the United States – and in Italy, where more than one hundred journals were registered in Florence alone.[7]

The popular press did not so much make rebellion heroic as make it ordinary. If Philadelphians in 1773 could read in the New York papers about the rebellion brewing in Massachusetts, rebellion became thinkable in the Quaker colony too (Ryerson, 1978: 43–44). If Norwich's citizens could read how thousands in Manchester had signed petitions against slavery, it became intolerable to allow slavers to go unblamed in Norfolk (Drescher 1982). If a man could read in his national press about how insurgents in another country overthrew their ruler, then ruler overthrow became conceivable everywhere. As Anderson writes of the French Revolution, "once it had occurred, it entered the accumulating memory of print.... The experience was shaped by millions of printed words into a 'concept' on the printed page, and, in due course, into a model" (1991: 80).

ASSOCIATIONS AND MOVEMENT NETWORKS

New associational forms that escaped the tight corporate boundaries of estate societies first developed around church and commerce before being adopted by reading clubs, reform groups, and antislavery societies embodying moral purposes. Latent conflicts between ordinary people and their opponents were transposed into pamphlet wars, ribald songs, and scatological cartoons and prints. If the Queen of France could be portrayed in print in a compromising position,[8]

---

[7] The 1848 figure for Paris is from Jacques Godechot, *Les Révolutions de 1848* (1971). For the developments of the working class press in Germany and Italy in 1848, see Godechot, et al., *La Presse ouvrière* (1966). On the explosion of new journals in Florence during and after the 1848 revolution, see Clementina Rotondi, *Bibliografia dei periodici toscani, 1847–1852* (1951).

[8] Antoine de Baecque analyzes the political pornographic pamphlet from 1787 on in his "Pamphlets: Libel and Political Mythology" (1989). Also see the description of "Body Politics" in Schama's *Citizens* (1989: 203–227) and the libels of Marie-Antoinette that he refers to. Schama writes, "It was her [Marie-Antoinette's] transformation in France to the `Austrian whore'... that damaged the legitimacy of the monarchy to an incalculable degree" (p. 205). Lynn Hunt, in her *Family Romance of the French Revolution* (1992), takes the subject up in penetrating detail.

and if aristocrats and commoners could talk politics in the same coffee shops and reading clubs, how long would it be before members of these classes joined in contentious collective action? Print and association made it possible for people in widely scattered towns and regions to know of one another's actions and join across wide social and geographic divides in national social movements. By the twenty-first century, they would routinely cross national frontiers in transnational social movements (see Chapter 12).

People have always come together in groups, both religious and secular. But until the late eighteenth century, corporate and communal organizations predominated. These, as William Sewell Jr. argues for the case of France, were aimed more at the defense of established and communal privileges than at the acquisition of new rights and benefits (1980; 1986). Rather than bring people together on behalf of emergent or contingent interests, corporate and communal ties divided them into insulated pockets, emphasizing corporate identities and differences, and not into broader solidarities and common interests. These corporate ties were limited to solid burghers, trade guilds, and clerics and left most of the population outside their protection.

But when people came together in groups for contentious purposes, their ties were most often founded on locality and personal proximity. The religious conflicts of the sixteenth and seventeenth centuries produced hundreds of militant groups across Europe, but few of them gave rise to durable associations, if only because – once established – their churches frowned on independent associations. In France, the Croquant movement, though organized through remarkably modern-seeming assemblies, was limited by local ties; its organizers were never able to construct a broader movement (Bercé 1990). In England, the infamous "Gunpowder Plot" – the origins of the modern Guy Fawkes Day – was organized by a network of Catholic friends and relatives, most of whom lived within easy reach of one another's homes in the Midlands.[9] So out of touch were they with the communities around them that they imagined that blowing up Parliament would trigger a general rising against the Protestant regime.

Early in the eighteenth century, a new kind of association developed to help occupational groups protect themselves against state expansion and to influence the passage of legislation in their favor. In England, where commerce was king, expansion of the excise tax stimulated such groups to lobby Parliament as early as 1697 for the leather trades, 1717 for tanners, and by the 1760s for glassmakers and brewers. "The levying of indirect taxes," writes John Brewer (1989: 233), "encouraged the emergence of organizations which transcended local and regional boundaries."

---

[9] "In this small world" (of English upper-class Catholics), writes Antonia Fraser, "which for security's sake perpetuated itself by intermarriage, it is perhaps simplest to state that almost everyone was related to almost everyone else." See her *The Gunpowder Plot* (1996), and especially the chart of the conspirators' relationships and the map of their residences in the Midlands. The quotation is from p. 35.

By the middle of the eighteenth century, a rich and varied associational life was developing in both Europe and North America. Government officials came to depend on them for information, and they, in turn, cultivated contacts with ministers and members of Parliament to improve their chances of gaining favorable treatment (pp. 232–234). But association would not remain for long within such narrow commercial confines.

The Modularity of Association

The new forms of association spread across the commercial societies of the Atlantic. In England, the antislavery agitation of the 1780s first appeared among dissenting sects before spreading to Manchester's industrial interests (Drescher, 1987: 61–63). The Yorkshire Association adopted the form of the correspondence committees, which had been invented by commercial lobbies (Read 1964) and which later traveled to America in subversive form. O'Connell's Catholic Association adopted the subscription tactic of the lobbies, asking his members to contribute a penny a year for emancipation. The Catholics' success was not lost on the parliamentary reformers, who used subscriptions to finance the Political Unions that extracted the Reform Act from Parliament (Tilly 1982). By 1832, the special purpose association had become a modular form of social organization (Tilly 1995b: Chapter 7).

England's American colonies were in some ways in advance of the metropole. The anti–Stamp Act movement of the 1760s was mounted by a network of local committees. With hardening of British financial policy in the 1770s, a new wave of committees and associations were formed. In 1772, the mechanics of Philadelphia formed a Patriotic Society, which Gordon Wood describes as the first organized nonreligious public pressure group in Pennsylvania's history (1991: 244). This was followed by similar moves in New York and Massachusetts in 1773, culminating in the formation of the Continental Association of 1774.[10] By the time Revere rode off to warn the colonists in Lexington and Concord that the British were coming, a national web of associations, couriers, and spies was in place.

As in England, religion was a cradle for associational development in America, but more so because of the weakness of the established church and the secular role of the churches in local communities (Moore 1994). Habits and forms of association learned in prayer meetings and to stamp out working on the Sabbath were applied to moral crusades and then to civic and social movements. This can be seen in the militant evangelical Protestantism of the Second Great Awakening. When historian Paul E. Johnson examined the social structure of the newly

---

[10] In addition to Maier's *From Resistance to Revolution* (1972), major sources are Richard Ryerson, *The Revolution Is Now Begun* (1978), for Philadelphia, Edward Countryman, *A People in Revolution* (1981), for New York, Richard D. Brown, *Revolutionary Politics in Massachusetts* (1970), for Boston and its hinterland, and Richard W. Walsh, *Charleston's Sons of Liberty* (1959) for the South Carolina city.

established city of Rochester, he found that by 1830, it already possessed a rich network of religious associations (1978). What was new in Rochester was not that a town on the Erie Canal had a large number of churches; after all, churches had been the organizing matrices of New England society for two hundred years. What was remarkable was how easily special-purpose associations were formed *across* denominational lines for secular purposes.[11]

Such cross-denominational coalitions would be instrumental in the moral crusades of the nineteenth century. It was from the associational crucible of evangelical Protestantism that such movements as anti-masonry, sabbatarianism, temperance, evangelical revivalism, and its most revolutionary product – abolitionism – would come.[12] A new social actor in American popular politics – women – first organized in church groups, before moving outward into movements such as temperance, abolitionism, and feminism (Cott 1977).

It was not so much formal organizations, but the informal social networks that lay at their heart, that were the sources of movements. Remember why Paul Revere was so successful in bringing the word of the British threat to the towns between Boston and Concord? It was because he had informal connections to a broad network of people from different social classes in the towns surrounding Boston. These in turn used their connections to spread the word to the surrounding countryside.

Shin-Kap Han reconstructed the network structure of the revolutionary movement in Boston by aggregating into blocks individuals whose names he found in these revolutionary groups. Figure 3.1, from Han's work, shows fourteen "structurally equivalent" blocks in the person-by-person network with identical ties to and from all the other actors in the network. Han's network structure shows how central Revere (#13) and Warren (#12) were in this network. When they are removed from it by Han, he reports that the network "becomes virtually hollowed out at the core" (2008: 154–155).

The same kind of network ties that Han found in Boston brought news of the events in Lexington and Concord across the colonies. As Richard D. Brown writes:

> The diffusion of information regarding the Battles of Lexington and Concord was at once contagious, spreading spontaneously from person-to-person and place-to-place, and prearranged and channeled through patriot networks. As a result, word of the bloody conflict moved with a rapidity, social penetration, and territorial reach never before witnessed in colonial America (1989: 247).

---

[11] For example, Paul Johnson shows how the sabbatarian movement in Rochester was organized by an organization of Protestant laymen from several local churches. See his *Shopkeeper's Millennium* (1978: 109).

[12] For some typical patterns of diffusion, see Donald G. Mathews, "The Second Great Awakening as an Organizing Process, 1780–1830" (1969). On the role of religion in producing movements for civic morality, see Clifford S. Griffin, *Their Brother's Keeper* (1960), and Ian R. Tyrrell, *Sobering Up* (1979). A study that emphasizes class, gender, and the political – as well as the religious – origins of abolitionism is Herbert Aptheker's *Abolitionism: A Revolutionary Movement* (1989).

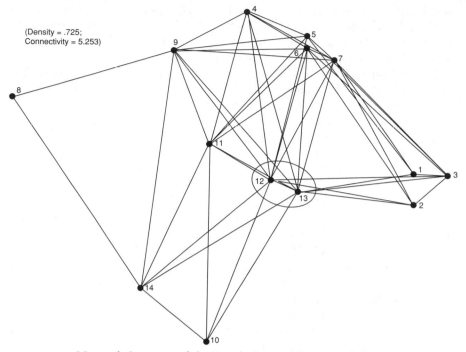

(Density = .725;
Connectivity = 5.253)

FIGURE 3.1. Network Structure of the Revolutionary Movement in Boston. *Note:* For layout, Gower metric scaling is used. Circles contain structurally equivalent blocks. Density and connectivity reported are measured between those blocks. *Source:* Shin-Kap Han (2008). "The Other Ride of Paul Revere," *Mobilization* 14: 143–162. Adapted with permission.

Informal networks would prove even more important in France, for legislation dating from the revolutionary Le Chapelier Law restricted formal association in that country. Under the old regime, guilds and corporations had been legal bodies, regulating trade and restricting practices, but workers' corporations and *compagnonnages* were illegal. With the liquidation of guilds by the Revolution, workers' combinations remained, but they were outside the law. It was only in the 1830s – and then briefly – that they took legal form, and their repression after 1834 forced workers to organize in clandestine networks until 1848 (Sewell 1986).

Informal organization was easier for members of the French middle class, for although legislation prohibited the discussion of politics in associations, by the 1830s, there were scores of cultural and musical groups, sporting associations, and "gentlemen's clubs" in the capital alone – *pace* Tocqueville (Harrison 1996: 42).

The same was true in rural areas in France. Similar to English coffeehouses, the popular *chambrées* that developed in the Midi were places where a man could drink with his friends without being overheard by outsiders or paying the hated tax on alcohol. Never a formal system of association, but rather a set of similar informal groupings modeled on the social *cercles* of upper status Frenchmen, the *chambrées* had enough in common to permit them to become centers of collective action when the opportunity arose. In such settings, republican newspapers could be read, a sense of solidarity developed, and the occasional traveler dropped by with news of what was happening in the wider world. At first tolerated by authorities, they were eventually feared as potential sites for subversion. "For the lower classes of Provence," concludes Maurice Agulhon, "to set themselves up as a *chambrée* was, just as much and perhaps even more than learning to read, to become accessible to whatever was new, to change and to independence" (1982: 150).

Informal groups like the *chambrées* help us to understand the subversive role that informal networks play in spreading new models of collective action. Painites, radicals, and reformers in England; Whigs and radicals in the American colonies; liberals, republicans, and *montagnards* in France; *carbonari* and freemasons in Italy – all used the tools of association developed by commercial, religious, and reformist groups when they were legal, but could relapse into informal networks in times of repression or demobilization. Less easily infiltrated by the police and less subject to factionalization than formal organizations, informal networks offered advantages during a time when governments were becoming increasingly wary of combination. They could develop and reside within friendship and family networks, "lying low" during times of repression and emerging actively during times of stress or opportunity. They were difficult to repress and control, for who could complain if a man wanted to drink with his friends in a private house or in the back of a café?

FRAMING CONTENTION

If print and association were both channels in the development of social movements, in combination they made for an explosive mix in providing the fuel for contention. As Eisenstein notes of the reading clubs and corresponding societies of the late eighteenth century, they had no fixed numbers of members, and, in the case of informal gatherings, no membership at all. But readers of the *Encyclopédie* and other similar periodicals were conscious of having a common identity.[13] To subscribe to such a journal linked readers to an invisible network with unknown others with similar views in communities whose amplitude could only be imagined and could easily be exaggerated – as their publishers had ample reason to do.

By the time of the French Revolution, the intersection between print and association was explicit. "To a greater extent than is often appreciated," writes Eisenstein, "the events of 1788–9 in France hinged on both a suspension of

---

[13] See Eisenstein's "Revolution and the Printed Word" (1986: 197). Also see Darnton's *The Literary Underground of the Old Regime* (1982), and Jack R. Censer and Jeremy Popkin, eds., *Press and Politics in Pre-Revolutionary France* (1987).

governmental controls over the printed word and on the freeing of associations." At the same time as the new government was convoking the Estates
General, it legalized Parisian clubs and freed a number of booksellers and printers from jail, resulting in what Lefebvre calls "an outpouring of pamphlets that
astonished contemporaries."[14] What followed were the first deliberate public
opinion campaigns in history. When, in 1792, the Republicans went to war
against their neighbors, it was through the press that they spread hatred of the
foreigner and induced young men to "volunteer" in the world's first *levée en
masse*.

England's history was both more pacific and more advanced in the connections between print and association. By the late eighteenth century, reform
associations were becoming skilled in using the press to advance their views.
As a strategic directive from the London to the Sheffield Corresponding Society
put it:

> ...if every [reform] society in the island will send forward a petition,
> we shall ultimately gain ground, for as much as it will force the members of
> the senate repeatedly to discuss the subject, and their deliberations, *printed in
> the different newspapers*, will most naturally awaken the public mind towards
> the object of our purpose (Read 1964: 45; emphasis added).

The link between print and association was even clearer in America. During
the Stamp Act controversy, according to Pauline Maier, the Sons of Liberty
in Connecticut "instructed local groups to 'publish their proceedings in the
New London Gazette.'" The same was true in Rhode Island and New York.
Printers were active members of the Sons of Liberty in Boston, Rhode Island,
and Pennsylvania. Long after the Sons were dissolved in 1766, "these papers
and others like them...remained a forum for public discussion" (Maier 1972:
90–91). They were part of the "weak ties" on which a strong social movement
could be built.

Weak Ties and Strong Movements

While newspapers circulated the idea of movement, movements expanded the
market for print, as people tried to share – if only vicariously – in what was happening around them. By their very mastheads, newspapers announced themselves as agents of movement. In Java in the early twentieth century, the founding of a journal called *The World on the Move* was followed by *Islam on the
Move*, *Workers on the Move*, and *The People on the Move* (Anderson 1990:
32). Through print, people as far apart as Messina and Warsaw, St. Petersburg
and Beijing could imagine themselves not only as Italians, Poles, Russians,

---

[14] Georges Lefebvre, *The Coming of the French Revolution* (1967: 54). At the same time, an
amnesty was granted to booksellers and merchants who had been arrested for distributing
tracts critical of the government, as Eisenstein points out in her "Revolution and the Printed
Word" (1986: 199).

and Chinese, but as Jacobins and *sans-culottes*, radicals, and communists, and their local enemies as feudatories and rentiers, aristocrats and capitalists. The weak ties among readers of the same newspapers, members of the same reading clubs, and people who occasionally met in the marketplace became the bases for social movement mobilization.

This is not to say that the strong ties of homogeneous groups at the base of social movements are *un*important. In institutional settings such as the factory or the mine, professional and family ties formed the basis of the primary solidarities at the base of militant social movements. But when it came to forming broader movements, strong ties might be mutually exclusive and thus inhibit broader solidarities. What movements needed to be successful was informal connective structures among heterogeneous and interdependent social groups and localities whose ties were weak (Granovetter 1973; Han 2008). Class solidarity was a tool in mounting strikes, but it was much less important than the weak ties we find in coalition formation – and could be even counterproductive – in the sustained interactions with authorities that were needed to build national social movements.

Remember Paul Revere's ride? Revere and his friend Warren were embedded in a network of weak ties. After the Boston "Tea Party" of 1773, writes Gladwell, "dozens of committees and congresses of angry colonists" sprang up around New England. They had no formal organization or established means of community but had ties across the colonies, both through brokers like Revere, who would "routinely ride down to Philadelphia or New York or up to New Hampshire, carrying messages from one group to another" (Gladwell p. 57) and by written messages. Through such connections, the news of what happened in Lexington and Concord spread up and down the coast of North America in a matter of days.

CONCLUSIONS

Primary associations and face-to-face contacts provided solidarity for social movements among people who knew and trusted one another. But it took the experience of reading the same journals, associating in the same groups, and forming coalitions across class and geographic lines to build the formal connective structures that allowed movements to be diffused to new publics, and the scale of contention to mount from the neighborhood and the locality to the region and the nation. Because of their largely local range, it was easy for historians to characterize the localities and the actors in earlier waves of collective action. Thus, geographer Andrew Charlesworth was able to pinpoint the social composition and geographic sites of English riots from 1548 to 1900 (1983), because most of these encounters involved a particular social category living in a limited territorial space and making a distinct set of claims on (usually visible) others. Sometime during the eighteenth century, we begin to see a broadening of claims, a widening of their geographic reach, and a more sustained capacity to mount collective action among coalitions of contentious actors. Maier found it in the cross-class and intercolonial spread of tax resistance in America in the 1760s (1972: 69, 87); Han found it in the interclass nature of the coalition that responded to Paul Revere's ride (2008: 155–156); Drescher observed it in the antislavery agitation in England (1987: 80–81); and Margadant saw it in the urban and rural, middle and lower class interaction in the 1851 insurrection in France (1979: Chapters 7–8). It was print and association – and especially the two in combination – that made possible such sustained campaigns of collective action on the part of broad coalitions making claims against elites and authorities. These created the national social movement.

But national movements needed more than the "push" provided by print and association. They also needed the pull of solidarities and common targets and a focal point for their claims. These they found in the driving force of capitalism and in the fulcrum of the consolidating national state. Both in Europe and in America, capitalism created new contacts, new identities, and new cleavages, while consolidating states offered new targets for contention. Social movements grew up around the thrust of capitalism and within the armature of the national state, as we will see in the next chapter.

4

States, Capitalism, and Contention

States and capitalism: the two major sources and targets of contentious politics. In the past, and especially in Europe, with its heritage of deep class divisions, the cleavages of industrial society were seen as the master source of contentious politics. Americans, with their longer history of civil politics and weaker class traditions, took a more pluralistic view. But whether dichotomous or plural, from the late nineteenth century onward, the notion that social cleavages are the source of contentious politics was the underlying assumption in most studies of social movements.

In the half-century after World War II – and especially since the 1960s – social scientists began to see the state as an autonomous actor in social conflict and no longer only – in Marx's memorable phrase – "the executive committee of the bourgeoisie."[1] This shift has had several sources. First, the failure of the working class to rise to the challenge of the student and antiwar movements in the 1960s shocked many who had thought class was the underlying basis of political conflict. Second, the development of a theory of the state led to the idea that states have an autonomous influence on class politics.[2] Third, social scientists began to explore the question of "post-industrial" politics, which, for many, came to mean "post-class" politics (Inglehart 1990).

As the result of these real-world and academic changes, a more interactive and iterative conception of state/society relations has developed, in which the state is seen not only as the *reflection* of society's dominant groups but as a *fulcrum* for the mediation of societal conflicts and a *regulator* of society's needs. Of course, few would argue that social cleavages are irrelevant to contentious

---

[1] Marx and Engel's exact phrasing in *The Communist Manifesto* was, "The executive of the modern state is but a committee for managing the common affairs of the whole bourgeoisie." R.C. Tucker, ed. *The Marx-Engels Reader,* 2nd ed. (1978: 475).
[2] The major figures in the United States in "bringing the state back in" were Peter Evans, Dietrich Rueschemeyer, Theda Skocpol and their collaborators (1985), and Charles Tilly (1990; 2006). In Britain, J.P. Nettl (1968), and in France, Pierre Birnbaum (1988) played leading roles in this movement.

politics, and most scholars assume that broad social changes are at the root of the mobilization of contentious actors. What has been challenged is the assumption that the state is no more than the "superstructure" of capitalist society, its role to simply process, facilitate, or suppress demands from society's "base."

Not only that: Regimes and state structures are increasingly seen as outcomes of societies' distinct histories of contention. If the American state is tolerant of certain (but not all) forms of contention, this surely has something to do with how the federal system was shaped by those conflicts (Elkins and McKitrick 1993). If the French state is "Jacobin" (i.e., centralized), this is the product of radical centralization by the Jacobins. And if the British state is "parliamentarized" (Tilly 2008), that surely results from Parliament's role as the fulcrum of contentious politics in early modern England.

Thus we can view contentious politics not only as the expression of societies' submerged groups putting pressure on the state, but as an intermediary set of processes between states and societies. Before turning to this interactive view, however, we need to explore how capitalism structured social scientists' views of social movements in the past, and where the state fit in that construction. Three major theorists – Marx, Polanyi, and Tocqueville – will serve to structure this discussion.

CAPITALISM AND CONTENTION

Observers of nineteenth century social movements were fixated on the class origins of movements, first with respect to the French Revolution – which had to be either "bourgeois" or peasant-based; then with respect to the formation of the modern English working class – which supposedly gained class consciousness through the Industrial Revolution and the mass factory; and finally with respect to the failure of socialism in America – which was thought to be based on the dominance of ethnicity over class among America's immigrant workers. In all three cases, class was the analytical pivot on which the emergence and outcomes of social movements were thought to turn: violent and class-based in France; class-based but peaceful in Britain; peaceful and not class-based in America.

But all three of these precepts turned out to be wanting:

- First, following the path-breaking work of E.P. Thompson, *The Making of the English Working Class*, the beginnings of class consciousness in Britain were pushed back well before the coming of the Industrial Revolution and the mass factory (1966).
- Then new research on the French Revolution raised doubts about its class nature and instead stressed its ideological and cultural underpinnings (Baker 1994, Chartier 1991, Furet 1979).
- Finally, in America, scholars such as Ira Katznelson (1981) argued that although ethnicity was a primary marker of *territorial* politics, in the factory, class reigned supreme. Indeed, to the degree that class politics was weak in

America, this was due more to repression of the working class than to predominance of ethnic identities. Identities are various, competing, and lodged in different institutional settings.

Yet class continued to tantalize scholars of both social movements and electoral politics (Przeworski and Sprague 1986; Bartolini and Mair 2009). For Bartolini and Mair, European Social Democratic Parties were *the* parties of the working class, while for Prezeworski and Sprague, these parties confronted an electoral dilemma: As it became clear that the proletariat would never constitute a majority of the population, their leaders realized that they would never come to power based on working class votes alone. As a result, these parties softened their electoral programs to appeal to an interclass constituency. As they write; "The quest for electoral allies forced socialist parties to de-emphasize that unique appeal, that particular vision of society, which made them the political expression of workers as a class, an instrument of historical necessity" (Przeworski and Sprague, p. 50).

What does any of this have to do with social movements? The answer is "plenty!" As the primary expressions of the working class movement – along with the trade unions – Social Democratic and labor parties faced the same dilemma that social movements face today: They cannot hope to effectively maneuver against more powerful opponents unless they form social coalitions. The long history of social movements shows that, except in times of exceptional crisis, movements are simply too weak or too ephemeral to represent the interests of a single class. Even when they continue to frame their claims in class terms and claim to represent the interests of the working class, they are forced to seek support among members of other classes and to broaden their appeals from class dialectics to appeal to broader interests and values.

The Marxian Synthesis

Karl Marx was the first theorist to propagate the view that the social movement of the nineteenth century would be class-based. He thought that as capitalism produced a more and more socialized mode of production, the resulting homogeneity of the working class would counteract its tendency to compete for jobs and would produce a class-based movement centered on the industrial proletariat. When intellectuals joined their efforts with those of the workers, they were "leaving" their class of origin as a sign of the coming collapse of capitalism (Tucker, ed. 1978: 481). When different classes formed coalitions – as in the *Eighteenth Brumaire of Louis Bonaparte* – this was the result of an intermediate stage of development that history would soon render archaic (in Tucker, ed., 604ff.).

Marx's logic was dichotomous: As capitalism became more concentrated and more exploitative, capitalists would become richer and more powerful, and intermediate sectors of the population would be forced into the proletariat. Ultimately, through the inherent contradiction between overproduction and exploitation, and propelled by the growing organization of the workers, the system would implode. As for the state, it was part of the "superstructure" of capitalist society, serving the interests of the dominant groups and suppressing those of the proletariat and its allies.

The societies that produced the movements we have encountered so far in this book were not yet the homogeneous industrial societies that Marx imagined, nor were they any longer the estate societies that preceded them. How could they have produced such powerful episodes as British antislavery, American independence, and the French Revolution? The answer is that the loose ties created by print and association, by newspapers, pamphlets, and informal social networks, made possible a degree of coordinated collective action that the supposedly "strong ties" of social class could not have constructed (Granovetter 1973). The proletariat was but one actor – and a divided one – in the societies that were developing in Europe and America even as Marx was predicting the collapse of capitalist society.

Consider the early English industrial workers. They were not easy to distinguish from their artisan and journeyman antecedents. When they cooperated with the latter in the popular movements of the late eighteenth and early nineteenth centuries, either the coincidence was thought to be accidental – like ships passing in the night – or a "declining" social formation of artisans and journeymen was being absorbed into its "rising" successor. But E.P. Thompson found distinct elements of working-class culture in the artisans and journeymen of the late eighteenth century. Craig Calhoun added to his finding the observation that the areas of England with the greatest levels of militancy were based not on heavy industry, but on small-scale artisanal enterprise (Calhoun 1982). The issue was more than providing a correct reading of English working-class history: If large-scale industry was not producing the kind of class politics that Marx foresaw in the English capitalism of his day, was it likely that advanced capitalism would ever produce a revolution?

Class was an ambiguous factor in the French Revolution. Far from representing a single social class, the Parisian *sans-culottes* who were responsible for some of the most electrifying *journées* of the Revolution were a coalition of middle-class intellectuals, artisans, and journeymen, with few representatives from the poorer strata (Levebvre 1967). What brought them together was not their social class, but dearth, ideology, and associational networks. It was through the diffusion of information and the formation of coalitions within movement organizations that claims were coordinated and collective action co-occurred among social groups with different social interests and identities.

The same was true in early America. Remember the Massachusetts movement that triggered the American rebellion in 1775? It too was an interclass coalition. Paul Revere was a high-ranking member of the artisanal class – one of "the middling sort" – in the highly stratified society of colonial Boston, but his friend Warren was a medical man with a degree from Harvard. While the provincial militia, or "Minutemen," who rose out of the bushes to harry the British soldiers with withering musket fire were mainly artisans and farmers, upper class merchants and men with degrees from Harvard were heavily concentrated in the groups that became important in the Revolution (Han 2008:

155–156). Socially and culturally, the formations that sustained the revolution were "poles apart," as Han writes. Revere and Warren were effective bridges "in spanning various social chasms and connecting disparate organizational elements" (p. 157). They were the agents of a social movement coalition.

Of course, all three of these movements arose before fully fledged capitalism had transformed the faces of Britain, France, and the United States. But when it had, class development turned out to be far more differentiated than what Marx had imagined. Not only did the middle class grow as capitalism expanded, belying Marx's image of a dichotomizing class structure; even those members of the working class who were "supposed to" frame their ideas around class interests were often more influenced by religion, regionalism, or nationalism than by their objective class membership. The most sustained social movements either had a nonclass basis or were constituted by coalitions of social actors whose relations were mediated by brokers such as Revere and Warren, or were organized by loosely coupled organizations.

The diffusion of contention through interclass coalitions has remained a central process in social movements up to the present day (Meyer and Rochon, eds. 1997). Think of the British Labour Party that developed toward the end of the nineteenth century: It was based on an intellectual Fabian elite, a network of cooperatives, and a trade union base from its beginnings. Or, consider the French Left, which was divided among intellectual social democrats, working class anarcho-syndicalists, and assorted peasant and middle class groups in the South. Even the Social Democratic Party of Germany, which saw itself at the proud keeper of the Marxist flame, had significant middle class support and a reformist trade union base, and was animated more by its ameliorative "minimal program" than by its revolutionary "maximal program." Class served more as a framing and a mobilizing symbol for these parties than as an objective determinant of political action.

But if it is assumed that Left-oriented parties were based on coalitions of classes, why did they fail to counter the power of capitalism with their power of numbers (de Nardo 1986)? One reason was that nonclass identities – religion, ethnicity, nationalism – competed with class for the loyalty of the lower classes. Another was that capitalism – because it depended on the mass production of cheap commodities – promoted relative prosperity among many of these groups.

But a third reason was that the logic of liberal capitalist states belied the simple dichotomous imagery of the Marxian synthesis. Both in Europe and in America, as capitalism developed, politics and policy brought together working and middle class, state and nonstate actors in shifting coalitions and combinations. And this takes us to the pioneering work of Marx's twentieth-century successor, Karl Polanyi.

Polanyi and the Great Transformation

Unlike for Marx, for whom the capitalist class drove inexorably toward its doom, for Polanyi, history was made up of a movement-countermovement interaction that was cyclical rather than linear. The growth of a market society in the early nineteenth century was driven by the ideology of liberalism that found coherent expression in a legislative and regulatory program based on naturalization of the market. This made it possible for the first industrializers to bring their economies out of their mercantilist and corporatist strictures and ignore the severe costs of the transformation for both traditional and new subordinate groups. In Polanyi's terms, "Economic society was subject to laws which were not human laws" (Polanyi 2001: 131). "The self-regulating market," he famously wrote, "was now believed to follow from the inexorable laws of Nature, and the unshackling of the market to be an ineluctable necessity" (p. 132).

This intellectual revolution was the essence of a social movement – not in the narrow sense of a political movement, but in the broader sense of a "social and cultural metaphor" that guided the political economy through its early stages of liberation from mercantilism.[3] It created a "common sense" in many sectors of society that free markets were the natural way to organize an economy. This was the ideology that justified the British bourgeoisie in enclosing the common lands that peasants had used for centuries as sources of water, wood, and pasture – a deprivation that drove them into the cities, where they offered a cheap labor force for the expanding capitalist system.

Polanyi did not believe that the market could *really* be disembedded from society; this is why he said that the "ineluctable necessity" of the "unshackling of the market" was *"believed"*: for Polanyi, the disembedding of the market from society was a cultural, not an economic, reality. "When Polanyi wrote that 'the idea of a self-adjusting market implied a stark utopia,'" writes Fred Block, "he meant that the project of disembedding the economy was an impossibility" (Block 2007: 3; Polanyi 2001: 139).[4] The believed-in myth of disembedded markets came into conflict with the realities of national protection. This was the contradiction, for Polanyi, that produced the collapse of the international economy in the 1930s.

The movement toward free trade, free markets, and free enterprise was contested almost from the beginning by "a countermovement." That countermovement, similar to the free market movement that triggered early capitalist development, could take reactionary, reformist, or even fascist forms. The earliest opponents of free enterprise in England were upper class landowners,

---

[3] I am grateful to Philip McMichael for providing me with this felicitous expression for the way Polanyi saw the market. For McMichael's own contribution and updating of Polanyi, see McMichael (2005).

[4] The problem, however, is that the precepts of the disembedded market were *believed in* by European policymakers and bankers, who insisted on their defense even as the international financial system was crumbling in the years after World War I. National states retreated into a countermovement that took the form, at best, of protected markets, and, at worst, of the authoritarian involution that produced fascism and Nazism. It was to avoid a similar collapse that post–World War II policymakers tempered the return to free trade. For this story, see John Ruggie's important work in Ruggie (1982 and 2008).

who were disturbed at the impact of new industries on the sylvan English countryside. The first English workingmen's groups were inspired by religious and utopian principles. And the fascist and Nazi movements that took control of Italy and Germany between the wars combined opposition to liberal capitalism with hatred of the Left.

But that was in the future: As early as the middle of the nineteenth century, just as capitalists and their supporters used their access to the state to enforce their demands to liberate the economy, middle class and religious reformers and their allies in government used access to the state to ameliorate the abuses of capitalism. The factory acts of the 1840s, the limitations of child and female labor, and, ultimately, unemployment and disability insurance were the product of reformist and even conservative elites protecting subordinate sectors of the population and trying to prevent revolutions.

Both movement and countermovement were imbricated within the state, and if the movement for free enterprise had the inside track – which it certainly did – the countermovement was not bereft of resources. If only because state actors were cognizant of the need to control the lower classes, reform efforts developed within, as well as against, the capitalist state. Rather than a dichotomization within society, capitalist development proceeded on the shifting tides of movement-countermovement interaction both within and outside the state. The state, rather than the "executive committee of the bourgeoisie," contained within it the *agency* for capitalist interests, but it was also the *fulcrum* of contention between social actors, and it was the *regulator* of capitalism. This came about not only as the result of the intricate relations between the state and capitalism, but because rulers, to make war, extract resources, and ensure internal control, built modern consolidated states.

Tocqueville and the Strength of the State

National states are so central a focus for the mobilization of opinion today that we often forget that this was not always so. During the centuries before the coming of absolutism in western Europe, national states worthy of the name could hardly be said to exist. "On the one hand," writes Norbert Elias in *State Formation and Civilization*,

> kings were forced to delegate power over part of their territory to other individuals. The state of military, economic and transport arrangements at that time left them no choice.... On the other hand the vassals representing the central power were restrained by no oath of allegiance or loyalty from asserting the independence of their area as soon as the relative power positions of the central ruler and his delegates shifted in favour of the latter (1994: 276–277).

In such a system, contention was constant, was largely territorially based, and changed its contours according to whether the monarch was temporarily ascendant or suffering a crisis.

From roughly the fifteenth century onward, this pattern began to give way, as the expansion of the money economy gave kings the power to pay mercenary soldiers, build roads on which to deploy them, and hire civil servants to collect taxes, administer rules, and tame provincial nobles. Where they could establish a rough balance between the aristocracy and the rising burghers of the towns, they developed a "royal mechanism," which led to the formation of absolutist states – as in France (Elias: Chapter 2). Where they were forced to share power with their nobles and eventually with an assertive merchant class, the result was a constitutional or a segmented monarchy – as in England and the Low Countries (Spruyt 1994).

During all this time, contentious politics did not cease, but its character changed from the more or less constant struggle over territory to alternating periods of war and relative peace, with outbursts of popular politics over land, religion, bread, and taxes increasingly taking intraterritorial form (see Chapter 2). Between the fifteenth and seventeenth centuries, popular contention developed among the triad of ordinary people, local rulers, and national claimants to power, particularly when wars and revolutions opened opportunities for ordinary people (te Brake 1998: Chapter 1). Each major episode of political change brought opportunities for ordinary people to ally with local rulers against national claimants, or to connect their fates to national leaders against local oligarchies. They usually lost, but not before affecting the type of national state that eventually emerged. As Wayne te Brake concludes,

> It was in the interstices and on the margins of these composite early modern state formations that ordinary people enjoyed their greatest political opportunities. By choosing to oppose the claims of some putative sovereigns, ordinary Europeans were often deliberately reinforcing the claims of constitutionally alternative or competitive rulers... (1998: 15).

And so they remain today. What changed were the consistency and the resources of ordinary people in contentious politics as the form of the state evolved, centering around plebiscitary leaders, constitutional parliaments, or both. Major changes took place between the late eighteenth and middle nineteenth centuries. This is not to say that national state building began only in the nineteenth century, but that state consolidation implying the creation of national forms of citizenship and identity dates from that period.[5]

Alexis de Tocqueville was the first to theorize the implications of these changes for collective action. In his *Democracy in America* and *The Old Regime and the French Revolution,* he taught that differences in patterns of state building produced differences in opportunity structures for social movements. Centralized states (e.g., France) aggrandized themselves by destroying intermediate bodies and reducing local autonomy. This left few openings for institutionalized participation; when confrontations did break out, as they did

---

[5] On the general relation between state consolidation and citizenship, see Charles Tilly, *Coercion, Capital and European States* (1990: Chapter 4). On the different national patterns leading to national citizenship, see Wayne te Brake, *Shaping History: Ordinary People in European Politics, 1500–1700* (1998).

in 1789, they were violent and were likely to lead to despotism because there was nothing to structure them. In contrast, in the United States, where civil society and local self-government were stronger, participation was both regular and widespread, channeling confrontation and allowing democracy to flourish. Tocqueville's underlying message was that state building creates an opportunity structure for collective action of which ordinary people take advantage. Tocqueville's vision will provide us with a convenient starting point for examining the relationship between state building and the rise of national social movements.

Tocqueville's image of a France bereft of intermediate bodies exaggerated both societal atomization and state strength, while his glowing picture of Jacksonian America underestimated the relationship between state building and contention in this country. For one thing, the bucolic image he drew of antebellum America left the relationship between association and contention in the shadows. As early as the 1790s, President Washington had sent a militia to subdue farmers in western Pennsylania who rebelled at paying the hated excise tax on whiskey (Gould 1998; Elkins and McKitrick 1993: 461–473). For another, the weak American state was a contingent result of the standoff between the states until, decades after Tocqueville studied it, the federal state was strengthened by the Civil War (Bensel 1990).

To begin with the second point, although the nineteenth century American state was not centralized, it was far from a *non*state. The Federalists had constructed an effective state for their purposes – achieving fiscal consolidation, debt reduction, diplomatic maneuver, and westward expansion (Bright 1984: 121–122). And although its military arm was considerably weaker than its European counterparts (the Revolution left a deep suspicion of standing armies), its armed might could expand remarkably quickly when it was needed for defense or for westward expansion (Katznelson 2002).

What of American contention? Tocqueville saw this through the red lens of the Terror that had decimated his family and his class. Finding nothing of the kind in America, he saw few social movements. But the United States in the late eighteenth and early nineteenth centuries was bursting with contention. The sabotage of British rule and the raising of a popular army in the 1770s; Shay's and Whiskey rebellions that required troops for their suppression; popular opposition to and support of the 1812 War; the frontier mobilization that produced Jackson's presidency; the religious fervor of the Second Great Awakening that "burned over" wide swatches of newly settled territory – these episodes and others escaped the neat institutional pluralism that Tocqueville thought he saw in his travels through America.

The center of gravity of American social movements was still local in 1832, and this contrasted with the national insurrections that Tocqueville had seen in France. But even before industrialization, there was a lively urban workers' movement with a strong dose of Painite republicanism (Bridges 1986; Wilentz 1984). Already, regional and national movements were developing a capacity for collective action in rough dialectic with the national struggle for power, laying the groundwork for temperance, abolitionism, and the first feminist movement in the world. The sectional conflict that had begun by paralyzing national policymaking in the 1820s ended in the most cataclysmic episode of contention in the nation's history – one that would turn the American state into a modern Leviathan (Bensel 1990). America might be decentralized, but it was hardly lacking in contention!

Of course, there were differences in state centralization, in association, and in the intensity of collective action between centralized France and localized America. But in both countries, state building provided an opportunity structure for emerging movements, and these movements helped to shape the future of each state. In both countries – and all over the West, for that matter – the expansion and consolidation of the national state prodded the social movement into existence, and ordinary people helped to shape the modern state. In the rest of this chapter, we will examine how state building provided opportunities for contentious politics during the modern phases of state consolidation in Britain, France, and the United States.

STATE BUILDING AND CONTENTION

Even before the Revolution of 1789, and in places more pacific than France, the national state was gaining unprecedented power to structure relations among citizens and between them and their rulers. Expanding states made war and needed roads and postal networks, armies, and munitions factories to do so. To finance such improvements, states could no longer rely on a surplus extracted from the peasantry but depended on the growth of industry and commerce, which, in turn, required that law and order be maintained, food be supplied, associations be licensed, and citizens gain the skills necessary to staff the armies, pay the taxes, and turn the wheels of industry (Tilly 1990).

These efforts at state building were not intended to support mobilization – quite the contrary. But they provided the means of communication through which opinion could be mobilized; they educated a mass citizenry, created a class of men experienced in public affairs, and led to financial exactions on citizens who were not always disposed to pay them. In addition, states that took on responsibility for maintaining order had to regulate the relations between groups; this meant creating a legal framework for association and providing mechanisms for social control more subtle than the truncheons of the army or the police. By these efforts, states not only penetrated society; they integrated it into a standard set of roles and identities that form the basis of modern citizenship. Within this matrix, citizens not only contested state expansion; they used the state as a fulcrum to advance their claims against others.

The most obvious example can be seen in the effects of the extension of male suffrage on the legalization of public gatherings. Bourgeois states might not wish to see workers marching on the prefecture or peasants milling around the village square, but even under a restricted suffrage, the meeting and drinking that attended election campaigns provided umbrellas under which even "undesirable" social actors and contentious forms of action could find shelter. Even without elections, as Raymond Grew writes, all states, "as if by irresistible mandate, encouraged easier nationwide communication and a minimal universal education.... Once citizenship became a formal matter of birth or oaths registered by the state, it remained so even though specific criteria could be altered" (1984: 94).

Three basic policies – making war, collecting taxes, and providing food – were part of the struggle waged by expanding states to ensure and expand their power. Although they began as pressures on citizens and as efforts to penetrate the periphery, each produced new channels of communication, more organized networks of citizens, and unified cognitive frameworks within which ordinary people could mount claims and organize. In states as different as liberal constitutional Britain, absolutist France, and colonial America, these policies became arenas for the construction of movements, and movements – or the fear of them – shaped the national state.

War and Contention in Britain

The most portentous changes were produced by war and colonization, not only because they raised taxes and granted governments more power, but because they mobilized people in an organized way and provided opportunities for collective action. Mobilization to make war had been a limited affair until rulers responding to the technical revolution in weaponry needed larger standing armies than their noblemen could lead or mercenaries could staff. The size of armies grew geometrically in the eighteenth century,[6] as did financial and logistical requirements for putting them in the field. From multinational assemblies of mainly mercenary battalions, armies became national,[7] and national mobilization – while it came nowhere near twentieth century levels – was great enough to cause severe social and financial dislocation – and sometimes revolution (Skocpol 1979).

In late eighteenth century England, both the formation of the party system and opportunities for mobilization were advanced by colonization and war making. Although the early years of the American war produced an increase in public support for the government, the later war years, with their disillusionment, financial strain, and fear of French invasion, brought attempts to mobilize resistance. These were at first elite-led campaigns centered on London. But the government's opponents eventually encouraged a broad-based and continuous attack on ministers on the basis of economic reform. It was in this context

---

[6] Samuel Finer reports that, while the number of French troops used against Spain in 1635 was 155,000, Napoleon mustered 700,000 for the Russian campaign in 1812. And while the Prussians assembled 160,000 men for the Seven Years' War, as many as 300,000 were recruited in 1814. For England, the numbers were always smaller, but growth was proportional: from the 75,000 troops assembled in 1712 to the 250,000 called up at the peak of the Napoleonic campaigns. See Finer's "State-and Nation-Building in Europe: The Role of the Military" (1975: 101).

[7] Finer notes that "as late as the third quarter of the eighteenth century, from one-half to one-third of the troops of any state would have been foreigners." See his "State and Nation-Building" (1975: 101–102).

that Wilkes made his famous plea connecting the war to parliamentary reform: "The American war," he argued, "is in this truly critical era one of the strongest arguments for the regulation of our representation" (Christie 1982: 65).

Although London politics was the spark for this movement, much of the opposition came from sections of the country – like Yorkshire – whose trade was badly hit by colonial boycotts of English goods, and then by the blockade of American ports. Clergyman Christopher Wyvill's Yorkshire Association began its activities with a platform combining a call for economic and parliamentary reform with an attempt to build a national network of county associations.[8] The Association drew up a petition, which gained nearly nine thousand signatures in Yorkshire and elected a committee of correspondence. The Tory government condemned the effort as an attempt to imitate the "seditious" American continental congress. War and state building were already leading to movement association.

The Gordon riots of June 1780 produced a reaction against extra-parliamentary association, and the Yorkshire and other branches of the movement petered out in the later years of the war (Read: 14–16). The reaction was intensified when the Jacobin phase of the French Revolution appeared to threaten British institutions (Goodwin 1979). But although Jacobin and Painite agitators were suppressed, the movements for economic and parliamentary reform and the war that fostered them established the future form of the social movement in England. "War made the state and the state made war," writes Charles Tilly (1975b: 42). But making war also created the space and incentives for social movements.

Provisioning Food in France

Not only in wartime, but around more routine activities of national states, collective claims were organized. A traditional function of European states was to regulate the supply and the price of food – in part, to tax it, but also to ensure subsistence and public order. In the past, the battle had been fought mainly by city burgesses trying to gain control of their hinterlands. But as cities grew, states expanded, and markets internationalized, national states became responsible for guaranteeing food supply and were held responsible for it when it failed.

The provisioning of food was never wholly free of public control. For example, the insistence that the trading and weighing of food be done in a public place was a way of ensuring not only its taxation, but minimal standards of quality and price (Kaplan 1984: 27 ff.). At one time or another, communities, manors, churches, and states were all involved in the control of food supply.

---

[8] Donald Read writes in his *The English Provinces* that it called for "opposition to that mercenary phalanx" that ruled the country, through the formation of "associations in the several districts of the kingdom, acting by their respective Committees, and by general deputation from the Associated Bodies" (Read 1964: 12).

But "only states unequivocally acquired greater power to intervene in the food supply over the long run" (Tilly 1975a: 436), because it was states that were ultimately threatened by dearth and the popular contention it could foster.

As in much else, the connection between provisioning food and preventing disorder was explicit under the French monarchy, because France was both large and centralized. According to an eighteenth century administrator, the prerequisite for order "was to provide for the subsistence of the people, without which there is neither law nor force which can contain them."[9] Indeed, the obligation to ensure subsistence came to be seen as a major responsibility of paternal kingship, for "what more solemn duty could a father have than to enable his children to enjoy their daily bread" (Kaplan 1984: 24).

Though conflicts over food frequently occurred when people felt that their right to subsistence was threatened, this situation was radicalized only "when states began to assure the subsistence of those populations most dependent upon them and/or threatening to them." These included, most notably, the armed forces, state administrators, and the populations of capital cities (Tilly 1975a: 393). Because all three expanded rapidly in the eighteenth century, it is no accident that subsistence crises and food rebellions punctuated that century – most notably in the years before and after 1789. With the spread of physiocratic ideas, the idea of freeing the price of grain came up against the prevailing paternalistic policy of ensuring subsistence to the cities – and especially to Paris.

Provisioning Paris was a special state responsibility, not only because of the city's enormous population, but because it was assumed (correctly, as it turned out) that Parisians were capable of overthrowing the government. The state thus made it its business to ensure not only the amount of food supplied to Paris, but also the quality of the grain and flour that entered the capital. The deepest conflicts arose in times of dearth between Parisian officials and the local communities that produced grain for the metropolis. "The fiercest intercommunity struggle for subsistence," writes Kaplan, "opposed the local market town to the vulturous capital" (p. 39).

The 1789 Revolution, though triggered by conflicts over taxation and parliamentary power, showed how deeply the national state had become involved in the provision of food. The municipal insurrections that followed the news of the fall of the Bastille were radicalized by the cry of "Bread at two sous!" (Lefebvre 1967: 125) Even the Jacobins, fearing to be outflanked on their Left when they took power, found it convenient to set maximum prices on bread, sending revolutionary armies to scour the provinces for grain. From a set of local, parochial, and episodic conflicts over subsistence, food provision became a pivot for the spread of revolution. It would remain an important element in each revolutionary cycle up to 1848.

---

[9] The administrator was Bertier de Sauvigny, whose unpublished manuscript from the Bibliothèque Nationale, "Observations sur le commerce des grains," is quoted by Steven Lawrence Kaplan in his *Provisioning Paris* (1984: 23).

Levying Taxes in America

The common denominator of all of the modern state's policies is its ability to raise revenue to support its other activities. The result is that fiscal problems, writes Gabriel Ardant,

> are to be found in the beginnings of great social changes, such as the liberation of the serfs of Western Europe, the subjugation of the peasants of Eastern Europe, wars for independence (that of Portugal as well as that of the United States), revolutions, the creation of representative governments, etc. (1975: 167).

The growth of the modern state was most often contested by revolts against the growing burden of taxes. The hated *gabelle* in France and the *dazio* in Italy led to revolts that flared up for years. In France, the monarchy's tactic of selling to tax "farmers" the right to collect taxes increased resentment against the burden, while making it easier to assault the collector. Tax revolts rose and fell, more commonly in peripheral than in core areas, but were by no means limited to the lower classes, as the history of relations between the French monarchy and the provincial *parlements* shows.

But it was only in the late eighteenth century that tax revolts became sufficiently broad-based and well-organized to feed into national movements. If the states of the late eighteenth century had a new fiscal problem, it was because their expanded ambitions required a degree of financial universalism that was contradicted by their dependence on their clerical and secular elites. Both paid few or no taxes, regarding the military role of the nobility and the spiritual role of the clergy as sufficient service to the state. Rulers who toyed with equalizing the burden of taxes had to face the prospect of losing the support of one or the other of their major allies (Ardant 1975: 213).

England's difference from the continental powers was that basic reforms in its tax system were never attempted, in part because the expansion of global trade – much of it British and carried in British ships – produced large revenues from the excise tax, and in part because the effective center of the British state was a Parliament in which landed proprietors held a majority of seats (Ardant 1975: 207). Revenue collection thus weighed lightly on the land, on which the wealth of the parliamentary elite depended,[10] and heavily on trade – particularly on trade with the colonies. What Americans called "The French

[10] According to Gabriel Ardant, in his essay "Financial Policy and Economic Infrastructure of Modern States and Nations" (1975: 202–203), between 1736 and 1738, English domestic revenues, on average, came from:

Land	17.5%
Windows, annuities, and functions	2.4%
Customs	24.6%
Excise	52.8%
Stamp	2.6%

and Indian War" brought these pressures to a head, because it was immensely more expensive to wage than any previous British struggle, and because Parliament chose to make the colonists pay for it rather than raise their own taxes (Ardant 1975: 204). But such a fiscal strategy was foolhardy, for the American colonists lived an ocean away and had their own provincial governments, which depended on much the same mix of revenues as the mother country.[11] The first major anticolonial revolution in history was a response to state building, indicated its limits, and demonstrated the power of movement to block a national taxation policy.

THE STATE AS TARGET AND MEDIATOR

Making war, provisioning cities, and levying taxes all stimulated new and more sustained episodes of collective action, particularly because making war required higher taxes and produced strains on provisioning. As the activities of national states expanded and penetrated society, the targets of contention shifted from private and local actors to national centers of decision making. The national state not only centralized the targets of collective action, it provided a fulcrum on which claims could be mounted against *non*state antagonists through the mediation of the state.

During much of the eighteenth century, as we learned from Charles Tilly's research in Britain (1995a: Chapter 2), the targets of the prevailing forms of contention in Britain were millers and grain merchants, local gentry, members of the community, and peripheral agents of the state such as tollgate managers or tax collectors. But from the late eighteenth century onward, with a brief inflection between 1789 and 1807, Tilly found a decisive movement of collective actors away from private and local targets and toward the use of public meetings, with Parliament as their main target. By the 1830s, Parliament had become the object of approximately thirty percent of the contentious gatherings that Tilly and his team found in Southeast England (1995a: 36).

State centralization not only made the national government a target for citizens' claims, it led to a broader framing of citizens' actions. The standardization of taxation, of administrative regulations, and of census categories encouraged the formation of coalitions of groups that had previously been opposed or indifferent to one other. Classifying citizens into what started out as pragmatic administrative groupings (e.g., payers of a certain tax, residents of particular cities, counties, or *départements*, soldiers conscripted in particular years) constructed new social identities or laid the bases for broader coalitions.[12]

---

[11] For example, New York's expenses were met from an import duty, an excise on various commodities, and a license fee paid by hawkers and peddlers. As in England, land was taxed only in times of war, leaving large landholders bearing a slim portion of the colonies' expenses, and cities like New York and Albany bearing disproportionate amounts of the tax. See Edward Countryman's *A People in Revolution* (1981: 83), for New York's revenue structure.

[12] The *départements* created during the French Revolution were an archetypical example. Constructed from mapmakers' calculations and named for whatever river happened to flow through

We see this integrative effect most clearly in the effects of taxation on collective action. As taxes shifted from a congeries of disparate duties on different classes of citizens to simplified national imposts collected by a central bureaucracy, tax revolts united diverse social groups and localities. Conscription had a similar effect – especially when resistance to it was linked to ideological or religious objections. The Vendée Rebellion was only the first in a series of such movements, ending, most recently, in opposition to the Vietnam War, in which the trigger for mobilization was resistance to the draft (Tilly 1964: Chapter 13). Through mass petitioning, public meetings, and demonstrations aimed at the state, there was now an alternative to attacking your enemies directly.

One result of these changes was a massive decline in the amount of violence attending contention (Tilly 1995a: 35). Another was the appearance of a number of forms of contention that were more integrated into the polity than earlier ones had been. A third was that states had to take account of popular will and be prepared to suppress it when it got out of hand. The two most characteristic areas of state growth in the nineteenth century – the expansion of the suffrage to most male citizens and the growth of a professional police force – were both linked to fear of popular contention.

Workers and the Ballot in America

The fundamental fact about American workers in the nineteenth century was that, as the result of a revolution for citizen rights that was won before an industrial working class existed, workers got the vote earlier than in Europe. This meant not only that (male) workers' collective action was channeled through the ballot, but that in the future, workers' participation would be territorially oriented. And since the bulk of the working class was urban from a very early stage, their collective action was directed at urban politics, where lively political machines could make use of their votes and provide them with channels for upward mobility.

These institutional factors made the American working class different from the one that was appearing in Western Europe. In 1830, American workers shared with their English cousins an artisan republicanism, understood the coming of the industrial system in similar ways, and used the same language of master and slave (Bridges 1986: 158). But the fact that they voted in an already electoralized state "changed the arena in which the newly created working classes struggled to achieve their goals" (p. 161). As Amy Bridges concludes, "sheer numbers, the search for allies, geographical dispersion or concentration, and the rules of the electoral game all affected the political capacity of the working classes" (p. 161).

them, the departments were designed to break up old provincial loyalties, especially in areas of late integration that had been indirectly governed by the monarchy. But in reaction to the state's territorial and fiscal policies, they eventually gave rise to administrative, and then to political identities.

Thenceforth, the integration of the waves of immigrants who fed the American industrial machine was shared between the unions – which organized workers on an occupational basis – and the urban political machines – which sought their votes on territorial lines (Katznelson 1981: 45–72). "Class" as an organizing category was far from absent in the factory, but in elections, it had to compete for workers' loyalty with territory and ethnicity, both of which were combined with party by electoral politics. The long-term institutional trends created by the American revolutionary settlement created – and shaped – political opportunities for the workers for generations to come.

Repression and Citizenship

Not all the long-term changes in state structure created opportunities for contention; many were deliberately designed to check popular politics. For once the idea of combining consistently on behalf of collective claims was widely diffused, fear of uprisings led states to strengthen the police and pass legislation restricting rights of assembly and association. It does not seem accidental, for instance, that the British created a professional police force after the Peterloo massacre, when uncontrolled troops had fired on unarmed workers demanding the vote.[13] A second major strengthening of police forces coincided with the increase in labor disputes, particularly when the mass strike was developed toward the end of the nineteenth century.[14] The rhythms of repression followed the pulse of popular politics.

In France, it was less the pressure of strikes than the fear of insurrection that kept authorities plotting new strategies of order. After each wave of revolutionary agitation (1789, 1830, 1848, and 1870–1871), new attempts were made to restrict collective action, both by limiting association and by preparing the forces of order for urban civil war. Both were draconian on the surface, but each adapted in the long run to the inexorable pressures of citizenship and civil society. With respect to association, "French law and administrative practice forbade the discussion of politics within [bourgeois] associations," writes historian Carol Harrison, but this did not prevent thousands of Frenchmen from joining them (1996: 45). It did give the state the power to investigate associations that it thought dangerous. But at each opening of political opportunity, new or revised forms of association sprang up, evading the authorities with their ingenuity or apparent innocence.[15]

---

[13] The sequence took until 1828 to complete. Robert Peel (hence, the "bobbies"), who had served the government in Ireland before becoming Prime Minister, created the predecessors of the English civilian police there, under the trying circumstances of colonial government. Similar to the Indian Civil Service, whose lessons were later transferred to Britain, the Irish colony was an experimental ground for later metropolitan innovations in state building.

[14] On this development, see Roger Geary, *Policing Industrial Disputes, 1893–1895* (1985), and Jane Morgan, *Conflict and Order: The Police and Labor Disputes in England and Wales* (1987).

[15] For example, the banquets that marked the Republicans' determination to widen the suffrage and set off the 1848 Revolution were replays on a larger scale of those that had marked

As for combating urban insurrection, the police won that battle. The barricades that had sprung up during the 1830 and 1848 revolutions corresponded
to a temporary balance of technical power between urban insurgents and
authorities. By June of 1848, the Parisian barricades could no longer resist
the determined firepower marshaled by the army, and most were blown apart
(Traugott 1995; Gould 1995). Under the Second Empire, the restructuring of
Paris by Baron Haussmann spelled the doom of the barricade as a defensive
weapon. For the tangled warren of streets in the old quarters of Paris, Haus-
mann substituted today's broad boulevards to facilitate the reduction of future
barricades by cannon fire.

But the successful repression of the barricade had a latent effect: It led to the
development of new tools of agitation by working class militants – mainly the
strike and the public demonstration (see Chapter 5). Both were less threatening
to republican order and were therefore harder to repress. By the late nineteenth
century, both a jurisprudence and the conventions of police practice led to the
institutionalization of these newer forms, culminating in the development of
the "service d'ordre," by which demonstrators largely agreed to police themselves (Bruneteaux 1996). The characteristic tools of twentieth century popular politics were born through a long-term dialectic between violent protests
and equally violent state repression, some but not all of it for protection of
capitalism.

This lesson can be generalized: As movements learned to use the appara-
tuses of national communications and consolidated states, governments had
to grudgingly accept forms of collective action whose legitimacy they had earlier resisted, while suppressing others and routinizing still others. The English
leaders who had condemned petitions in favor of Wilkes as subversive were
eventually forced to accept mass petitions and political associations as legitimate. There was a reaction during the war with France, but, by the early
1800s, voluntary associations were so common that innkeepers routinely kept
their funds and papers in locked boxes (Morris 1983: 95–118). By the 1830s,
the private association for group purposes was a familiar part of the political
landscape (Tilly 1982).

At the same time, violence and the threat of violence were treated ruthlessly,
especially in the United States, where the federal presence on the ground was
thin, but where state militias, private detective agencies, and the courts were
widely used to repress strikers. In the long run, even immigration and race
became a tool in the control of worker militancy: If Irish workers went on
strike, they could be replaced by impoverished Poles or Italians; and if white
workers organized, the more easily controlled black underclass could be put
in their place. If we measure the amount of suppression by the overall number
of deaths during industrial conflict, rather than by central state repression, it

the transition to the Orléanist regime in 1830. On neither occasion could the authorities curb
Frenchmen's natural propensity to dine together and socialize (Corbin 1994; Tocqueville 1987).

turns out that American labor relations were more repressive than in Britain or France. So much for the weak American state!

The progress of the social movement was never smooth, not even in liberal Britain, for once the Revolution of 1789 broke out on the continent, even mild reform movements such as the British one raised suspicions of sedition among frightened elites. Books and pamphlets were censored and radical associations banned, and even moderate ones lost membership. "The result of this confusion and the inexpedient policies that flowed from it," observe Malcolm Thomas and Peter Holt, "was often the creation of revolutionaries where none had previously been." Governments, they conclude, "helped to create and sustain that very danger to themselves that they supposedly wished to avoid" (1977: 2).

War and the threat of war increased repression and the threat of repression in the United States as well. During the same decade in which the British were repressing reformist movements, Washington's successor, John Adams, watched with growing concern as his Vice President, Thomas Jefferson, began to ready himself for the Presidential election of 1800. Backed by a Republican press incensed that revolutionary France was left to fight alone against its former colonial master, Jefferson launched a series of political attacks on Adams and the Federalists as the pre-electoral season heated up. Under political assault and bolstered by the argument that France was readying an army to attack its former ally, the Federalists pushed through a series of repressive laws – the Alien and Sedition Acts – designed to deter Republican-leaning immigrants from supporting the French cause. Even a member of Congress, Matthew Lyon, was arrested under the Act (Stone 2004: 48–54). Even a "quasi-war" on the part of an incipient state led to increased contention and its repression.

But by the second half of the nineteenth century, in both Europe and America, movements and their potential for disruption had led national states to broaden (male) suffrage, accept the legitimacy of mass associations, and open new forms of participation to their citizens. In a very real sense, citizenship emerged through a rough dialectic between movements – actual and feared – and the national state. From the post-revolutionary American suffrage reforms to the British factory legislation of the 1840s to the unemployment and health reforms of Imperial Germany, a Polanyian movement-countermovement interaction was evident. As Bright and Harding point out, "contentious processes both define the state vis-à-vis other social and economic institutions and continually remake the state itself" (1984: 4).

CONCLUSIONS

It is a good time to recapitulate what has been argued in this and the last two chapters. Contentious politics has characterized human society from whenever human society can be said to have begun. But such actions usually expressed the claims of ordinary people directly, locally, and narrowly, responding to immediate grievances, attacking opponents, and almost never seeking coalitions with other groups or political elites, except when religion or war brought them together. The result was a series of explosions – seldom organized and usually brief – punctuating periods of passivity.

Sometime in the course of the eighteenth century, a new and more general repertoire of collective action developed in Western Europe and North America. Unlike the older forms, which expressed people's immediate grievances directly, the new repertoire was national, autonomous, and modular. It could be used by a variety of social actors on behalf of a number of different claims and could serve as a bridge among them to strengthen their hand and reflect broader and more proactive demands. Even inherited forms such as the petition were gradually transformed from the tool of individuals seeking grace from superiors into a form of mass collective action.

The root causes of this change are difficult to tease out of a historical record that has been mainly collected by those whose job it was to repress rebellion. But as we saw in Chapter 3, two main kinds of resources helped to empower these early movements: print and association. Both were expressions of capitalism, but both expanded beyond the interests of capitalists to fuel the spread of social movements. The commercial press not only spread information that could make potential activists aware of one another and their common grievances, it also equalized their perception of their status with that of their superiors and made it thinkable to take action against them. The private association reflected existing solidarities, helped new ones to form, and linked local groups into movement networks that could contest the power of national states or international empires. Social coalitions, sometimes purposeful and sustained, but often contingent and provisional, took concerted collective action against elites and opponents in the name of general programs.

Although it was capitalism and its cleavages that drove the creation of the countermovement, the framework for contention was increasingly the national state. In making war, provisioning cities, and raising taxes, the state became both a target for claims and a place in which competing groups could fight out their disputes more or less peacefully. Even when access to the state was denied, the standardizing and unifying ambitions of expanding states created opportunities for less well-endowed people to mimic and adapt the stratagems of elites.

Why did this system break down between the world wars in Europe, and why did it occur when it did? Polanyi provides us with a plausible answer: As long as the uneasy relationship between free enterprise capitalism and the countermovement remained in balance, states were insulated from the categorical inequalities of capitalist society (Tilly 1998). It was only when policymakers blindly insisted on the disembeddedness of the free enterprise economy from society that the international financial system collapsed, and a great depression emerged. But that depression, which produced the most ruthless social movements in modern history, fascism and Nazism, also produced a resurgence of democratic movements in the American New Deal – a reformist welfare state that saved capitalism from itself. What this means is not that class and capitalism do not matter in modern capitalist states, but that contentious politics forms around a number of axes of cleavage and conflict, rises and falls with the rhythm of changes in opportunities and threats, and helps to reshape the state, as we will see in Chapter 5.

PART II

POWERS IN MOVEMENT

5

Acting Contentiously

In the summer of 2008, as the administration of George W. Bush was winding down in the midst of a massive financial crisis, many Americans were outraged at the bank bailouts that Bush's Treasury Secretary, Henry Paulson, was designing. They were upset that a supposedly "small-government" administration was planning to dole out billions to financial institutions whose reckless habits had thrown the economy into a tailspin. The fact that Paulson had come from the bedrock of financial capitalism, Wall Street, made these heartland Americans – some of them older people living on fixed incomes – even angrier.

But the restlessness at the base of American society hit its stride only when the new Democratic administration came to power in January 2009. All through the 2008 campaign, Barack Obama had hammered the Republicans for fiscal irresponsibility, poor economic planning, and getting into bed with the bankers. But only days after his election in November, it was clear that his administration would be climbing into the same bed. By appointing a treasury secretary, Timothy Geithner, who had played a key role in the bank bailout, and an economic advisor, Larry Summers, who had, in the Clinton administration, approved banks' expansion into dangerous derivatives, Obama was signaling to financial markets that government support for banks that were considered "too big to fail" would not end with the Bush administration.

Aiding the banks was one thing; quite another was the new administration's plan for far-reaching healthcare reform. How, these outraged citizens asked, could the government think of expanding healthcare when millions of Americans were out of work, tax receipts were declining, and state governments were teetering on the edge of bankruptcy? Obama argued that healthcare reform, once it kicked in, would have a positive effect on the budget and that the public would gain from expanded access to healthcare and near-universal coverage. But healthcare reform was complicated (the bill that eventually came before the House of Representatives was over 2,000 pages long), and it was soon apparent to the wounded Republicans that it would provide them with a weapon with which to recoup their losses from the last election. Soon public outrage and

Republican calculations congealed in what came to be called "the Tea Party movement."

THE TEA PARTY

This "movement" did not begin at the grassroots, as its more militant supporters liked to claim. Instead it was triggered on the floor of the Chicago Mercantile Exchange, where "an excitable cable-news reporter named Rick Santelli, a former futures trader and Drexel Burnham Lambert vice-president," sounded the alarm about the new administration's plan to provide assistance for homeowners facing foreclosure. "'President Obama, are you listening?' he shouted, and he added that he'd been thinking of organizing a Chicago Tea Party in July" (McGrath 2010: 42). The agitation attracted the attention of Glenn Beck, Fox News avatar of the populist right, who founded what he called "the 9.12 project." Beck went well beyond opposing the financial mess and healthcare reform to excavate every shibboleth of the "values" Right: "things like honesty and hope and courage" and more politically tinged principles such as belief in God and hard work and independence. "Government," Beck proudly declared, "cannot force me to be charitable" (ibid). By the end of the following week, dozens of small protests were occurring simultaneously around the country, "evoking the legacy of early New England colonists in their revolt against King George" (p. 43). By February 2010, when a national Tea Party convention was held in Nashville, more than 500 Web sites had sprung up to oppose the Democrats' plans for major healthcare reform.

The activists' main expressions recalled the disruptive politics of the 1960s: At hundreds of town meetings and demonstrations, Tea Partiers followed the advice of Keli Carender (a.k.a. "The Liberty Belle") from Seattle: "Unlike the melodramatic lefties, I do not want to get arrested," she wrote. "I do, however, want to take a page from their playbook and be loud, obnoxious, and in their faces" (McGrath, p. 43). By the summer of 2009, when Democratic Party leaders went back to their districts to call for healthcare reform, thousands of Americans exploded at town hall meetings demanding to know why the government was threatening to reform healthcare. In the fall, more than 300,000 protesters gathered outside the Capital to protest both healthcare reform and the bailouts, and to question the loyalty and even the U.S. citizenship of President Barack Obama.[1] At least at the outset, they were not so much Republican as populist – combining outrage at the government's bailout of the Wall Street bankers with opposition to "socialized medicine," with a tinge of racism against an African American President, all of it bound together by a thread of the antigovernment libertarianism that has been a staple of opposition

---

[1] The so-called "birthers' movement" was made up of people who determinedly insisted that President Obama was not an American citizen, having been, in their view, born in Kenya, and therefore had been unconstitutionally elected. For more information, go to their Web site at www.birthers.org; visited February 7, 2010.

to central governmental power since the opposition to the Federal Constitution (Elkins and McKitrick 1993: Chapter 1; Friedberg 2000). But that was not the end of the Tea Party's string of contentious actions. From haranguing politicians at town meetings to holding public demonstrations to organizing picnics complete with geezers dressed up as George Washington (McGrath, p. 42). Tea Party activists soon turned to the electoral arena.

When, in late 2009, beloved Democratic Senator Ted Kennedy died and his long-safe Democratic seat came up for election, many Tea Party adepts flocked to Massachusetts to campaign for little known but telegenic Republican candidate, Scott Brown. Traveling around the state in his pickup truck and disguising his lack of concrete policy proposals under a blanket pledge to become "the forty-first vote against the Obama health care proposals," Brown swept to victory against the hapless Democratic candidate, then Lieutenant-Governor Martha Coakley. And in the congressional and gubernatorial elections of 2010, Tea-Party-backed candidates pushed their way into electoral contests in Alaska, Delaware, Nevada, New York and elsewhere against mainstream Republicans.

From a disruptive campaign against runaway government spending, the Tea Party had become a player in American politics.[2] And although a few George Washington look-alikes still wandered the lobbies of its first national convention, fewer outrageous placards were evident, and leaders such as Judson Phillips, the founder of the social networking site that sponsored the convention, was looking forward to the movement's transformation into an electoral political action committee (PAC). "If we just go out and hold signs and protest," he said, "that's not going to win the election" (*New York Times,* February 7, 2010, p. 1).

WHAT'S HAPPENING HERE?

Think of the forms of action that we have encountered in this brief narrative:

- Harassing politicians at local town meetings
- Organizing demonstrations outside of Congress
- Holding picnics and rallies to mobilize support at the grassroots level
- Dressing up in period costumes
- Supporting candidates in elections
- Organizing a national convention
- Setting up a political action committee to support candidates.

---

[2] As the 2010 congressional elections approached, Democrats from swing districts in places as far apart as Arkansas, Nevada, and Illinois began to shy away from healthcare reform and from activist government in general. By February, a group calling itself "Tea Party Nation" organized a for-profit National Tea Party Convention, with Republican vice presidential candidate and right-wing media star, Sarah Palin, as its keynote speaker (www.teapartynation.com/, visited February 3, 2010).

In this story, we see the two major properties of how people act contentiously. First, activists can employ a wide variety of forms of action. This flexibility allows them to adapt to changes in their environment, to combine the actions of broad ranges of actors, and to force political leaders to deal with new issues. From petitioning to holding public meetings to mounting demonstrations in public squares, all the way to disruption and outright violence, one of the key features of social movements is their capacity to employ a wide array of performances and combine them in contentious campaigns that navigate the boundaries of the polity while drawing on a broader "repertoire of contention." That repertoire, its three major variants, and how it intersects with state actors and the forces of order are the first topics of this chapter.

Second, the forms of action change, both over the long term as repertoires evolve in response to changes in states and capitalism, and in the shorter term, in response to changes in political opportunities and constraints. These changes can be either incremental or paradigmatic, as we will see in the final sections of this chapter. They sometimes lead the same actors to move toward different forms of action and sometimes change the meaning of the same actions from transgressive to contained. This takes us to the two key terms developed by Charles Tilly in his work on contentious politics: "performances" and "repertoires."

PERFORMANCES AND REPERTOIRES

In the traditional repertoire we sketched in Chapter 2, most actions were direct, often violent, and were usually aimed at achieving immediate redress from close-range opponents. Modern forms of contention are aimed at demonstrating a claim, either to objects of the claim, to power holders, or to significant third parties. This makes contentious politics a form of representative politics – however disruptive – and instills in it symbolic and cultural elements, even in the most violent forms such as terrorism, guerilla warfare, and civil war.

Social protest as performance was already becoming evident in the French Revolution, when forms of dress and public display became politicized (see Chapter 7). The nineteenth century – with its development of the political march, the public demonstration, and the turnout – reinforced the trend toward protesting through ritualized public performances. But only in the twentieth century – when public opinion, the media, and national states began to mediate between claim makers and their targets – did contention become a true performance for the benefit of third parties. With the development of mass media and the growing role of states and third parties in determining the outcomes of protest, the performance of political contention became both routine and professional. The very term we use to designate orderly marches through city streets – the "demonstration" – is itself a performative term.

In this new century, electronic communication has made some forms of physical performance less effective, while other forms – such as use of the Internet– have become more so. For example, protests against the stolen Iranian election of 2009 were organized largely through new means of electronic communication – cell phones, the Internet, Facebook, and Twitter – that had only recently been imported from the West. As we will see later, this provides the possibility for distant mobilization on the part of exiles or Diaspora nationalists, but it also offers repressive regimes the possibility of suppressing protest by jamming the airwaves or closing off Internet access, as the Iranian regime did to impede protests during the celebration of the founding of the Republic in February 2010 (*New York Times,* February 15, 2010), and as the Chinese government does today.

But new forms of "offline" performance have been steadily invented too, such as the "Seattle repertoire" of theatrical tactics, which included wearing costumes such as the giant puppets that first appeared at the anti-World Trade Organization (WTO) protests of 1998 and were diffused around the world (Wood 2004; Graeber 2009, Smith 2001). Since the turn of the century, and especially among "global justice" protesters, a new performative repertoire has been gaining ground. But it is not absent from the new populist right either. We saw this in the popular use of revolutionary costumes and the evocation of the Boston Tea Party around the country in 2009–2010.

What is it about protest performance that makes it appealing to organizers of contentious politics? First, protest performances add amusement or excitement to public politics; second, they help solidarity to grow through the interaction of the "performers" in protest actions. But the most important reason they are appealing is that they disrupt the routines of life in ways that protesters hope will disarm, dismay, and disrupt opponents. Disruption is the common coin of contentious politics and is the source of the innovations that make social movements creative and sometimes dangerous.

The repertoire of contention offers movements three broad types of collective action – disruption, violence, and contained behavior. These actions combine to different degrees the properties of challenge, uncertainty, and solidarity. The most dramatic forms, *violent ones,* are the easiest to initiate, but under normal circumstances, they are limited to small groups with few resources who are willing to exact damage and risk repression. The opposite forms, *contained ones,* offer the advantage of building on routines that people understand and that elites will accept or even facilitate. This is the source of its numeric predominance in the repertoire, but also of its institutionalization and lack of excitement. The third set of forms, *disruptive ones,* break with routine, startle bystanders, and leave elites disoriented, at least for a time (Piven and Cloward 1977). Disruption is the source of much of the innovation in the repertoire and of the power in movement, but it is unstable and easily hardens into violence or becomes routinized into convention.

We can illustrate this variety and flexibility in the modern repertoire of contention through the range of actions I found in a study of the protest movements of the late 1960s and early 1970s in Italy. Between 1967 and the mid-1970s, a vast wave of protests, strikes, and demonstrations and the beginnings of organized violence arose in Italy. In a detailed catalogue of

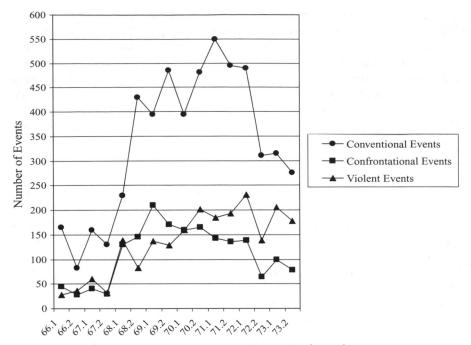

FIGURE 5.1. Italian Contention, 1966–1973. *Source:* Author's data.

"protest events," collected from Italy's major newspaper of record, the *Corriere della Sera*, I tried to track these three main forms of contention across this period. Figure 5.1 summarizes my Italian findings for the period 1966–1973, aggregating the many specific forms of contention found there into disruptive, violent, and routine forms of action.

Other protesters are just as flexible as Italians. When comparing the ecological movement in France and Germany, Dieter Rucht found that, at one time or another, antinuclear protestors in both countries used forms of collective action that were expressive or instrumental, confrontational, violent, or contained, and that came together in campaigns, skirmishes, and battles (1990). Writing of the American Women's movement, Anne Costain found that "Movement groups changed from working inside the institutions of government... to more electorally focused events and rising political protest" (Costain 1992: 126–127). Suzanne Staggenborg found that women's activities ranged between "teas held at churches to discuss change in the laws and endless trips to the state legislatures" and "counter-hearings" and "speak-outs" (Staggenborg 1991: 29, 44). Although their continent has a well-deserved reputation for political violence, Latin Americans are extremely versatile in how they engage in contentious politics. In a study of 1,318 contentious challenges between 1981 and 1995 in seven countries of the region, James Franklin found 369 demonstrations, 151 strikes and boycotts, 150 violent protests, 79 additional cases of violent threats, 35 hunger strikes, and 486 "revolutionary actions" (Franklin 2009: 707).[3]

Of course, overlaps and combinations can be seen among disruption, violence, and routine politics. Disruption easily escalates into violence, but it can also evolve into routine forms of action; violence aims at destruction of people or property, but it also has symbolic elements; and frequent interactions have been reported between routine politics and violence (Auyero 2007). In Part III of this book, we will turn to some of these interactions; for the sake of clarity, in this chapter we will deal separately with disruption, with violence, and finally with contained forms of collective action.

DISRUPTION AND INNOVATION

At the core of contention is the power to disrupt through the invention of innovative ways of performing protest. Disruption has always taken a variety of forms, from the attack on a wrongdoer's house and the assault on a miller's grain store in the eighteenth century to the barricades of the nineteenth century to the sit-ins and sit-down strikes of the twentieth century to the disruption of computer networks in our century. In its most direct forms, disruption is no more than the threat of violence: "If you do not produce grain or money," the challenger seems to be saying "or do not cease to use the machines that are destroying our livelihood, you may suffer physical harm."

However, in contemporary forms of contention, disruption has a more indirect logic. First, it provides evidence of a movement's determination. By sitting, standing, or moving together aggressively in public space, demonstrators signal their identity and reinforce their solidarity. Second, disruption obstructs the routine activities of opponents, bystanders, or authorities and forces them to attend to protesters' demands. Finally, disruption broadens the circle of conflict. By blocking traffic or interrupting public business, protestors inconvenience bystanders, pose a risk to law and order, and draw authorities into what was a private conflict.

Disruption need not threaten public order, but it can profoundly affect social and cultural expectations. In the 1960s and 1970s, the women's movement taught Americans that political causes can be advanced through personal means (Evans 1980). For example, a primary battlefield for American feminism has been the family – even on the part of nonmilitant women who would never consider themselves feminists. Another recent arena has been the Catholic Church, where "women religious" developed a discursive but highly disruptive critique of hierarchy and patriarchy (Katzenstein 1998: Chapter 6). A third

---

3 Franklin used full-text news wire reports from wire services indexed on LexisNexis and Keesing's Record of World Events and Facts on File for Argentina, Brazil, Chile, Guatemala, Mexico, Nicaragua, and Venezuela. This richer and broader source makes his findings only roughly comparable to the findings in Tarrow (1989), which were based only on a daily reading of Italy's major newspaper of record, *Corriere della Sera*.

was the HIV/AIDS movement, in which groups including the AIDS Coalition to Unleash Power (ACT-UP) used performative techniques, such as the public display of quilts commemorating those who died of AIDS (Gould 2009).

Consider the essentially performative nature of hunger striking. Until the late nineteenth century, only scattered evidence of this form of protest appeared in the historical record, largely from among prisoners who had no other means of self-expression than putting their lives in danger by fasting (Siméant 2009). The practice became more visible among prisoners in Czarist Russia in the period before the Russian Revolution (pp. 14–15). But it was only with the British and American suffragettes at the turn of the twentieth century and Northern Ireland's IRA prison protests in 1914–1918, and again in the 1970s, that hunger striking was widely used (pp. 15–17).[4] Why do prisoners and others engage in the self-destructive practice of hunger striking? Siméant provides the answer: "The hunger strike is the expression of an indignation which is aimed, through shock, to interrupt the ordinary course of things" – to disrupt normality (pp. 26–27).

Protesters have also invented new forms of direct action, which, instead of demonstrating a claim in public, perform protest by directly attacking the issue at hand. Italians called this "the practice of the objective," for example, lowering transit costs by getting onto buses without paying their fare. Ecological groups have perfected these forms of direct action. For example, tree sitters in the American Northwest protest clear-cutting by camping out in trees for more-or-less long periods. Gandhi's followers protested the British occupiers' monopoly of textile manufacture by weaving cloth on hand-held looms. This takes us to the issue of nonviolence as disruption.

The Nonviolent Repertoire

Social movement actors innovate to maintain solidarity, attract new supporters, and keep opponents off balance. To the march ending in a demonstration in a public place, the twentieth century added the tools of nonviolent direct action and the sit-in. In places as far apart as pre-independence India, the American South, and Greenham Common, England, nonviolent direct action became a staple of protesters (Chabot 2002, Cortright 2009, Sharp 1973). Although evidence has revealed the use of organized nonviolence farther back in history,[5] the practice first received formal theorization by Mohandas Gandhi after he and his followers used it against South African discrimination, and then to

---

[4] Such performances are not, however, universal; for example, Israel Waismel-Manor finds it almost completely absent in Israel but common in the United States (2005).

[5] Gene Sharp, in *The Politics of Nonviolent Action*, finds nonviolence as far back as the Roman plebeians, who, rather than attack the consuls, withdrew from Rome to a hill later called "the Sacred Mount" (1973: 75). He also finds examples of it in the American Revolution, in Hungarian resistance against Austrian rule in the nineteenth century, and in the general strike and shutdown of governmental functions that defeated the Kapp putsch in Weimar Germany (pp. 76–80).

oppose British colonial rule in India. Although the tactics of this movement were peaceful, Gandhi was quite clear about its disruptive aims. In initiating the 1930–1931 nonviolence campaign in India, he wrote the following to the British Viceroy: "It is not a matter of carrying conviction by argument. The matter resolves itself into one of matching forces" (quoted in Sharp, p. 85).

Although it began as a tool of anticolonial nationalism, nonviolent direct action became modular, spreading to a variety of movements in the 1960s and 1970s as a tool of strategic choice, even when it was not formally theorized (Chabot 2002). It was employed in the American Civil Rights movement, during the Prague spring in 1968, in the student movements of the same year, by European and American peace and environmental movements against nuclear arms and nuclear energy, by opponents of the Marcos regime in the Philippines, by opponents of military rule in Thailand and Burma, and in the overthrow of dictator Slobodan Milosovic in Serbia in 2000.

The innovative nature and the modularity of the nonviolent repertoire were demonstrated dramatically by its use by antiabortion protesters in the United States. Here, a movement that rejected much of the cultural and ideological baggage of the New Left adopted the tactic of blocking the entrances of abortion clinics and resisting nonviolently as its militants were being carried off by the police.[6] Even in authoritarian systems, where nonviolent protest would be smartly repressed, opposition movements have become skilled at mounting unobtrusive, symbolic, and peaceful forms of disruption that avoid repression while symbolizing contention. Long before state socialism collapsed in the former Soviet Union and East Central Europe, opponents of those regimes developed a broad repertoire of symbolic actions, passive resistance, and spray-painting graffiti on walls (Bushnell 1990). The more closed citizens' access to legitimate participation has become, the more sensitive citizens are to the meanings of symbolic forms of protest. Thus slaves in Portuguese-run Brazil developed forms of dance that appeared to be exotic African-derived amusements but were actually imitations of colonists' behavior as seen by the slaves.

The Instability of Disruption

But there is a paradox in disruptive forms of contention. Because disruption spreads uncertainty and gives weak actors leverage against powerful opponents, it is the strongest weapon of social movements. But when we analyze modern cycles of collective action, we see that disruptive forms are by no means the most common or the most durable (Tarrow 1989: Chapter 4). Look back

---

[6] The movement's effectiveness was demonstrated by the increasing unwillingness of American doctors or hospitals to perform abortions during the 1980s, and by the shame and guilt induced in women who were forced to go through with unwanted pregnancies. The antiabortion movement is dealt with sensitively by Suzanne Staggenborg in her *The Pro-Choice Movement* (1991: Part 3). Some organizational and tactical aspects are analyzed by John McCarthy in his article, "Pro-Life and Pro-Choice Mobilization" (1987). Also see Kirstin Luker's *Abortion and the Politics of Motherhood* (1985).

at Figure 5.1: It shows that the forms of contention coded as "disruptive" (e.g., the street or train blockade, the sit-in, the occupation of buildings) reached their height in the exciting days of 1968–1969, when students, workers, and others were in the streets. But by the numeric peak of the cycle, these disruptive forms had declined and contained forms of action (e.g., strikes, marches, meetings) had become more numerous. Not only that, but forms such as the sit-in and the assembly had been routinized, even in the factories, where nonunion-controlled factory councils were formed in the early days of the cycle, and these forms were adopted by the unions and conventionalized (Tarrow 1989: Chapter 6).

Why should the rate of innovation decline in the course of a movement's development? One reason is that – as we saw in the later stages of the Tea Party movement – the lure of politics draws activists toward more contained forms such as lobbying, publishing, media politics, and elections that will attract less committed supporters. This was what Frances Fox Piven and Richard Cloward found for the National Welfare Rights Organization that they studied in the 1960s. So determined were its leaders to gain political influences that they turned the movement into a mass membership organization and lost its disruptive power (1977: Chapter 5).

A second reason for the decline in innovation is that disruption depends on maintaining a high level of commitment among participants. This can seldom be sustained for very long, especially when police are determined and elites are united. Each invention of a new tactic is ultimately met by new police tactics (McAdam 1983). Short of violence, organizers run out of new ways to challenge authorities, embolden supporters, and keep the public interested and amused. They themselves soon run out of energy and can eventually "burn out." In a study of French and German "alter-global" protesters, Ariane Jossin found that three years after her first interviews with them, "the spirit of global activism that was very much alive before, had declined in the lives of the interviewees" (Jossin, in press: ms. p. 56).

Third, faced by determined police and unified governments, the marginal members of social movements – usually in the majority – tend to slip back into private life, leaving the field in the hands of the most militant activists, who are more likely to choose violence than to maintain an uncertain relation with authorities. Disruption splits movements into moderate majorities heading toward institutional politics and militant minorities – often goaded by police and authorities – more likely to descend into violence (della Porta and Tarrow 1986). In Chapter 10, we will return to the bifurcation of disruptive movements through the dual processes of institutionalization and escalation.

Most important, over the medium-long term, what begin as disruptive forms of contention become conventionalized, just as the strike and the demonstration did in the nineteenth and early twentieth centuries (see below). This means that, except at the extremes, we cannot classify a particular form of contention as disruptive or contained; its degree of disruption declines as it becomes more acceptable, more routinized, and more legitimated by law and practice. I will return to this process of routinization later in this chapter. First, I will distinguish between disruption and violence.

THE CHALLENGES OF VIOLENCE

Violence is the most visible trace of collective action, both in contemporary news coverage and in the historical record. On any recent day, look at a daily newspaper: It may record, among other items, accounts of the civil war in Sudan, guerilla fighting in Afghanistan, suicide bombings in Iraq or Pakistan, brawls between immigrant workers and local thugs in southern Italy, police repression of demonstrators in Iran, violence between soccer fans in Congo, attacks of guerillas on Israeli settlements, and ritualistic killings of young Muslim women in England or the Middle East who have defied their families by wanting to marry outside their faith.

Violence can take so many forms that even the term "collective violence"is an approximation. In addition, violence and nonviolent forms of contention are often found within the same movement, which is another reason to embed the study of violence within a broader framework of contentious politics. For example, in her study of the South African Anti-Apartheid movement, Gay Seidman pointed out that scholars have too readily classified the movement led by Nelson Mandela as "nonviolent." In actual fact, she writes,

> the armed struggle played a key role: it attracted popular support to the anti-apartheid movement, it demonstrated the persistence of resistance to white supremacy despite recession, and it served as a badge of commitment for anti-apartheid activists (Seidman 2001: 111).

In *The Politics of Collective Violence* (2004), Charles Tilly arrayed collective violence into seven major categories according to the degree of coordination among actors and the salience of the short-run damage inflicted. Figure 5.2 places six forms of collective violence on this grid, above the larger category of "individual aggression," in which the degree of damage inflicted may be great, but coordination is absent.

Tilly's six forms bleed into one another but can be distinguished as follows:

> *brawls* – highly violent but involving low levels of coordination – are attacks between individuals in groups in a previously nonviolent gathering; examples include barroom fights or battles at sporting events.
>
> *opportunism* – at a slightly higher level of coordination – is when individuals shielded from social control use damaging means to pursue forbidden ends, as in examples of looting after natural disasters, gang rape, or revenge killing.
>
> *scattered attacks* – less violent and slightly more coordinated than the first two forms, these occur when, in the course of nonviolent interaction, like a party conference or a march, some participants engage in damaging acts, like sabotage, assaults on government agents or arson.

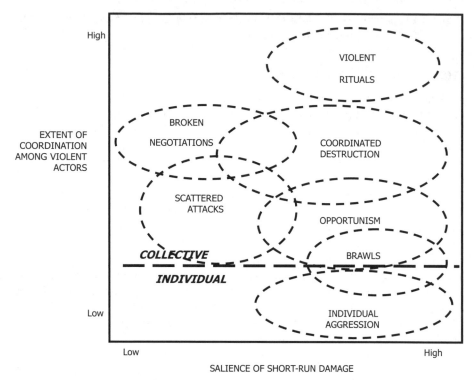

FIGURE 5.2. A Typology of Interpersonal Violence. *Source*: Charles Tilly, *The Politics of Collective Violence*, p. 15. Copyright © 2003 Charles Tilly. Reprinted with permission of Cambridge University Press.

broken negotiations – higher on the coordination scale but less certain to result in actual violence– occur when agreements cannot be reached or when negotiations break down between opponents, one of whom escalates the conflict by threatening violence, as when demands for change in a government by military leaders lead to a military coup.

coordinated destruction – both very violent and highly coordinated – occurs when persons or organizations that specialize in coercive means deliberately undertake a program of damage to others: examples include war, many forms of terrorism, and genocide.

violent rituals – at the top of the scales of coordination and the certainty of violence – occur when an organized actor follows a culturally known script to inflict damage as it competes for priority with others, as in the lynching of "uppity" African Americans in the Old South or in gang rivalries.[7]

---

[7] These descriptions merely paraphrase Tilly's longer definitions and lists of examples in *The Politics of Collective Violence* (2003). Each type is then elaborated and examined in detail in a separate chapter of his important book.

Note that although the incidental forms of violence that Tilly charts in the lower part of Figure 5.2 are most widespread, it is the coordinated forms of violence – such as guerilla movements, terrorism, and civil wars – that make their mark in the history books. Yet even these major episodes demonstrate the importance of incidental or opportunistic violence, as we will see from a rapid survey of the recent literature on civil war.

Warring Movements

As the Soviet Empire began to collapse in the early 1990s, a series of militant Islamist movements, taking their inspiration from the Iranian Revolution of 1979, challenged both secular regimes such as Egypt and royal theocracies such as Saudi Arabia. In North Africa, one such movement took control of the Sudan, while another fought to the death against the Algerian government. Nowhere was their triumph more electric than in Afghanistan, where, following a fight over the spoils of the defunct Socialist regime, the fundamentalist Taliban came to power as the victors in a civil war.

Fundamentalist Islam was not alone in creating turbulence around the globe. In Central Africa, a genocidal war in Rwanda in 1994 produced a mass migration into neighboring states and fed a devastating civil war in Zaire, whose corrupt leadership was overthrown in 1997. In Southeast Asia, challenges arose to both the Indonesian and the Burmese military dictatorships – the first with success, and the second failing. In Latin America, in 1995, a rebellion in Chiapas held the world's attention for almost a year (Olesen 2005), while in 1997, a desperate guerilla movement was able to hold hundreds hostage in the Japanese embassy in Peru.

The new century, if anything, exacerbated this picture of violence and political decay. The civil war in Sudan gave way to a rebellion in the Western region of Darfur, followed by genocide by government-backed militias. In Iraq, the American invasion of 2003 unleashed Sunni-Shi'a conflicts that had been suppressed under the dictatorship of Saddam Hussein. In South Asia, the long stalemate between Pakistan and India gave way to explosions of communal conflict, culminating in the massacre in Mumbai in 2008. And then of course, the endless civil war between Jews and Arabs in Israel/Palestine was punctuated by factional fighting between two groups of Palestinians in Gaza (Alimi 2007; Tilly and Tarrow 2007: Chapter 8).

Scholars of social movements have been stunned by these events, some applying models of mobilization from the West to violent challenges elsewhere, and others studying these challenges by applying new methods and theories. A whole new specialty of "security studies" responded to the threats of fundamentalist Islam, with no reference to the social movement canon. New methods of analysis drawing on microeconomic models have been employed to examine large numbers of these violent conflicts (Collier and Hoefler 2004; Fearon and Laitin 2003) and by applying variants of rational-choice theory (Kalyvas 2003; 2006; Weinstein 2006). Some of the best work combines theories derived from microeconomic models with detailed case materials (Collier and Sambanis, eds. 2005; Wood 2000 and 2003; for a review, see Tarrow 2007).

The most striking departure from the violent patterns of the past has been the partial replacement of interstate war by civil wars. A civil war occurs when two or more distinct military organizations, at least one of them attached to the previously existing government, battle each other for control of major governmental means within a single regime (Sambanis 2004). Over the last twenty years, civil wars have raged in Colombia, Iraq, Israel/Palestine, Kashmir, Nepal, Peru, Uganda, Guatemala, and Sudan. Scandinavian scholars have done annual tallies of major conflicts, counting as civil wars those armed conflicts between governments and other actors in which at least twenty-five people die during the year (Harbon and Wallenstein 2009). These cases range from regimes in which the major parties fight for control of a single national government (e.g., Nepal) to others in which at least one major party seeks to escape entirely from a central government's jurisdiction (e.g., the Philippines).

Scholars have divided armed conflicts since World War II into these four categories:

- *Extrasystemic war,* which occurs between a state and a nonstate group outside its own territory, the most typical cases being colonial wars
- *Interstate war,* between two or more states
- *Intrastate war,* between the government of a state and internal opposition groups without intervention from other states – e.g., civil wars
- *Internationalized internal war,* between the government of a state and internal opposition groups, with military intervention from other states (Strand, Wilhelmsen, and Gleditsch 2004: 11)

Figure 5.3, adapted from Harbon and Wallensteen's work (2010), shows colonial wars declining, then disappearing after 1975; interstate wars fluctuating but never predominating; and internationalized civil wars reaching their maximum during the 1980s, then declining around the turn of the century, only to increase again after 2003. In terms of sheer frequency of conflict, it is civil wars that have predominated during the last decades over all other types of violent conflict. Why is this so? It occurred in part because of militant nationalist and religious ideologies and in part because of the opportunities for violence that they trigger.

In his book on civil wars, Stathis Kalyvas distinguished between the central ideological/political cleavage at the center of civil war conflicts and the varieties of local conflicts and violence at their periphery. Referring to two great political theorists – Thomas Hobbes and Karl Schmitt – Kalyvas developed two parallel models of civil war violence: a *Hobbesian* model in which violence is privatized (e.g., roughly coinciding with Tilly's brawls, opportunism, and scattered attacks), and a *Schmittian* model, which "stresses the fundamentally political nature of civil wars and its attendant processes"; this corresponds roughly to

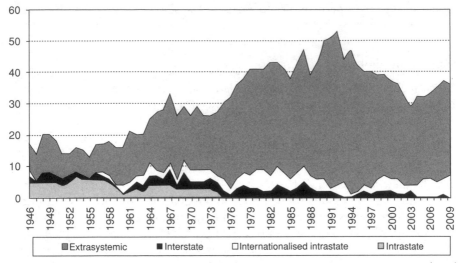

FIGURE 5.3. Numbers of Armed Conflicts by Type, 1946–2009. *Source*: Reproduced with permission from Lotta Harbom and Peter Wallensteen (2010). "Armed Conflicts, 1946–2009." *Journal of Peace Research* 47: 501–509.

Tilly's coordinated destruction and violent rituals (Kalyvas 2006: 475–476). Kalyvas found both Hobbesian and Schmittian elements in the civil wars he studied, and – most important – he argued that the extreme brutality of civil war violence results not from one or the other, but from their interaction and from the alliances they foster between those whose violence is the result of "Schmittian" ideological commitments and those who take advantage of the central ideological conflict to attack people they don't like or fear (2006: 381–386). Translating the complexities of Kalyvas' argument into the abstract terms of Tilly's paradigm, we can say that the explosion of a "Schmittian" central conflict into civil war violence triggers "peripheral" brawls, opportunistic violence, and scattered attacks among people who may have lived side by side for generations, but seize the opportunities offered by a central conflict to attack one another.

Kalyvas' insight can be extended to other forms of violence, both historical and contemporary. For example, during World War II, when Poles and Rumanians turned on their Jewish neighbors with knives and pickaxes, they did so because of the opportunity offered by the presence of Nazi invaders who were engaged in a "Schmittian" genocidal campaign. In a contemporary example, the invasion of Iraq by American and coalition forces in 2003 opened opportunities for violence between Shiite and Sunni groups who had lived in more or less uneasy peace under the repressive regime of Saddam Hussein. Rather than bringing social peace to Iraq, war – the most general form of collective violence – opened opportunities for scattered attacks between religious groups that broadened into a civil war.

Suppressing Violence

Given the relative ease of initiating violence, it is striking that – over the long run – violence has become rarer than other forms of collective action (della Porta 1995: 216). The change began with the rise of the national state in the West, as it suppressed private armies and took control of organized violence to build its own monopoly of power. We saw evidence of this change in Chapter 2 from Tilly's research on British collective action. As Britons shifted from the brawls, the *charivari,* and the rick-burnings of the mid-eighteenth century to the petitions and demonstrations that dominated the historical record in the nineteenth, private violence declined, and contention migrated to Parliament (1995a and b). We also see it in our own century in the growing availability of legitimate forms of nonviolent protest and their acceptance by government authorities.

Every polity draws lines between collective action that is *forbidden, permitted,* or *facilitated* (McAdam et al. 2001). We can find all three in authoritarian China. The Chinese Communist authorities *facilitate* official or sponsored protests, similar to those that erupted after the accidental bombing of the Chinese embassy in Belgrade by American planes in the Balkan Wars. But the Chinese government also *forbids* mobilization across social sectors or geographic areas, because it threatens the central control on which Communist Party power is based. On the other hand, small-scale or local protests are often *tolerated,* both because they are often directed at local authorities whom the central government likes to monitor and occasionally see punished for corruption, and because protests reveal where dissent is brewing and where problems can be addressed (O'Brien ed. 2008; O'Brien and Li 2005).

Liberal democratic governments, in contrast, tolerate a much broader range of forms of contention, sponsor relatively few, and mainly forbid violent or threatening forms of contention. This does not mean that they are generally tolerant, for such governments have a range of forms of suppression other than state violence with which to suppress dissent (see Chapter 8). For example, since September 11, 2001, the United States has enormously increased its invasion of citizens' privacy (Sidel 2004). But it has not notably increased its repression of actual protest.

As long as violence remains a possibility behind protesters' actions, uncertainty reigns and collective actors gain psychological leverage vis-à-vis opponents. But where violence occurs or is even likely, this gives authorities a mandate for repression (Eisinger 1973) and turns sympathizers away. When this happens, organizers are trapped in a spiral of military confrontation with authorities that, in the modern age, is virtually impossible for them to win. This may be why practically all of the modular forms of collective action that have developed as staples of the contemporary repertoire in democratic states are nonviolent. Or more specifically, as we saw in the Tea Party movement, why disruptive protesters often adopt contained forms of action.

CONTAINED COLLECTIVE ACTION

It is easiest for people to employ a form of collective action that they know how to use, and this is what best explains the predominance of contained forms over all others. Look back again at Figure 5.1: You will see that the largest numbers of events were not disruptive nor violent but were the strikes, marches, demonstrations, and meetings that are the stock-in-trade of modern contentious politics. Why was this? Most modern forms of contention have become part of a repertoire that is generally known and understood. Coordinated through a process that resembles the "contracts by convention" outlined by Russell Hardin in his work on collective action (1982), they involve at least the tacit coordination of participants' implicit expectations (Schelling 1960: 71). And because they require relatively little commitment and involve low risk, they can attract large numbers of participants. These are the major appeals of contained forms of contention such as the strike and the demonstration.

Conventionalizing the Strike

The strike is an organized withdrawal of labor or cooperation with the intended effect of stopping production, reducing profits, or impeding the flow of public or private business. The strike offers a good example of how forms of contention that began as forbidden practices are ultimately conventionalized. The first use of the term "strike" in English seems to date from the actions of the eighteenth century sailors who "struck" the sails of their ships as a sign of their unwillingness to work (Linebaugh and Rediker 1990: 240). But the emergence of the term "strike" in many European languages about the same time suggests that the strike had multiple origins (Tilly 1978: 159).

Though mainly associated with industry, the strike form has come to include a variety of social actors, few of whom could be regarded as "proletarian."[8] As it became generally known that strikes could succeed, striking spread from skilled to unskilled workers, from the large factory to smaller firms, from the withholding of labor to the withholding of produce, from industry to agriculture, and from there to the public services. By now, the strike has become a virtual part of the institutions of collective bargaining, with its own jurisprudence, rituals, and expectations among both challengers and opponents.

Strikes developed as a means for workers to put pressure on management, but in the course of the nineteenth century, they also became a way of building

---

[8] As late as the 1872 French census, writes Ronald Aminzade, though artisans in both handicraft and industrial production "constituted only 21.9% of the labor force and 29.5% of the working class, handicraft artisans alone accounted for 72% of the strikes during the years from 1830 to 1879." See his *Class, Politics and Early Industrial Capitalism* (1981: 77–78).

class solidarity. This was reflected in the increase in mutual support across occupational and geographic lines (Aminzade 1981: 81–82) and the growing ritualization of the strike. Strikers could parade within the precincts of the factory, carrying banners and tooting horns, chanting slogans, and singing songs of solidarity to induce their workmates to join them. Solidarity sometimes was imposed, by "sending to Coventry" a worker who refused to down his tools when a strike was called.

Strikes could be combined with other forms of contention: occupations, marches, industrial sabotage, petitions, and legal actions. Assemblies prepare the workers for a strike and elect strike committees; organizers in an especially militant sector try by example to bring out workers in other sectors; pickets block the gates of the plant to keep raw materials out. Strikers who want to gain community solidarity can march from the factory through working-class neighborhoods in "turnouts," which – at their most successful – induce merchants to close their shutters and housewives to join their marches. From a spontaneous withdrawal of labor, the strike became the major means through which workers build and express solidarity, demonstrate their challenges, seek external support, and negotiate their differences with opponents from a position of enhanced, if temporary, power.

Demonstrating in Public and for the Public

Similar to the strike, the protest demonstration began as a disruptive direct action that eventually was institutionalized. Owing much to the traditional form of the religious procession, it developed when challengers moved from one target to another, either to attack opponents or to deliver demands. Public demonstrations are connected historically with democratization; it was in the democratic phase of the 1848 Revolution that the demonstration appeared in its full modern form, for the leaders of the new French Republic could not refuse the people the right to present their petitions (Favre 1990: 16). From that time on, the typical form through which all types of French movements made themselves known was the peaceful demonstration in a public place. By the late nineteenth century, the demonstration had become the major means by which unions and mass parties publicized their demands and demonstrated their strength in numbers. By the twentieth century, it had become part of the political process.

In contrast to strikes, which require some relationship to the withholding of labor or of a product to attract supporters, the use of demonstrations spread rapidly from place to place and from social actor to social actor. Demonstrations could be employed on behalf of a claim, against an opponent, to express the existence of a group or its solidarity with another group, or to celebrate a victory or mourn the passage of a leader. Demonstrations thus became the classical modular form of performance of collective action.

As demonstrations became legalized, similar to the strike, they gave rise to a jurisprudence and a culture (Hubrecht 1990; Champagne 1990). Rather than allowing the police to manhandle demonstrators, organizers began to employ their own parade marshals (Cardon and Huertin: 199), developed a repeated sequence of routes, slogans, and signs, and had a regular marching order. Different ideological families favored one route or another, so that the political coloration of the group could often be determined from its itinerary. Even the roles of nonparticipants – the press, the forces of order, bystanders, and opponents – eventually became part of the demonstrative performance (Favre: 18–32).

Repressive states almost always see demonstrations as potential riots, which leads to the repression of peaceful protesters and sometimes – as in the events of January 1905 in Russia – to revolution. Constitutional states have come to accept demonstrations as a normal, and even an advantageous, practice, as indicated by the fact that demonstrators receive police protection and even guidance. In Washington, D.C., in Rome, and in Paris, organizers are offered advice by the police on how best to run a demonstration (McCarthy and McPhail 1998; della Porta, Fillieule, and Rieter 1998). From an unruly movement of protesters from one place to another, the protest demonstration has become the major nonelectoral expression of civil politics.

REPERTOIRE STABILITY AND CHANGE

Over time, many changes have been made in the repertoire of contention, some resulting from changes in the state and capitalism, and others from the internal evolution of particular performances. Some repertoires give way to new ones more easily than others. We can distinguish among four main types of repertoire:

- *No repertoires,* which is the use of forms of contention that fail, make no impression on popular memory, or are no longer relevant to people's claims. The "armed demonstration" in mid-nineteenth century France was such a case (see Chapter 2).
- *Weak repertoires,* which have somewhat more purchase, develop amid special circumstances such as war, repression, or immigration, and give way to new performances when those circumstances change. When the former Soviet Union emerged from state socialism, the tradition of "samizdat" (self-published clandestine writing) lost its relevance (Fish 1995; Mendelson and Gerber 2005).
- *Ritual political performances* sometimes evolve when performances lose their original meaning but are preserved for symbolic reasons (Kertzer 1998; Muir 1997). May Day began as a day of protest but evolved into a ritualized festival of labor.[9]

[9] For example, May Day began in July 1889, when a congress of French trade unionists proposed that "a great international demonstration should be convoked, on the same day all over the world, to put governments on notice to reduce the workday to eight hours" (Tartakowsky 2005: 14).

• *Strong repertoires* are performances that retain their original meaning in popular memory and continue to have purchase in popular politics.

The American "Strong" Repertoire

In the United States today, the repertoire was strongly marked by the period Americans remember as "the sixties." Three major developments marked a shift in performances that culminated in the "strong" repertoire of today:

First was the practice of "marching on Washington" in major set-piece demonstrations culminating in rallies before the Lincoln Memorial. The sixties' marches on Washington evolved out of the veterans' marches of the 1930s and from the civil rights march that A. Philip Randolph threatened to organize in 1941, just as the United States was mobilizing for its part in World War II (Kryder 2000). There are elements of ritual in Americans' marches on Washington, but there were changes too. For example, antiwar protesters marched across the Potomac to the Pentagon, which they surrounded in a mock levitation. Eventually organizers learned to provide mobile TV monitors for demonstrators who were too numerous or too far away to see the speakers (McCarthy and McPhail 1998). The march on Washington became a culturally embedded part of a strong repertoire.

The second new practice was the dedication of a period of time – usually the summer – to a particular campaign. Summers have always brought out more protesters than other periods of the year, if only because of the more clement climate and the fact that students are off from school. Mississippi's "Freedom Summer" was the most notable example of the choice of a finite period of time in which to concentrate the energies of militants on a particular goal – in that event, to register African Americans to vote (McAdam 1988). Other campaigns such as Vietnam Summer and Labor Summer soon followed.

The third development was the disruptive practice of sit-ins, blockages, and building occupations. First at lunch counters, then at bus stations, and finally wherever public segregation was practiced, the sit-in became the most important new performance in the American strong repertoire. Though the sit-in has a family resemblance to the factory occupations of the 1930s (Piven and Cloward 1977), it gained its power from the presence of a new actor in public life: television. If the public saw spitting thugs brutalizing well-dressed young black men sitting quietly at lunch counters, it would be hard to ignore the contradiction between the American claim of freedom and the reality of segregation. "The whole world is watching," wrote Todd Gitlin (1980).

Despite the resilience of strong repertoires, practices of contentious politics often change in imperceptible ways that are visible only at some distance. We can chart the itineraries of repertoire change within four major categories: *the institutionalization of disruptive forms* of contention; *innovation at the margins* of inherited forms; *tactical interaction with police* and other actors; and *paradigmatic change*.

The Institutionalization of Contention

We saw earlier how the strike and the demonstration gradually became part of the existing repertoire. The pattern of institutionalization is almost everywhere the same: As the excitement of the disruptive phase of a movement dies and the police become more skilled at controlling it, movements institutionalize their tactics and attempt to gain concrete benefits for their supporters through negotiation and compromise – a route that often succeeds at the cost of transforming the movement into a party or interest group (Piven and Cloward 1977).

At times, forms of disruption that invite repression are discarded as participants learn to avoid them. Such was the case for the "armed demonstrations" used by the French Montagnards during the 1851 insurrection against Louis Napoleon's coup d'état.[10] At other times, forms of confrontation are themselves institutionalized as authorities learn to tolerate them or facilitate their use. And at times, to win concessions that supporters demand or authorities proffer, leaders move from confrontation to cooperation. This is particularly true when a political ally comes to power – as occurred in the democratization of South Africa in the mid-1990s (Klandermans, Roefs, and Olivier 1998).

Institutionalization frequently results in what sociologists have called "goal displacement" – the suppression of a movement's original radical goals for more moderate ones. This was how European social democratic parties eventually gave up their "maximum program" for what were originally seen as short-term "minimal goals." Such changes are often adopted for tactical reasons – for example, the threat of police repression, or the desire to attract the support of moderates. But once a movement's chosen form of action crystallizes into convention, it becomes a known and expected part of the repertoire. As Franz Kafka metaphorically wrote in one of his most prescient fables:

> Leopards break into the temple and drink to the dregs what is in the sacrificial pitchers; this is repeated over and over again; finally it can be calculated in advance, and it becomes a part of the ceremony.[11]

Innovation at the Margins

Even within inherited forms of collective action, innovation often occurs incrementally. For instance, using the general form of the demonstration, demonstrators can march in costume, brandish pitchforks, wave monkey wrenches to display their militancy (Lumley 1990: 224), or carry props that symbolize their goals. Feminists wear witches' costumes to ridicule feminism's stereotyping by male opponents (Costain 1992: 49). Peace marchers don skeleton outfits to

---

[10] "In taking arms against the government," writes historian Ted Margadant, "they appeared to engage in an intrinsically violent form of collective action.... But as an instrument of military force," he continues, "it was hopelessly outclassed by the French army." See Margadant's *French Peasants in Revolt* (1979: 267).

[11] From Franz Kafka, *Parables and Paradoxes* (1937: 92–93).

symbolize their fear of nuclear holocaust. And protesters against sexual crimes against children march in white clothing – as they did in Belgium in 1996 – to symbolize the purity of the victims (Hooghe and Deneckere 2003).

In the short run, innovation at the margins may simply enliven a familiar form of collective action by adding elements of play and carnival to its basic form. But over the long run, innovations in a given performance can transmute into wholly new forms. For example, the hunger strike in India began as poor Indians sat outside the doors of rich men who refused to pay them what they were owed (Siméant 2009: 13). And when four African American students sat in at a lunch counter in Greensboro, North Carolina, the lunch counter sit-in became well known to potential demonstrators and through the public at large. Ultimately, it became a modular form of contention (Andrews and Biggs 2006).

Tactical Interaction

Innovation in collective action forms often results from the interaction between protesters and their opponents. This can be seen in the history of industrial relations. When employers used the tactic of locking their workers out of a factory to defeat a strike, workers invented the sit-down strike and added the factory occupation to their repertoire (Spriano 1975). By the time the French Popular Front was elected in 1936, the factory occupation had become routine, with its characteristic rituals, roles, and activities (Tartakowsky 1996: 56–57). Lockouts eventually were made illegal in most countries to protect the legality of the strike and to defend factories from potentially damaging occupations.

The same interactive process occurred between the American Civil Rights movement and the Southern police who tried to repress it. Doug McAdam determined from a detailed analysis of the movement's actions that each time its leaders approached a crisis in participation or opposition, the threshold of collective action was raised to a new level – using its tools selectively and creatively to outguess opponents and increase participation (1983). For example, the use of public marches expanded when it appeared that police chiefs like "Bull" Connor were responding to them by the violent arrest of hundreds of demonstrators before the eyes of the nation. In response, police chiefs more subtle than Connor began to use more restrained tactics.

Paradigmatic Change

Given the long, slow, historical evolution of the repertoire of contention, it may seem surprising to use the term "paradigmatic" change for the forms that people use to express their claims. And indeed, given the need to root collective action in cultural expectations, paradigmatic change is rare and unusual (Tilly 2008). That it does sometimes occur, however, can be gathered from examples that have been used in this chapter and in preceding chapters. The shift from rigid to modular forms of contention in the eighteenth century; the invention of the strike and the demonstration in the nineteenth; the development of nonviolent forms of resistance in the twentieth; and the invention and rapid diffusion of suicide bombing in this century – these could not be explained if no breakthroughs were made in the way people mount claims and how authorities respond to them.

Part of the reason for what seem like sudden breakthroughs is undoubtedly that protest routines are "sticky": Cultural familiarity and the habits of organizers may lead people to continue to employ familiar forms rather than more appropriate or effective ones long after they lose their force. As a result, when a new form is "discovered," its appropriateness becomes immediately obvious. For example, part of the reason for the rapid diffusion of the democratization movements in East Central Europe in 1989 was the discovery that many citizens felt the same way as the early protesters, and that ordinary means of public expression would be tolerated and could succeed (Kuran 1991; Lohmann 1994).

The same was the case for the diffusion of the "electoral model" of opposition to authoritarian regimes in Southeastern Europe and Eurasia. The strategy of using outrage at stolen elections began in Slovakia and Serbia in the late 1990s (Bunce and Wolchik 2006). Once it was shown that mobilizing against corrupt authoritarian regimes could succeed, election revolutions spread across the region, and beyond – to the Caucasus and into Central Asia. There, of course, their success was much weaker, which takes us to the need to examine the other three powers in movement – networks and organizations, framing and identity construction, and political opportunities – to which we turn in the next three chapters.

CONCLUSIONS

To many scholars writing in the 1990s, the industrial West seemed to be becoming a "social movement society" (Meyer and Tarrow, eds. 1998). This concept was developed to describe two related, but not identical phenomena: first, that more and more people seemed to be using what had previously been seen as unconventional forms of political action; and second, that as these forms continued to be used, they were becoming conventionalized.

For example, Sarah Soule and Jennifer Earl's (2005) analysis of protest events in the United States suggests that protest events increased in size between the 1960s and the 1980s.[12] The United States was not alone: when Dieter Rucht and his colleagues examined contention from major newspapers for the years 1950–1988 for West Germany and for both halves of Germany

---

[12] From the World Values Study, we know that the U.S. propensity to protest has increased. The World Values Survey data can be found at http://www.worldvaluessurvey.org/. Recent data from the General Social Survey suggest a flattening and possible reversal between 1996 and 2002. In the latter year, just over 6 percent reported having participated in a rally or protest in the previous 5 years, compared to just over 9 percent in the former year. However, the differences are too small to reach statistical significance.

over the following decade, they found a dramatic increase in the numbers of protests in the 1960s, and smaller, but still substantial, increases over the next three decades (Rucht 1999). Most of this increase in protest occurred in the more contained forms of participation – such as petitions and peaceful demonstrations – while the violence that erupted in the 1960s and the 1970s largely subsided (Caren et al. ND: ms. p. 5). (An exception was the violence against immigrants and minorities in Europe, which grew rapidly in the 1990s.)

The increase in terrorism, guerilla warfare, and civil strife elsewhere in the world in the last decade presents another form of "social movement society." Was it the result of the end of the constraining influence of the Cold War? A result of failing states and newly mobilized populations? Or was the world bifurcating into two different repertoires of contention: peaceful, contained, and increasingly institutionalized contention in the West, and violent, uncontrolled, and destabilizing contention in the rest of the world? Only a long-term comparative analysis of the performances and repertoires of contention across the planet will answer this question.

In the meantime, we have seen how social movements combine challenge, solidarity, and uncertainty in their actions. They maintain support and grow, in part because they have available a known, well-understood script of modular forms to build upon. And they innovate around that basic script, much as jazz musicians improvise on a basic tune. But the presence of a large number of protest events does not, in itself, constitute a social movement. Actors first must find ways of coordinating contention and organizing themselves to sustain mobilization – tasks that depend on their capacity to build on existing social networks and to construct more formal organizations to maintain solidarity and aggregate resources. These are the "internal" powers through which social movements are constructed and maintained; we turn to them in the next chapter.

6

Networks and Organizations

Tan Guocheng is hardly a self-styled labor leader. Age 23 and introverted, he grew up among rice paddies and orange groves far from China's big factory towns. But last month, an hour into his shift at a Honda factory in the southern city of Foshan, Mr. Tan pressed an emergency button that shut down his production line. "Let's go out on strike!" he shouted. Within minutes, hundreds of workers were abandoning their posts (*New York Times,* June 14, 2010, p. B1).

China is hardly a place where we would expect to find widespread labor insurgency. And, indeed, Tan was fired soon after leading the strike in Honda's transmission plant and went back to his native Hunan. But the action at the Foshan Honda factory triggered strikes all over the Eastern Chinese industrial zone, especially in Japanese-owned firms, which had come to China to take advantage of its cheap and, until recently, docile labor force. Not only that: Unlike most Chinese industrial actions before 2010, which had focused on poor working conditions and wages, this one made a new demand – the right to form a labor union independent of the party-controlled All-China Federation of Trade Unions. Similar to the Solidarity union in Poland, which we will turn to later, Chinese workers were beginning to understand that without representation, their material demands would go unanswered.

Tan Guocheng was not alone; realizing that his monthly salary of \$175 was inadequate to allow him to find an apartment and marry, he tried to recruit fellow workers in secret talks on the factory floor during breaks. "A week before the strike," the *Times* continues,

15 or so workers from Mr. Tan's workshop had a meeting outside the factory one night to discuss the plan. . . . A 20-year-old worker named Xiao Lang, also from Hunan, agreed to help lead the strike". . . . By agreement, when Mr. Tan hit that emergency stop button at 7:50 a.m., Mr. Xiao was doing the same thing on a separate, nearby production line. Within minutes, workers were marching through the factory rallying others to join the strike (p. B10).

Honda, with orders to fill and in the midst of a shortage of skilled labor to run its technologically advanced transmission plant, quickly gave in to the workers' demands and ultimately agreed to a large pay raise.

WHAT WAS HAPPENING HERE?

No one should expect that the Communist Party–controlled industrial labor system in China will transform into a free industrial relations system in short order, or that striking workers elsewhere would get the same deal as the Honda workers in Fonshan. (Indeed, in the city of Zhongshan, Honda workers who tried to copy the Fonshan example went back to work after receiving minimal concessions, and many were replaced.) But the story of the success in Fonshan is interesting for what it tells us about networks, organizations, culture, and opportunities:

- First, Tan Guocheng trusted another Hunanese immigrant to launch the strike simultaneously in another workshop. This pattern of native-place solidarity, familiar from Chinese labor history (Perry 1993), builds on cultural affinities, as well as on workplace solidarity.
- Second, the two Hunanese workers acted only after forming a network of 50 workers – many of them also from Hunan – who had agreed to support the plan (*New York Times*, p. B10).
- Third, as the workers quickly realized, the solidarity of a small and provisional network of activists would not be sufficient to guarantee their gains; they called for an independent union to bargain on their behalf in the future.
- Finally, it was not through fear or generosity that Honda management gave in to the strikers; the outcome was a result of the opportunity structure provided by (1) a shortage of skilled workers, (2) the new industrial relations laws that the Chinese government had passed in 2008 and was attempting to impose on reluctant factory managers, and (3) the fact that the local authorities were often their shareholders (*New York Times*, June 21, 2010).

In the last chapter, I showed the variety of ways in which social movements engage in collective action. I argued that they do not invent forms of contention out of whole cloth but instead innovate within and around culturally embedded repertoires. In this chapter and the next two, I will turn to the three other powers in movement:

- How challengers build on and appropriate social networks and organizations
- How they combine emotions and identities with cultural repertoires and make meanings around them
- And how they attempt to seize and transform political opportunities.

None of these powers in movement alone ensures the emergence or the outcomes of social movements. But taken together, they produce the movement campaigns, the cycles of contention, and the outcomes that we will turn to in

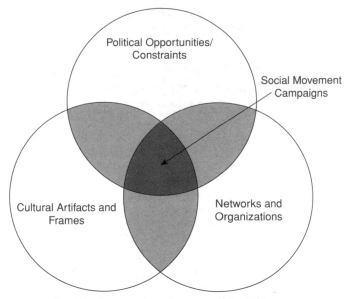

FIGURE 6.1. The Intersecting Elements of Social Movements

Part III. Though I will deal with them here in separate chapters, the three resources overlap considerably (McAdam, McCarthy, and Zald 1996). Figure 6.1 maps the intersections of these three powers to lay out the agenda for the rest of this section and to emphasize their interactive nature.

The Bases of Movements

Organizing contention draws upon cultural artifacts, historical memories, and political traditions. But note the ambivalence in the very term "organization" (Clemens and Minkoff 2004: 156). If we looked only at formal modes of organization, we would miss seeing how episodes such as the strike at the Honda factory in Foshan arose and, more generally, how organizational forms grow out of the initial interaction between protesters and opponents, as the following episode suggests.

SOLIDARITY AT THE LENIN SHIPYARD

On June 30, 1980, Polish Communist authorities announced an increase in meat prices, triggering a vast wave of contention that would ultimately undermine the country's Communist system and pave the way for the collapse of the socialist bloc. As Jan Kubik tells the story:

> The next day workers in several factories . . . went on strike. During July the strike wave engulfed several regions. On August 14, 1980, several dozen workers began an occupational strike in the Gdańsk Lenin Shipyard. As the strike in

the Shipyard grew and the workers from other plants joined in, the authorities agreed to grant wage increases and met some other demands, but only for the Lenin employees (Kubik 2009: 3073).

The chance always existed that the Gdansk workers would accept the wage increases and go back to work, but under pressure from their base, their representatives ultimately refused, and the strike spread. As Kubik continues,

> During the night of August 16 the Inter-factory Strike Committee (*MKS*) was formed and immediately formulated a list of twenty-one demands, including a demand to create a trade union independent from the Communist Party. By the end of the month over 700 thousand people were on strike in about 700 enterprises in all 49 regions of Poland (ibid.).

The strike soon broadened beyond the confines of an industrial dispute, as intellectuals and artists, peasants and students, and even state workers lent their support, and Catholic clerics offered certification for the strikers by identifying the workers' claims with the country's deep religious beliefs (Kubik 1994), By September, more than thirty Interfactory Founding Committees had emerged along the lines of the original one, forming an independent trade union – "Solidarity" – with a National Coordinating Committee (KKP) as its governing body. By now, the new union had about three million members.

Of course, an independent trade union and a state socialist regime could not coexist for long. With each move forward by the union, the state intervened with delays, challenges, and occasional repression (Kubik: 3074). On December 13, 1981, martial law was declared, Solidarity's leaders were rounded up, and the regime survived for eight more years. But although the struggle for a free trade union movement changed its form, it was far from over. As Kubik writes, "A multi-faceted 'underground society' emerged, whose activities ranged from clandestine publishing and private theater performances to spectacular rallies and marches often dispersed by the special riot police units" (ibid. p. 3075). Slowly, but with increasing determination, Solidarity emerged from its secret networks and formed a National Council in 1987. After a new wave of strikes, a series of roundtable discussions was held in January 1989, and national elections were mounted in June – elections that Solidarity candidates won with overwhelming support. What had begun as an isolated strike of shipyard workers on the Baltic coast produced the first noncommunist government in a state socialist regime.

This story has been told and retold in many versions, but for students of contentious politics, it offers three main lessons:

- *First,* it shows how organizations emerge out of episodes of contention through interaction with authorities, allies, and third parties.
- *Second,* it shows that these organizations begin as local networks, spread through the diffusion of contention, and ultimately either disappear or scale upward to regional and national levels.

- *Third,* it shows that the key to organizational survival is not the formal properties of organizations, but the interpersonal networks within them, which can survive even when the formal organization has disappeared.

Modes of Organizing

Ever since social movements became a force for change in the modern world, observers and activists have puzzled over the effects of organization on movements' capacity for contention. Some theorists argued that without leadership exercised through organizations, rebellion remains "primitive" and soon disintegrates (Hobsbawm 1959). Support for Hobsbawm's position comes from William Gamson's *The Strategy of Social Protest* (1990), which was based on research on 53 American challenging groups and showed that the groups that were most successful in achieving policy outcomes developed centralized and hierarchical forms of organization.

Yet others are persuaded that, far from inspiring people to action, organizational leaders can deprive them of their major power – the power to disrupt (Piven and Cloward 1977). This is what Frances Fox Piven and Richard Cloward found in their analysis of the welfare rights movement that emerged in the United States in the 1960s. Theoretical support for Piven and Cloward's position came from Robert Michels' famous "Iron Law of Oligarchy," which held that, over time, organizations displace their original goals, become wedded to routine, and ultimately accept the rules of the game of the existing system (Michels 1962; Clemens and Minkoff 2004, Rucht 1999).

As must be obvious, some leaders, working through certain kinds of organizations, in particular situations, *do* transform contention into successful movements and sustain conflict with opponents, but others do not. Equally obvious, some movements emerge without formal leadership, often producing leaders out of the experience of struggle – or from cognate groups from which they borrow resources or organizational forms. Organizations provide movements with strategic and tactical leadership, and with a focal point for the interaction of activists – a mechanism for framing how events and relationships are interpreted (see Chapter 7) and a source for recruiting new members and identifying future leaders.

How are we to explain this diversity of organizational roles? The first task is to distinguish among three different meanings of movement organization:

A first meaning is *the organization of collective action at the point of contact with opponents*. They can be controlled by formal organizations, by coalitions of organizations, or by no one in particular. We saw this in the organization of the strike and factory occupation of the Lenin shipyard in Gdansk. A second, more common meaning of the term is the *advocacy organization* – or formal associations of persons "that make public interest claims either promoting or resisting social change that if implemented would conflict with social, cultural political or economic interests or values of other constituencies or groups" (Andrews and Edwards 2004: 483). We saw this in the formation of the national Solidarity union in Poland. The third meaning of organization refers to the *connective structures or interpersonal networks* that link leaders and followers, centers and peripheries, and different parts of a movement sector with one another, permitting coordination and aggregation, and allowing movements to persist even when formal organization is lacking. We saw these in the underground structure of Solidarity activists during the period when the union was declared illegal under martial law.

Interpersonal networks are the most basic structure: They socialize and build movement identities; they offer participation opportunities to individuals sensitive to a particular issue; and they shape individual preferences before individuals join a movement (Passy 2001). They can also exercise a social control function for individuals with low levels of commitment. Most important, they are the sites for the normative pressures and solidary incentives out of which movements emerge and are sustained.

Movements are not based on networks alone; without some degree of formal organization, movements frequently fade away or dissipate their energies. The problem for movement organizers is to create organizational models that are sufficiently robust to structure contention but are flexible enough to reach out to the informal networks and communities of protest (Diani 2009) that connect people to one another. The following cases from the nineteenth century history of European contention illustrate the importance of all three factors in the history of social movements.

THE SOCIAL DEMOCRATIC MODEL

In the decades that followed the 1848 revolutions, and as the Industrial Revolution took hold in continental Europe, a new social actor appeared – the industrial proletariat – forming out of capillary structures in the factory and linked to a new set of labor organizations. Mainly middle class organizers and intellectuals took charge of the socialist and labor parties that formed at the summit with links to trade unions, cooperatives, mutual insurance schemes, and even recreation centers. In the most well developed case, the Social Democratic Party of Germany (SPD), these sprawling structures gave the imposing impression of a "state within a state" (Roth 1963).[1]

But between the centralized organizations of European Social Democracy and the informal networks of workers at the base, no natural or social set of connective structures was apparent. In some countries, such as France,

---

[1] Such was the prestige of the SPD that its organizational model was imitated to different degrees in Central, Northern, and Eastern Europe, and even, for a time, in the United States. On the formation of the Swedish Socialist Worker's Party (SAP), see Donald Blake, "Swedish Trade Unions and the Social Democratic Party: The Formative Years" (1960). On the Austrian Party and its relation to the German model, see Vincent Knapp, *Austrian Social Democracy, 1889–1914* 1980: Chapter I). On the influence of German Marxism on the development of Russian Social Democracy, see John Plamenatz, *German Marxism and Russian Communism* (1954: 317–329).

the distance between syndicalist-oriented workers and reformist parliamentary socialists was so great that competing organizations were formed. In Britain, the unions were stronger, and the Labour Party took hold more slowly. In America, socialism found its natural home mainly among immigrants from Europe, and apart from a brief flowering around the turn of the century, was soon submerged by repression and nativism.

It was the German Social Democrats who, with characteristic determination, undertook to formalize relations between summit and base into a rigid hierarchy and to make them permanent. Discipline and dues paying were expected of those who joined, and collective actions were periodically organized to advance the movement's goals. From a scattered network of insurgent groups and secret societies, the workers' movement grew into a vast, formal, and hierarchical organization. The result was the creation of a single organizational structure that frightened the Imperial regime to the point of its temporarily banning the party for a time, but, ultimately, to vitiate the movement of its creativity and leave it incapable of facing the threat from Hitler's brownshirts in the 1930s.

This was the model of organization – the central European working-class party – that Michels had in mind when he formulated his "Iron Law of Oligarchy." In such an organization, he argued, organizers became more wedded to the survival of the organization than to revolutionary action by the proletariat, with the risks it imposed. If the movement's militancy melted away once representation for the lower classes was achieved, no one should have been surprised. One group of competitors was anything but surprised; they had chosen a very different organizational model.

The Anarchist Counter-Model

Even as German Social Democrats were building a "state within a state," in other parts of Europe and in America, activists were developing competing organizational models. The most serious challenge came from the anarchists – whose political theory and practice were opposed to Social Democracy in every respect. Where the Social Democrats were led by politicians and intellectuals who aimed to take over the bourgeois state through elections, the anarchists distrusted politics and sought to create producers' cooperatives from below. Where Social Democrats organized over the long haul and eventually turned to parliamentary means, anarchists hoped for an explosive moment that could be advanced through the mechanism of the general strike.

The anarchists resisted the tendency to become a party. Their instinctive organizational model was provided by Pierre-Joseph Proudhon, who had theorized that a network of workers' associations, democratically organized and loosely linked in a voluntary federation, could eventually replace both the state and capitalism.[2] But lacking an organizational template similar to that of their

---

[2] Basic materials on this poorly understood movement will be found in Daniel Guérin, *Anarchism: From Theory to Practice* (1970).

opponents, they surged into different forms in different parts of Europe in close approximation to different local economic and political conditions.

It was in Eastern and Southern Europe that economic conditions were most backward and political organization least developed, and it was here that anarchism became a mass movement. The Russian *narodniki* (populists) had first hurled themselves at the Czarist power structure, imagining that their personal courage and bravery would unleash the rebellious potential they thought lay hidden in the peasants. The latter responded with indifference, if not hostility, and long prison terms and doleful memoirs were the lot of many of these activists.

In Italy, the story ended just as badly. Hounded by the police and the authorities, the Italian anarchists encapsulated themselves into tight cells in which they hatched utopian schemes and plotted the overthrow of the state. As Daniel Guérin writes,

> Free rein was given to utopian doctrines, combining premature anticipations and nostalgic evocations of a golden age. . . . The anarchists turned in on themselves, organized themselves for direct action in small clandestine groups which were easily infiltrated by police informers (Guérin 1970: 74).

Whereas the hierarchical model of Social Democracy turned movements into parties, the anarchists' obsession with action and their allergy to organization transformed them into a sect and, ultimately, to the world's first terrorist network.[3]

Competitive Legitimation and Diffusion

These two models of organization – hierarchical national organizations and decentralized cells of militants – grew out of particular political-historical configurations, with their centers, respectively, in the rapidly industrializing German Empire and in the less-developed Southern and Eastern peripheries of Europe. But the durability of the former and the militancy of the latter led to imitation throughout Europe and the Americas. For regardless of their rooting in particular settings, organizational forms tend to become legitimized as cultural artifacts. As Debra Minkoff writes,

> Those organizations that prove themselves able to take advantage of environmental opportunities and overcome competition for scarce resources serve as models for future action by other groups. As models become established, they secure the legitimacy of this type of collective response (Minkoff 1995; also see Hannan and Freeman 1989).

But the "legitimacy" of organizational forms does not depend on their inherent appeals alone. For one thing, they intersect with different societal traditions of organization; for another, their actions trigger different combinations of

---

[3] The parallels to today's transnational Islamist terrorist network are tempting, but the anarchists were far less connected transnationally and appear to have been more susceptible to police infiltration.

governmental facilitation or repression, which, in turn, reshape their forms; and for a third, their competition leads to greater success for some forms of organization than for others (Clemens and Minkoff 2004: 164; Minkoff 1994). Movement organizations develop in interaction with cultural artifacts, power holders, and other movements. The success of these two models led to recurring polarities of organization in social movements around the world.

Recurring Polarities

Although Social Democracy eventually lost its mass base in the working class, the new form that it invented – the class-mass party – endured through two world wars and a depression, and gave way to a new type – the professional-ized cadre party – only after the 1960s (Muir 1997). And although classical anarchism all but disappeared with the Bolshevik revolution, the urge to foster participatory decentralization was reborn in the participatory movements of the 1960s in both Europe and the United States, in the peace movements of the 1980s, and in the global justice movement after the Seattle anti-World Trade Organization (WTO) campaign of 1999. Both models grew out of different cul-tural and ecological soils but, once invented, similar to the forms of collective action examined in Chapter 5, they became modular.

As in the past, these organizational polarities were competitive. By the early 1960s, most of the American Civil Rights movement had become institutional-ized (Piven and Cloward 1977: Chapter 4). From the streets of Selma, the battle for civil rights gravitated to the lobbies of Congress and to community organi-zations that were subsidized by government and foundations. The movement was soon constrained by the rules of the game of ordinary politics (Piven and Cloward: Chapter 5). Not even the riots following the murder of Martin Luther King turned mainstream civil rights organizations away from their institutional frameworks, although it did shift their programs onto a more progressive path.

The same was true of the new women's movement, which – despite its ene-mies' image of wild-eyed "bra burners" – was highly institutionalized from the start. Groups such as the National Organization of Women (NOW) and the National Abortion Rights Action League (NARAL) quickly became profession-alized, maintaining a high level of organizational activity (Minkoff 1995: 40) and directing their activities mainly toward Congress and the Administration (Costain 1992). The same shift could be seen in the environmental organiza-tions that grew out of the 1960s in Europe (Minkoff 1995; Dalton 1994). In both Minkoff's and Dalton's studies, only a very small proportion of the groups engaged primarily in protest. "As such organizations begin to dominate the movement sector," write Clemens and Minkoff, "it becomes increasingly diffi-cult for younger, smaller, and more decentralized organizations . . . to establish a national presence" (Clemens and Minkoff 2004: 264).

The positive result of such institutionalization was that the strength and numbers of the advocacy sector grew rapidly from the 1960s onward. Focusing on environmental organizations in America, Robert Brulle and his associates

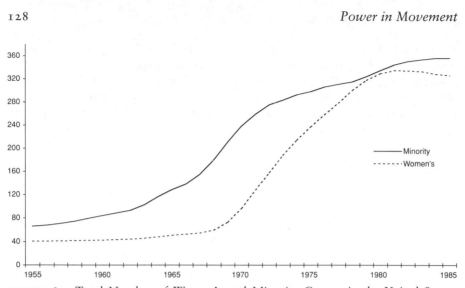

FIGURE 6.2. Total Number of Women's and Minority Groups in the United States, 1955–1985 (3-year moving average). *Source:* Courtesy of Debra Minkoff, from her *Organizing for Equality: The Evolution of Women's and Racial-ethnic Organizations in America, 1955–1985.* Rutgers University Press, 1995.

found a near tripling in their numbers between 1960 and 1970 and another doubling between then and 1990 (Brulle et al. 2007). Using data on women's and minority groups from the Encyclopedia of Associations, Minkoff found a sixfold expansion of these organizations from a total of 98 in 1955, to 688 thirty years later (1995: 61). The largest growth was seen in advocacy and advocacy/service-oriented groups, with smaller growth rates for groups specializing in cultural and service provision alone, and no growth at all for groups oriented toward protest (p. 62; Fig. 3.2). Figure 6.2, drawing on Minkoff's work, traces three-year moving averages for the growth in the total number of women's and minority group organizations in the United States over this period.[4]

THE NEW GRASSROOTS ALTERNATIVES

But at the same time as advocacy and service organizations were gaining a near-monopoly at the national level, a contrary tendency was at work. It grew out of dissatisfaction with the steady institutionalization of these mainstream organizations among a generation of activists who had experienced the failures of these groups and disliked the compromises they had made. Just as anarchism measured its progress in competition with European Social Democracy, radical American activists split off into or formed decentralized organizations to carry the fight to the heart of organized capitalism, white supremacy, and male

---

[4] Group data of Brulle et al. are based on a wider range of sources and will be found in their 2007 article, p. 265.

hegemony. In the civil rights field, Black Power and black nationalist groups challenged mainstream civil rights organizations. In the women's rights sector, splits took place over race and sexual preference, and some groups took on the same sect-like characteristics seen earlier in European anarchism. As for the New Left, elements of the Students for a Democratic Society (SDS) radicalized before giving way to the Weather Underground, a clandestine organization organized for armed struggle.

Similarly, in Western Europe, parts of the New Left that were critical of the "long march through the institutions" drew sharp lines between their continued militancy and the growing moderation of their opponents. Some – similar to their anarchist predecessors – ended up in clandestine cells from which they launched armed struggle (della Porta 1990; 1995: Chapter 8); others competed for worker support with the party-linked trade unions. Institutionalization and radicalization were contrary but symbiotic trends that fed off each other and led in opposite political directions, as we will see in Part III.

The same competitive polarization can be seen in the movement against neo-liberal globalization today. While sedate nongovernmental advocacy organizations (NGOs) navigate the corridors of national and international institutions on behalf of environmental, developmental, and climate change goals, radical direct action groups have taken to the streets around international summits, sometimes engaging in armed conflict with police and authorities. This division was already evident at the anti-WTO countersummit in Seattle in 1999, where two coalitions of activists opposed this expression of global neo-liberalism (Levi and Murphy 2006). It was also evident at the Copenhagen UN Climate Change Conference in 2009. There, thousands of activists represented two competing networks: on the one hand, social movement groups that challenged delegates to put the welfare of the planet ahead of their national interests and, on the other, representatives of nongovernmental organizations anxious to work with the official delegations to hammer out agreements to control the climate. (Hadden 2010; Reitan 2010). Each move toward institutionalized movement organizations triggered contrary moves in the direction of grassroots models of organization.

Amending the Iron Law: Organizational Hybrids

Social Democracy and anarchism were not the only forms of social movement organization that developed in the nineteenth century. Nor does the polarity between bureaucratic organizations and grassroots radical groups exhaust the varieties of movement organization today. In both periods, movement entrepreneurs built hybrid forms of organization shaped by their evolving goals, their organizational cultures, and the patterns of political opportunity and constraint they faced in their environments (Campbell 2005; Clemens and Minkoff 2004; Bennett et al. 2008). In fact, the variety of organizational forms today is, if anything, even broader than in the past, because they include a range of local, regional and national, centralized and decentralized, and membership and nonmembership organizations, and they draw on the new digital forms of media.

John McCarthy has identified a wide variety of action types of social movement organizations (2005: p. 196). They range from the classical federated structure we met in European Social Democracy all the way to free-standing local groups, through a variety of regional and networked organizations. In addition, the advent of online recruitment and mobilization has created a gamut of new kinds of organizations and quasi-organizations that Michels could never have imagined. The broad variety of types of movement organizations identified by McCarthy suggests that we may need to soften Michels' "iron law."[5] For example, focusing on peace organizations in the United States, Bob Edwards and Michael Foley divided the universe of social movement organizations into four types that differ in size and in taxable status, as well as in organizational form, membership, tactics, and issue focus (Edwards and Foley 2003).[6]

This is no new development: Nineteenth century American civic organizations had already developed organizational hybrids. Corresponding to the structure of American federalism, many national umbrella organizations were linked to networks of local affiliates through traveling agents (Skocpol et al. 2000). In fact, what Tocqueville saw as self-generated grassroots associations were often started by national agents who would travel around the country creating local affiliates. This allowed local trust networks to be built into national organizations and provided the "free spaces" in which ordinary citizens could take initiatives that more centralized organizations could not have mounted on their own (Evans and Boyte 1992). It also freed umbrella organizations from financial responsibility for their local affiliates, through a pattern that has grown into the "franchising" of not-for-profit organizations in our generation (McCarthy 2004: 221).

In the 1960s and 1970s, in both Western Europe and the United States, such loosely coordinated hybrid organizations were theorized by both scholars and activists (Rosenthal and Schwartz 1989; Evans and Boyte 1992; Zald and Ash 1966). Luther Gerlach and Virginia Hine called this wave of movement organizations "decentralized, reticulated and segmented," "composed of a great variety of localized groups or cells which are essentially independent, but which can combine to form larger configurations or divide to form smaller units" (1970: 41). For example, Elizabeth Armstrong shows how gay-lesbian

---

[5] The durability of Michels' imagery – if not agreement with his theory – can be illustrated by the titles of two of the essays on which this chapter draws: Elisabeth Clemens' and Debra Minkoff's "Beyond the Iron Law" (2004) and Dieter Rucht's "Linking Organization and Mobilization: Michels' Iron Law of Oligarchy Reconsidered" (1999). A Google search for "Iron law of oligarchy" produced an astonishing 1,020,000 hits!

[6] Edwards' and Foley's four types include numerous, but generally quite small groups that operate without tax-exempt status; small non-national groups of the same type; large, non-national tax-exempt groups; and national organizations (2003: 87). Their point is that most research has been based on the highly more accessible large national organizations, and this produces a skewed picture of social movement organizations.

activists in San Francisco shaped new organizational forms that coupled identity building with concrete activities such as biking or music (Armstrong 2005). As Evans and Boyte argue, at the heart of successful democratic movements are "environments in which people are able to learn a new self-respect, a deeper and more assertive group identity, public skills, and values of cooperation and civic virtue" (pp. 17–18).

American community organizers extended the model of decentralized, segmented, and reticulated organizations into the city. First theorized by activists such as Saul Alinsky (1971) and Harry Boyte (1980), community action organizations took a variety of forms, including individual membership organizations (like the recently disbanded organization ACORN), coalitions, and church-based organizations (McCarthy and Castelli 1994). The most successful are affiliated with federations of religious congregations. Linked nationally by well-organized "networks," faith-based community organizations of both left and right are significantly more effective than other types of urban movements in gaining organizational power, imparting skills and a sense of efficacy to members, and building cross-race coalitions, because they are able to transform religious identities into activism (Swarts 2007).

THE TYRANNY OF DECENTRALIZATION

However, such loose patterns of organization as those described earlier have the defects of their virtues. While encouraging the autonomy of the base and exhilarating activists with a sense of participation, they permit – and indeed encourage – a lack of coordination and continuity. For example, although the women of the Greenham Common peace camp kept the British army at bay for months during the peace movement of the 1980s, their devotion to internal democracy permitted conflict to break out over the issue of whether to allow male comrades to spend the night there (Rochon 1988: 82). Similarly, in the women's groups that Judith Hellman studied in Italy, personalism became a kind of "tyranny" that made formal decision making difficult and left non-initiates feeling excluded (1987: 195–196). More recently, conflicts broke out among the planners of the Northwest Social Forum in Seattle and minority groups that complained that their issues were being sidetracked by organizers' global justice commitments (Hadden and Tarrow 2007).

Nor can these organizations always maintain themselves as easily as their predecessors did through churches, cooperatives, or trade unions – what Verta Taylor (1989) has called "abeyance structures." For one thing, twenty-first century social life, organized around the family, the TV screen, and the cellphone, does not offer as many opportunities for sustained interpersonal interaction as our ancestors found in the pub, the parish church, and the bowling league; for another, the sheer density of formal associations in contemporary society offers numerous alternatives for individuals in search of organizations to join. And as the result of the looseness of control in such decentralized organizations, they easily break into factions (Meyer 1990).

Where European Social Democracy solved the problem of coordination by encapsulating the working class into permanent organizations, and anarchists tried to inspire mass revolt by mounting dramatic attacks on authority, today's hybrid movements thrive because they need no special organized efforts to maintain them over time and across space. But their weakness is that autonomy at the base sometimes excludes strong connective ties between center and periphery, making it difficult for leaders to implement coherent strategies or control their membership.

Networks within and beyond Organizations

Formal organizations rise and fall with cyclical frequency, along with the waves of contention whose enthusiasms they reflect (see Chapter 10). Whether formal or informal, centralized or decentralized, they rest on networks of activists whose friendships, interpersonal trust, and shared perceptions are transformed into movement actions and programs (Diani and McAdam eds. 2003; Diani 2004). When they draw on existing social networks, social movement organizations (SMOs) can mobilize supporters rapidly and put pressure on opponents through established institutions.

Some networks are based on trust, others on information or resource exchange, still others on instrumental alliances. Charles Tilly focuses only on "networks of trust" (2005b), but Delia Baldassari and Mario Diani make a distinction between solidarity-based "social bonds" and instrumentally driven "transaction" networks (2007). Sometimes networks are horizontal; at other times they are vertical. Movements form between initiates within movement clusters, and sometimes between the leaders of adjacent organizations. Networks can link leaders across organizations and can link activists within movement clusters. Sometimes ties are strong, as in Tilly's networks of trust, but often they are weak (i.e., information or resource generating). They can also be based on co-participation in events, in which case they may be shifting and short-lived (Mische 2008: Chapter 5).

Mark Granovetter (1973) has argued persuasively that weak ties can serve as better bases for mobilization than strong ones, because the latter are more likely to be exclusive and to exclude potentially useful allies. But much depends on the type of goal that links members of the network. While consensus movements such as Mothers Against Drunk Driving and broad reformist movements such as Civil Rights prospered on relatively weak networks, high-risk groups such as the Italian Red Brigades depended on the extremely strong ties of family and close friends whose ties had been hardened in the heat of combat (della Porta 1990; 1995).

Not only do movement organizations build on networks; acting collectively can *create* networks. Mische describes how activists move through overlapping organizational networks, bringing with them identities, projects, and styles of work as they move through different organizational settings (2008). Situations of risk, excitement, or repression create trust among people who may not have known each other beforehand or understood that they had claims in common. When reforms are accomplished, mobilization declines, or repression bites, activists without tight links to organizations tend to disappear into "abeyance structures" – inactive potential groups that can come to life when new crises or opportunities arise (Taylor 1989). We saw how this happened in Poland after martial law was declared and Solidarity was disbanded. But it also happens in liberal societies. When a new cycle of contention appears, informal contacts from the last wave of activism can be reactivated (Buechler 1986; Blocker 1989).

Social networks can form bridges both laterally and over time. *Laterally,* ties between individual activists can help create formal coalitions between contemporary organizations. In his work on Italian environmental organizations, Diani found that, even in Italy, where the gaps between Catholic and Marxist subcultures were deep, informal ties between members of different environmental organizations helped to develop a common collective identity among members and bridge organizational gaps (1995). *Over time,* bridges among activists can lead them from one organizational site to another. Over time, bridge building was evident in Paul Lichterman's work on American community activists (Clemens and Minkoff 2004: 157). Lichterman found that "the individual activist's sense of commitment is highly portable; it can be carried from group to group, in concert with other activists and imagined communities of activists who validate personalized politics" (1996: 34). This takes us to the trajectories of movement organizations.

Organizational Trajectories

The density of movement organizations rises and falls in different historical periods. In America, the 1820s constituted a watershed for the creation of (mainly church-based) organizations. In Europe, the 1890s were a crucible for the formation of working-class organizations. The period since the 1960s has been a period of organizational innovation, both in the social movement field and more broadly. This occurred not only because those decades produced a tidal wave of new movements; the same period also saw the development of technical, managerial, and communications innovations that movement organizations could use to find members and maintain support. Two kinds of innovations were important for growth of movements: internal and external.

EXTERNAL INNOVATIONS

The most important external development was the enhanced availability of the media – and especially of television – in diffusing the influence of movement organizations. From Civil Rights marchers braving police dogs and hoses, to the New Left's public draft card burnings, to the spectacle of gay or lesbian activists "coming out," to Tea Partiers decked out as revolutionary militiamen, television's appetite for dramatic visual images is a tool that is nurtured and exploited by movement organizers. If movements can transmit their messages to millions of people across the airwaves – encouraging some to follow their example and larger numbers to take notice of their claims – it becomes possible to create a social movement without incurring the costs of building and maintaining a mass organization. The media thus play an important role in "co-producing" protest events (Walgrave and Manssens 2000).

A second set of external changes revolves around the increased amount of money, free time, and expertise available to young people since the beginning of the postwar boom years (McCarthy and Zald 1973; 1977). Not only has disposable family income risen substantially, by the 1960s, young people were targeted as a choice market for consumer goods and as the center of a new youth culture (McAdam 1988: 13–19). Both in Europe and America, young people entered universities in much larger numbers, where they had more free time and were exposed to broader currents of ideas than in the past. If nothing else, this has produced many more "conscience constituents" to lend their numbers and skills to minority movements (Marx and Useem 1971). Young people are also more attuned to the cultural changes brought about by globalization, and thus are more likely than their elders to associate with causes beyond their borders (Jung 2009).

A third set of external changes consists of the financial and administrative resources available to movement organizations from foundations, from governments, and even, in some cases, from business and civic groups (McCarthy and Zald 1973; Jenkins and Eckert 1986).[7] Particularly for the Third World nongovernmental organizations that blossomed in the 1980s and 1990s, foundations, the United Nations, the European Union, and several international human rights groups are major funding sources (Keck and Sikkink 1998; Joachim and Locher 2009; Smith 2008). As we will see in Chapter 12, external support can be a mixed blessing; external support makes it tempting for local leaders to ignore relations with constituencies, leaving the door open to defection and fragmentation. But where repression or its threat constrains organizations from collecting funds or soliciting new members, external funding and sponsorship can provide a lifeline.

INTERNAL INNOVATIONS

Organizers have been quick to take advantage of the same advances in communication and fundraising as more conventional political and interest groups – first through the mimeograph machine, then through the use of direct mailing lists, and more recently, with the fax, the cell phone, and e-media. As a result of these changes, organizers can now mount and coordinate collective action rapidly across a broad sweep of territory in competition with parties, interest groups, and even the government (Bennett et al. 2008). Even in authoritarian

---

[7] Note that Jenkins and Eckert, in their "Channelling Black Insurgency" (1986), find that foundation support did not coincide with the most insurgent phase of the Civil Rights Movement, but with the more institutionalized, more moderate phase in the late 1960s and early 1970s.

China, where the Internet is closely controlled, news of the strike at Foshan was instantly communicated through cell phones to Zhongshan and other factories in the region.

Movement organizations have also learned to draw on the appeal of celebrities – the rock stars, folk singers, and movie stars who lend their names and their talents to movement campaigns (Meyer and Gamson 1995, Lahusen 1996) – and of professionals – for example, scientists and technical experts who lend their authority and their expertise to the ecological, antinuclear, and peace movements (Nelkin 1975). Similarly, the American women's and gay movements in the 1980s depended on the professional services of feminist or gay lawyers, who lent a legalistic tone to much of their activity (Mansbridge 1986; d'Emilio 1992: 192). Finally, the peace and antinuclear movements have depended heavily on the expertise and prestige of physicists, and anti-genetic seed campaigners have used the expertise of soil biologists and ecologists.

PROFESSIONALIZING LEADERSHIP

Professionalization was nothing new for the large mass parties and movements of the past; this was what worried Michels most about the loss of the revolutionary drive of the Social Democratic Party of Germany (SPD). But what we see in movements today is a new type of professional, who is not dependent on mass membership but specializes in the diffusion of information and the construction of temporary coalitions among groups of activists. Possession of such skills makes it possible to mobilize a large reservoir of support at short notice, allowing movement organizations to be both small *and* professional.

Of course, this also means that movement organizations are likely to have smaller memberships than class-mass parties and trade unions in the past. Theda Skocpol (1999) and Robert Putnam (2000) have both argued that today's movement organizations depend less on active memberships than on largely passive "checkbook" supporters. "Membership of this kind," writes John McCarthy, "rarely provides the opportunity for widespread activist involvement for members, nor is it likely to provide any face-to-face contact among checkbook members or between them and SMO leaders" (McCarthy 2005: 195).[8]

Tradeoffs and tensions may result from professionalization (Staggenborg 1991) – for example, tensions between paid and volunteer staff; those between organizational maintenance and grassroots mobilization; and tensions between lobbying and protest.[9] In research carried out on civil society groups in the

---

[8] Evidence suggesting that European movement organizations have smaller memberships today than in the past comes from Hanspeter Kriesi's work on new social movement organizations in four European democracies (1996). Kriesi finds that, with the exception of Greenpeace, organizations created since 1965 had much smaller memberships than those created before that date (p. 172).

[9] In a personal communication to the author, Ann Mische points out that this has been particularly important in Brazil, as many grassroots movement and party activists were drawn into

European Union, a great deal of tension was uncovered between the professional Brussels-based leadership of these groups and their mostly volunteer national affiliates (Imig and Tarrow 2001).

FRANCHISING, APPROPRIATING, AND BURROWING
WITHIN INSTITUTIONS

In part in response to the problems of gaining broad support without bureaucratic membership organizations, many movements have "franchised" local organizations, which remain independent but use the name of the national organization and receive their publicity in return for financial contributions and cooperation in joint campaigns (McCarthy and Wolfson 1993: 4–6; McCarthy 2005). Franchises allow a small national umbrella organization to coordinate the activities of a broad base without expending scarce resources on maintaining the formal connective structures of a large mass organization. A successful case of such "franchising" was the Committee for Nuclear Disarmament (CND) in Britain in the 1980s (Maguire 1990). Another is MADD (Mothers against Drunk Driving) in the United States (McCarthy and Wolfson 1993). A third are the loose and evolving relations between the national Tea Party movement and the congeries of local groups that supported right-wing candidates in local and state races around the United States in the 2010 congressional elections.

In addition to franchising, many contemporary movements draw upon the resources of organizations and associations not created primarily for collective action. This is what Doug McAdam has called "social appropriation" (1999 [1982]). This practice allows movements to use the infrastructures of more stable organizations and to mobilize into movement campaigns people who would not be interested in permanent movement activity. In her comparative study of coalitions to oppose free trade in the Americas, Marisa Von Bülow found that those Latin American networks that had found homes within national organizations were the coalitions most likely to survive (Von Bülow 2010).

Movements often develop *within* institutions, when their structures and ideologies are used to develop contacts among networks of dissidents and those espousing their ideologies – literally conceived – against their official bearers (Zald and Berger 1978). With its sprawling structures and official dogma, the Catholic Church has long provided a home for such heterodox movements. In the 1960s and 1970s, Christian "base communities" developed in Catholic Europe (Tarrow 1988) and supported insurgencies in Latin America (Levine 1990). More recently, a movement for gender equality has developed within

professional roles as the Workers' Party took power, or into nongovernmental advocacy organizations (NGOs), which receive foreign assistance and thus can support a paid staff. I am grateful to Professor Mische for this comment, as well as for other suggestions that have improved this chapter.

the female monastic orders of the Catholic Church in America (Katzenstein 1998).[10]

Digitizing Movement Organization

Finally, perhaps the most dramatic change in social movement organizing in the last few decades has been the impact of the Internet and, more generally, of electronic communication. From "hactivism" to "meetups," from using the Internet to diffuse information and propaganda to employing it to bring people to international sites of protest over great distances, the Internet has rapidly become a basic tool of movement organizers and has given rise to enormous excitement among both activists and publicists.

The Internet and the many interactive communication and social networking technologies that now operate over it serve not just communications functions; they serve many other purposes as well. For example, when Edna Reid and Hsinchen Chen coded the Web sites of 84 extremist groups in the United States and the Middle East, they found that in addition to their communications functions, these sites worked to increase fundraising, share ideology and propaganda, provide training and recruitment opportunities, and overcome environmental challenges from law enforcement and the military (Reid and Chen 2007). Internet links also connected members of these "families" of extremist movements – for example, Reid and Chen found hyperlinks with different extremist American groups in the neo-confederate, the Christian identity, the white supremacist/neo-Nazi, and militia clusters, but found fewer links between these extremist families (p. 182).

Technologies that operate over the Internet offer so many different kinds of support to social movements that it may be reductive to regard them as simply vehicles for "message transmission." When combined with their social implications, digital media have become a partial substitute for traditional forms of social movement organization as well. Writing of the transnational "global justice" movement, for example, W. Lance Bennett and his collaborators note that "electronic networks... constitute *organizational structures* (such as decentralized campaign networks, interactive protest calendars and planning sites, and social forums) joining diverse and often widely dispersed activists" (Bennett, Givens, and Willnat 2004).

Bennett has made a powerful case that the digital media are changing the nature of activism in important ways, including extending the range of social networks transnationally; diminishing the relative importance of local and national "off-line" organizations as bases for activism; increasing the advantages of resource-poor organizations within broader movements; making it easier to link specific targets in faraway places to ongoing campaigns; and combining face-to-face interactions with virtual performances (Bennett 2003).

---

[10] Ann Mische reminds me that nuns sometimes describe themselves as "the original uppity women."

The few empirical studies we have of the Internet's influence on political participation and activism tend to support Bennett's claims (Fisher et al. 2005; Nah,
Veenstra, and Shah 2006; Reid and Chen 2007; Rohlinger and Brown 2009).

Some technological enthusiasts have seen these new technologies entirely
remapping social movement organization and strategy (Rheingold 2003), but
we should be cautious before drawing so far-reaching a conclusion (e.g., see
Hellman 1999, on the Zapatista rebellion). Rather than displacing traditional
organizations, access to the Internet combines with personal networks and
organizations in recruiting people to take part in demonstrations. And similar
to earlier forms of communication, access to e-media varies by country and
by social power. Assessing Internet access internationally, Charles Tilly and
Lesley Wood found that Internet hosts per thousand varied from 295.2 in the
United States to a mere 0.02 in Paraguay. "To the extent that internationally
coordinated social movements rely on electronic communication, they will have
a much easier time of it in rich countries than poor ones" (Tilly and Wood 2009:
104–105).

Nevertheless, the Internet has opened up new windows of opportunity to
movement groups with the strategic vision and the tactical skills to use it effectively. It is interesting to note that conservative groups seem to have been slower
off the mark than progressive ones in taking advantage of it. Perhaps because
of their structural advantage in power and their greater financial resources, the
American neo-conservative movement has been slow to build an online infrastructure (Karpf 2009a). Not so their progressive opponents: The progressive
group MoveOn.org was quick to turn the methods of electronic communication to their purposes and to help to elect Barack Obama in 2008 (Karpf 2009a
and b, Streeter 2007).

CONCLUSIONS

There is no single model of movement organization and no single organizational trajectory. In fact, heterogeneity and interdependence are greater spurs to
collective action than homogeneity and discipline, if only because they foster
interorganizational competition and innovation. Encapsulation of the European working class into mass parties and unions was a solution for the long
term that left workers unprepared for contention when crises struck. The anarchist countermodel was an organizational weapon for the short term that led
to sectarianism and isolation. Contemporary innovations of transitory teams,
professional movement groups, decentralized and differentiated organizations,
and e-media-bolstered protest campaigns are variations on and combinations
of these experiences. What underlies the most successful of them is the role
of informal connective tissue operating within and between formal movement
organizations.

The dilemma of hierarchical movement organizations is that if they perma-
nently internalize their bases into organizations, they will lose their capacity
for disruption. But if they move in the opposite direction, they will lack the

infrastructure to maintain a sustained interaction with allies, authorities, and supporters. The new hybrid forms of organization that have developed since the 1960s offer partial solutions to this problem. While umbrella organizations at the summit offer general guidance, financial support, and the use of their "name brands," decentralized units at the base can absorb or create networks of trust that are free to develop their own programs and engage in forms of action appropriate to their settings.

Campaigns run by such hybrid organizations are not limited to their own activists; through loosely coupled social networks and the media, they can periodically activate broader "protest communities" – sets of activists sharing a bedrock willingness to engage in sustained participation in protest activities (Diani 2009). These communities of activists bolster small organizational cores and diffuse information about protest events to those they may have met in other organizational settings (Bennett et al. 2008). At the extreme end of the continuum, Internet-based movements have practically no permanent organizations and depend on "virtual networks," which offer complete autonomy at the base but no mechanism to ensure their continuity or survival.

Hybrid forms of organization have the vices of their virtues. Slogans such as "a movement of movements" make good copy among activists who treasure autonomy but, lacking mechanisms to control their base, organizers may see their supporters go off in all directions. Peaceful demonstrations organized in their name can be infiltrated by violence-seeking outsiders; programs designed to cast a wide net can be undercut by radical fractions determined to provoke opponents; small groups with particular claims may be diverted from the organization's broader goals. In the case of Internet-based movements, umbrella organizations lack even the ability to monitor the activities of their supporters. In such decentralized and loosely coupled movements, the center of gravity of decision making descends to the lowest level at which activists possess the skills to create a new Web site.

Yet a certain vitality is evident in the new forms of hybrid organization that was lacking in their more disciplined and centralized predecessors. For decentralization and looseness are not merely structural properties; they bring with them a code of diversity and inclusiveness that Donatella della Porta, in her work on the European Social Forum (2005), has referred to as "multiple belongings and flexible identities." We will turn now to how these belongings and identities are constructed.

7

Making Meanings

At 11 AM on December 6, 1992, in the holy city of Ayodhya, in the Indian state of Uttar Pradesh, a group of young men carrying hammers and iron rods erupted into the Babri mosque. This mosque, which was built during the Moghul (i.e., Muslim) domination of India, stood on land that had supposedly held a temple to the Hindu god Ram. The young men, or *kar sevaks,* were volunteers loosely affiliated with three Hindu nationalist groups: the Rashtriya Swayamseveak Sangh (RSS), the Vishwa Hindu Parishad (VHP), and the rapidly rising Bharatiya Janata Party (BJP), which had gained almost a third of the votes in the 1991 elections and governed the state (Jaffrelot 1996: 558). Although Hindu nationalism was on the rise all over India, it was particularly volatile here in the North (Brass 1974, Jaffrelot 1996, Mehta 1993).

By lunchtime, as the police stood by, the mosque's idols, collection boxes, and portraits were carried off by the crowd. By 2:55 PM, the left dome of the building had caved in; by 4:35, the right one fell too, and the central one followed a few minutes later. "Even before that," continues Christophe Jaffrelot, "Muslims were attacked in Ayodhya town and many houses whose inhabitants had fled were set ablaze." After the demolition was complete, the *kar sevaks* constructed a temporary temple in which Hindu images were placed (p. 455).

That day's carnage was not an isolated event. Even under the British Raj, to avoid communal violence, the British had divided the space inside the mosque between Muslims and Hindus. But from partition of the subcontinent in 1947

---

[1] My all-too-brief account of this long and tangled story is based on the accounts of Ved Mehta, "The Mosque and the Temple: The Rise of Fundamentalism" (1993); Pradeep Chhibber and Subhash Misra, "Hindus and the Babri Masjed: The Sectional Bias of Communal Attitudes" (1993); Christophe Jaffrelot, *The Hindu Nationalist Movement and Indian Politics* (1996); and Ashis Nandy et al. *Creating a Nationality: The Ramjanmabhumi Movement and Fear of the Self* (1998); and on the kind advice of my colleagues, Ron Herring and Mary Katzenstein.

onward, because Hindus believed the mosque was built on the site of a Hindu temple, conflict swirled around possession of the site:

- In 1949, icons of Lord Ram appeared in the mosque, and both Hindu and Muslim parties launched civil suits for its possession. The then-secularist government, declaring the site "disputed," locked the gates.
- In 1984, a movement was started by the VHP and the BJP under the leadership of L.K. Advani to build a Hindu temple to honor Ram.
- In 1986, a district judge ordered the opening of the disputed structure to Hindus, but the central government resisted.
- In 1989–1990, the VHP intensified its activities by laying foundations of the Ram temple on property adjacent to the mosque.
- In 1990, the first attempt to attack the temple was made.

Although these events gravitated around the symbolic importance of Ayodhya, they were part of a broader movement challenging the secular foundations of the Indian state and seeking to identify it with the majority Hindu religion. In the 1980s, a TV series popularizing the story of the Ramayana played a leading role in creating a new national Hindu identity (Rudolph 1992). At the same time, the BJP began to employ in its election campaign a new repertoire of aggressive, religiously tinted rituals. Excited marchers in religious/political processions frequently would enter Muslim neighborhoods, stones would be thrown at them, and, in reply, young Hindu hotheads would loot businesses and burn houses (Jaffrelot, p. 392). These processions-turned-riots raged across the subcontinent to the point that one expert called them an "institutionalized riot system" (Brass 2003). Religious imagery and political theatrics also came together in the *Rath Yatra* – a religion-tinged chariot procession – by which BJP leader Advani criss-crossed the country during the 1990 elections. Advani traveled more than 10,000 km in a symbol-bedecked vehicle meant to evoke the chariot used by Hindu hero Arjuna on his way to battle. As he came closer to Ayodhya, he was arrested in the state of Bihar, initiating another cycle of violence (Jaffrelot: 418–419).

The worst violence followed the Adyodha demolition, especially in the city of Bombay (now Mumbai), where a local nativist organization, the Shiv Sena, took advantage of the excitement over the mosque's destruction to stir up anti-Muslim violence (Katzenstein, Mehta and Thakkar 1997; Jaffrelot p. 459). As in Ayodhya, the police took the side of the militants. By January 1993, more than 500 people were dead, the majority of them Muslims, thousands had fled, and others were forced to move into protected Muslim neighborhoods.

The controversy did not end there. The courts and the central government went back and forth for years over the responsibility for the demolition of the mosque, over whether there had ever been a Hindu temple on the site, and over the future of the site. A high-level commission by retired Supreme Court Justice S.M. Liberhan was appointed to look into all these questions and propose a solution. It was only in 2009 that the Liberhan report was submitted to the government.[2] It condemned just about everybody but proposed no solution to the dispute over ownership of the mosque.

WHAT IS HAPPENING HERE?

What can we learn from this series of explosive incidents between Muslims and Hindus, secularists and religious militants, in South Asia? We could, of course, inscribe the story in the empirically rich and theoretically provocative literature on communalism (Brass 1974). We could also see it in the light of theories of nationalism, which has a long and intimate relationship with religion (Aminzade and Perry 2001). We could see it as the fuel of political party conflict (Chandra 2004) and public opinion, which was divided over the demolition of the mosque (Chhibber and Misra 1993). Or we could see it in the light of theories of civil society and social capital (Varshney 2002). Instead, I will use this sequence of events to help explicate the complex, subtle, and confusing issue of how meaning is made in contentious politics. For what the coalition of Hindu nationalist forces was trying to do through the contentious events they stage-managed was to construct a new and militant national identity built on the Hindu religion.

All movement leaders proffer symbolically laden messages to gain support from followers, attract fence sitters, and mark themselves off from opponents. This is one reason why public actions of movements take the form of "performances": Their performances compete for public space with entertainment, news, other movements, and government attempts to monopolize the formation of opinion. A performance is at once a spectacle and an action that is part of a repertoire of contention (see Chapter 5). At times, actors emphasize the spectacle aspect, both to attract the attention of the media and to set themselves off from conventional political actors. But performances are also goal-oriented, as when the *Rath Yatra* was used to attract supporters in an election campaign.

Over the past two decades, students of social movements and contentious politics have recognized that movements do not simply seek instrumental goods; they also make and manipulate meanings. But analysts differ about just how movements make meaning. At least three main mechanisms can be extracted from the recent "cultural turn" in the study of social movements:

First, movements *frame contentious politics.* Starting with the work of David Snow and his collaborators, students define framing as the construction of an interpretive scheme that simplifies and condenses the "world out there," just as journalists "frame" a story by selectively punctuating and encoding objects (Snow and Benford 1992: 137). We saw such a process of framing when the Ayodhya militants framed their attacks on Muslims as the need to defend Hindu tradition. As a pamphlet put out by the RSS in 1988 put it, "My temples have been desecrated, destroyed. Their sacred stones are being

---

[2] http://news.bbc.co.uk/2/hi/south_asia/8125927.stm. Accessed March 9, 2010.

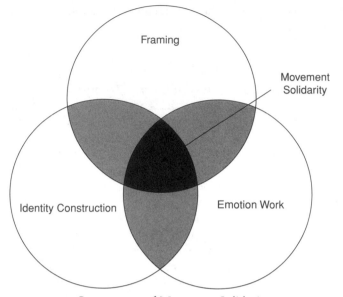

FIGURE 7.1. Components of Movement Solidarity

trampled under the aggressor's feet. My gods are crying. They are demanding of me for reinstatement in all their original glory" (quoted by Jaffrelot, p. 391).

Second, movements *define, crystallize, and construct collective identities.* Starting with the pioneering work of Alberto Melucci (1988), scholars have increasingly seen identities not as an "essentialist" component of collective action, but as a constructed set of boundary mechanisms that define who "we" are, who "they" are, and the locations of the borders between them. Attacking the Ayodhya mosque was a product of the attempt to reconstruct a nationalist identity around a religious one and define Muslims as outside that identity (Nandy et al. 1998).

Third, scholars have increasingly focused on how movements *reflect, capture, and shape emotions* to mobilize followers. In the Ayodhya episode, the RSS constructed the image of Ram as an *angry* god (Jaffrelot, pp. 391–392) who feels humiliation at the alleged aggression of Muslims and is anxious to assert his lost prerogatives. His anger was used to justify the rage of his followers and, thus, to justify their violent acts.

Scholars of social movements who have taken the cultural turn have wrestled over which of the three – framing, identity construction, or emotion – are the most important parts of the culture of contention. What seems clear is that all three are important elements in creating solidarity among potential movement participants and activating them. We will best understand this combination if we can show how framing, identity, and emotions are combined in episodes of contentious politics. Figure 7.1 lays out the agenda for this chapter and indicates what will have to be shown: that framing, identities, and emotions intersect to produce the solidarities with which social movements interact with allies, opponents, and authorities.

Framing Contention

In an important series of papers, David Snow and his collaborators adapted Erving Goffman's (1974) concept of framing to the study of collective action, arguing that a special category of cognitive understandings – collective action frames – relates to how social movements construct meaning for action.[3] A frame, to repeat Snow and Benford's definition, is an interpretive schemata that simplifies and condenses the "world out there" by selectively punctuating and encoding objects, situations, events, experiences, and sequences of actions within one's present or past environment (1992: 137).

Framing, according to Bert Klandermans, "is a process in which social actors, media and members of a society jointly interpret, define and redefine states of affairs" (1997: 44). Collective action frames may "underscore and embellish the seriousness and injustice of a social condition or redefine as unjust and immoral what was previously seen as unfortunate but perhaps tolerable" (Snow and Benford 1992: 137). Social movements are deeply involved in the work of "naming" grievances, connecting them to other grievances, and constructing larger frames of meaning that will resonate with a population's cultural predispositions and communicate a uniform message to power holders and to others (p. 136).

Goffman's term "framing" originally applied to how an *individual* constructs reality, but in the social movement tradition that grew out of his work, scholars have focused on how *movements* frame specific grievances with collective action frames that dignify claims, connect them to others, and help to produce a collective identity. But the concept can be enlarged to relate to how entire episodes of contention, their actors, and their actions are interactively framed by participants, their opponents, the press, and significant third parties (McAdam et al. 2001: 45). Framing is carried out not only by social movement organizers, but also by the media, by other sources of information, and by the state. Indeed, framing goes well beyond how a movement's goals are strategically formed to a much broader set of interpretive processes, which build on inherited understandings and engage in "framing contests" between challengers and their opponents (p. 48).

Movement entrepreneurs do not simply adapt frames of meaning from traditional cultural symbols; if they did, they would be proffering to their

---

[3] For their most important theoretical contributions, see Snow, Rochford, Worden, and Benford, "Frame Alignment Processes" (1986); Snow and Benford, "Ideology, Frame Resonance, and Participant Mobilization" (1988), and "Master Frames and Cycles of Protest" (1992); Robert Benford, "Frame Disputes within the Disarmament Movement" (1993); and Robert Benford and Scott Hunt, "Dramaturgy and Social Movements" (1992). Also see the synthesis of this work in Snow's "Framing Processes, Ideology, and Discursive Fields" (2004).

followers nothing more than reflections of their societies' values – a move that would inhibit them from challenging these values. They orient their movements' frames toward action, and fashion them at the intersection between a target population's inherited culture and its own values and goals.[4] But sometimes they try to transform inherited frames. This was the goal of the Hindu nationalists who attempted to transform the inherited secular frame of Indian nationalism into one based on the symbols of its majority religion (Nandy 1995).

The process of frame alignment is not always easy, clear, or uncontested. First, movement leaders have to compete with authorities, the media, and the market for cultural legitimacy. These are competitors with immensely powerful cultural resources at their disposal. Second, movements that adapt too well to their societies' cultures can alienate their most militant supporters – for what society has dominant values that do not support existing power arrangements? Third, ordinary people often have their own "reading" of events that may differ from those constructed by their leaders. A considerable effort at consensus mobilization is often necessary to break constituents of their inherited habits of thought. In doing so, two kinds of strategies are often employed: injustice framing and bricolage.

Injustice Framing

A recurring mode of discourse in contentious politics is built around what William Gamson calls an "injustice frame" (1992a: 68, 73). In the same vein, writes Barrington Moore Jr., any movement against oppression "has to develop a new diagnosis and remedy for existing forms of suffering, a diagnosis and remedy by which this suffering stands morally condemned" (1978: 88). Similarly, Doug McAdam argues that "before collective action can get underway, people must collectively define their situations as unjust" (1999 [1982]: 51). "Injustice," concludes Gamson, "focuses on the righteous anger that puts fire in the belly and iron in the soul" (1992b: 32).

But it is no simple matter to convince normally passive people that the indignities and inequalities of everyday life can be challenged. Contention may point to a grievance, identify a constituency, and name an enemy. But, writes Gamson, "it is insufficient if individuals privately adopt a different interpretation of what is happening. For collective adoption of an injustice frame, it must be shared by the potential challengers in a public way" (1992a: 73). Inscribing grievances in frames that identify an injustice, attribute the responsibility for it to others, and proposing solutions to it is a central activity of social

---

[4] This is what Snow and his associates call "frame alignment" (1986). In their article, they describe four alignment processes through which movements formulate their messages in relation to the existing culture of politics. The first three – "frame bridging," "frame amplification," and "frame extension" – make only incremental innovations in symbolism. But a more ambitious strategy is the fourth one – "frame transformation." It is the most important framing device in movements that seek substantial social change (pp. 467–474).

movements. This is what the Hindu nationalists did in reconstructing the myth of the destroyed temple in Ayodhya; this allowed them to convince majority Hindus that the very existence of a mosque on this holy ground demanded collective action (Jaffrelot, pp. 401–402).

Bricolage

The French term *bricolage* ("do-it-yourself") was imported to political science by Richard Samuels (2003) to describe the mixture of traditional and modern themes employed by Italian and Japanese leaders in building their states. Social movement leaders often do the same: Familiar themes are arrayed to entice citizens to become supporters; and new themes are soldered onto them to activate them in new and creative directions. Bricolage pulls together accepted and new frames to legitimate contention and mobilize accepted frames for new purposes. Symbols and frames can serve to unite diverse actors; at the same time, their meanings can be ambiguous and multivalent across different movement constituencies, which allows leaders to attract diverse constituencies that come together behind ambiguous symbols.

Consider the American Civil Rights movement. It both built on and tried to transform the traditional American frame of rights. Americans instinctively frame their demands in terms of rights, but for African Americans, rights most often have been honored in the breach. However, the Civil Rights movement of the 1960s drew centrally upon this frame, which then become the "master frame" of many other movement sectors during the cycle of contention of the 1960s (Snow and Benford 1992).

The first reason for the dominance of the rights frame was that the earliest terrain of the Civil Rights movement was the courts. As Charles Hamilton writes, this context "created a cadre of constitutional lawyers who became in a real sense the focal points of the civil rights struggle" (1986: 244). A second reason was more strategic: Equal opportunity was a useful bridge between the movement's main internal constituency, the southern black middle class, and the white liberal "conscience constituents," whose support the movement wanted. For the black middle class, equality of opportunity was a worthy enough goal, while white liberals were most offended by the contradiction between the value Americans place on rights and the denial of equal opportunity to African Americans.

But was the Civil Rights movement's concept of "rights" no more than the traditional costume of American consensus? If so, why did the movement have to await the 1960s to act, and how did it achieve as much as it did? The answer is that only through "bricolage" between the traditional rights frame and the new and innovative forms of nonviolent collective action did rights become the central collective action frame of the movement (Chapter 5 and Tarrow 1992). Using this combination, the movement's leaders elaborated a practice of militant quiescence within the most traditional institution they possessed – the black Church. It was not the inherited grammar of rights but the combination of this traditional frame with the creative action of nonviolent resistance that turned quiescence into action.

Costumes of Consensus

But there is a paradox in the bricolage of inherited and creative movement framing: between developing dynamic symbols that can bring about change, and evoking symbols that are familiar to people who are rooted in their own cultures. Gregory Maney and his collaborators described the relationship between inherited symbols of consensus and oppositional frames of challenge in the antiwar movement in the United States before and after the watershed of the Iraq War in 2003. As public anger at the September 11th attacks rose, the antiwar movement faced a dilemma: Opposing every aspect of the government's rush to war in Iraq would condemn the movement as un-American; supporting the war would undercut the movement's basic ideology. The solution of the main trunk of the antiwar movement was to embrace nationalist identities in the months after 9/11, but to revert to pre-9/11 patterns after the Iraq War began (Maney et al. 2009).

In the months following the attacks on the World Trade Center and the Pentagon, Maney and his collaborators found a persistent attempt by peace movement leaders to "harness hegemony" – as opposed to "challenging hegemony." But as the misrepresentations of the Bush-Cheney administration about weapons of mass destruction became ever more evident, the body bags began returning from Iraq, and after the disclosures of torture at Abu Ghraib, the antiwar movement leaders began, in the words of Maney et al., "challenging hegemony." They found that during periods of massive public sympathy and support for the government – for example, immediately after 9/11 and following the successful invasion of Iraq in 2003 – the peace movement tended to emphasize symbols of hegemony. In contrast, after the Iraq War turned into a quagmire, the movement emphasized symbols that "challenged hegemony."

Why does it seem so difficult to construct truly oppositional symbols that challenge hegemony? One reason may be that movement leaders genuinely wish to remain within the boundaries of a political consensus – this was certainly true of most of the American peace protesters. Another is that the reach of the state is so great that even messages of rupture are often framed in terms of consensus. But a third reason relates more directly to the structure of communication in today's societies: Movements that wish to communicate with a broader public must have the internal resources to "perform" protest (Glenn 1997; Meyer and Gamson 1995), or they must use the media to do so, and the media are often allergic to the framing of issues that appear to challenge political consensus.

Media Framing

Although first the press and then radio have been highly influential in the construction of contention, it was television with its unique capacity to encapsulate complex situations in compressed visual images that brought about a revolution in movement tactics. The extent of this revolution first became evident during the 1960s in the American Civil Rights movement. That movement, write Richard Kielbowicz and Clifford Scherer, "was television's first recurring news story largely because of its visual elements" (1986: 83). The coincidence of the movement's appearance with on-site TV newscasting helped it in three ways: first, television brought long-ignored grievances to the attention of the nation, and particularly to viewers in the North; second, it visually contrasted the peaceful goals of the movement with the viciousness of the police; and third, television was a medium of communication for those *within* the movement. TV helped to diffuse information on what the Civil Rights movement was doing through the visual demonstration of how to sit-in at a lunch counter, how to march peacefully for civil rights, and how to respond when attacked by police and fire hoses.

Similarly, but with more violent results, broadcasting by the media of the destruction of the Babri Mosque in India helped to diffuse the legitimacy of violence and stoked the riots that followed across the country (Jaffrelot: 458). Television was a co-producer of collective action. As two scholars of the media's effect on movements conclude, "for members of the audience whose own experiences resemble those of the televised cases, such media attention can serve to cultivate a collective awareness, laying the groundwork for a social movement" (Kielbowicz and Scherer: 81).

Religious figures have become adept at using the media to diffuse their political messages. From France, the Ayatollah Khomeini and his followers used radio and cassettes to diffuse their anti-Western critique of the Shah of Iran's government; in America, Christian fundamentalists broadcast their messages using television and radio from venues as diverse as the pulpits of neighborhood churches and the gridirons of football stadiums; in the 1990s, Islamist terrorist groups began to use media messages to diffuse their versions of religiosity across the Islamic world; and in 2010, a little-known Florida minister used television to broadcast his intention to burn a stack of Qu'rans on the anniversary of September 11th. His publicity stunt failed, but only after the President, the Defense Secretary, the U.S. commander in Afghanistan, and platoons of religious figures begged him to desist (*New York Times*, September 11, 2010, p. 1).

The most dramatic example of the role of the media in framing contention was the staging of a massive demonstration by Chinese students in Tienanmen Square in 1989 in protest against Communist Party corruption and authoritarianism (Esherick and Wasserstrom 1990). Students not only drew on traditional symbols of Chinese political theater, but as in other episodes of the 1989 revolutions, they used theatrical forms strategically to gain the sympathy of the international media audience, which they knew represented their only hope of putting external pressure on Chinese authorities (Calhoun 1994a: Chapter 3). The monument to freedom that they rolled onto the square had roots in Chinese political culture, but it also had a disarming resemblance to the Statue of Liberty.

The media provide a diffuse source for consensus formation that movements on their own cannot easily achieve in that they provide differential "standing" for different actors in a conflict (Ferree et al. 2002). New information and new ways of interpreting it often appear first in public space, only later giving rise to collective action frames on the part of movement entrepreneurs. Once formed, movements can take advantage of coverage by sympathetic journalists (Gitlin 1980: 26). More often, however, the media choose to frame a story in a certain way because it sells newspapers or attracts viewers. At least in a capitalist society, the media are in business to report on the news, and they stay in business only if they report on what will interest readers, or on what editors believe will interest them.

Media framing tends to focus on what "makes" news. This reinforces the shift from disruption to violence often found in protest cycles (Gans 1979: 169). The single student in a peaceful antiwar protest who throws a rock at a police line and the transvestite marching in garish drag in a gay rights march make better copy than well-dressed marchers, no matter how many, parading peacefully down a city street. In this way, the media "accentuate the militant strains found in any collection of activists" (Kielbowicz and Scherer: 86), providing incentives for disruptive or violent elements in otherwise peaceful movements.

CRYSTALLIZING IDENTITIES

In Year V of the French Revolution, writes historian Lynn Hunt, the commissioner of the revolutionary executive power in Grenoble wrote:

> It is a contravention of the constitutional charter... to insult, provoke, or threaten citizens because of their choice of clothing. Let taste and propriety preside over your dress; never turn away from agreeable simplicity.... Renounce these signs of rallying, these *costumes of revolt,* which are the uniforms of an enemy army.[5]

The commissioner was in a position to know. In the decade in which he wrote, the French produced the first systematic attempts to reshape political culture around new forms of dress, holidays, salutations, public works, and monuments.[6] As the Revolution spread, so did its symbols. Self-declared republicans wore austere dress to mark them off from "aristocrats," which came to mean anybody who wore elegant dress and refused to display the signs of republican virtue (Hunt: 1984: 75–76). Supporters of the Revolution would challenge citizens who dared to be seen on the street in elegant dress; even the

[5] Archives Nationales, III Isère 9, Correspondance, 1791–1853, "Adresse du Commissaire du pouvoir exécutif près l'administration centrale du départment de l'Isère." Quoted by Lynn Hunt in her *Politics, Culture, and Class in the French Revolution* (984: 52).

[6] The most thorough treatment of the festivals of the French Revolution is Mona Ozouf's *Festivals and the French Revolution* (1988). The symbol of Marianne, goddess of liberty and the Republic, has been magnificently studied by Maurice Aghulon in his *Marianne au combat* (1979).

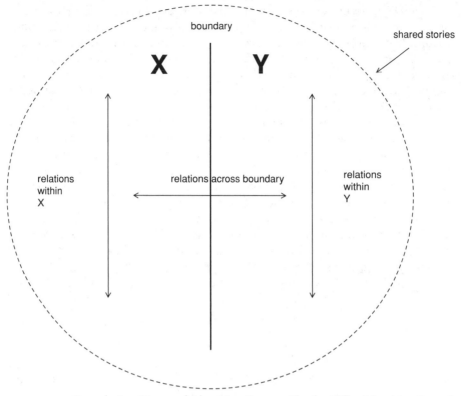

FIGURE 7.2. Boundaries, Ties, and Identities. *Source:* Charles Tilly, *Identities, Boundaries and Social Ties,* p. 8. Copyright © 2005 Paradigm Press. Reprinted with permission.

King had a Phrygian bonnet stuck on his head before he lost it after the failure of his flight to Varennes (Schama 1988: 603–604).

The story that Hunt tells about the "costumes of revolt" in the French Revolution reveals how contentious politics constructs, crystallizes, and politicizes collective identities.[7] As Tilly writes, "A crucial set of identities is categorical; it pivots on a line that separates Xs from Ys, establishing distinct relations of Xs to Xs, Xs to Ys, and Ys to Ys" (2005: 61). Between identities are boundaries, whether spatial, gender- or class-based, ethnic, religious, and so forth. Figure 7.2 lays out this simple paradigm from Tilly's work on the relations among identities, ties, and boundaries.

---

[7] The locus classicus of collective identity theory is found in Alberto Melucci's *Challenging Codes: Collective Action in the Information Age* (1996). Issues of identity formation in social movements are central to several major collections in the social movement field: Hank Johnston and Bert Klandermans' *Social Movements and Culture* (1995), Enrique Laraña, Hank Johnston and Joseph Gusfield's *New Social Movements* (1994), and Aldon Morris and Carol Mueller's *Frontiers in Social Movement Theory* (1992).

Categorical identities are overlapping and multiple; the same individual who is a mother at home may be a worker in the factory, a union member in the hiring hall, a bowler in the bowling league, and a protester on the street. That is often far too pluralistic a set of identities around which to mobilize a challenge to powerful enemies. Movements must often struggle to politicize the meaning of identities and to activate boundaries, as the Hindu nationalists did when they strove to militarize the image of the god Ram and portray Muslims as aggressors. This is why movements often try to suppress identities that fit badly with their goals, trying instead to create what Mische calls "provisional homogeneity along a reduced identity dimension" (2008: Chapter 10).

The Hindu nationalists were not alone: German National Socialists built boundaries between themselves and other "races" based on their own supposed "Aryan" superiority and on the degenerate characteristics of Jews, Gypsies, and Slavs. When they settled in Palestine, European Zionists fought to discard the image of the Eastern European Jew as urban, mercantile, and designing for a new one that would be agrarian, productive, and courageous. Similarly, Islamist militants construct boundaries between the true faith of the Prophet and the westernization of Arab government elites. And American nativists – many of foreign origin – rail against the supposed inferiority of undocumented immigrants from South of the border.

Perhaps the best documented effort at identity change was that of American civil rights leaders who worked to create a new and more positive image of "the new negro" in a community in which lightness of skin color had been seen as a sign of status. As Martin Luther King wrote after the Montgomery bus boycotts,

> Our non-violent protest in Montgomery is important because it is demonstrating to the Negro, North and South, that many of the stereotypes he has held about himself and other Negroes are not valid. . . . In Montgomery we walk in a new way. We hold our heads in a new way (quoted in McAdam et al. 2001: 319).

The implication was clear: The movement was more than an instrumental effort to change the bus seating laws in Montgomery; it was working to create more generally a new collective identity among Southern blacks.

Movements require solidarity to act collectively and consistently; constructing identities around its claims is one way of doing so. Thus, feminists identify themselves not with a particular program of reforms, but with women's oppressed fate since the dawn of time; climate change campaigners present themselves as representatives of the interests of humanity; and well-paid, skilled "aristocrats of labor" identified themselves as the suffering proletariat. Sometimes the myths create what Tilly calls "lineaments of durable connection among core participants." "But," he concludes, "most social movements remain far more contingent and volatile than their mystifications allow" (Tilly 1998: 133). For example, as Israeli society evolved from scattered *kibbutzim* and *moshavim* defending their perimeters from Palestinian attackers to a military/industrial powerhouse, the myth of the intrepid farmer making the desert bloom gave way to a new image of a high-tech, high-income country.

Although such identity claims are often the outward apparel that movements wear to mark their members off from others, the solidarity of their militants is often based on more intimate and specialized solidarities, such as the "communities of discourse" that Mary Katzenstein found among American Catholic women (1995); or the workplace solidarity that Rick Fantasia noted among the workers he studied (1988); or the community solidarity that Paul Lichterman described in the community group he studied in California (1996). Often a movement has to negotiate among a variety of identity claims. For example, in his research on Hartford's progressive community, Stephen Valocchi discovered three different forms of identity: movement identity, held by those whose primary identification was with the movement culture they had inherited from the 1960s; organizational culture, among those whose primary loyalty was to a movement organization; and what he calls "biographical identity," among those whose identity was associated with a broad social category (Valocchi 2008: 66).

Building a movement around strong ties of collective identity – whether inherited or constructed or, more often, some combination of the two – does some of the "work" that would normally fall to organization. According to Jo Reger and her collaborators, "Activists are often faced with the task of building solidarity among a diverse membership, which can require very careful, deliberate identity work." Especially in movements in which identity construction is crucial – such as the women's, gay men's, and lesbian movements – "Disagreements about who 'we' are – or should be – can become quite costly, taking time and resources away from other activist tasks and even alienating participants or fragmenting the movement" (Reger et al. 2008: 3).

Given the importance of establishing legitimacy and certifying a movement as an authentic representative of the constituency it claims to represent, identity construction is probably most important during the emerging phase of the movement, becomes less important as it is institutionalized, and disappears with the movement's establishment in speaking for its constituency. But because most individuals negotiate among a variety of identities, the politicized identity that a movement claims may need to be constantly reinforced, especially after mobilization has peaked. Second, competing movement organizations may each claim to be the constituency's authentic representative, producing competition over identity. Third, toward the ends of protest cycles, militants may raise the walls of their collective identity higher, finding increasingly narrow definitions of identity and rejecting alliances as a form of "selling out" (Chapter 10).

DOING EMOTION WORK

Much of the "work" of meaning-making is cognitive and evaluative, that is, identifying grievances and translating them into claims against significant others. But to maintain solidarity among activists and to transform claims into action, emotion work needs to be done. Emotions, writes Verta Taylor, are the "site for articulating the links between cultural ideas, structural inequality, and individual action" (1995: 227). She writes, "it is emotions that provide the ‘heat,’ so to speak, that distinguishes social movements from dominant institutions" (p. 232).

Nationalism is a ready source of emotional energy. Lacking the fine mechanical metaphors of class dialectics, it possesses a great emotional potential, especially when it is linked to religious or ethnic appeals. As Benedict Anderson ironically asks, while contrasting the many monuments to nationalism with the lack of memorials to social class, "Could one even imagine a Tomb of the Unknown Marxist"? (1991: 10). Feminism has also led to recognition of the force of emotionality in social movements. "Scholars of the women's movement," writes Verta Taylor, "have pointed to both the love and caring, on the one hand, and the anger, pain, and hostility, on the other, that characterize feminists' interactions" (1995: 229).[8] But as the story at the beginning of this chapter suggests, it is though religion that "hot cognitions," infused with emotion, reinforce or create solidarity and produce the most volatile and even violent movements.

The Muhammad Cartoons

On September 30, 2005, a Danish newspaper, *Jyllands-Posten*, published twelve satirical cartoons of the prophet Muhammad, ostensibly as a protest against what the paper believed was self-censorship on the part of the Danish press out of fear of repercussions from Islamist extremists.[9] Protests by Muslims living in Denmark, who make up four percent of the population in that small country, were immediate. These reactions to the cartoons were restrained and led to no violence. But after two months of relative silence, punctuated by a letter of protest from ambassadors from Muslim countries to the Danish prime minister, protest began to grow, with twenty protests in December, twenty-four in January, more than one hundred in February, and more than sixty in March (Lindkilde 2008: 225). Seventeen different Muslim organizations were direct claim makers in Denmark alone, while another 27, primarily local ones, were indirectly involved (p. 227).

More surprising, this Danish-based protest movement escalated to the transnational level, and this time the protests were far from peaceful. As Thomas Olesen writes, "The images that linger are those of embassies on fire and angry crowds burning Danish flags." In contrast to the Danish

[8] See, in particular, Leila Rupp's "Imagine My Surprise" (1980) and Barbara Ryan's *Feminism and the Women's Movement* (1992).

[9] My main sources for this narrative are Olesen (2007) and Lindekilde (2008). For the cartoons themselves, which were subsequently republished all over the world, go to www.humanevents. com/article.php?id=12156. Accessed March 11, 2010.

government, which responded to the protests with firm, if flagging support for freedom of the press, Middle Eastern governments were ambivalent. In several countries, state-controlled newspapers were sharply critical of the Danish government, calling for a boycott of Danish goods and condemning the cartoons as "a crime against the Muslim world" (Olesen 2007: 42). Demonstrations were held in Egypt, Palestine, Yemen, Indonesia, Turkey, Syria, Lebanon, Afghanistan, Iran, and the Philippines, with arson attacks against Danish offices in Damascus and Beirut (p. 44). Death threats and rewards for the assassination of the cartoonists followed, and several were forced temporarily into hiding.

Different Emotion Cultures

Sociologist Arlie Hochschild has pointed out that particular groups form their own "emotion cultures" (1990). This has given rise to a rich tradition of quasi-ethnographic research on "emotion work" (Aminzade and McAdam 2001; Goodwin, Jasper and Polletta, ed. 2002; Gould 2009; Jasper 1998; Polletta 2006), with particular emphasis on religion, gender, and nationalism. Movements often attempt to stimulate particular emotional responses by talking about them (Gould 2009). By saying "we are not afraid, one can become less afraid; by saying 'we are angry,' one can feel angry."

Some emotions – such as love, loyalty, and reverence – clearly are more mobilizing than others – such as despair, resignation, and shame. Some – such as anger – are "vitalizing," while others – such as resignation or depression – are "de-vitalizing." Optimism and confidence are frequent accompaniments to protest, but so are anger, indignation, fear, compassion, and a sense of obligation (Polletta and Amenta 2002: 305). Many movements are built around the deliberate cultivation of hatred or anger. The long and tortured struggle between Catholics and Protestants in Northern Ireland cannot be understood, except as the deliberate stoking of mutual hatreds. The rape of Muslim women by Bosnian Serbs was aimed at least as much at desensitizing their own solders as it was at humiliating their victims (Eisenstein 1996: 167). Even racial pride – cultivated by a sector of the Black Power Movement in the United States in the 1960s – involved formalized expressions of verbal violence (Gitlin 1995: Chapter 1).

Much depends on the constituent base of the movement, on the emotion culture of the society in which it emerges, on the phase of the movement's development, on its interaction with significant others, and on surrounding opportunities and constraints. High points of contention may produce emotional pivots around which the future direction of a movement turns. Over time, movement entrepreneurs will strain to re-evoke these emotional pivots through rhetoric, ritual, and gathering at the sites of injustice or of past victories. For example, movements against anti-immigration laws in France often re-evoke the memory of the deportation of Jews and others by the wartime Vichy regime by marching from the Gare de l'Est, which was their point of debarkation to the gas furnaces.

But emotion cultures are never as simple as "one movement = one emotion." During different phases of their life cycles, movements draw on a broad repertoire of emotions (Aminzade and McAdam 2001). For example, Deborah Gould's analysis of the lesbian/gay community's response to AIDS ranges from fear of repression to shame to initial repression of anger, followed by pride in the community, and, finally, anger, when conventional tactics appeared ineffective in gaining government support for victims of the disease (Gould 2009; Aminzade and McAdam, p. 35). Student movements are particularly expressive of a wide range of emotions over their life cycles, ranging from enthusiasm and solidarity in their early phases, to anger and outrage at the indifference of authorities and the brutality of the police at their heights, to despair and burnout during their decline.

But even this is too simple a picture of the repertoire of emotions in movement cycles. Movements mobilize emotions not in a vacuum but in relation to significant others:

- To movement allies whose emotion culture may be very different from that of the movement's primary constituency
- To bystander publics that the movement may wish to attract by toning down its emotional temperature
- To the media, which movement leaders know to be indifferent to emotional subtleties but alert to extreme expressions of emotion that will attract readers or viewers
- To the forces of order whose repressive tactics may goad the movement's militants into acts of revenge
- And to public officials, whose indifference to the movement's goals may lead to anger or disillusionment, or both

CONCLUSIONS

The "cultural turn" in social science has enriched the repertoire of social movement scholars by bringing framing, identity construction, and emotions to the center of attention. But it will do more harm than good if it results in a species of paradigm warfare in which emotion is chosen over rationality, identity politics over instrumental politics, and movement framing over the social construction of broad episodes of contentious politics. Even assuming that the basic language of a movement is its symbolism, how is that message received and interpreted over time and across space among different social subjects? Will it be understood in its original form, like Holy Scripture? Must it be reworked and readdressed to local constituents according to their own preconceptions? Or will it be applied selectively and in combination with indigenous cultural symbols by movement entrepreneurs?

Most important, how does a movement message change in response to the responses of significant others? In 1994, when the Zapatista rebels launched attacks on government forces in Chiapas, Mexico, they drew heavily on the symbolism of landless peasants everywhere. But when the movement gained resonance in the capital and in North America and Europe, it was mainly as an "indigenous movement," and the message of movement leaders shifted from peasant-based claims to demands that were heavily inflected with the symbolism of indigenous Indians oppressed by five hundred years of white and mestizo power. The cultural turn is a refreshing departure from the heavy structuralism that had weighted down previous accounts of contentious politics (see Chapter 1), but if it fails to connect framing, identity, and emotion to the political process, it risks becoming every bit as deterministic as its structuralist predecessor.

What is the solution? Framing, identity construction, and emotions cannot be simply read like a "text," independent of the strategies of movements and the conditions in which they struggle. Out of a cultural reservoir of possible symbols, movement entrepreneurs choose those they hope will mediate among the cultural understandings of the groups they wish to appeal to, their own beliefs and aspirations, and their situations of struggle to create solidarity and animate collective action (Laitin 1988). To relate text to context, the grammar of culture to the semantics of struggle, we need to turn from framing, identity construction, and emotions to how movements intersect with their contexts. We need to examine, in particular, the structure of opportunities and the constraints in which they operate. We turn to this important intersection in the next chapter.

8

Threats, Opportunities, and Regimes

A COLLAPSING REGIME

In the late 1980s, contentious politics arose in the highly centralized and police-and-party controlled Soviet Union. Mark Beissinger documented the rise and dynamics of contentious politics there – which began as a wave of peaceful demonstrations, strikes, and protest marches, but evolved into violent nationalist-inspired riots and militarized conflicts (Beissinger 2002). Figure 8.1 shows what Beissinger found when he employed a protest event analysis to see what was happening during the last years of the Soviet Union:

How could so massive a wave of political contention develop in so centralized a regime after decades of repression? The simplest answer was provided by Alexis de Tocqueville. Because people act on opportunities, he observed, "the most perilous moment for a bad government is one when it seeks to mend its ways" (1955: 176–177). Tocqueville was writing of the collapse of the French Old Regime; had he been present two hundred years later, he might well have applied his theory to the Soviet Union. There, as in France in the 1780s, an international power mired in corruption and torpor and unable to compete with a more dynamic market-oriented society (Bunce 1985; cf. Skocpol 1979) sought to reform itself from within. Incoming party secretary Mikhael Gorbachev was convinced that his country could not survive as a world power without reform. As a result, the late 1980s "engendered a process of liberalization that sparked an explosion of organized extra-state political activity" (Fish 1995: 32).

As was to be expected in so centralized a system, liberalization began at the top, with a change in official thinking and policy on both foreign policy and questions of participation and association. Gorbachev had proposed a modest concept of socialist pluralism, which "amounted to de facto toleration of the formation of some small, non-state citizens' organizations" (Ibid.). But it did not take long for the new possibilities he offered to stimulate more independent initiatives. For example, a group called "Memorial," dedicated to investigating

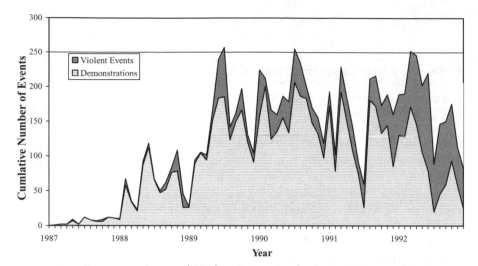

FIGURE 8.1. Demonstrations and Violent Events in the Soviet Union and Its Successor States, 1987–1992. *Source:* Original data provided by Mark Beissinger, from his *Nationalist Mobilization and the Collapse of the Soviet State.* Cambridge University Press, 2002.

the crimes of Stalinism, quickly formed; another, called "Citizen's Dignity," dedicated to promoting human rights, soon followed (Ibid.); and eventually, a reform faction developed within the ruling Communist Party, calling for movement toward a multi-party system.

To some extent, Gorbachev's desire for liberalization was based only on the idea of stimulating more open discussion (*glasnost*). But he quickly realized that without a renovation of the political class, his plans would be stymied by official obstruction. As a result, he transformed the usually formalistic elections to the USSR Congress of People's Deputies into "the first even partially open and competitive national election in the history of the Soviet Union" (Fish, pp. 35–36). Although the election's rules reserved a third of the seats for party-controlled representatives, it conferred on independents the mantle of legitimacy. "Perhaps of greatest moment," writes Steven Fish, "the balloting engendered the closest thing that the populace had ever known to a real election campaign" (p. 35).

But the reformers were few and disorganized. Lacking internal resources and possessing weak connective ties and little mutual trust, they divided into competing factions and parties (Fish, pp. 35. ff). What they profited from was external support – like that accorded them when the secretary of the Moscow Communist Party Committee, Boris Yeltsin, gave informal support to a conference of political discussion groups called "Social Initiative for Perestroika" (p. 32). External help also appeared from the coal miners of the Kuzbass and the Donbass, who went on strike in 1989, and from Eastern Europe, where Gorbachev's reforms – and particularly his removal of the threat of Red Army intervention – triggered a wave of democratization movements

(Fish, pp. 39–41). These "allies" – both conscious and involuntary, internal and external – added to the confidence of insurgents in the USSR that change was inevitable.

Not all the stirrings of dissent were aimed at democratization. Soon after liberalization began at the center, long-repressed nationalist sentiments began to stir in the Soviet Union's far-flung minority republics. First in Georgia and the Baltic states, then in Armenia, Ukraine, and the central Asian republics, separatist movements began to mobilize. In many cases, they resorted to violence against other ethnic groups or the center; in some, such as Kazakhstan, Communist Party elites turned into peripheral nationalists practically overnight (Tilly and Tarrow 2007: 104–105). Beissinger's data in Figure 8.1 show that as the cycle of contention gathered steam, more and more of it took violent forms, mainly from among nationalist groups in the periphery of the USSR, who threatened and were threatened by other groups and by the state.

As 1990 dawned, these developments were accompanied by a decline in the state's capacity for repression. As Fish concluded:

> The center and the party could prevent, obstruct, and coerce; but they could no longer even pretend to initiate, create, and convince.... A motley conglomeration of autonomous social organizations, spearheading a popular movement for democracy, had rendered power visible.... In doing so, they had begun to push it toward its demise (p. 51).

Seeing the growing prospect of the regime's collapse, in August 1991 conservative elements in the Communist Party elite launched a countermovement, bringing tanks onto the streets of Moscow, and threatening a return to the harsh Stalinist regime that Gorbachev had tried to liquidate. The threat was opposed by Yeltsin, who rallied the populace and other elements of the army in a dramatic standoff at the Moscow White House. The coup plotters were defeated, but Gorbachev's power was broken, and Yeltsin emerged as leader and officiated over the dissolution of the Soviet Union (Bonnell, Cooper, and Freiden 1994).

WHAT IS HAPPENING HERE?

First, in a pattern strikingly close to what Tocqueville would have predicted, a cycle of reform begun at the top triggered *a spiral of opportunities and threats*. It offered political opportunities to groups seeking liberalization through institutional means. This encouraged other groups, who mobilized, using the opportunities they opened. Third, this sapped the elite's will to resist and ate away at the centralized structure of the USSR. Fourth, a countermovement threatened both reformers and peripheral nationalists and was defeated, finally, by Yeltsin, an opportunistic reformer who put together a coalition built around the core Russian Republic.

The turbulence unleashed by Gorbachev's reforms not only produced opportunities; it posed a number of *threats* – to members of the elite whose positions in the state and in the Communist Party apparatus were threatened by them;

to the majority Russian ethnic group whose dominant position was under-cut by peripheral separatism; and to "certified" minorities whose position in some peripheral Republics was threatened by others, such as the Ajerbaija-nis, who were attacked by minority Armenians in Nagorno-Karabakh. Threats and opportunities combined in a major challenge to the Soviet regime, bringing about its eventual collapse.

Finally, we saw a process typical of the beginning of *regime change:* com-binations of old and new repertoires; new actors like Memorial alongside old ones like the Communist Party and newly revived ones like the separatist move-ments, which took advantage of the chaos at the center to stake their claims; threats of revanchment from party and military elites attempting to stop the slide to democracy and dissolution. Opportunities, threats, and regime change came together in the former Soviet Union, producing a new and hybrid form of regime.

In this chapter, I will examine, first, political opportunities, then threats; finally, I will turn to how changes in regimes intersect with processes of con-tentious politics.

Opportunities and Threats

Contention increases when people gain access to external resources that con-vince them that they can end injustices and find opportunities in which to use these resources. It also increases when they are threatened by costs, which out-rage their interests, their values, or their sense of justice, but they still see a chance to succeed. When institutional access opens, rifts appear within elites, allies become available, and state capacity for repression declines, challengers see opportunities to advance their claims. When these are combined with high levels of threat but declining capacity for repression, such opportunities pro-duce episodes of contentious politics, sometimes producing changes in regimes.

It is time to define these terms:

Opportunities I will define, following Jack Goldstone and Charles Tilly, as "the [perceived] probability that social protest actions will lead to success in achieving a desired outcome" (2001: 182). "Thus," they continue, "any changes that shift the balance of political and economic resources between a state and challengers, that weaken a state's ability to reward its followers or opponents or to pursue a coherent policy, or that shift domestic or outside support away from the regime, increases opportunities" (pp. 182–183).

Threats, which are often seen as only the "flip side" of opportunities, are actually analytically distinct. Threat relates to the risks and costs of action or inaction, rather than the prospect of success. "Let us label the costs that a social group will incur from protest," continue Goldstone and Tilly, "or that it expects to suffer if it does not take action, as a 'threat.' A group may decide to bear very high costs for protest," they conclude, "if it believes the chances of success are high, but the same group may decide to avoid even modest costs of protest if it believes the chances of succeeding are low" (p. 183).

Regime Change: Regimes consist of regular relations among governments, established political actors, challengers, and outside political actors, including other governments. Regime change is change that inserts new actors into these relations, reduces the power of regime members, or imposes new relations among them (Tilly and Tarrow 2007: Chapters 4 and 5). Not all changes in the balance of opportunity and threat change regimes, but all regime change is based on changes in opportunities and threats

One way of understanding the importance of threat in triggering contention is suggested by the "prospect theory" of the late Stanford psychologist Amos Tversky (see Quatrone and Tversky 1988). Tversky and his collaborators argued that individuals react differently to prospective gains and losses. They claimed that individuals employ decisional heuristics that are contextually contingent. "An individual's attitude toward risk depends on whether the outcomes are perceived as gains or losses, relative to the reference point" (p. 722; also see Berejikian 1992).

But this does not mean that resource-poor people or those living under authoritarian regimes are always bereft of opportunities. It is how threats and opportunities combine, rather than shifts in the prospect of success alone, that shapes decisions regarding collective action (Goldstone and Tilly 2001). Just as minority ethnic groups seized the opportunity of chaos at the center to nibble away at the Soviet Union, my research in Southern Italy showed how desperately poor peasants seized parts of the *latifundia* in the rapidly opening opportunity structure when fascism was defeated at the end of World War II (Tarrow 1967). In the very different circumstances of highland Peru, poor peasants seized the land they claimed their ancestors had lost when the opportunity structure opened (Hobsbawm 1974). In the Soviet Union in the late 1980s and early 1990s, shifts in opportunity and threat were sufficiently great that a momentous change in regime transpired.

FROM SOCIETAL TO POLITICAL STRUCTURATION

Before the 1960s, most students of social movements stressed long-term structural threats or short-term deprivations as the sources of collective action. Initially, observers in both Western Europe and the United States were struck by how changes in modern society had expanded the incentives for contention. They focused on the "why" of mobilization – for example, whether "life-space" changes or "post-material attitudes were spurring contention. But they could not easily explain why people would lend support to movements during certain periods of history and not others, and why some countries within the West were experiencing more sustained contention than others. To answer those questions, it was necessary to trace how underlying social structure and mobilization potential were transformed into action. In such a transformation, the role of political opportunities and constraints was crucial, as observers of the 1960s could see from an earlier episode of contention: the Great Depression.

STRIKE WAVES AND POLITICAL OPPORTUNITY

The relationship among threat, opportunity, and mobilization can be illuminated by looking at the differences in working class mobilization in different Western countries in the 1930s. Other things being equal, workers are more likely to go on strike in boom times than in depression.[1] The logic of the connection is clear: Prosperity increases employers' need for labor, just as tight labor markets reduce the competition for jobs. As workers learn this, they demand higher wages, shorter hours, or better working conditions. As a result, other things being equal, the strike rate follows the curve of the business cycle upward when a declining unemployment pool leaves employers prey to the pressure of the labor market and downward when the demand for labor declines.[2]

The depression of the 1930s saw the rise of a number of worker mobilizations in Europe and the United States. We would normally expect such an economic crisis with widespread unemployment to depress contention. But in some countries of the West, industrial workers struck, demonstrated, and occupied factories in response to sackings and reductions in pay, while in others they did not, or they allowed themselves to be repressed. While workers in Britain languished through most of the Great Depression and German workers were brutally repressed by the Nazis, French and American workers reacted to the crisis with unprecedented levels of contention.

How can we explain the increase in industrial insurgency by hard-pressed workers in France and the United States, while in Germany and Britain, workers accepted their fate? The answer, I propose, lies in changes in the opportunities and threats that surrounded the different working classes. Strike waves were felt in France and the United States in the 1930s, and not in Germany or Britain, because the reform administrations that came to power in France in 1936 and in America in 1933 showed a willingness to innovate in political-economic relationships and a reluctance to support the suppression of labor. Of course, all the Western working classes suffered the threat of unemployment in the Great Depression, but it was the opening of political opportunities and the relaxation of threats of repression offered by the French Popular Front and the American New Deal that encouraged labor insurgency in those countries, and not the depth of workers' grievances or the extent of their resources.

Returning to the present, we will see that political opportunities are seized and transformed by a variety of challengers under many different conditions. Our first task will be to classify the dimensions of opportunity that help shape movements. The second will be to specify threat more precisely, and to show

---

[1] A long and somewhat technical literature is available on the relations between economic conditions and strikes. The most thorough summary and assessment is found in John Kennan's "The Economics of Strikes" (1986) in the *Handbook of Labor Economics*, eds. Orley Ashenfelter and Richard Layard.

[2] The most synthetic interpretation of the economic sources of the wage explosions of the late 1960s is David Soskice, "Strike Waves and Wage Explosions, 1968–1970: An Economic Interpretation." in Colin Crouch and Alessandro Pizzorno, eds. *The Resurgence of Class Conflict in Western Europe Since 1968*. Vol. 2, (1978).

how both police repression and general suppression discourage protest. The third will be to investigate how state structure and prevailing strategies of the state shape contention. We will also see that political opportunities are not the result of objective structures; they must be perceived to bring about mobilization, and this depends on the unleashing of a number of mechanisms of contention (McAdam et al. 2001).

Dimensions of Opportunity and Threat

By the concept of political opportunity, I mean consistent – but not necessarily formal or permanent – dimensions of the political environment or of change in that environment that provide incentives for collective action by affecting expectations for success or failure (Gamson and Meyer 1996). Compared with theorists of resource mobilization (see Chapter 1), writers in the political opportunity tradition emphasize the mobilization of resources *external* to the group.[3] They also emphasize mechanisms in the immediate environment that trigger mobilization such as the following:

- The attribution of opportunity or threat
- The availability of potential allies
- The formation of coalitions, both on the margins of and within the polity
- The framing of entire episodes of contention

Political opportunities sometimes center on particular groups – as our example of workers in the 1930s suggested – and opportunities for protest are greater in some regions or cities than in others (Agnew ed. 1997: Part 4; Eisinger 1973). But frequently, movements emerge because general prospects for mobilization have expanded – as was the case when the American peace, student, and women's movements of the late 1960s took advantage of a generally widening opportunity structure (see Chapter 10). Some movement sectors are particularly affected by changes in opportunities – as was the peace movement in the 1980s (Meyer 1990) – but more often, opportunities signaled to some are also perceived and taken advantage of by others.

"OBJECTIVE" AND PERCEIVED OPPORTUNITIES

Political opportunities may not be apparent all at once to all potential challengers. Indeed, there is no such thing as "objective" opportunities – they must

---

[3] The ultimate source of political opportunity theory was Charles Tilly's *From Mobilization to Revolution* (1978: Chapter 4). Also see David Snyder's and Tilly's article, "Hardship and Collective Violence in France" (1972). Explicit building blocks in the United States were Doug McAdam, *The Political Process and the Development of Black Insurgency* (1999 [1982]), Anne Costain, *Inviting Women's Rebellion* (1992), Suzanne Staggenborg, *The Pro-Choice Movement* (1991), and David Meyer, *A Winter of Discontent: The Nuclear Freeze and American Politics* (1990). Explicitly comparative use of the concept was made by Herbert Kitschelt in his "Political Opportunity Structures and Political Protest" (1986), and in Tarrow, *Democracy and Disorder* (1989a) and "Struggle, Politics and Reform" (1989b).

be *perceived* and *attributed* to become the source of mobilization (McAdam et al. 2001: Chapter 2; Meyer and Minkoff 2004). This means that communication and learning are important mechanisms in mobilization around opportunities. It also means that short-term changes in opportunity cannot compensate for weaknesses in cultural, ideological, and organizational resources (Kriesi 1995).

Individuals and groups may be constrained from acting collectively by threats of repression that are more apparent than real. This was undoubtedly the case in Eastern Europe and the former Soviet Union before 1989, because citizens were unaware of how weak their regimes really were (Kuran 1991; Lohmann 1994). By the same token, insurgents may launch themselves into action because they see opportunities but fail to perceive the threats that authorities hold in reserve. This was the case during the "Hundred Flowers" campaign in Maoist China, when the apparent opening of the regime was a pretext to bring dissidents into the open, where they could be identified and repressed.

The perception and attribution of opportunities have two crucial correlates.

First, what we might call "pseudo-opportunities," that is, when opportunities are perceived but have little or no objective existence. This can lead to disaster, as it did for the second group of strikers at the Honda plant we saw during the 2010 strikes in China (see Chapter 6).

Second, the sequencing of opportunities within cycles of contention (see Chapter 10). Early challengers who achieve success reveal the vulnerability of elites and institutions to weaker players, who may believe they will enjoy the same advantages as their predecessors (McAdam 1995). But weak actors who attempt to follow in the footsteps of stronger ones may be doomed to failure, either because they lack the same level of resources or because authorities have learned how to organize against them. Both of these were the causes of failures among the later "color revolutionaries" in Central Asia in 2002–2005. Insurgents in this region attempted to follow the examples of the Slovakians, Serbs, and Ukrainians whose electoral revolutions had succeeded, but without their resources; after authorities had become aware of the danger, their challenges were savagely repressed (Bunce and Wolchik 2006).

Although some scholars have expanded the use of the term "opportunities" to include "discursive opportunities" (Koopmans and Olzak 2004; Bröer and Duyvendak 2009) and "organizational opportunities" (Kurzman 1998), such conceptual expansion risks allowing virtually any change in the environment to be seen as part of "opportunity structure."[4] For this reason, it seems more useful to restrict the concept to factors in the environment that visibly and proximately open up the prospect of success (Goldstone and Tilly 2001). Most important among such factors are (1) opening of access to participation for new

---

[4] Other scholars have further expanded the concept to include other dimensions, for example, to "gendered opportunity structure" (McCammon 2001) or the "legal opportunity structure" (Pedriana 2006).

actors; (2) evidence of political realignment within the polity; (3) availability of influential allies; and (4) emerging splits within the elite. For the same reason, it seems most useful to limit the concept of threat to the state's and other actors' capacity or will to control dissent.

INCREASING ACCESS

Sensible people do not often attack well-fortified opponents when opportunities are closed; gaining some access to participation can provide them with such incentives. But are people who possess full political rights any more likely to engage in contention than those with none? Peter Eisinger argues that the relationship between protest and political opportunity is not linear but curvilinear: Neither full access nor its absence produces the greatest degree of protest. Eisinger explains that in closed systems, contention is restrained by fear of repression, while in fully open ones, prospective protesters turn to more institutionalized channels. Taking his cue from Tocqueville, Eisinger (1973: 15) writes that protest is most likely "in systems characterized by a mix of open and closed factors."[5] His research on American cities demonstrated that urban protest movements in the 1960s were most likely to emerge at intermediate levels of opportunity.

SHIFTING ALIGNMENTS

A second element that can encourage contention is the instability of political alignments. In democratic systems, this is measured most centrally by electoral instability. Especially when they are based on new coalitions, the changing fortunes of government and opposition parties create uncertainty among supporters, encourage challengers to try to exercise marginal power, and may even induce elites to compete for support from outside the polity. The importance of electoral realignments in opening opportunities can be seen in the American Civil Rights movement. Throughout the 1950s, racial "exclusionists" in the Southern wing of the Democratic party were weakened by defections to the Republicans, while the number of Democratic "inclusionists" was growing stronger (Valelly 1993). The decline of the Southern white vote and the move of African American voters to the cities, where Jim Crow was less oppressive, increased the incentive for the Democrats to seek black electoral support. With its razor-thin electoral margin, the Kennedy Administration was forced to move from cautious foot dragging to seizing the initiative for civil rights.

---

[5] Eisinger's claim was based on more than a Tocquevillian hunch. Operationalizing opportunity structure in American cities through differences in the formal and informal political structures of local government, he studied the behavior of urban protest groups in a sample of fifty-three cities during the turbulent 1960s. He found that the level of activism of these groups was highest not where access was open or closed, but at intermediate levels of political opportunity.

DIVIDED ELITES

Conflicts within and among elites can also encourage outbreaks of contention. Divisions among elites not only provide incentives to resource-poor groups to take the risks of collective action, they encourage portions of the elite that are out of power to seize the role of "tribunes of the people." History provides numerous examples of divided elites bringing resources to emerging movements. Splits within the elite played a key role in the challenges to communism in East Central Europe, especially after Gorbachev warned the Communist states of the region that the Red Army would no longer intervene to defend them. This was seen by wobbling elites as a signal to join the opposition. Splits in the elite were also important in the transitions to democracy in authoritarian Spain and Brazil in the 1970s and 1980s, where the divisions between soft-liners and hard-liners provided openings for opposition movements to exploit (O'Donnell and Schmitter 1986: 19; Bermeo 1997). Finally, splits in the elite enabled the success of the Sandinista guerillas in coming to power in Nicaragua (McAdam et al. 2001: Chapter 7).

INFLUENTIAL ALLIES

A fourth aspect of political opportunity is the presence of influential allies. Challengers are encouraged to take collective action when they have allies who can act as friends in court, as guarantors against repression, or as acceptable negotiators on their behalf. As we saw earlier, both through Yeltsin's apparent support for their efforts and through the independent activities of the miners and East European dissidents, challengers in the USSR gained both confidence and models for collective action. William Gamson's book on contention in the United States (1990) provides historical evidence for similar processes in democratic systems.[6] And as we will see in Chapter 12, external actors such as transnational nongovernmental advocacy organizations (NGOs) can sometimes be crucial allies of domestic human rights groups in the global South (Keck and Sikkink 1998).

These mechanisms of opening and closing political opportunity are arrayed differentially in different systems and change over time – often independently, but sometimes in close connection with one another. For example, splits among elites and political realignments can work together to induce disaffected groups to seek support from outsiders. When minority factions of the elite ally with outside challengers, challenges from inside and outside the polity combine in major cycles of contention (see Chapter 10). And these elements of opportunity

---

[6] William Gamson's research shows a correlation between influential allies and movement success. In the 53 "conflict groups" he studied, the presence or absence of political allies was closely related to whether or not these groups succeeded (1990: 64–66). In studying American Farmworker movements in the 1940s and 1960s, Craig Jenkins and Charles Perrow found a similar contrast: The advantage of the United Farm Workers in the 1960s lay in the presence of external constituencies that their predecessors in the 1940s had lacked (1977).

are malleable and need to be seen in connection with repression and the threat of repression.

Making and Diffusing Opportunities

Contentious collective action demonstrates the possibilities of collective action to others and offers even resource-poor groups opportunities that their lack of internal resources would deny them. This occurs when "early risers" make claims on elites that can be used by "spin-off movements," which have fewer resources (McAdam 1995). Moreover, early risers can expose opponents' points of weakness that may not be evident until they have been challenged. Their actions can also reveal unsuspected or formerly passive allies both within and outside the system. Finally, the efforts of early risers create "master frames" and can pry open institutional barriers through which the demands of other groups can pour.

Once collective action is launched in part of a system on behalf of one type of goal by a particular group, the encounter between that group and its antagonists provides models of collective action, master frames, and mobilizing structures that produce new opportunities. These secondary effects take three general forms: the expansion of a group's own opportunities and those of cognate groups; the dialectic between movements and countermovements; and the unintended creation of opportunities for elites and authorities.

EXPANDING ONE'S OWN OPPORTUNITIES

Challengers are strategic actors, but they are not always strategically astute. Some surge forward without looking to left or right, taking the initial disorganization or unpreparedness of their targets as permanent weakness. Inexperienced protesters often underestimate the reserves of their opponents. But challengers may also be strategically more savvy. William Gamson's research showed that the most successful groups that he studied in American history sought not new advantages but increased access (1990). That access could then become a new and more durable opportunity structure for the same actors. The same was true of the Solidarity activists in Poland in 1980–1981; their insistence on recognition of trade union rights over immediate advantages was aimed at guaranteeing them future opportunities. It may also prove true of the emerging Chinese labor movement, a shift that we saw hints of in Chapter 6.

EXPANDING OTHERS' OPPORTUNITIES

One of the most remarkable characteristics of contentious politics is that it expands opportunities for others. Protesting groups put issues on the agenda with which other people identify and that demonstrate the utility of collective action that others can copy or innovate upon. For example, as we saw in Chapter 7, the American Civil Rights movement expanded the doctrine of rights that became the "master frame" of the 1960s and 1970s (Hamilton 1986).

Collective action embodies claims in dramatic ways that show others the way. This was the case for Latinos and other minority ethnic groups who took advantage of the opportunity structure opened by the efforts of the black-led Civil Rights movement (Browning, Marshall and Tabb 1984). Together, these cognate movements can eventually constitute an alliance system (Kriesi et al., 1995). These others, however, may not be particularly friendly to the groups that expand their opportunities.

MOVEMENTS AND COUNTERMOVEMENTS

Not only does expansion of opportunities affect a movement's "alliance system," a movement that offends influential groups can trigger a countermovement (Meyer and Staggenborg 1996). Movements that employ violence invite physical repression. Movements that make extreme forms of policy demand can be outmaneuvered by groups that pose the same claim in more acceptable form. And when a movement's success threatens another group in the context of heightened mobilization, this can lead to outbidding and counterprotest. For example, the spiral of conflict between the American Pro-Choice and Pro-Life movements shows how movements create opportunities for opponents. The access to abortion rights that was decreed by the Supreme Court in the early 1970s galvanized Catholics and fundamentalist Protestants to organize against abortion clinics. This Pro-Life movement became so dynamic that it was a major force in defeating the Equal Rights Amendment (Mansbridge 1986). Eventually, a radical offshoot of Pro-Life called "Operation Rescue" used such radical direct tactics in the early 1990s that it stimulated a countermobilization campaign by the usually legalistic Pro-Choice forces (Meyer and Staggenborg 1996).

MAKING OPPORTUNITIES FOR ELITES AND PARTIES

Finally, protesters create political opportunities for elites – both in a negative sense, when their actions provide grounds for repression, and in a positive one, when opportunistic politicians seize the opportunity created by challengers to proclaim themselves tribunes of the people. Protesters on their own seldom have the power to affect the policy priorities of elites. This is so both because their protests often take an expressive form, and because elites are unlikely to be persuaded to make policy changes that are not in their own interest. Reform is most likely when challenges from outside the polity provide a political incentive for elites within it to advance their own policies and careers. As we will see in Chapter 11, perhaps the most enduring outcome of the French May movement was an educational reform on which the protesters had only minimal impact.

Political opportunism is not a monopoly of left or right, parties of movement or parties of conservation. The conservative Eisenhower Administration responded in essentially the same way to the Civil Rights movement as the liberal Kennedy Administration did – for the simple reason that both were concerned with electoral realignment and wished to minimize the foreign policy damage of American racism (Piven and Cloward 1977: Chapter 4). The Obama campaign of 2008 took advantage of the more radical peace movement that had arisen in opposition to the Bush Administrations' wars in Iraq and Afghanistan, just as the Republican party took advantage of the anti-incumbent mood of the electorate in 2010 to embrace the surging "Tea Party."

When are parties and interest groups most likely to take advantage of opportunities created by movements? They appear to do so mainly when a system is challenged by a range of movements, and not when individual movement organizations mount challenges that can be easily repressed or isolated. That is to say, reformist outcomes are most likely when political opportunities produce general confrontations among challengers, elites, and authorities, as in the cycles of contention that will be examined in Chapter 10.

DECLINING OPPORTUNITIES

The opening of opportunities provides external resources to people who lack internal resources. It opens gates where there were only walls before, alliances that did not previously seem possible, and realignments that appear capable of bringing new groups to power. But because these opportunities are external – and because they shift so easily from initial challengers to their allies and opponents and, ultimately, to elites and authorities – political opportunities are fickle friends. The result is that openings for reform quickly close or allow new challengers with different aims to march through the gates that the early risers have battered down.

Thus, the 1989 revolutions in Eastern Europe that many thought would bring democracy to a part of the world that had been denied freedom for a half-century produced few working democracies, several neo-Communist states, a number of countries that disintegrated into separatist conflict – like Yugoslavia – and a number of hybrid regimes with representative institutions and an authoritarian core (Beissinger 2002). Even in East Germany, which was rapidly absorbed into a stable Western democracy, the democratic Civic Forum that led the way to unification in 1989 was swept aside by the established political parties, while the successor to the old Communist party remained an electoral force. Movements are evanescent because they influence political changes that can precipitate their own decline.

The shifting nature of political opportunities does not mean that they do not matter for the formation of social movements. Just as Lenin and the Bolsheviks came to power in Russia in 1917 as the result of the opportunity of the First World War, it was the opportunities provided by Gorbachev's reforms that stimulated collective action in the former Soviet Union and in East Central Europe in 1989. But if contention migrates from challengers to their allies, from movements to countermovements, and from outside the polity to elites and parties within it, this occurs not only because of changes in opportunity, but because of changes in the level and character of threat as well.

Suppression and the Threat of Suppression

Before we begin, it will be important to distinguish between physical threats from authorities and more general mechanisms of suppression of dissidence. Some forms of suppression go beyond overt coercion, and some *non*-state actors also have resources to suppress dissent. In what follows, I will limit the term "repression" to mean physical coercion of challengers, and will use the broader term "suppression" to mean the social control of dissidence.[7]

Suppression is a more likely fate for movements that demand fundamental change and threaten elites than for groups that make ameliorative claims (Gamson 1990: Chapter 4). It is also obvious that, although authoritarian regimes suppress social movements, representative ones facilitate them. But several aspects of repressive regimes encourage some forms of contention, and some characteristics of representative regimes take the sting out of movements. We will have much more to say about different types of regime in the final section of this chapter.

The possession of repressive tools by a state does not mean that they will be freely employed. During the period from the 1970s onward, the United States became objectively a far more repressive regime (Soule and Davenport 2009). For example, imprisonment and incarceration rates increased, more money was spent on corrections, police increased the use of deadly force against ordinary citizens, and police forces equipped themselves with paramilitary forces, in part to control public protest. As Sarah Soule and Christian Davenport conclude of the period up to the 1990s, "across a wide variety of indicators, the United States is systematically becoming more aggressive with regard to how citizens are treated by the police" (Soule and Davenport 2009: 2, 5).

Not only that, but since September 11, 2001, the American state has dramatically expanded its apparatus of intelligence and surveillance. For example, two students of constitutional law, Eric Posner and Adrian Vermeule, list eight major areas of Bush administration policies after 2001 that affect the rights of Americans and others:

- Heightened search and surveillance powers
- Ethnicity-based search and surveillance
- Coercive interrogation
- Immigration sweeps and surveillance
- Terrorism and material support statutes
- Military trials
- Military action
- Detention of enemy combatants outside the theatre of hostilities (Posner and Vermeule 2007: pp. 7–9)[8]

---

[7] Jennifer Earl, to whose work the following section is in debt, prefers the term "protest control" to "suppression," but appears to mean very much what I do by "the social control of protest." See her introduction to the special focus issue of *Mobilization* 11(2006: 129–144) on repression.

[8] Posner and Vermeule excluded censorship from among the Bush policies, but this is correct only if we ignore the extraordinary expansion of the areas of information that the government claimed falls within national security limits.

TABLE 8.1. *A Reduced Typology of Protest Control*[9]

	Coercion	Channeling
State Agents Tightly Connected With National Elites	Military action against protests; FBI counterintelligence	Cutting off funding; tax law on nonprofits
State Agents Loosely Connected With National Elites	Local policing of protest; local police counterintelligence programs	Permitting requirements for protest; financial aid restrictions on students convicted of crimes
Private Agents	Violence by countermovements; private threats made by a countermovement	Elite patronage limited to specific goals or tactics; company towns

Source: Adapted from Jennifer Earl, "Tanks, Tear Gas and Taxes: Toward a Theory of Movement Repression," 2003.

Although a rhetorical rollback of some of these repressive techniques occurred under the Obama Administration, underneath the liberal rhetoric, the American state has normalized most of them (Margulies forthcoming).

The threat to protesters and potential protesters is not limited to the use of overt instruments of repression. Using the term "protest control" rather than "suppression," Jennifer Earl (2003) outlines a typology that distinguishes among twelve different kinds of control, which combine three fundamental dimensions: (1) the identity of the actor engaging in protest control (e.g., state agents closely connected to national elites, (2) state agents loosely connected to them and to non-state actors); and (3) the form of the action (outright coercion versus channeling to encourage or discourage certain types of actions), and whether the actions are covert or overt. Table 8.1 reports Earl's typology but for simplicity excludes the visibility of protest control. Earl's work shows that we cannot reduce the potential or actual threats to protesters to the overt use of police violence against them, as we will see below.

COERCIVE CONTROL

Coercion of protesters (the left hand column of Table 8.1) was the major recourse of most regimes until the 20th century, even in liberal polities such as the United States, where no national police force existed, but where state militias and private detective agencies were often employed to repress strikers. However, direct repression began to lose its sting after World War I, when major expansion of the concept of civil liberties was achieved by the courts (Stone 2004). Thus, although antiwar protesters, radicals, and anarchists were severely repressed during that war, by the 1930s many of the court decisions

[9] This is a reduced version of the typology presented in Earl (2003), which combines her categories of "observed" and "unobserved" forms of protest control.

that condemned them had been reversed (pp. 226-ff.). Posner and Vermeule even see a "libertarian ratchet" in American civil liberties from the 1930s on (pp. 146–149).

The invention of nonviolent resistance helped to neutralize the effectiveness of coercive methods, because nonviolent protesters appeared to welcome incarceration (Sharp 1973). In response to the strategic weapon of nonviolent protest, the police and the courts began to accept as legitimate forms of action that they had previously repressed. Thus, the sit-in, punished almost universally by incarceration when it was first employed, was increasingly accepted in the 1960s as a form of speech. Diffused among progressive and liberal groups in the 1960s, the sit-in even spread to their ideological enemies in the 1980s, as the antiabortion movement gained ground (Staggenborg 1991).

CHANNELING CONTENTION

Perhaps because of the growing ineffectiveness of coercive controls, states have turned to some degree toward what Earl calls "channeling." Though outright repression is more brutal and frightening, evidence indicates that increasing the costs of organization and mobilization is a more effective strategy for reducing contention in the long run (Tilly 1978: 100–102). For example, when Steven Barkan compared Southern cities that used the courts to block civil rights activities versus those that used the police to repress them, he found that the former were able to resist desegregation longer than the latter (1984). Similarly, during the McCarthy Era, American conservatives found it easier to increase the costs of membership in the Communist Party than to ban strikes or demonstrations. More recently, Egyptian authorities have found that an effective way of discouraging the use of the Internet for communication among dissidents is to require patrons who use Internet cafés to register their identity cards at the entrance to the café.[10]

Suppressing the preconditions for collective action is not easy to accomplish and has its own costs. First, financial and administrative costs are associated with generalized channeling. For example, because Egyptian authorities do not know who the potential protesters are, they must make Internet café owners register the ID cards of all patrons, even those who simply want to play computer games. Because the National Security Agency after 9/11 did not know which insurgents were planning to penetrate America's defenses, it monitored all telephone and Internet traffic between the United States and foreign countries, thus breaking American privacy laws (Sidel 2004). And because the Supreme Court claims it cannot distinguish between speech that helps terrorists move toward peaceful contention and that which contributes to violence, in 2010 it supported a provision of the U.S Patriot Act that bans all such "helpful speech" when it is used to tell groups that have been declared terrorist by the government how to participate peacefully (*New York Times*, June 22, 2010).

[10] I am grateful to Joel Beinen for this information.

The second and more subtle cost of channeling is that repressing organizations silences constructive critics, as well as opponents of the regime, and blocks information flow upward. One reason why the Soviet Union disintegrated as quickly as it did after 1989 was that independent organizations that might have signaled minor causes of dissent had been silenced. In such cases, when collective action does break out, it turns from a trickle into a torrent as people learn for the first time that others like themselves oppose the regime (Kuran 1991). The Chinese authorities today tolerate some grassroots protest because local protesters provide information about sources of dissent that allows central authorities to identify the perpetrators of abuse at the local level (O'Brien, ed. 2008).

State toleration for nonviolent contention is a double-edged sword (Meyer and Tarrow 1998). On the one hand, it provides a relatively risk-free means of giving large numbers of people the sense that they are acting meaningfully on behalf of their beliefs. But on the other hand, it deprives organizers of the weapon of outrage. Violent and capricious police who throw sincere young protesters into jail are easier to mobilize against than are reasonable-sounding public authorities who organize seminars for demonstrators and protect their right to free speech (della Porta and Reiter, eds. 1997). If we are entering a "social movement society," overt repression will be far less important than the indirect control of contention.

PROTEST MANAGEMENT OR QUIETER PROTESTERS?

After the 1960s, when American and European courts and authorities began to tolerate new forms of protest, it seemed as if the police had moved systematically toward a strategy of peaceful protest management. During this period, Sarah Soule and Christian Davenport found that "aggressive policing of protest" (defined as police use of force and/or violence) had declined. A slight increase was noted in the early 1980s and again in the early 1990s, but generally, a de-escalation of protest policing occurred (Soule and Davenport 2009: 9).

What was the reason for this change from overt coercion to peaceful protest management? One theory emphasizes a deliberate shift in public policy to recognize the legitimacy of protest (McCarthy and McPhail 1998; della Porta and Reiter, eds. 1997). A second possibility is a change in the degree of "threat": Police may employ coercive tactics only when they are threatened by more aggressive forms of contention, such as organized violence.

Both hypotheses are plausible, but in their systematic analysis of protest and police behavior in the United States between 1960 and 1990, Soule and Davenport found the strongest support for the second one – that the decline in police coercion after the 1960s was the result of a decline in aggressiveness of protesters and an increase in "quieter" forms of action (2009: p. 12 and Table 1). In their view, the de-escalation of police coercion was directly related to the de-radicalization of the repertoire of contention. But such an inference is also compatible with the first hypothesis, that is, increased state reliance on the "channeling" of protest may have produced both a decline in coercive means and a shift on the part of protesters to quieter forms of contention.

THE EFFECTS OF COERCION ON PROTEST[11]

A question that has produced an enormous outpouring of research involves the effect that protest control has on subsequent mobilizations (see the review in Earl 2006 and Earl and Soule 2010). Some researchers (e.g., DeNardo 1985, Muller and Weede 1990) argued that the use of coercion reduces protest participation by increasing its costs. Others argued that coercive methods have exactly the opposite effect – radicalizing individuals and thus increasing the amount and severity of protests (Opp and Roehl 1990). Still others see curvilinear patterns in the relationship between protest and repression (Lichbach and Gurr 1981, Francisco 1996; 2004), while others see no overall pattern and suspect that these relationships are situationally based and depend on interactions among protesters, opponents, and third parties (Earl and Soule 2010: 76).

The heterogeneity of these findings has led skilled researchers, including Karen Rasler, to conclude that the relationship between protest and repression can be understood only in light of the intergroup dynamics of the political process (1996). Others, including Jennifer Earl (2005) and Earl and Soule (2010), have focused on the effects of specific repressive actions, such as the impact of arrest on the future behavior of protesters and on different forms of police intervention. The most challenging proposal is Tilly's, who suggested that, rather than attempting to uncover general laws about the protest/repression relationship, researchers should focus on alternative causal pathways that involve interaction among protesters, the police, the authorities, and significant others (Tilly 2005; Johnston 2006).

Following Tilly's surmise, we would expect the protester/police relationship to be very different during a phase of radicalization such as the Palestinian Intifada (Alimi 2006, 2009) or the Iranian Revolution (Rasler 1996), then during declining mobilizations, as after the 1960s in the United States (Earl and Soule 2006). Charles Brockett's work on Central America supports just such a temporally differentiated hypothesis (1995). Brockett found that repression was more ferocious when the guerilla movements were weak, and that it let up as the movement gained mass support. We would also expect police behavior to differ greatly between different forms of regime – a broad subject that we turn to now.

---

[11] This section is much in debt to Jennifer Earl's (2003 and 2006) summaries of the literature on the effects of police control on mobilization, and to her's and Sarah Soule's article, "The Impacts of Repression" (2010).

TABLE 8.2. *State Strength and Prevailing Strategies as Structuring Principles for Contentious Actors*

Prevailing Strategy	State Strength	
	Weak States	Strong States
Exclusive	Formalistic inclusion; strong repression; veto possibility but no substantive change	Full exclusion; strong repression; no possibility of veto or substantive change
Inclusive	Full procedural integration; formal and informal access; weak repression; possibility of veto but no substantive concessions	Informal cooptation; weak repression; no possibility of veto but substantive concessions

Source: Adapted from Hanspeter Kriesi, "The Political Opportunity Structure of New Social Movements: Its Impact on Their Mobilization," p. 177. 1995.

Regimes and Opportunities

Until now, we have focused mainly on changes in the opportunity/threat equation. But more stable aspects of opportunity/threat condition contentious politics. One set of factors revolves around the concepts of "state strength," centralization, and decentralization; a second deals with states' prevailing strategies toward challengers; and a third relates to the overall structure of the regime and the role of protest in regime change.

In his and his collaborators' work on "new" social movements in Western Europe in the 1970s–1980s (1995; Kriesi et al. 1995), Hanspeter Kriesi distinguished between weak and strong states and between two poles of dominant state strategies toward opposition – "exclusive" and "inclusive" strategies. Kriesi's typology is reproduced with some modifications in Table 8.2. Of course, many actual states are found between the poles of strong and weak states and somewhere between inclusive and exclusive strategies. But let us take Kriesi's typology as a heuristic starting point and modify it as we consider some real-world variations.

STATE STRENGTH, CENTRALIZATION AND DECENTRALIZATION

In its most common form, the argument from state strength would run something like this: Centralized states with effective policy instruments at their command attract collective actors to the summit of the political system, while decentralized states provide a multitude of targets at the base.[12] Strong states

---

[12] The major published source is Peter Evans, Dietrich Reuschmeyer, and Theda Skocpol, eds., *Bringing the State Back In* (1985). Also see Richard Valelly's *"The Two Reconstructions: The*

also have greater capacity to implement the policies they choose to support; when these are favorable to challengers' claims, the latter will gravitate toward conventional forms of expression; when they are negative, violence or confrontation ensues.[13] In contrast, it would follow that because weak states allow criticism and invite participation, they can deal with the most challenging elements of popular politics through the institutional political process, as the United States did after the race riots of the 1960s (Lipsky and Olson 1976).

Federalism and local home rule are particular invitations to movements to shift their actions into institutions, because they provide alternative sites for participation (Tarrow 1998a). In her research on the American Temperance movement, Ann-Marie Syzmanski showed how the movement's middle-class women leaders shifted strategically between levels of the federal system, and from proposing constitutional amendments to local organizing (1997). Such strategic flexibility and "venue shopping" are typical of decentralized systems and are less available to movements in more centralized states.

Different degrees of centralization were a major source of the differences that Tocqueville saw between France and the United States. In France, he argued, the centralized *ancien régime* had snuffed out local initiative and associational life, so that when contention broke out in the 1780s, no civil society was available to absorb it, distill it into separate channels, and make reform possible without revolution (Tocqueville 1955). In America, in contrast, decentralization helped local associations and local decision making to flourish (1954). A pluralistic polity made it possible to avoid the "excess of democracy" that the French Revolution had engendered (Tarrow 1998a). Similar contrasts emerged between the French and American student movements that emerged in the 1960s. The first exploded only in early 1968, diffused rapidly, and soon moved rapidly into the political arena, triggering a political convulsion that threatened the Fifth Republic. The second produced a much longer, more decentralized series of protest campaigns at campuses around the country and was diffused into various rivulets of the New Left.

But decentralization is a double-edged sword. Tocqueville did not stay in America long enough to see how federalism would allow the Southern and Northern states to develop along radically different lines – the one slaveholding, the other free – developing conflicts that festered for decades before exploding in a savage civil war. Similarly, although federalism did not cause the collapse of Communism in the former Soviet bloc, it was only the three federal systems – Czechoslovakia, the USSR, and Yugoslavia – that collapsed under the strain; in the third, a civil war broke out (Bunce 1999).

Struggle for Black Enfranchisement. (2004), which compares American state structures and party systems over time.

[13] For example, Herbert Kitschelt traces differences in the environmental movements of France, Germany, Sweden, and the United States to such institutional differences in state structure. See his article, "Political Opportunity Structure and the Political Process" (1986).

PREVAILING STRATEGIES

But when taken alone as a guide to action, the concept of state strength lacks agency. As Table 8.2 suggests, some states – whether strong or weak – have a dominant strategy toward challengers that is inclusive, responding to and absorbing their demands. Prevailing strategies intersect with state strength in interesting ways. In their research on protest events in four European countries, Kriesi and his collaborators found that Switzerland (which they code as a "weak" state with an inclusive state strategy) had a high level of mobilization and a low level of violence and confrontation. At the other extreme, France (which they code as a strong state with an exclusive strategy) was found to have a lower level of routine mobilization and a higher level of confrontational protest (1995: 49).[14]

Of course, "strength" and "weakness" are relational values that vary for different actors, for different levels of the state, and in different historical periods. With respect to different actors, the degree and constancy of repression vary according to the legitimacy of the actor, its social strength, and how its actions are likely to affect other actors. For example, in his detailed analysis of protest and repression in South Korea in 1990 and 1991, Taehyun Nam found that the state was less tolerant to the protest of workers than of students and to mixed-dissident protest, and it was more tolerant to peasants' protests (2006: 431). Similarly, the American state – which would be "inclusive" in Kriesi's overall typology – has usually been quite "exclusive" in the face of attacks on property or from groups suspected of disloyalty. As a result of this difference, the American state presents an open door to groups that advance modest goals – the so-called "consensus movements" studied by McCarthy and Wolfson (1992) – but sets up a barricade against those who are thought to challenge capital or national security.

Similar differences can be found at different levels of the polity. When Ann-Marie Szymanski's temperance activists found the national state too strong to crack in the nineteenth century, they turned to state legislatures and local governments, where they could concentrate their strength more effectively (Szymanski 1997). Does this make the American state "strong" or "weak"? That depends on where it is challenged and on who is challenging it. For example, Peter Eisinger found that urban protest in the 1960s was far more common in "unreformed" mayor-council cities than in reformed council-manager ones (1973).

"Strength" and "weakness" with respect to the control of contention also vary in different historical periods. Neither state strength nor prevailing

---

[14] Note that Kriesi and his collaborators found a lower level of mobilization for France only in the so-called "new" social movements; traditional class-based movements were more vigorous. These findings are contested by the enormous level of street protests described by Olivier Fillieule in his book *Stratégies de la Rue* (1997), based on close examination of French police files on protests.

strategies are exogenous of political factors, which change as the result of wars, elections, party realignments, and shifts in public opinion. A state that is "strong" in the hands of a unified majority or under a strong leader can easily become "weak" when that majority is divided, or opposition to it grows. And a state that is strong when it enjoys the confidence of business weakens when inflation soars and capital moves abroad. When a new political configuration appears – for example, with the perceived threat to domestic security after 9/11 – the supposedly weak American state turns stronger and is ready to roll back civil rights and civil liberties (Margulies 2006; Sidel 2004; Vitale 2007).

Temporary divisions in the political elite are easy to mistake for a structurally weak state. Thus, from the defeat of the Federalists and the election of Jefferson in 1800 until the Civil War, the regionally divided American elite limited the size of the American state. When that war reduced the South both militarily and politically, the state became much stronger – a "Yankee Leviathan," in Richard Bensel's terms (1991). Conversely, the "strong" French state under General de Gaulle was weakened under his less charismatic and ideologically divided followers after the 1960s, and France became one of the most protest-prone countries in the West (Fillieule and Tartakowsky 2008).

WAR, COERCION, AND CONTENTION

Although the American state may have been "weak" in some absolute sense when Tocqueville studied it in the 1830s, in the train of two World Wars, the Cold War, and the War on Terror, the American state has become a national security state that can hardly be considered "weak." Similarly, the British state, which shares America's tolerance of peaceful dissent, has constructed a dense network of CCTV cameras – 4.2 million of them, or about one for every fourteen people.[15]

Wars ratchet up the coercion of dissatisfied minorities and those who oppose the decision to go to war. From the opposition to the Alien and Sedition acts in the 1790s, to the jailing of Americans unwilling to serve in the Civil War, to the persecution of pacifists and radicals who opposed entry into World War I, to the internment of Japanese-American in camps in World War II, to the oppression of Communists and "fellow travelers" in the Cold War, wars and "quasi-wars" have strengthened the American state and ratcheted up coercion of minorities and opponents. As Elizabeth Kier and Ronald R. Krebs write: "Democracies often compromise their principles during crises: Executive authority grows, rights of due process are set aside, and freedom of expression suffers" (2010: 1).

Yet a contrarian view suggests the following: The long-term effect of war making for democratic regimes may actually be positive. In his historical analysis of war and state building, Charles Tilly argued that the requisites of war making obliged rulers to build stronger states, collect taxes, conscript soldiers,

---

[15] See http://news.bbc.co.uk/2/hi/uk_news/6108496.stm. Accessed March 19, 2010.

and expand the reach of the state (Tilly 1990). To gain consent for war and inspire citizens to support war-making efforts, rulers extended rights, expanded protection, and ultimately created the modern welfare state. War, Tilly maintained, created the conditions for "white-hot bargaining" between citizens and their states. In the twentieth century, war gave a push to women's suffrage, to the GI Bill of Rights, to votes for 18-year-olds, and to the expansion of modern civil societies. Though the short-term effect of war is often repressive, the indirect effect of war may reinforce the capacity of citizens to make claims on the state.

Regimes, Opportunities, and Threats

Strength and weakness, prevailing strategies toward protest, historical and spatial differences, and war and citizenship come together in the concept of regime. Tilly (2006: 19) classifies regimes along two main axes:

- *Governmental capacity*: the degree to which governmental actions affect distributions of populations, activities and resources within the government's jurisdiction, relative to some standard of quality and efficiency
- *Democracy:* the extent to which persons subject to the government's authority have broad, equal rights to influence governmental affairs and to receive protection from arbitrary governmental action (p. 21)

High-capacity democratic regimes produce an enormous concentration of social movements. This is obvious when we recall that social movements depend on regime-backed rights, notably rights of association, assembly, and speech (Tilly, p. 188). Low-capacity regimes exert significant control over contention close to their operating bases – especially in the capital – "but intervene in contention much less vigorously, effectively, and continuously outside of that zone" (p. 211). High-capacity undemocratic regimes throttle the development of independent civil society organizations and repress dissent and, as a result, produce few and mainly unsustained social movements. Lacking regime-backed rights, they tilt away from channeling and toward the coercion of contention. Lacking the sensitivity to the buildup to consent that comes from a highly developed political society, when contention appears, it erupts violently.

CONCLUSIONS

This typology, as Tilly would have been the first to admit, is largely static. It is also unidirectional, predicting forms and levels of contention from stable aspects of regimes. And it assumes that the state is a natural unit isolated from global and transnational trends. What we need to do next is begin to look at the dynamic relations between social movements, political contention, and regimes, and at the embedding of national patterns of contention in world politics. This we will attempt to do in Part III. In Chapter 9, I will return to the general issues raised in Chapter 1 regarding the relational nature of contention. In Chapter 10, employing this approach, I will turn to the cyclical patterns of the rise and fall of contention in different types of regimes. In Chapter 11, I will examine the impact of contention on regimes, policies and citizen politics. And in Chapter 12, I will turn to the transnational embedding of contentious politics.

PART III

DYNAMICS OF CONTENTION

9

Mechanisms and Processes of Contention

In Part II of this book, we moved progressively through four of the main powers in movement:

- In Chapter 5, we saw that it is disruption – not violence or convention – that characterizes the most vital insurgent movements. But movements that rely only on disruptive mass action risk slipping into violence and conflict with the police, while those that adopt conventional forms of action may suffer from cooptation of their goals and decline, as the public becomes bored and activists defect.
- In Chapter 6, we saw that social movements depend to a varying extent on three levels of organization: the social networks at their base, the organization of collective action, and some degree of formal organization – however rudimentary. The key to movement dynamism is the social networks that lie at the heart of formal organization and can survive even when these organizations disappear or are repressed.
- Chapter 7 showed that collective action is constructed not only out of organizations, but also out of cognitive frames, collective identities, and emotion work. An uneasy balance is always present between inherited – but passive – mentalities, and action-oriented – but unfamiliar – transformative frames.
- Finally, in Chapter 8, we saw that movements form in the context of widening opportunities and collapsing constraints, but in making opportunities for others, for opponents, and for elites, movements may create the conditions for their own irrelevance or repression.

From time to time in Parts I and II, the powers in movement were seen to be interdependent. For example, innovation in the repertoire of contention can also produce organizational inventions; the organization of collective action often creates frames for the future; identities constructed in the heat of struggle can be called upon when new struggles arise; and opportunities and threats that have produced major clashes are remembered by both challengers and authorities, who create forms of organizations to encourage or prevent their

repetition. But these connections between the powers of movement were incidental to the main task of Part II, which was to explore each of the main powers
in movement. In this concluding section of the book, we will turn more deliberately to the interactions among them by developing a relational approach
to the dynamics of contention.

INTERACTIVE CONTENTION

That interactions take place among repertoires, organizations, frames, identities, opportunities, and threats has long been recognized by students of
contentious politics. Without using this precise language, an older tradition
of scholarship wove narratives in which these elements were to some degree
present. In the stories of the Tea Party, the Babri Mosque, the Chinese Honda
strike, and the collapse of the USSR, opportunities, framing, organization, and
contentious performances came together. But so far, we have not devised a
means for systematically bringing these elements together and putting them in
motion. This remains a fundamental issue in the study of contentious politics,
but some progress has been made in this regard.

Over a decade ago, a group of scholars led by Doug McAdam, John
McCarthy, and Mayer Zald, recognizing the intersection of frames, opportunities, and mobilizing structures, organized a comparative volume in which
each author was explicitly invited to "cross over" from one of the major powers
in movement to another (McAdam, McCarthy, and Zald, eds. 1996). Their volume, *Comparative Perspectives on Social Movements*, made progress toward
an integration of these three topics, but it was limited by a static ontology.
Frames, opportunities and threats, and mobilizing structures were recognized
as interactive elements in contentious politics, but how they joined in the process of contention remained implicit for most of the authors they assembled –
including this one (Tarrow 1996).

One reason why this integration remained incomplete was that the subject
of research was often seen as a single actor – a social movement or, even more
narrowly, a movement organization. It was recognized that movements operate
in a broader field of action, but the dynamics of that field, the interaction
between movements and other actors, and the intersection of contentious and
routine politics remained theoretically unspecified. A second reason was that
most of the raw materials for analysis came from a relatively narrow geographic
area: the reformist social movements of North America and Western Europe.
The study of Third World movements, revolutions, civil wars, strike waves,
and terrorism seemed too far removed from the social movements of the West
to draw upon empirically or theoretically, and was left to area specialists to
excavate.

A third reason – and the most important one – was that the mechanisms and
processes that connect the elements in a contentious episode too often were
left unspecified. Actors responded to opportunities and threats; they framed
their movements around collective action frames; and they created movement

organizations or activated old ones. The action in this model was locked into the boxes of a static paradigm, rather than in the mechanisms and processes that connect the elements in the paradigm to each other and to other actors. Not only that: Except for the path-breaking work of Charles Tilly, the independent impact of particular performances on the dynamic of contention was seldom brought into the equation (Tilly 2008).

In the decade and a half since the publication of *Comparative Perspectives*, a mechanism-and-process approach to social action has gained ground, both in the social sciences in general and in the study of contentious politics in particular. A first move in this direction was actually made in the 1980s by David Snow and his collaborators, who specified different forms of social movement framing (Snow et al. 1986). Students of diffusion, such as Sarah Soule, were also studying mechanisms – particularly the complex of mechanisms that constitute diffusion (Soule 1997; 2004). McAdam himself had made a creative move in the direction of a relational analysis of contention in his work on the strategic interaction between the Civil Rights movement and authorities in different Southern cities (1983). More recently, David Meyer and Suzanne Staggenborg examined the interaction between movements and countermovements (1996, 1998) in a dynamic framework, and Ann Mische specified a variety of relational mechanisms in her study of networks of Brazilian youth movements (Mische 2008).

Specifying the mechanisms among actors in episodes of contentious politics can help to put these episodes in motion. Mechanisms are a delimited class of changes that alter relations among specific sets of elements in identical or closely similar ways over a variety of situations (McAdam et al. 2001; *Mobilization* 2011). Mechanisms compound into processes, regular combinations and sequences of mechanisms that produce similar transformations of those elements. Some mechanisms and processes – such as the attribution of opportunity or threat, the adoption of new performances, and the construction of new identities – have already appeared in this book. Others will be elaborated in this chapter and in the rest of Part III.

What is so different about this mechanism-and-process approach to contentious politics? We can begin to understand how it differs from the correlational approach that has been dominant in the social sciences by thinking of the differences between the physical and biological sciences. Some social scientists yearn for explanations such as those in physics that ask how input and output variables co-vary. Mechanism-based explanations are different: Their logic comes closer to the logic of biology, in which the goal is to show how different mechanisms combine into small-scale processes such as reproduction, or large-scale ones such as evolution. The equivalent in the study of contentious politics consists of small-scale processes such as diffusion and scale shift (Givan, Roberts, and Soule, eds. 2010) or large-scale ones such as revolutions, democratization, or nationalism (McAdam et al. 2001: Chapters 7–9). Students of mechanisms and processes are less interested in the "why" of contentious politics than in its "how." In this respect, they are closer to the strong advocates of "process tracing" in comparative and international politics than to traditional variable-based analysis (George and Bennett 2004).

But students of mechanisms are not *un*interested in variable-based analysis; they see mechanisms as the connective fabric between variables of interest to students of contentious politics. Take the well-known correlation between membership in informal networks and activism that we explored in Chapter 6. That correlation could be the result of several different mechanisms: of the social control that leading members of a group impose on other members; of the mutual trust that produces a propensity to take risky action (remember Tan Guocheng and his Hunanese network in Chapter 6); of simple (and even provisional) proximity of interests; or of the activation of underlying norms of the community by interaction within the network. Identifying a link between networks and collective action is only the first step in a causal analysis; identifying the causal mechanism or mechanisms that produce that correlation is a far more important step that often is left inferential by analyses of correlation.

We can distinguish four main ways of getting at mechanism-process accounts of contentious politics:

- *Common process accounts*, which identify similar streams of contention and ask whether recurrence of a given process helps to explain the similarity among those streams; thus, Valerie Bunce and Sharon Wolchik identify similarities in the process of challenging electoral fraud in eleven post-Soviet systems in their work on the so-called "color revolutions" (2011).
- *Local process accounts*, which take processes whose operation analysts have established in other settings and apply them to particular instances – often combining more than one well-established process for a more complete explanation; thus, Daniel Sherman applies the concepts of political opportunity and influential allies to his work on low-level radioactive waste, finding that the first does not correlate with success or failure of anti-sitting movements, but that the second does (Sherman 2011).
- *Process generalization accounts*, which concentrate on the process itself, asking in general how it arises and what effects it produces under different conditions. In this spirit, Bogdan Vasi investigates the local conditions affecting the rise and diffusion of the movement against the U.S. Patriot Act (Vasi 2011).
- *Site comparison accounts*, which seek to identify significant differences in the frequency, origin, or consequences of certain processes across different types of sites. In a site comparison account, Katie Furuyama and David Meyer compare the process of certification of two ethnic-American movement organizations (Furuyama and Meyer 2011).

What's Up, DOC?

In the early 2000s, an attempt was made to draw these insights together in a comparative and historical exploration of the mechanisms and processes of contention in a variety of settings, in *Dynamics of Contention* (henceforth "DOC"; McAdam et al. 2001). Together with Doug McAdam and the late Charles Tilly, we tried hard to build a relational approach to contentious politics by specifying the major mechanisms and processes that appear not just in social movements, but in strike waves, civil wars, revolutions, and so forth. The book focused to some extent on the factors contributing to the emergence of contentious action and to some extent on its outcomes, but most of its message centered on the processes of contention between inputs and outcomes.

For example, its authors tried to show that – however different the actors and however great the intensity of contention – major episodes such as Spanish democratization, the Nicaraguan Revolution, the failed rebellion in China in 1989, and nationalism in the former Soviet Union shared a number of key mechanisms and processes. Three main types of mechanisms were identified and explored in the book:

- Dispositional mechanisms, such as the perception and attribution of opportunity or threat
- Environmental mechanisms, such as population growth or resource depletion
- And relational mechanisms, such as the brokerage of a coalition among actors with no previous contact by a third actor who has contact with both.

Sometimes a single mechanism, such as the emergence of new coordination, can initiate a new episode of contention. But no complex outcome ever results from the operation of a single causal mechanism. Take brokerage – the production of a new connection between previously unconnected actors; it will have a major effect only through the activation of additional mechanisms, such as those that produce diffusion (see below). Through the new connection, ideas, frames, and practices flow that affect claim making at both the origin and the destination of the diffusion process. Often these new ideas, frames, and practices themselves facilitate coordination between sites. In Chapter 12, we will see how a very few key ideas that came out of meetings and protests in the late 1990s activated the coordination of a wave of international days of action targeting international financial institutions.

All three types of mechanisms – dispositional, environmental, and relational – are combined in complex cycles of contention. Think of the run-up to the American Civil War: It combined a major environmental mechanism (the growth of population in the North and West while the South's population remained static); a major relational mechanism (the brokerage of a coalition between Western small farmers seeking "free land for free men" and northern Abolitionists); and a dispositional mechanism (the growing opposition between a Northern work culture and a Southern culture of gentility). No single mechanism could have produced a war between the states, but this combination of mechanisms created a spiral of opportunities, threats, and uncertainties.

Although *Dynamics* stirred up a lively scholarly discussion when it was published, even specialists who were sympathetic to its approach made three justified complaints about the book. First, it tossed off mechanisms and processes with abandon without defining or documenting them carefully, much less showing how they worked. Second, it remained unclear what methods and evidence students and scholars could use to check out its explorations. Third, instead of making a straightforward presentation of its teachings, the book reveled in complications, asides, and illustrations (see *Mobilization* 2003).

Happily, *Dynamics* was not an isolated effort. In the last decade, the mechanism-and-process approach has made great progress in the broad field of contentious politics, especially among younger scholars. For example, in a 2011 issue of *Mobilization*, a number of mostly younger scholars came together to explore and extend the mechanism-and-process approach. Mark Beissinger applies a mechanistic approach to the "color revolutions" in the former Soviet bloc; Roger Karapin surveys a number of mechanisms in the American Women's movement of the late nineteenth century to trace spirals of opportunity and threat; Dan Sherman examines the mechanisms that were triggered in local opposition to the storing of low-level radioactive waste in the United States; Michael Heaney and Fabio Rojas demonstrate how coalition formation and narrowing affected the American peace movement between the beginning of the Iraq War and the election of Barack Obama; and Bogdan Vasi shows how opposition to the U.S. Patriot Act diffused during the same period (all in *Mobilization* 2011).

In this and the next three chapters, I will explore how a relational approach based on mechanisms and processes can help us put the powers in the traditional canon of social movement theory into motion. In the next chapter, the approach will be employed to examine "cycles of contention" – the trajectories of complex episodes of contentious politics. In Chapter 11, it will be used to examine the major outcomes of movements. In Chapter 12, the approach will be applied to examining a major challenge to the state-based nature of the literature on social movements – transnational contention. Here I will simply illustrate some of the key mechanisms that drive the dynamics of contention.

Mechanisms of Mobilization and Demobilization

Mobilization is perhaps the most basic process in the study of social movements; without it, no collective action would take place. Touching off the process are broad change processes that affect both challengers and authorities. These are the types of processes – such as appropriation of a surplus and accumulation of capital – that Marx had in mind with his macro-historical model of the factors that he predicted would lead to revolution. The political process begins when these processes become manifest. They manifest themselves in four main ways of interest to the process of mobilization:

- Both challengers and those they face engage in interpretation of what is happening – they frame the field of contention.

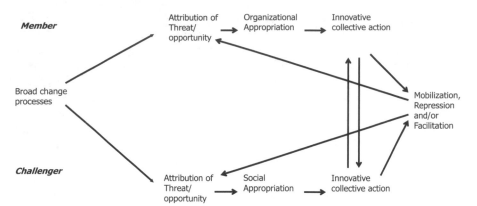

FIGURE 9.1. A Dynamic, Interactive Framework for Analyzing Mobilization in Contentious Politics. *Source:* Adapted from Doug McAdam, et al., *Dynamics of Contention*, p. 45. Copyright © 2001 Cambridge University Press. Reprinted with permission.

- Both challengers and those they face perceive opportunities and threats in these processes.
- Both challengers and authorities create or appropriate resources, organizations, and institutions to take advantage of opportunities and ward off threats.
- Challengers engage in innovative collective action to attract supporters and impress or threaten authorities, while the latter organize to oppose or appease them.

The result is mobilization, followed by its repression or facilitation or some combination of the two, resulting in demobilization. A simple version of this process, reducing the players to a single challenger and a single authority, is presented in graphic form in Figure 9.1 from The *Dynamics of Contention* project (also see McAdam 1999 [1982]).

Note that, in reality, most episodes of contention are far more complex than the sketch in Figure 9.1. They involve challengers who do not always agree on their aims or their methods, authorities who are often divided between those who favor repression and those who favor facilitation, and the media that play an important role in framing the episode for a broader public, as well as bystanders and third parties. The purpose of the diagram is to illustrate the essentially *relational* nature of contentious politics. It suggests that we cannot predict the outcome of any episode of contention by focusing only on a single movement or movement organization's mobilization and demobilization. As opportunities widen and information spreads about the susceptibility of a political system to challenge, not only activists, but also ordinary people, begin to test the limits of social control. Clashes between early challengers and authorities reveal the weak points of the latter and the strengths of the former, inviting even timid social actors to align themselves on one side or another.

Once triggered by a situation of generally widening opportunities, information cascades outward and political learning accelerates. As Hill and Rothchild write, "As protests and riots erupt among groups that have long histories of conflict, they stimulate other citizens in similar circumstances to reflect more often on their own background of grievance and mass action" (1992: 193).

During such periods, as we will see in the next chapter, opportunities created by early risers provide incentives for new movement organizations to be created. Even conventional interest groups are tempted by unconventional collective action. Alliances are formed – often across the shifting boundary between challengers and members of the polity. New forms of contention are experimented with and diffused. A dense and interactive "social movement sector" appears, in which organizations cooperate and compete (Garner and Zald 1985). This depiction of the process of mobilization is not fundamentally different than the classical social movement canon, but it is more explicit in focusing on the arrows in the paradigm in Figure 9.1, rather than on the content of the "boxes" that they connect.

Mechanisms of Demobilization

The social movement field has developed to a high degree our knowledge of the process of mobilization; it has been far less successful in analyzing the processes of *demobilization* that inevitably follow it. Note that I used the plural process*es* of demobilization, because the evidence suggests that, once episodes of mobilization are triggered, so many other actors and institutions are activated that it is not possible to talk about a single process of demobilization. Turning to the mechanisms that we see in demobilization, we can isolate five important ones:

- *Repression* or, more generally, control of contention (see Chapter 8), but also its opposite
- *Facilitation*, which satisfies at least some of the claims of contenders, who may also retreat from the struggle because of
- *Exhaustion*, the simple weariness of being in the streets or, more subtly, irritation and the strains of collective life in a movement.

Finally, two linked but opposing mechanisms are often simultaneous:

- *Radicalization* – the shift of social movement organizations, or parts of them, toward increased assertiveness, and
- *Institutionalization* – the incorporation of some other organizations or parts of them into the routines of organized politics.

In the next chapter, as we trace the mechanisms and processes in several cycles of contention, we will encounter all these mechanisms in different combinations. Here we turn to three processes and mechanisms that we find in all major processes of mobilization: campaigning, coalition formation, and diffusion.

Campaigning and Coalition Formation

A campaign is a sustained, organized public effort making collective claims on targeted authorities (Tilly and Tarrow 2007: 119). It can constitute new actors, a recognizable set of people who carry on collective action, making and/or receiving collective claims. But it can also activate coalitions of different actors who come together instrumentally around collective claims and disperse when the campaign is over. In contrast to a one-time petition, declaration, or mass meeting, campaigns extend beyond any single event.

Campaigns contain public performances, but they also contain media efforts, educational activities, and lobbying. A campaign always links at least three parties: a group of self-designated claimants who claim, *inter alia*, to represent a particular constituency; some object(s) of claims; and a public of some kind. Claims may target government officials, but the "authorities" targeted can also include owners of property, religious functionaries, and others whose actions (or failures to act) significantly affect the welfare of the claimed constituency.

Campaigns often grow out of single protest events and take their shape around the initial conflict in those events and their organization. Remember how the Solidarity network emerged from a single industrial dispute in Gdansk? Its demand for a free trade union and the invention of a (literal) "round table" to meet with Communist Party and government officials became the template for a broader campaign that soon spread around the country, involving not only workers but intellectuals, farmers, state officials, and even some elements of the ruling Communist Party.

The Solidarity movement helps us to identify a second key process: coalition formation. Coalitions I define, with Margaret Levi and Gillian Murphy (2006), as "collaborative, means-oriented arrangements that permit distinct organizational entities to pool resources in order to effect change." Many factors can produce the desire to form a coalition, including ideological proximity (Park 2008), the desire to pool resources (Staggenborg 1986), the need to combine against a common threat (McCammon and Campbell 2002), the urge to produce solidarity among the members of neighboring categories (Van Dyke 2003), and, in institutionally structured environments, the desire to put together a minimum-winning coalition (Levi and Murphy 2006). The most important incentive to forming a coalition involves helping a group gain in numbers, unity, legitimacy, and political influence against more powerful enemies (Hathaway and Meyer 1997).

Campaigns are mounted and coalitions formed almost always when weak actors challenge stronger ones or elites or authorities (Meyer and Corrigall-Brown 2006). For example, Jürgen Gerhards and Dieter Rucht studied two protest campaigns in Berlin, in which literally hundreds of separate organizations combined in protest coalitions against more powerful actors (Gerhards and Rucht 1992). Such broad coalitions are particularly notable in transnational campaigns (see Chapter 12 and Bandy and Smith, eds. 2004). But they are important in all rapidly changing situations in which old alignments are coming apart, new issues are suddenly placed on the agenda, old social movement organizations have become set in their ways, and new ones are still in the process of formation – in other words, during cycles of contention.

Diffusion and Scale Shift

The process of diffusion results from people's decisions to take advantage of opportunities that have been demonstrated by other groups' actions. It occurs when groups make gains that invite others to seek similar outcomes; when someone's ox is gored by demands made by insurgent groups; and when the predominance of an organization or institution is threatened, and it responds by adopting collective action (Soule 2004).

Students of contention Rebecca Givan, Kenneth Roberts, and Sarah Soule have identified three main pathways of diffusion:

- *Direct or "relational" diffusion*, "whereby repertoires or frames are transmitted through personal contacts, organizational linkages, or associational networks"
- *Indirect diffusion*, "as when instantaneous global communications project images that elicit demonstration effects among social actors that are otherwise unconnected"
- *Mediated diffusion*, "such as when two activist groups are not directly connected to one another, but are each connected to a third, mediating group or actor" (Givan, Roberts, and Soule 2010: p. 2).

Diffusion occurs in all major episodes of contentious politics, but during cycles of contention, when existing relationships are destabilized (Koopmans 2004), newly mobilized actors are especially attentive to what others are doing and are less constrained than they might have been to behave in expected ways. Diffusion does not require direct contact when homologies between actors are present, and actors learn what others like themselves are doing. Thus, Sarah Soule found that the spread of the shantytown performance across American college campuses could best be explained among educational institutions that were similar along certain dimensions. "The construction of categories of similarity served as indirect channels between colleges and universities . . . , leading to the diffusion of the shantytown tactic during the student apartheid movement" (2004: 298).

The importance of indirect pathways of diffusion points to the role of the media in diffusion processes. Daniel Myers (2000) shows that national media attention was associated with the spread of the 1960s urban riots at the national level, while smaller riots that received only local media attention increased riot propensity only at the local level. The Internet, of course, plays an even broader role in diffusing contention because it is not limited by local or national boundaries. But although diffusion through the Internet may have greater "reach" than direct diffusion or diffusion through traditional media, it lacks the interpersonal ties needed to create trust between initiators and adopters;

thus coordinated contention that spreads through the Internet may be less easily sustained than contention that diffuses through these more traditional forms.

Scale Shift

Sometimes, contention diffuses to different levels of the polity, where actors encounter a different set of incentives and constraints, sometimes even spreading to other states or to international institutions. This is what has been called "scale shift" (Tarrow and McAdam 2005). It differs from horizontal diffusion in that it triggers institutional routines that threaten collective actors who were relatively safe at lower levels, or engages elites in transactions that lead to at least partial institutionalization of claims. Scale shift can move contention upward in a polity – for example, when national elites respond to a set of local protests by bringing in national armed forces to repress them or by defending the rights of protesters against oppressive local elites. The former is what Soviet elites attempted to do when peripheral minorities protested in the Baltic states in 1988–1991; the latter was the response of the Eisenhower and Kennedy administrations when the Southern states were refusing to allow African American students to register for classes: they sent in the troops and turned a regional dispute into a national conflict over civil rights.

Scale shift can also move contention downward in a polity, when national issues are taken up at the local level. An important part of the "Tea Party" episode occurred when members of Congress returned to their districts for summer recess and were harangued by angry residents for their support of the Obama Administration's healthcare plans. We will see examples of both upward and downward scale shift in the next chapter.

CONCLUSIONS

These explorations of some of the major mechanisms and processes in contentious episodes lay the groundwork for the analyses to follow. Our relational approach suggests, first, why I think it is not particularly fruitful to examine the trajectories of single social movements apart from their interactions with significant others. In general cycles of contention, policy elites respond not to the claims of any individual group or movement, but to the overall degree of turbulence and to the demands made by elites and opinion groups, which only partially correspond to the demands of those they claim to represent. These are the issues we will turn to in the next chapter.

A relational approach also tells us why it is difficult to examine how one social movement's efforts produce, or fail to produce, the policy outcomes the group desires. From the point of view of the outcomes of social movements, the important point is that, although movements usually conceive of themselves as outside of and opposed to institutions, acting collectively inserts them into complex political networks, and thus within the reach of the state. If nothing else, movements try to enunciate demands in terms of frames of meaning that are comprehensible to a wider society; they use forms of collective action drawn from an existing repertoire; and they develop types of organization that often mimic the organizations of those they oppose. The outcomes of episodes of contention are the main subject of Chapter 11.

The relational approach will also help us to place national episodes of contention in a broader geographic framework, as we will do in Chapter 12. So far, our discussions have been limited to national polities, and this is a reasonable limitation, given that social movements arose with the national state, and that their major opportunities and constraints are bounded by national polities. But in the last decade or so, contention has broadened beyond national boundaries. Chapter 12 will examine the mechanisms and processes of this expansion. The conclusions will turn to what this may mean for the place of the national state in the world polity.

10

Cycles of Contention

THE FIRST MODERN CYCLE[1]

In the winter and spring of 1848, rebellions broke out all over Europe. In parts of the continent, the bad crop yields of the previous years were the main cause, but in other areas, harvests had been improving.[2] In some countries, disputes over the suffrage were the trigger for the agitations, but in others, the vote had already been expanded to the middle class, and in others this became an issue only after agitation erupted. Finally, religious and ethnic cleavages were the source of the struggles in some countries, while in others, no communal conflict was visible.[3] Yet from the start, the uprisings of early 1848 struck observers as a single event of continental importance – what we will call a *cycle of contention*. Echoes of these events were felt as far away as Latin America (Weyland 2009).

Although revolution first stirred in Switzerland and Italy, eventually spreading to France, Germany, Austria, Hungary, and the Balkans, the shadow of the first French Revolution chilled the souls of the royal rulers who had returned to power in 1815. That revolution focused primarily on political rights. But as this one gathered force, the social question began to emerge. In his 1847 program

---

[1] The following section summarizes parts of the analysis in Sarah Soule and Sidney Tarrow, "Acting Collectively, 1847–1849: How the Repertoire of Collective Action Changed and Where It Happened" (1991).

[2] For a survey of the main background causes of the revolutions in the various European countries, see Roger Price, *The Revolutions of 1848* (1989), and the excellent basic bibliography he provides.

[3] Generally speaking, religious cleavages were dominant in Switzerland, ethnic and nationalist ones in the Hapsburg Empire outside of Austria, and issues of political representation in France, Germany, and Austria itself. Although the national question came to dominate the Italian *quarantotto*, it began with agitations for liberal reform in Rome and the Kingdom of the Two Sicilies; only as it moved northward to areas controlled by the Hapsburgs did it take on a nationalist coloration. In France and Germany, although food riots occurred in the early stages of the conflagration, the major axes of conflict involved representative institutions and workers' rights.

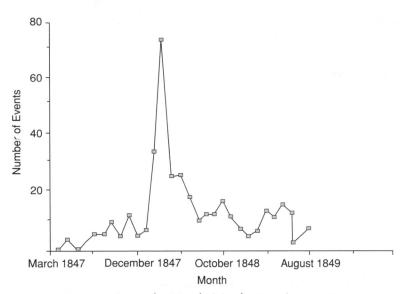

FIGURE 10.1. 1848 Events by Month, March 1847–August 1849

for the moderate opposition, Tocqueville foresaw this expansion into the social: "The time is coming," he prophesied, "when the country will again be divided between two great parties; soon the political struggle will be between the haves and the have-nots; property will be the great battlefield" (1987: 12–13).

Tocqueville's fears were exaggerated. The 1848 Revolution was not yet the social revolution of the future, but it frightened elites by spreading more rapidly than any revolution in the past.[4] Following the tumult of the early weeks, the specter of social revolution empowered democrats and frightened liberals all over Europe, and it threw constitutional monarchists into the hands of the Right. The revolutionary coalitions soon broke up, and, after a period of retreat, conservative governments recovered their self-control and swept the insurgents from the field.

Yet as long as the revolutionary cycle lasted, all regimes were threatened or overturned, and people marched and met, organized assemblies and committees, and erected barricades. Rulers scurried to places of safety or rushed through reforms to forestall further rebellion. Figure 10.1, coded from François Godechot's chronology (1971), demonstrates the dramatic rise and fall in both conflict and response by combining the number of contentious public events for all major European states for which he provides information for the years 1847

---

[4] Marx understood this well. As he shrewdly writes, in his *Eigtheenth Brumaire,* "Bourgeois revolutions, like those of the eighteenth century, storm more swiftly from success to success ... soon they have attained their zenith and a long depression lays hold of society.... Proletarian revolutions ... criticize themselves constantly, interrupt themselves continually in their own course, come back to the apparently accomplished in order to begin it afresh ... " (1978: 597).

through 1849.[5] Godechot's chronology provides us with a graphic picture of what revolution looked like in mid-nineteenth century Europe.

Contention rose all over Europe, but a more detailed analysis of Godechot's data tells us how much they differed – from a single peak of contention in France and Austria to a more punctuated cycle in Italy and Germany; from mostly violent encounters in Hungary and the Balkans to a mixture of transgressive and contained contention in Belgium and France (Soule and Tarrow 1991; Weyland 2009); and from liberal claims in the West to nationalist demands in the South and East. But apart from Godechot and a few others, the historical literature has constructed the 1848 events as A Single Thing: The People rose up; they sent their rulers temporarily packing; after a time, they were defeated.

Seen from a distance, this picture is not inaccurate: What it lacks is a disaggregated account of the initial conditions and strategic decisions, as well as the mechanisms and processes through which mobilization engaged elites and authorities, led to coalitions and protest campaigns, radicalized and divided, and ultimately gave way to very different outcomes. It also lacks an account of the mechanisms that combined with each other and with different contexts to produce these different outcomes from place to place.

To understand the 1848 events, and to help us examine more recent cycles of contention, we can disaggregate that "Great Event" into a number of mechanisms and processes:

- *Making Opportunities:* Although propagandists for the revolutionaries and many academics emphasized the deep cleavages in their societies, in fact contention began in cautiously liberalizing regimes, such as Belgium and Switzerland, where reforms opened the way for moderates to seek expansion of the suffrage. Even in backward Italy, it was reforms promised by a newly elected Pope that encouraged insurgency. In France, it was the legal "banquet" campaign by the liberals that offered democrats the opening that led to the violent February Days. It was only when these opportunities were exploited and the vulnerabilities of authorities exposed that contention spread to the lower classes and to more authoritarian regimes to the East.
- *Innovation in the Repertoire:* As in many of the cycles that followed, the peak of contention was marked by expansion of new forms of collective action – public meetings, demonstrations, barricades – as well as by more traditional violence against landowners, bakers, and Jews. The barricades that spread rapidly across Europe were the most dramatic form of action and the best remembered (Traugott 1990; 1995; 2010). But traditional public meetings and conventions marked most of these revolutions too, as well as violence, especially when the revolutions moved East, and ethnic groups used the disorder to take vengeance on their enemies.

[5] No information is provided by Godechot for Scandinavia (except for the brief war between Denmark and Prussia over Schleswig-Holstein); none for Greece and Portugal; and none for the European parts of the Ottoman Empire. For a more detailed analysis of his data and of some of the problems that they present, see Soule and Tarrow, "Acting Collectively."

- *Protest Campaigns and Coalition Formation:* No single social group advanced the revolution. As liberal and conservative gentlemen were holding sober meetings and learned conferences in Paris and Berlin, republicans were organizing demonstrations, workers and artisans were building barricades, and peasants were attacking landlords and taking over forest reserves. These objective coalitions would eventually fall apart, but in the "springtime of peoples," it seemed to supporters as well as to elites that entire societies were rising up in unison. These campaigns were often halting and disorganized, but they provided models for future political campaigns.

The dynamics of the conflict described some major processes that were briefly sketched in the last chapter:

- *Diffusion:* As in past episodes, France was the epicenter of contention. Once Paris revolted, agitation spread to Italy, Belgium, Germany, Austria, and the rest of the Hapsburg Empire. As it spread, the same signature repertoire of committees, public meetings, and barricades appeared over and over. The barricades themselves were an instrument of diffusion; people heard about them and rushed to copy what the French had done in the streets of Paris.
- *Exhaustion:* The initial euphoria of the "springtime of peoples" soon evaporated; people wearied of life in the streets; some went home, others joined liberal governments, still others turned to reaction. *"Post coitum omnia animal triste,"* writes Aristide Zolberg, quoting the old adage to reflect the disillusionment that follows waves of contention (1972: 205–206).
- *Radicalization/Institutionalization:* No single pattern of radicalization was noted, but in many places, campaigns begun in parliaments and public meetings encouraged people to organize in the streets. As the revolutions progressed beyond the effervescence of the spring of 1848, the peaceful demonstration and the public meeting began to disappear from Godechot's chronology. In France, the banquet campaign gave republicans the opportunity to outbid their competitors; in Italy, liberal reformers in the North gave Garibaldi and other radicals the signal to launch assaults; and in the Habsburg domains, the agitations for a more Lliberal monarchy triggered violent revolts by subject peoples in the Balkans. Yet the same revolutions also saw attempts at institutionalization, especially where liberals and moderates met to attempt to work out constitutional compromises between monarchy and representation.
- *Restabilization:* Normalization took two main forms: repression and facilitation. In France, a new Republic was declared and elections organized. In Switzerland, a Confederation was created under the control of Protestant liberal cantons. But in October, the Kaiser retracted the reforms he had conceded in Prussia the previous spring. In the Balkans and in Italy, order was restored with the intervention of the foreign armies. By the end of 1848, a picture of almost unrelieved armed strife, foreign intervention, and the collapse of popular collective action emerges from Godechot's chronology.

Similar to many other protest cycles, the 1848 Revolution left the most bitter memories where the hopes it generated were highest. At first welcomed across Europe, the 1848ers were soon denounced for their "hollow rhetoric, their mystical idealism . . . and their generous illusions" (Sigmann 1973: 10). In Germany, the year was soon labeled "*das tolle Jahr*" (the crazy year), while the British ambassador to Paris wrote that 1848 left "almost every individual less happy, every country less prosperous, every people not only less free but less hopeful of freedom hereafter" (quoted in Postgate 1955: 266). In Italy, even today, the expression to "*fare un quarantotto*" (i.e., "to make a 48") has come to mean to create confusion.

But something is missing from this picture: It leaves out authorities, who do not sit idly by as challengers contest their rule. They can respond weakly or strongly, selectively or generally, intelligently or stupidly, to the emergence of contention, setting a pattern of interaction that affects, and often empowers, other challengers (Goldstone 1998; Koopmans 2004). These factors establish broader cycles of contention than the individual movements that have filled most academic treatments of contentious politics, and lead to divergent outcomes that cannot be encapsulated in a simple parabola of contention. In combination, they determine whether a burst of contention will sputter out like a roman candle or ripen into a cycle of contention – or a revolution. It is to understanding when and how contention broadens into general cycles and revolutions, and when it gives way to rapid normalization, that this chapter is devoted.

Definition and Elements of Cycles

By a "cycle of contention," I mean a phase of heightened conflict across the social system, with rapid diffusion of collective action from more mobilized to less mobilized sectors, a rapid pace of innovation in the forms of contention employed, the creation of new or transformed collective action frames, a combination of organized and unorganized participation, and sequences of intensified information flow and interaction between challengers and authorities. Such widespread contention produces externalities, which give challengers at least a temporary advantage and allow them to overcome the weaknesses in their resource base. It demands that states devise broad strategies of response that are repressive or facilitative, or a combination of the two. And it produces general outcomes that are more than the sum of the results of an aggregate of unconnected events.

Particular movement campaigns also exhibit cyclical behavior, as David Meyer's work on nuclear weapons protest showed (1990; 1993). These single-issue or single-constituency oriented cycles do not overlap perfectly with the broader society-wide cycles of contention, but aggregate to form them. The same has been true of environmental campaigns; they arose as part of the "new social movement" cycle in the 1970s (Kriesi et al. 1995), but then took on a life of their own, to eventually converge in the "climate change" cycle of the first decade of this century (Hadden 2010).

When we turn to social scientists' research on cycles, we find an odd paradox. Though recognizing their importance for social movements, scholars have been more apt to pay attention to individuals, movements, and movement organizations than to the broad waves of contention that mark much of modern history. Even students of revolution have often ignored the role of particular movements within revolutionary cycles (but see Goldstone 1998). This has occurred in part because of the tendency to see revolutions as unique Great Events, distinct from other forms of contention, rather than as processes (for an exception, see Tilly 1993). Once we understand them as processes, their analogies with and differences from other forms of contention are set in relief.

The idea that entire systems go through cyclical dynamics has been found mainly among three main groups of scholars: cultural theorists who see changes in culture and political and social change interrelated (Brand 1990; Rochon 1998; Swidler 1986); political historians and historical economists who look for regular cycles of political or economic change (Schlesinger 1986; Hirschman 1982); and social theorists who see changes in collective action resulting from changes in states and capitalism (Elias 1994; Tilly 1986: Chapter 1). The first group of scholars emphasized the globality of cycles, the second their regularity, and the third their derivation from structural change.

In recent years, sociologists and political scientists have begun to examine the internal dynamics of cycles of contention. Much of this work focuses on the dynamics of particular systems.[6] In an in-depth analysis of the French Revolution, William Sewell Jr. embedded his analysis of the taking of the Bastille in a broader dynamic of contention and ideological rupture (Sewell 1996). Focusing on Italian protest event data, this author showed how transgressive contention grew out of, and eventually transformed, routine politics in that country (Tarrow 1989). Focusing on the first Intifada, Karen Rasler found a similar pattern of radicalization to what I found in Italy (2004), but Carol Mueller found a different dynamic in the East German protest cycle of 1989 (1999). Working in the United States, David Meyer (1993) and Jeff Larson and Sarah Soule found different dynamics in different sectors of contention. Larson and Soule also found a high level of tactical overlap between sectors connected to the growth in numbers of protest events (Larson and Soule 2009).

Much of this work grew out of the political process approach that was surveyed earlier in this study. Working mainly in Germany, Ruud Koopmans applied a version of that approach to that country's cycle of new social movements (Koopmans 1993; Kriesi et al. 1995). Hanspeter Kriesi's foundational dataset was the source of Jai Kwan Jung's innovative event history study, which

---

[6] A major study in progress, led by Sarah Soule, with her collaborators Susan Olzak, John McCarthy, and Doug McAdam, will allow scholars to trace the emergence and permutations of the 1960s cycle in the United States. For the dataset and code book, go to /www.stanford. edu/group/collectiveaction/cgi-bin/drupal/. Published and unpublished reports from the study will be found at www.stanford.edu/group/collectiveaction/cgi-bin/drupal/node/13. I am grateful to Soule for this information and for her advice on earlier versions of this chapter.

demonstrated a different logic during the mobilizing and demobilizing phases of the cycles he studied (2010). Summarizing this rich tradition of research – including his own – Koopmans advises,

> ... we must move beyond single movements, and consider dynamic inter-actions among a multitude of contenders, including not only challenging protesters, but also their allies and adversaries – elite and nonelite, as well as the whole range of forms of claims-making from the most conventional and institutionalized, to the most provocative and disruptive (2004: 21).

That is exactly the approach of this chapter, and indeed, of the entire book. Within such periods, organizations and authorities, and movements and interest groups, members of the polity and challengers interact, conflict, and cooperate. The dynamic of the cycle is the outcome of their interaction. "Actions," writes Pam Oliver, "can affect the likelihood of other actions by creating occasions for action, by altering material conditions, by changing a group's social organization, by altering beliefs, or by adding knowledge" (1989: 2). These actions create uncertainty and transmit information, opening the way for new actors and undermining the calculations on which existing commitments are based. This leads regime supporters to trim their sails, and opponents to make new calculations of interest and alliance. The outcome depends less on the balance of power between and the resources of any pair of opponents than on the generalized structure of contention and the responses of elites, opponents, and potential allies to each other. This is why, as we will see below, although the beginnings of such cycles are often similar, their endings are far more disparate.

Opportunities and Cycles

The generalization of conflict into a cycle of contention occurs when political opportunities are opened for well-placed "early risers"; when their claims resonate with those of significant others; and when these give rise to coalitions and conflicts among disparate actors and create or reinforce instability in the elite. This co-occurrence and coalescence are furthered by state responses rejecting the claims of the early risers – thereby encouraging their assimilation to other possible claimants, while lowering constraints and offering opportunities for broader contention.[7]

Of course, as Chapter 8 emphasized, an opportunity unseen is an opportunity that, for all practical purposes, does not exist. This gives particular importance to the mechanism of "signaling" and to the media of communication through which both the determination of challengers and the vulnerability of their targets are signaled. During periods of increased contention, information

---

[7] Jack Goldstone argues that "where the existing regime and policies are widely viewed as undesirable, the environment for protest is highly supportive. Under such conditions, the emergence of a protest movement, and its mild handling by the state, is likely to encourage others.... this sequence tends to build to form a society-wide cycle of protest" (1998: 141).

flows more rapidly, political attention is heightened, and interactions among groups of challengers and between them and authorities increase in frequency and intensity. This gives particular importance to information brokers and to communities of discourse that are prepared to interpret new information in new ways to potential challengers (Rochon 1998).

Cycles of contention are usually remembered for big, bold, and system-threatening claims, but the early demands that trigger a cycle are often narrow and group-specific, similar to the middle-class demands for suffrage expansion that led to 1848 in France. These narrowly focused claims do three important things. First, they demonstrate the vulnerability of authorities to contention, signaling to potential allies that the time is ripe for their own claims to be translated into action. Second, they "challenge the interests of other contenders, either because the distribution of benefits to one group will diminish the rewards available for another, or because the demands directly attack the interests of an established group" (Tilly 1993: 13). Third, they suggest convergences between challengers and members of the polity that result in cross-sectoral coalitions.

Some scholars have found strong connections between the opening of political opportunities and the rise of cycles of contention (Alimi 2006, Brockett 1995, McAdam 1999 [1982], Osa 2001, Tarrow 1989); others have found negative relationships between openings and collective action (Inclán 2009); and still others have found a more differentiated picture (Meyer 2004). Most interesting is how different phases of a protest cycle increase, reduce, or produce changes in opportunities. Recently, in his reanalysis of the Kriesi et al. data on new social movements in Europe, Jai Kwan Jung goes even further: He finds that while the classical political opportunity model helps to explain the emergence of contention at the outset of protest cycles, it bears no detectable relationship to contention during the demobilization phase (Jung 2010).

PHASES OF OPPORTUNITY AND CONSTRAINT

Once opened, spirals of opportunity do not work in the same ways for everyone and for the entire length of a cycle (Karapin 2011). The opportunities that are opened to "early risers" in a cycle may not be available to late-comers, and these early risers themselves create opportunities for others – not only to others sympathetic to their cause. Thus, as we saw in Chapter 8, the democratic reformers who tipped the Communist regime over the edge in the Soviet Union created opportunities for peripheral nationalists who sought to break away from the USSR, but not always in democratic directions (Beissinger 2002). Moreover, not all those who are inspired by the demonstration effect of "early risers" have the resources to succeed. The democratic reformers against the hybrid authoritarian regimes in Eastern Europe and the Balkans at the turn of the new century created opportunities that weaker opposition movements in Central Asia thought they could take advantage of against stronger and more ruthless regimes, but they mainly failed (Bunce and Wolchik 2011; Beissinger 2007).

Doug McAdam, whose work on the Civil Rights movement inspired much of the recent work on cycles (1999 [1982]), has suggested a sharp distinction between "initiator" and "spin-off" movements. Though based on American data, McAdam's theory also resonates with the findings of Charles Brockett in Central America, who distinguished sharply between early and late stages of a cycle in terms of the willingness and capacity of regimes to repress insurgents (1995). Lorenzo Bosi found that changes in opportunity in Northern Ireland directly affected how insurgents framed their movement (2006).

The findings of these authors do not invalidate the idea that, in certain periods of history, insurgency appears in many parts of a society. On the contrary, they reinforce the caution expressed earlier that such periods cannot be studied *en bloc* as if they were single "movements," but must be disaggregated into innovations they produce, campaigns and coalitions, and mechanisms of mobilization and demobilization. Let us begin with innovations in the repertoire (Goldstone 1998).

Innovations in Cycles

At any time, innovations in how people challenge authorities are likely to gain the notice of elites, other groups, and the media (Koopmans 2004: 24–26). "Occasionally," Koopmans notes, "dissident groups are able to invent new combinations of identities, tactics, and demands. These creative moments are extremely important, for they may provide the initial sparks that expose regime weaknesses" (p. 25). Cycles of contention are often touched off by such innovations. Think of the unanticipated defeat of the British at Lexington and Concord that we saw in Chapter 3; or the taking of the Bastille by a rag-tag army of the poor in 1789 in Paris (Sewell 1996); or the Sunday demonstrations in Leipzig that helped to set off the collapse of the East German state in 1989 (Lohmann 1994). In all of these episodes, an innovation in protest performances both attracted supporters and left elites at least temporarily unprepared.

Different cycles of contention become identified with specific forms of action and with changes in the repertoire. The barricade in the 1848 revolutions; the factory occupations in the industrial conflicts following World War I and in the 1930s (Spriano 1975; Piven and Cloward 1977); the sit-ins during the American Civil Rights movements (Andrews and Biggs 2006); and the shantytown constructions during the anti-Apartheid movement in the 1980s (Soule 1997) – these innovations became symbols of their respective cycles of contention and helped to keep the flame of mobilization alive, often after its initial fuel was consumed.

Of course, not all the innovations that appear in these periods of generalized contention survive past the end of the cycle. Some are directly linked to the peak of contention, when it seems as if anything is possible and the world will be transformed (Zolberg 1972). Others depend on the high level of participation and information flow characteristic of the peaks of cycles and cannot be sustained when mobilization declines and the media turn to other issues. Some are eventually abandoned when they fail to move elites to respond to claims (Soule 1999), while others are limited by the threat of repression. The forces of order may be temporarily disoriented when they face unexpected masses of challengers on the streets, but when elites regroup, tactics that seemed unassailable at the height of the cycle can be easily crushed or discouraged (Gillham and Noakes 2007; Wood 2007).

Cycles often produce new or transformed symbols, frames of meaning, and ideologies to justify and dignify collective action. Cycles of contention are the crucibles within which new cultural constructs born among critical communities are created, tested, and refined (Rochon 1998; Valocchi 1999). These enter the culture in more diffuse and less militant form, where they can serve as sources for the symbols of future movements. As we saw in Chapter 7, the rights frame at the heart of the African American Civil Rights movement eventually became a "master frame" for a number of other movements during the cycle of the 1960s and 1970s (Snow and Benford 1992).

Organizational growth coincides with these additions to the repertoire. The emergence of a cycle is often marked by the appearance of "spontaneous" forms of action, but even at this phase, both previous organizational traditions and newly organized movements shape their direction and outcomes. Nor do "old" organizations necessarily give way to new ones in the course of the cycle: Many existing organizations – such as the National Association for the Advancement of Colored People (NAACP) at the height of the Civil Rights movement – adopt the radical tactics of their competitors and adjust their discourse into a broader, more aggressive public stance. In Italy in 1968, after the traditional trade unions were upstaged by the emergence of spontaneous shopfloor committees, they adopted these innovations and eventually institutionalized them as part of their repertoire (Regalia 1984).

Dynamic Elements in Contentious Cycles

Early students of revolutionary cycles, including Crane Brinton (1965), posited a set succession of stages, much like those that characterize biological development or the stages of disease. We now know that too many factors vary around the central processes of widespread contention for such unilinear models to help in comparing different revolutions. States may respond with repression, with facilitation, or with the combination of selective repression and partial reform that seems to be the most successful way to normalize the situation. If nothing else, external factors – such as foreign troops in the 1848 revolutions – intervene, shifting the internal balance of power and bringing the cycle to an abrupt close (Koopmans 2004: 39).

Perhaps reacting against the rigidity of stage theories, some students of revolution turned away from the internal processes by which cycles of contention develop, focusing on the recurring conditions that lead to revolution (Skocpol 1979, 1994; Wickham-Crowley 1992) or delving into historical narrative, often filled with rich evidence about agency or contingency. The best of these studies theorized narratives for relatively short periods and condensed events (Sewell 1996) or constructed general narratives out of sets of personal stories (Selbin 1993; 2010). But it is rare to find a theorized narrative that explains why a cycle will move inexorably forward up to a certain point and then sometimes will just as rapidly decline.

We do not possess a powerful enough general theory to allow us to delineate all the recurring elements in all cycles of contention (Koopmans 2004: 29). If we did, it might so flatten the different species of contention as to be of little use, as Goldstone points out (1998: 125–126). What we can propose is a series of causal mechanisms that transform distinct challenges into generalized contention, and we can compare these mechanisms in cycles in which conditions and outcomes may be similar or different.[8] Three sets of mechanisms appear to be present in a wide range of cycles: diffusion, exhaustion, and radicalization/institutionalization.

THE DIFFUSION OF CONFLICT

What is most distinctive about cycles of contention is not that entire societies "rise" in the same direction at the same time (they seldom do), or that particular population groups act in the same way over and over, but that the demonstration effect of collective action on the part of a group of "early risers" triggers a variety of processes of diffusion, extension, imitation, and reaction among groups that are normally more quiescent and have fewer resources to engage in collective action.

A key characteristic of cycles is the diffusion of a propensity for collective action from its initiator to formerly unrelated groups and to its antagonists. The former respond to the demonstration effect of a challenge that succeeds – or at least escapes suppression – to add their efforts to those of the earlier risers; the latter respond to threats to their interests posed by the successes of these early risers. This produces the countermovements that are a frequent reaction to the onset of contention (Meyer and Staggenborg 1996) and – in cases of collapsing states – to the spirals of retaliatory violence that can lead to civil war (Kalyvas 2007). Ethnic violence spreads not because people like to imitate what other people do, but because the mobilization of one ethnic identity triggers reactions on the part of others who fear that their survival or their interests will be threatened by gains made or by early risers.

Another recurring property of diffusion is what we called "scale shift" in the last chapter. This is a question not only of the spread of contention, but of its shift to levels of the polity in which new opponents, new potential alliances, and different institutional settings shape its progress. This can make contention more transgressive or more contained. It was when the Tienanmen Square

---

[8] This is the same procedure that Ruud Koopmans adopts in his synthetic essay on "Protest in Time and Space" (2004). He proposes a slightly different set of key mechanisms in his essay than the ones elaborated here.

Rebellion of 1989 began to spread from Chinese students to workers and others that the regime sent in the army to repress it. On the other hand, it was when the American "freeze" movement of the 1980s shifted from town meetings and campus protests to the national level that it was taken up by a wing of the Democratic Party and lost its transgressive edge (Meyer 1990).

Cycles of contention have broad paths of diffusion, some of which are traceable from large cities to the rural periphery or from the periphery to the center. They often spread from heavy industrial areas to adjacent areas of light industry and farming, along river valleys, or through other major routes of communication. They spread among members of the same ethnic or national groups, whose identities are activated by new opportunities and threats, as was the case among Serbs, Croats, and Muslims in the former Yugoslavia in the early 1990s. Widespread contention brings about uncertainty and fear, and the breakdown of functional ties that this produces increases the salience of preexisting ties such as ethnicity, religion, or other forms of mutual recognition, trust, and cooperation. It is around growth of such trust networks out of spirals of retaliatory violence that militant nationalist groups are formed (Tilly 2005).

EXHAUSTION

Although street protests, demonstrations, and violence are exhilarating at first, as movements organize, activists argue over methods and goals, and divide into factions, they involve risk, personal costs, and, eventually, weariness and disillusionment. What results is a decline in participation – one that can be encouraged when political authorities and the forces of order are intelligent enough to bide their time and wait for exhaustion to take hold, as occurred in the spring of 1848.

But participation does not decline at an equal pace for all sectors of a movement. Those at the periphery of a challenge, lacking strong motivation, are the most likely to defect, while those close to its core are most likely to persist. As a general rule, the former are more moderate in their actions; as they defect, their absence shifts the balance of the core conversely; because the latter are more militant, they are more likely to support radicalization of contention. Unequal rates of defection between the center and periphery of a movement shift the balance from moderate to radical claims and from peaceful to violent protest.

This unequal decline in participation poses a dilemma for movement leadership. Aware that their strength lies in numbers, they may respond to the decline in participation by embracing more moderate demands and attempting to compromise with opponents. Conversely, to keep the support of more militant elements, they may attempt to keep the fire alive by making radical claims and intensifying contention. In either case, the differential decline in support leads to polarization between those willing to compromise with authorities and those who seek continued confrontation. This leads to a complementary pair of mechanisms: radicalization and institutionalization.

RADICALIZATION/INSTITUTIONALIZATION

"Why is it that some social movements engaged in politics of contention experience splintering and adoption of more unruly and violent forms of contention on the part of member factions – a process commonly labeled radicalization – whereas others do not?" So asks Israeli political scientist Eitan Alimi, when introducing his paired comparison of two Jewish settler contentious campaigns against their exclusion from Palestinian lands (forthcoming). Other movements shift to contained forms of contention, structured by elections, negotiation, and institutionalization. What is most interesting about cycles of contention is that radicalization and institutionalization can occur at the same time and are mutually constitutive (Meyer 1993; Tarrow 1989).

Cycles of contention stimulate competitive mobilization among organizations in the same social movement families (Tarrow 1989). Competition may arise from ideological conflicts, from competition for space in a static organizational space, or from personal conflicts for power between leaders. Whatever its source, a common outcome of competition is radicalization: *a shift in ideological commitments toward the extremes and/or the adoption of more disruptive and violent forms of contention*. Radicalization also results from increased state pressure on insurgents. As Koopmans deduced from his work on Germany; "If the regime offers few channels of access, responds by repression and is unwilling to reform, radicalization will be the dominant outcome" (2004: 29).

Radicalization, according to Alimi, also results from lack of coordination. Comparing the largely nonviolent Gaza Strip pullout versus the violence of the Amona evacuation from the Palestinian West Bank in February 2006, he writes,

> in the Gaza Pullout case it was the willingness and ability of leaders from the various actors involved to voluntarily form and maintain a set of rules of engagement, expectations, and tacit understandings based on formal or informal contacts, exchange of information, dialogue and negotiations – labeled here as *infrastructure of coordination*. . . . Conversely, it was the disintegration of this same infrastructure of coordination during the run up to Amona that facilitated the saliency of perceptual and environmental mechanisms, and in the process triggered radicalization (forthcoming, p. 4).

Of course, increased access and government concessions may whet the appetite of some protesters. This is why institutionalization often accompanies radicalization. By this term, I mean *a movement away from extreme ideologies and/or the adoption of more conventional and less disruptive forms of contention.* Just as some activists are pushed into extreme forms of action by competition, repression, and frustration, others will seek accommodations with elites and electoral advantage, and to do so, they moderate their goals. Think of the Tea Party activists we met in Chapter 5: As they moved from raucous town hall meetings to the electoral arena, they moderated their claims to appeal to centrist Republican Party voters.

Radicalization and institutionalization are, of course, contrary processes, and only the most inchoate and decentralized movement organizations engage in both simultaneously. But as I have argued earlier, protest cycles are *not* unified movements, and they seldom come under the control of single movement organizations. More often, the growth in popular participation in the upward phase of a cycle invites organizational proliferation, and these new organizations compete for space with each other and with early risers.

Competition between radicals and moderates often takes the form of a conflict over violence. When moderate leaders institutionalize their tactics to retain mass support, radical competitors may employ confrontational tactics to gain the support of the militants and prevent backsliding. The former have a repugnance for violence, while the latter often use it and sometimes elevate it to a higher form of politics to justify its use against their enemies.

The battle between the Girondins and the Jacobins in the radical phase of the French Revolution was a good historical example of such conflicts. It was triggered by a dispute over whether to execute the King, with the Jacobins calling for regicide, and the Girondins, who opposed it, soon following Louis XVI to the guillotine. Within the British Chartists, a long debate about the virtues of physical versus moral action took place. And as we have seen, on the European Left, anarchists and Social Democrats were divided over the violence of the former and the moderation of the latter.

In recent decades, movement cycles have produced similar polarizations between institutionalization and radicalization. Jai Kwan Jung's reanalysis of the Kriesi data clearly shows that the demobilization phase of the "new social movement" cycle was marked by a combination of violence and institutionalization (2010). Even within the largely peaceful American Civil Rights movement, the debate between the older, moderate wing of the movement and the young firebrands who challenged it for leadership was about both violence and the wisdom of pushing for radical economic gains, as opposed to consolidating the political rights won in the early 1960s. As the movement's center of gravity shifted from South to North, a peaceful mass movement gave way to the practice of organized violence and thence to movement collapse. But here we must bring a third element into play – the reactions of the state.

Repression and Facilitation

In his synthesis of research findings and theory on cycles of contention, Ruud Koopmans sees the ends of such cycles as what he calls "restabilization." He writes, "The contraction of protest waves is best conceptualized as a process of *restabilization* and reroutinization of patterns of interaction within the polity" (2004: 37). By this term, Koopmans does not simply mean the contraction of contention; what he means is that at the end of protest cycles, "*the relationships between actors* become more stable" (p. 38). But what remains unspecified is how these relationships become stabilized. I identify two major mechanisms – repression and facilitation – and describe how they interact with the dynamics of radicalization and institutionalization already under way.

REPRESSION

As we saw earlier, governmental repression can take many forms and can operate with varying effectiveness. "Where the government is able to focus its repressive measures squarely on the movement supporters," writes Goldstone, "and uses violence and imprisonment to curtail their actions, repression is likely to either end the movement or drive it underground." But where repression is unfocused, inconsistent, and arbitrary, or where it is limited by international or domestic pressures, "the movement is likely to attract supporters while becoming more radicalized in its goals and actions" (Goldstone 1998:130).

Authoritarian regimes typically respond to contention with extreme repression, as was the case in the response to the Tienanmen Square Rebellion in China in 1989 (Calhoun 1995a). But extreme forms of repression are less typical of contemporary cycles in democratic societies than they are in authoritarian regimes. Far more common is the selective facilitation of some groups' claims and the selective repression of others. For example, Goldstone points out how rulers in the Philippines, Colombia, and Kenya successfully worked to split off elites from peasants and workers (1998: 139–142).[9] By negotiating with some elements among a spectrum of contenders, these governments encouraged moderation and split off the moderates from their radical allies.

But restabilization is never easy: Especially when it coincides with the decline in mass support and polarization inside the movement, the policy of facilitation and selective repression can push radicals into more sectarian forms of organization and more violent forms of action, and can push moderates into the arms of conservatives. At the extreme, the combination of partial demobilization, polarization, and selective repression and facilitation can produce terrorism (della Porta 1995: Chapter 6).

FACILITATION

As we will see in the next chapter, governments often respond to protest waves with reform. But reform seldom takes the shape demanded by protesters. This is not only because protesters typically make their claims in extreme form, but also because claims are raised in competition with competing and complementary claims and are processed through a mixture of state and nonstate actors and veto groups. What cycles of contention often do is increase the marginal power of intermediate groups, which claim the mantle of change without engaging in transgressive behavior. This was why Martin Luther King emerged as a symbol of the Civil Rights movement – when much of the heavy lifting was done by more aggressive groups such as the Student Nonviolent Coordinating Committee (SNCC) and the Congress of Racial Equality (CORE). It is only in

---

[9] But more rigid authoritarianisms – similar to that of the Shah of Iran – were doomed by a pattern of repression that was indiscriminately aimed at economic, religious, and technical elites, thus creating a national cross-class coalition against him (Goldstone 1998: 138–139).

revolutionary cycles that the radical wings of a spectrum of challengers gain enough purchase to outbid their competitors.

Revolutionary and Nonrevolutionary Cycles

Even the casual reader will notice that I have dealt indifferently with a truly revolutionary cycle – 1848 – and with more recent cycles of contention, such as the 1960s, which few would call revolutionary without seriously stretching that concept. This conflation of revolutionary and nonrevolutionary cycles is an intended provocation, for so isolated has the study of revolution become that we need to remember that revolutions are a species of contention driven by many of the same processes and mechanisms we have canvassed above – mobilization, signaling, diffusion, radicalization, institutionalization, repression, and facilitation.[10]

As we have seen earlier, parallels between cycles of protest and revolutionary processes abound. To see them, we need, first, a distinction between revolutionary situations and revolutionary outcomes (Tilly 1993). While revolutionary situations are moments of deep fragmentation in state power, revolutionary outcomes are effective transfers of state power to new sets of actors. A full-fledged revolution combines the two. Great revolutions typically fall into several phases: situation-outcome-new situation-outcome, and so on, until some set of political actors consolidates its hold over the state and beats down the next round of challengers.

With hindsight, we can say that a revolution can occur when states have lost the capacity to maintain their basic functions, and when at least two contenders claim sovereignty (Tilly 1993).[11] We can see such a situation in stark outline with the outbreak of the Russian Revolution in February 1917. The Czar's government had lost both control and legitimacy because of its wartime failures. When the opposition was strengthened by defections at the front and the state was weakened by interrupted food supplies in the cities, and sapped by peasant discontent, Lenin and his Bolsheviks consolidated their support by calling for "bread, land, and peace."

Because so many potentially revolutionary situations exist in these terms, as in protest cycles, we can only trace those that will produce revolutions by careful analysis of the political process that leads from revolutionary conditions to revolutionary outcomes. In both movement cycles and revolutions, a successful challenge by one previously disadvantaged actor simultaneously (1) advertises the vulnerability of authorities, (2) provides a model for effective claim making,

[10] See Goldstone, 1998, for an important challenge to the tradition of separating the analysis of revolutions from social movements.

[11] Tilly specifies this as more than one contender for power, each of which has substantial support from within the population. When some regimes fall apart, however, they turn out to have little support from any substantial group within society – as when the apparently powerful Shah of Iran fled ignominiously because it turned out that he had little support.

(3) identifies possible allies for other challengers, (4) alters the existing relations of challengers and power holders to each other, and (5) thereby threatens the interests of yet other political actors who have stakes in the *status quo*, thus activating them as well.

Such a situation becomes revolutionary if and when the elites in place reject all competing claims and when some challengers with claims to sovereignty gain power, then league together to fortify their positions against new challengers – a process that eventually splits mobilized actors between regime members and outsiders, demobilizes some outsiders, and drives the remainder toward increasingly risky actions. The dynamic processes described earlier can help to distinguish such revolutionary routes from more ordinary cycles of contention. When elites respond to broad-ranging claims from coalitions of challengers by blind repression and refusal of concessions to any of them, a sense of outrage and heightened solidarity counteracts the process of polarization and halts defections. Goldstone puts it this way:

> In the case of a revolutionary movement, while it may begin as a movement to achieve certain policy or attitudinal goals, it evolves into a collaborative effort of diverse groups with diverse policy goals into a movement that aims to overthrow the state. It evolves in that direction precisely because the state adopts a repressive stance of resolute resistance: it prohibits or sharply circumscribes movement actions, strongly opposes all who ally with the movement, and may eliminate the movement and its supporters (1998: 128).

A mechanism that helps to turn a movement cycle into a revolutionary one is the defection of members of the elite to the opposition because they are outraged by the government's brutal repression and lack of flexibility, or because they have the desire to advance their own interests and values, or both (McAdam et al. 2001). This was the great – and largely unexpected – aspect of the 1989 "revolutions" in Eastern Europe, when even police associated with the dreaded German Democratic Republic held back from attacking demonstrators in Leipzig and East Berlin and a number of regime elites turned from "apparachniks" into "entrepreneurchiks" (Solnick 1998).

Revolutionary situations, then, resemble the opening of new social movement challenges to the existing polity. One becomes the other to the extent that challenges multiply, put at risk the stakes of all existing potential actors in the system, and lead to governmental choices that both repress all opposition and unwittingly throw advantages to the regime's most determined opponents. Social movements, protest cycles, and revolutions, as Goldstone concludes,

> are not different *genera* of social phenomena. . . . But neither are they simply the same phenomenon, differing only by degrees from mild to extreme. Instead, they are best thought of as a family of related phenomena, originating in a similar set of circumstances, but evolving and diverging in consequence of distinct patterns in the interplay between protest movements, state response, the broader social environment, and cultural evaluations of state and protest actions (1998: 142–143).

The Ends of Cycles

Viewed from a distance, waves of collective action from the 1848 revolutions to twentieth century revolutionary cycles to the more contained waves of contention in Europe and America since the 1960s describe parabolas from institutional conflict to enthusiastic peaks of contention, to ultimate collapse, or – in the case of successful revolutions – the consolidation of new regimes. In a simple version of cyclical theory, after gaining national attention and state response, peaks of conflict are marked by the presence of organizers who try to diffuse the insurgencies to broader publics. As participation is channeled into organization, the parts of the movements that emerge in the early phases of the cycle take on a more political logic – engaging in implicit bargaining with authorities. As the cycle winds down, exhaustion and polarization spread, and the initiative shifts to elites and parties.

But the multipolarity of the interactions in these cycles and the diverse reactions of the authorities to challenges make their endings far less similar than their beginnings. The diffusion of collective action from early risers to late-comers, the shift of political opportunities from early challengers to their allies and elites, the different choices governments make about which groups to repress and which to facilitate, and splits between radicals and moderates – these increase the number and variety of interactions in the course of the cycle and – as in the wake of the 1848 revolutions – send them off in divergent directions.

CONCLUSIONS

What then do cycles of contention leave behind? In the next chapter, we will turn to the complicated issue of outcomes and impacts, but it may be useful to conclude this chapter with a look at what happens to the movement organizations created during such cycles. Hanspeter Kriesi has proposed a broad array of organizational trajectories from the common core of the "new social movements" that emerged in Western Europe in the 1970s and 1980s (1996). Based on whether constituents participate in politics directly or indirectly and whether they make claims on authorities or within society, Kriesi identifies four main trajectories, which are reproduced in Figure 10.2.

First, of course, is the process of *institutionalization,* which combines the formalization of the internal structure of an SMO with moderation of its goals. This is the pattern that Michels identified in European Social Democracy as it adapted its "minimal programme" to the routines of parliamentary democracy. But many of the actual trajectories of movement organizations break Michels' "Iron Law" (Clemens and Minkoff 2004); three other trajectories emerged from the "new social movement" cycle that Kriesi studied:

First, he identified a processs that he called *commercialization,* that is, the transformation of a movement organization into a service organization or profit-making enterprise. This is the process that Hayagreeva Rao found in

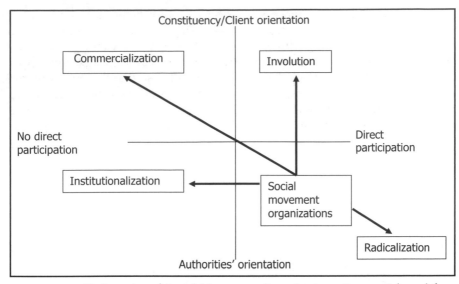

FIGURE 10.2. Trajectories of Social Movement Organizations. *Source:* Adapted from Hanspeter Kriesi, "The Organizational Structure of New Social Movements in a Political Context." In Doug McAdam et al., *Comparative Perspectives on Social Movements*, p. 157. Copyright © 1996 Cambridge University Press. Reprinted with permission.

the trajectory of the American consumer movement (1998), and that Michael Lounsbury found in the transformation of the American recycling movement (2005). Both began as mission-oriented movement organizations and gradually transmuted into commercial or nonprofit organizations. Another example comes from the European "autonomous" cooperative sector, which grew out of the environmental movement and drew on the desire of veterans of the movement to live a "green" way of life.

Second is the process of *involution* – a path that leads to exclusive emphasis on social incentives. Many of the communes that grew out of the American sixties' experiences shifted from active participation in politics to the cultivation of personal and religious development. In a more informal way, women's consciousness-raising groups in the 1970s sometimes evolved into self-help groups.

Finally, Kriesi identifies a third alternative to the Iron Law – *radicalization,* or "reinvigorated mobilization," which we saw in the escalation of collective violence in the American Weathermen and the Italian advocates of armed struggle. Indeed no Iron Law exists, but a variety of exits from activism are present, apart from the exhaustion and privatization that was the modal outcome predicted by Hirschman (1982) and others after the 1960s cycle.

Kriesi's typology is useful because he identifies the variety of ways in which classical movement organizations evolve. It also helps us to place movement cycles in broader ranges of history. It suggests the variety of ways in which a contentious cycle leaves sediments in its wake, and it helps us to understand how future social movement organizations can mobilize activists even after the cycle has ended. By joining self-help groups, working for service organizations, supporting parties and interest groups, and sometimes radicalizing, activists can keep up their contacts with old friends and comrades, so that they are available for mobilization when the next cycle of contention appears. But because the outcomes of protest cycles are never as uniform as their beginnings, we need to give particular attention to movement outcomes, which is the subject of Chapter 11.

Struggling to Reform[1]

"Struggling to reform": What a strange term to use in introducing a discussion of the impacts of social movements! Movement activists demand fundamental social change, the recognition of new identities, entry into the polity, the destruction of their enemies, or the overthrow of a social order – but seldom just "reform." Indeed when, as we saw in the last chapter, movements empower a general cycle of contention, claims become so broad and elites so besieged that profound changes are forced onto the agenda. Nevertheless, as I will argue in this chapter, few movements "succeed" in achieving their demands in anything like their original form. At best, they contribute to collective goods that benefit those they claim to represent; at worst, the structure of politics through which new claims are processed forces them into a common crucible from which reform is the best they can expect. The political process, this chapter will argue, is not only the context within which claims are made (Amenta 2006), but the mechanism through which claims are structured, narrowed, and often reversed (Lipsky and Olson 1976; Piven and Cloward 1977).

THE AMBIGUITY OF POLICY OUTCOMES

For many years, analysts of social movements have bewailed our lack of knowledge of their policy outcomes (Giugni 1998; Marx and Wood 1975). In the absence of convincing information on movement outcomes, a number of taxonomies have been produced – almost as many as there are studies of the subject. The best-known typology is also the simplest and the most often used – that of William Gamson. In his classic, *The Strategy of Social Protest*, Gamson distinguished between challengers who receive new advantages and those who gain acceptance (1990: Chapter 1). This produced his familiar fourfold

[1] Of all the chapters in this book, this one has had the longest life. It is the descendant of an occasional paper by the same title, published by the Cornell University Western Societies Program and revised with the title "Struggle, Politics and Reform" (Tarrow 1989b).

classification of "full response" and "defeat" at the two extremes, and "coop-tation" and "preemption" in between (Chapter 3). Tom Rochon and Daniel Mazmamian added a third type of outcome – changes in social values (1993). Paul Schumaker identified five kinds of system responsiveness, ranging from "access responsiveness" to "impact responsiveness" (1975), and Paul Burstein and his collaborators added "structural impacts" to Schumaker's list of five (1991).

Recently, this lacuna in social movement research has begun to be filled, and an entire research network has been formed to advance our knowledge of movement outcomes.[2] But as recently as 2008, Marco Giugni still bewailed the unevenness of our knowledge about the outcomes of social movement activities (2008: 1592). Part of the problem is that although it is possible to correlate the timing of outcomes with the timing of movement efforts, it is not as easy to identify particular movement actions as the cause of specific outcomes. Movement actions often coincide with changes in public opinion, interest groups, parties, executives, and administrators, not to mention the impact of other movements (Amenta 2006: 30; Giugni 2008).

The relationship between movements and policy outcomes becomes even more complicated when we recognize that the *targets* of contention – elites, authorities, other groups – respond in different ways to similar opportuni-ties. Looking at Latin American responses to contentious challengers, James Franklin identified four pure types of response – concession, repression, toler-ation, and a combination of concession and repression (2009). Joseph Luders explored these variations in the responses of different Southern states to the Civil Rights movement (2010). Marie Cornwall and her collaborators showed that state legislators and challengers responded differently to the same signals in the women's suffrage movement (2007). While French authorities responded to the "Events of May" with studied restraint, Italian authorities responded to less vigorous threats with uncontrolled violence (della Porta 1995).

Two examples will suffice to illustrate the wide array of factors that can complicate the relationship between movements and policy outcomes:

First, As Paul Burstein writes in his analysis of the struggle for equal employ-ment opportunity legislation, it was "adopted as the result of social changes that were manifested in public opinion, crystallized in the civil rights and women's movements, and transformed into public policy by political leaders" (1985: 125).

Second, benefits to minority groups such as Latinos in the United States might have been the result of efforts of the Latino Rights movement, but they were also the indirect result of the efforts of African American rights campaigners, whose efforts opened the gates through which other ethnic groups could pour (Browning, Marshall, and Tabb 1984).

---

[2] Visit the network's Web site at moveout.statsvet.uu.se/. Literature reviews by Amenta and Caren (2004), Bosi and Uba (2009), Earl (2004), Meyer (2005), and Giugni (2008) are good syntheses of recent findings on the outcomes of movements.

The relative weight of different factors in producing policy outcomes has been a bone of contention. While some, like Burstein and Linton (2002) have seen public opinion washing out the influence of movements in producing political outcomes, others, including Katrin Uba (2009), find no firm support for this hypothesis. And while some scholars think movements have a direct effect on outcomes, others see these effects as indirect, and still others see "joint effects" of movement actions, favorable political opinion, and the presence of influential allies (Amenta 2006, Giugni 2008, Giugni and Yamasaki 2009, Kolb 2007).

International waves of movement or opinion sometimes generate the conviction that change is the result of movement efforts, even in places where movements are weak or absent. For example, the passage of women's suffrage all over the industrialized world was more the result of a transnational wave of opinion resulting from women's sacrifices during the First World War than the product of the women's movement's resources or tactics. Similarly, after the early risers of Poland, Czechoslovakia, and East Germany revolted in 1989, the collapse of other Communist governments was more the result of elite defection than of the strength of domestic movements. The co-occurrence of movement action and political outcomes is difficult to trace to the actions of particular movements.

Strikes and Other Outcomes

Partial exceptions to this complexity are the results of strikes. A series of scholars have analyzed the effects of labor violence, contextual variables, group size, and duration and nature of demands on the outcomes of strikes.[3] The results are not uniform, but for countries as different as late nineteenth century Italy, the United States at mid-twentieth century, and Poland in the 1990s, researchers converge on the finding that "strike threats and strikes were effective in gaining concessions from the government or employers" (Osa 1998). But strikes are somewhat special: The actors are known to each other; the demands are clearly stated and can be quantified; the duration of the protest is short; and the workers are usually autonomous of other groups. In contrast, in broader cycles of contention such as those described in Chapter 10, movements are seldom unified; their demands are often imprecise and utopian; and the dynamic of political change in general may have more to do with their success than their direct efforts.

That is no reason for cynicism. "Success" for some movements may consist more of establishing a collective identity than of achieving policy success (Melucci 1996; Pizzorno 1978; Whittier 1995). It may also consist of placing issues on the political agenda that would not get there without the movement's efforts. And it may leave organizational and cultural residues around which new supporters can mobilize supporters in the next cycle of contention

---

[3] See Taft and Ross (1969), Snyder and Kelly (1976), Shorter and Tilly (1974), and Conell (1978).

(Earl 2004). This has led to an increasing emphasis on "collective goods" outcomes of movement activity, on biographical and cultural change, and on the outcomes of general cycles of contention such as those examined in the last chapter, rather than on the specific goals of individual movement organizations. When state elites are faced by a multitude of relations with allies and challengers, competitors and constituents, they respond not so much to the demands of any single movement as to the generalized conflict structure they face. In such a confrontation, they are more likely to look for lowest-common denominator solutions that will defeat their enemies, reestablish social control, and satisfy allies and supporters than to respond piecemeal to group claims.

The presence of allies within the polity is a particularly important factor in producing such mottled outcomes (Amenta 2006; Lipsky 1968; Jenkins and Perrow 1977). In fact, serving often as brokers between challengers and power holders, allies extract "rents" and can have a greater effect than the movements themselves in shaping elite responses (Burt 1997). The political process gives third parties, interest groups, movement allies and opponents, and state administrators a key role in shaping policy responses. Edwin Amenta takes this observation to its logical conclusion, arguing that

> Challengers' action is more likely to produce results when institutional political actors see benefit in aiding the group the challenger represents.... To secure new benefits, challengers will typically need complementary action from like-minded institutional actors, or other movement organizations, or both (2006: 24).

Amenta's observation is not as obvious as it may sound. For when political parties of the Left take power, progressive movements allied to it may forfeit their disruptive capacity to avoid rocking the political boat (Kriesi et al. 1995). For example, MoveOn.org lost its struggle to end the wars in Iraq and Afghanistan when the Obama administration, which it had helped to elect, came to power in 2009. As Michael Heaney and Fabio Rojas concluded from their extensive research, "The results show that the antiwar movement demobilized as Democrats, who had been motivated to participate by anti-Republican sentiments, withdrew from antiwar protests when the Democratic Party achieved electoral success, if not policy success in ending the wars in Iraq and Afghanistan" (Heaney and Rojas 2011).

That said, what are the factors that can help a movement to succeed? Most students agree that the power to disrupt brings about short-term success. For example, upon reviewing the recurring waves of welfare reform in the United States, Frances Fox Piven and Richard Cloward wrote, "relief arrangements are initiated or expanded during the occasional outbreaks of civil disorder produced by mass unemployment" (1972: xiii). Similarly, the Tillys concluded from their study of a century of conflict in Europe that "no major political rights came into being without readiness of some portions of those (protesting) groups to overcome the resistance of the government and other groups" (1975: 184).

Other scholars have focused less on disruption than on the expansion of participation to new groups to explain movement success (Jenkins and Perrow 1977; Tarrow 1989a and b). In particular, the access of new actors to the polity puts new issues on the agenda. Thus, enlargement of Western electorates to include the working class in the early twentieth century shifted the domestic power balance to parties of progress, which promptly passed welfare legislation and legalized strikes. But it did not noticeably increase the presence of workers in the political elite, and the welfare states that these "progressive" governments created helped the middle classes as much as or more than their working-class supporters (Esping-Anderson 1990). Where suffrage movements failed – for example, as the Swiss women's suffrage movement did for decades – this occurred because "opposition parties never launched an electoral challenge that might have prodded governing parties into action," and elites closed ranks rather than unbalance a carefully constructed internal consensus (Banaszak 1996: 215–216).

Other scholars have pointed to the internal resources, the organizational forms, and the "appropriate strategies" of challengers as clues to their success or failure. For example, whether their organizations are centralized or decentralized; how factionalized they are; whether their demands are far-reaching or limited; whether they have selective incentives to distribute to supporters; and whether they use violence or peaceful means against opponents.[4] Others have focused on environmental changes – such as whether or not a challenging group emerges during a systemic crisis or during more ordinary times (Goldstone 1980). In his extended study of the Townsend movement, Amenta focuses on the phase of the policy process in which a movement attempts to have influence, arguing that the "agenda-setting phase" is when a challenger is most likely to be influential (2006: 28).

But if so many variables appear to explain movement success or failure, how can we identify the factors that are most likely to explain the variance in outcomes? In a multivariate reanalysis of Gamson's data, Homer Steedly and John Foley found that success was related, in order of relative importance, to the nondisplacement (i.e., nonthreatening to elites) nature of their goals, the number of alliances, the absence of factionalism, specific and limited goals, and the willingness to use sanctions against opponents (Steedly and Foley 1979). Most of these variables would have to be regarded as "internal" to a movement, but the importance of alliances in Steedly and Foley's work, as well as Goldstone's findings on the role of periodic political crises (in Goldstone, 1980) and Amenta's research on the Townsend movement (2006), suggests

---

4 William Gamson's *Strategy of Social Protest* (1990) is the required starting point for the analysis of the internal facets of movements that lead to their success. A number of works followed the publication of Gamson's research, some supporting his findings, while others came up with different results. For a thorough review on the replications and criticisms following the publication of Gamson's study, see Marco G. Giugni's "Introduction: How Social Movements Matter" in the volume edited by Giugni with Doug McAdam and Charles Tilly, *How Movements Matter* (1998).

that a combination of internal and contextual, organizational and political, and structural and strategic factors must be present to produce movement success.

Moreover, although cycles of contention such as those that Goldstone identified can produce temporary coalitions for reform, they are usually too brief, too divided, and too dependent on temporary opportunities to provide permanent support once the fear of disorder disappears (Piven and Cloward 1977; Tilly 1998: 262). The rare successes and the frequent reversals of movement policy successes are best expressed by the subtitle of Frances Fox Piven and Richard Cloward's eloquent book, *Poor People's Movements* (1977): "How They Succeed and Why They Fail."

But because they so often fail, because other actors are so often responsible for their supposed successes, and because it is so difficult to assign a particular outcome to a particular movement, why should we care about movement outcomes? The answer is that we can assign a variety of *kinds of outcomes* to movements, apart from policy success or failure. Three kinds of long-term and indirect effects of movements are important:

- The first is their effect on the political socialization and the future activism of the people and groups who participated in them.
- The second are the effects of their struggles on political institutions and practices.
- And the third are their contributions to changes in political culture.

The Political Is Personal

"What we remember most" after the intoxication of a protest cycle, writes Aristide Zolberg, "is that moments of political enthusiasm are followed by bourgeois repression or by charismatic authoritarianism, sometimes by horror but always by the restoration of boredom" (1972: 205). Albert Hirschman goes further, citing a "rebound effect," in which individuals who have thrown themselves into public life with enthusiasm return to private life with a degree of disgust proportional to the effort they have expended (1982: 80).

Why so much disillusionment and such retreat to private life? One reason is that the early participants in a cycle of contention often see it whirl off in directions they never imagined. When two of the founders of the American republic – John Adams and Thomas Jefferson – looked back at what their generation had wrought, they were far from happy. Instead of the republic of virtue they had sought, "America had created a huge, sprawling society that was more egalitarian, more middling, and more dominated by the interests of ordinary people than any that had ever existed" (Wood 1991: 348). Hating the commercial culture that was sweeping the country, Jefferson never appreciated "how much his democratic and egalitarian principles had contributed to its rise" (p. 367). "All, all dead," he wrote to a friend near the end of his life;

"and ourselves left alone amidst a new generation whom we know not, and who knows not us" (p. 368).

Jefferson's disillusionment resulted from the gap between the ambitiousness of his vision for America and the revolution's actual outcomes. The same was true for many 1960s activists in both Europe and the United States; their later disillusionment was in direct proportion to their early utopianism. Activists with narrow goals, such as those in Gamson's studies (1990: Chapter 4) or in the "consensus movements" studied by John McCarthy and Marc Wolfson (1992), are less likely to emerge disillusioned from a protest campaign. But people such as the early participants interviewed after the Italian cycle of contention were more likely to be disillusioned as their utopian projects gave way to party political bargaining (Tarrow 1989a).

Disillusionment may be only a short-term result of activists' disappointment and exhaustion. Through the skills they have learned in struggle, the extension of their beliefs to new sectors of activity, and the survival of friendship networks formed in the movement, activism begets greater readiness to join movements or other civil society groups in the future and directs people toward the service professions and toward making changes in their life courses.[5] In describing his hopes for Freedom Summer, Student Nonviolent Coordinating Committee (SNCC) organizer Bob Moses in 1964 spoke of the "annealing process" that had occurred in Mississippi. For movement activists, "in the 'white heat' of that Mississippi summer . . . , politics became the central organizing force in their lives." From that time forward, "everything else – relationships, work, etc. – got organized around their politics" (McAdam 1988: 186–187).

Other movement cycles led to similar accretions of militancy and politicization. In Indonesia, for those who joined the radical Socialist Youth after World War II, according to Benedict Anderson,

> the tidal-wave rage for politics roared on out of control. Each person felt as though he, she, could not be truly alive without being political, without debating over politics. . . . Politics! politics! No different than rice under the Japanese Occupation (Anderson 1990: 38).

Movement participation is not only politicizing; it is empowering, not only in the psychological sense of increasing people's willingness to take risks, but in affording them new skills and broadened perspectives. Describing her return from Mississippi to the University of California in the fall of 1964, a Freedom Summer volunteer told McAdam, "Everybody knew about the summer project and everybody wanted to ask me what it was like and . . . I was an authority, an

---

[5] The following section is based on the summary by McAdam, "The Biographical Impact of Activism" (1999: 118–22), and on the more detailed analysis in McAdam, Van Dyke, Munch, and Shockey, "Social Movements and the Life-Course" (1998).

instant authority on the civil rights movement" (McAdam: 170). As a result of their politicization, many former Mississippi Summer activists would play key roles in the Free Speech Movement in Berkeley and, later on, in the national student, antiwar, and women's movements (p. 203).

Activists in the women's movement were particularly enriched by their experiences in the Civil Rights movement. Young women who had participated in civil rights activities learned from their experience that their male counterparts often were no less sexist than their opponents. Their resentment, added to the self-confidence they had gained in the South, was a key ingredient in the founding of the new women's movement (Evans 1980: Chapters 4 and 5). Interviewed twenty years later, former Freedom Summer women volunteers were more often involved in contemporary social movements than their male counterparts and were more likely to belong to political organizations (McAdam 1988: 222).

The narratives of other sixties militants, however, tell a mixed story. For some, the sixties left positive memories and produced an enduring activist orientation. For example, Jack Nelson, a successful New Orleans attorney who had taken on a series of cases for the Civil Rights movement in the early 1960s, used the following terms to describe the personal impact of his activity to historian Kim Rogers:

> I changed *my* life. And, rather than trying to change the world by using this person, that organization, I probably started to change my life... And, you know, I said, wait a minute, I gotta change. And I changed, and then everything just came naturally (1993: 172).

Not that everything came as naturally to all sixties activists as it did to Nelson. The more radical Congress of Racial Equality (CORE) and SNCC activists interviewed by Rogers found their postmovement years disappointing. Increasingly cynical about politics, they "despaired of meaningful change through the political process, remaining highly interested but ambivalent about politics, and often yearning for the collective intensity of their pasts" (p. 174).

From One Activism to Another

Mainly generated by films like "The Big Chill," a myth has grown up that former activists routinely discard their radical ideas and turn their talents to exploiting the mainstream. But the evidence for this is slim, and there is much evidence to the contrary. Movement involvement not only politicizes people; it can also radicalize them. Jack Blocker recorded this for the temperance activists of nineteenth century America, who began with attempts at moral persuasion, turned to more aggressive tactics when these tactics failed, and posed more ambitious demands of policymakers (Block 1989: xvi). The same was true of returning Freedom Summer volunteers; when McAdam compared their attitudes to those of applicants who chose not to go to Mississippi, he found that the first group had moved leftward ideologically, while the second remained more moderate.[6]

But neither apathy nor radicalization was the most typical outcome for the generation of the 1960s. Most former activists from that period continued to be active in one or another form of social movement, public interest group, or political activity; others moved from direct-action social movement organizations (SMOs) into service organizations, self-help groups, and parties and interest groups that had a family relation to their original movement homes (see Chapter 10). Only a few became professional movement activists.

These findings have been replicated in a number of studies in both the United States and abroad. In America, nearly half of the former Freedom Summer volunteers McAdam interviewed were active in at least one social movement twenty years later; former Italian activists were likely to be active in one of the country's traditional leftwing parties, in the Green party, or in a social movement (Lange, Irvin, and Tarrow 1989); similarly, former Japanese activists were frequently active in a leftwing political party or movement after graduation (Fendrich and Kraus 1978: 245).

Of course, not all the biographical outcomes of the 1960s activist generation have to do with politics. During the 1970s, writes McAdam, "the activist sub-culture was slowly disintegrating, leaving the volunteers who remained active more and more isolated as the decade wore on" (1988: 205). McAdam calculates that 47 percent of the Freedom Summer volunteers who married after that summer went through a divorce between 1970 and 1979. Among the applicants who chose not to go to Mississippi, the comparable figure was less than 30 percent (p. 208). The personal costs of activism were disproportionately high for women volunteers (pp. 220–221), not necessarily because they preferred a celibate life, but because they were isolated by their independence and Leftism from a political culture that was moving to the Right.

Both in the United States and in Western Europe, former activists suffered occupational instability, changing jobs and extended unemployment more often than nonparticipants. Many of the Freedom Summer volunteers delayed entry onto the job market to continue their activism, entering it only during the stagnant 1970s and never making up for lost career time (McAdam 1988: 109–212). The same was true of former leaders of the Italian movement, *Lotta continua*, many of whom were still working on the margins of the job market when they were interviewed in the mid-1980s.[7] But Western Europe was different from the United States in one important way – in affording members of

---

[6] Similar results were reported after the cycle of contention in Italy: When Carol Mershon compared the attitudes of Italian factory organizers recruited during the "Hot Autumn" of 1969 versus those of their peers, she found the former group to be more likely to see industrial relations in stark class terms (1990: 311–315); Peter Lange and his collaborators found similar effects among Communist Party militants (Lange, Irvin, and Tarrow 1989: 34–36).

[7] Tarrow, *Democracy and Disorder* (1989a: Chapter 11). This observation is based on too few cases to present statistically, but occupational marginality was true of most of the former leaders interviewed.

TABLE 11.1. *Percentage Differences between Those Who Did and Those Who Did Not Engage in New Left Activities, for Three Age Cohorts (b. 1943–1964)*

	Engaged in New Left Activities?	
	Yes (N = 192)	No (N = 897)
Cohabited before marriage	48%	32%
Never married	18%	13%
Has not had children	35%	23%
Mean age at marriage	23.41	21.98
Mean age at birth of first child	26.89	24.26

Source: Adapted with permission from Doug McAdam, "The Biographical Impact of Activism" 1998: 126.

the sixties generation professional outlets in the still-lively mass parties of the Left or the trade unions that were lacking in the United States, where mass parties were absent and the union movement was in decline in the 1970s (Cowie 2010).

In addition to more common divorces, according to McAdam's findings for Freedom Summer veterans and for a larger sample of young Americans (1998: 122–124), participation in New Left activities in the 1960s and 1970s appears to have been associated with a greater tendency for cohabitation before marriage and slightly lower rates of marriage and childless marriage (McAdam 1999: 127). For simplicity, Table 11.1 reproduces only McAdam's simple bivariate results for the larger sample of Americans, although his results were robust for the more complex multivariate models he presents as well (pp. 127–134).

No doubt, personal commitments count for much in the maintenance of activism. But those sixties activists who were still active in Western Europe or the United States decades later were often embedded in networks of former activists – they kept the faith by keeping in touch. As Debra Minkoff writes,

> National SMOs play a critical role in civil society and the production of social capital by providing an infrastructure for collective action, facilitating the development of mediated collective identities that link otherwise marginalized members of society, and shaping public discourse and debate (1997: 606).

FAILED EXPLOSIONS AND SLOW-SPREADING SPARKS

If policy success is difficult to predict for individual movements, and if movement activists often exhaust their energies in the full flush of a cycle, what are the long-term effects of cycles of contention on institutions and practices?

Another way of putting the question is whether their ultimate impacts are proportional to the intensity of their emergence, or whether it is only through incremental growth and generational reproduction that cycles have a long-term impact. The movements we have dealt with in this chapter differ along one key dimension – the degree to which they emerged as full-blown disruptive movements or as slow-growing incremental ones.

In recent years, political scientists have given a great deal of attention to what has come to be called "path dependency," that is, how the nature of the emergence of a collective phenomenon influences its future shape.[8] This "historical-institutional" approach has not yet found its way into the study of contentious politics, but it may help us to understand the connections between how a particular movement emerges and its long-term prospects. Does a movement that emerges explosively and enjoys immediate success have a proportional long-term effect? Or will movements that emerge slowly and incrementally have a more permanent effect? To investigate this question, I will compare two different movements. The first – the French student movement – was the wonder of the Western world when it erupted in May 1968; together with the labor movement that seized the political opportunity to go on a general strike, it paralyzed the Fifth Republic and indirectly forced President de Gaulle to resign. The second – the American women's movement – was slow-starting, appeared only as an offshoot of the Civil Rights movement, and worked, for the most part, within the institutions of American politics. The two movements arose at slightly different stages and had different constituencies, but they both were a part of broader cycles of contention in which they were important elements.

The Exploding French Student Movement[9]

May 1968 in France presents a near-laboratory case for studying the political impact of an explosive wave of protest. As two of its most acute observers argued on its twentieth anniversary,

> despite the retreat of the movement and its rejection in the ballot box, the Events (e.g., of May 1968) were the carriers of potentialities that, by one means or another, durably mortgaged the French political scene in a way that had to be immediately faced (Capdevielle and Mouriaux 1988: 219, author's translation).

The protest wave of May 1968 was followed the next autumn by a major educational reform, the Orientation Law for Higher Education, which

---

[8] The literature on path dependency is vast. For key findings, see Collier and Collier (1991), Mahoney (2000), and Pierson (2004). To my knowledge, no one had applied the path dependency approach to contentious politics except for Tilly, with respect to his theory of repertoires of contention (see Chapter 5).

[9] The following section summarizes my article, "Social Protest and Policy Reform: May 1968 and the Loi d'Orientation in France" (1998b).

addressed the sclerotic structures of higher education against which the students of May had mobilized. But by September, only a few students were still in the streets, and the initiative had shifted from the students to reformers, and from there to educational interest groups and the conservative government. As a result, the reform was scaled back and ultimately emasculated. A brief review of how this happened will silhouette how opportunities narrow and reforms are reshaped as protest cycles end, and how elites reconstitute their position after a cycle of contention.

In the early spring of 1968, leftwing students in the newly created University of Nanterre demonstrated on a variety of grounds against arbitrary administrative authority, as well as against more global targets. Their eruption into the courtyard of the Sorbonne in early May was met by a combination of police repression and governmental uncertainty. When they were roughly hauled off in police vans, middle-class Parisians were incensed. And when news of the outrage was diffused to other areas of the country, every university in the country and a number of secondary schools were shut down. Diffusion also spread to France's working class, which was poorly unionized but highly militant, especially in the atmosphere of spreading disorder that the students' rebellion had fostered.

As the movement of May spread, to the natural self-intoxication of the students was added their leaders' desire to broaden their appeal. As a result, the concrete issues of university governance were displaced by utopian demands: "Replace capitalist domination!" "Release the imagination!" It seemed to many, as Zolberg would later write, that a New World was just around the corner (1972). Surrounded by contestation on many sides, the authorities were placed on the defensive. When the movement spread to the working class, the government understood that it was facing a potential revolution.

Resisting civil strife by restraining repression was the first task the government undertook; preventing an alliance between the working class and the students was the second; getting the economy moving again was the third; and reclaiming middle-class votes was the fourth. To accomplish the first goal, the Paris Prefect of Police clamped down on police violence – indeed, 1968 marked a permanent change in the practice of protest policing (Bruneteaux 1996; Fillieule 1997). To accomplish the second goal, Prime Minister Georges Pompidou negotiated dramatic wage increases with the unions to get them back to work and to isolate the students in their university redoubts (Bridgford 1989). To effect the third, a devaluation redressed the shift of income to wages (Salvati 1981).

Frightening the middle class with fear of revolution was the fourth goal of the government, and this was accomplished both by President de Gaulle's overture to the army and by a massive counterdemonstration by his supporters. When the parties of the Left allowed themselves to be pushed into announcing their readiness to form a government, de Gaulle had the opportunity he needed. The National Assembly was dissolved, the opposition was soundly defeated, and the Gaullists and their allies returned to power with an overwhelming majority.

In the months following the June 1968 elections, the government boiled down the jumble of demands for educational change that had erupted in May into a major reform law – the *loi d'orientation*. A new, centrist but loyal Gaullist, Edgar Faure, was appointed Minister of Education and was given *carte blanche* to remake higher education around the goals of participation, multidisciplinarity, and autonomy of the universities.[10] Such a major change in the hidebound structure of French higher education could not have been introduced if it had not been for the impulse of a major political earthquake. But no one would call the *loi d'orientation* a "success" for the radical movement of May 1968.

Movements seldom produce their major effects directly, but rather do so through their interaction with more conventional political forces (Amenta 2006). The French students had no plan for university reform, and, by September, their influence had been weakened by splits in the movement and by the weariness of the public with disorder (Tarrow 1998b). As the threat represented by the Events receded and the center of gravity shifted to the political arena, the students' leverage was sharply reduced. Similar to the "processing" of racial crisis (Lipsky and Olson 1976) and the retraction of welfare reform (Piven and Cloward 1972) in the United States in the same period, an explosive movement was politically processed into a modest reform.

The Slow-Moving American Women's Movement

While students were the "early risers" in the French cycle of 1968, if there was ever a movement that seemed dependent on others, it was the "new" American women's movement of the 1970s. Changes in employment had brought many more women into the workforce; public attitudes toward the status of women were changing; these events were not the work of the movement. In terms of activism, many of the founders of the "new" women's movement gained their first political exposure in Civil Rights and in the New Left (Evans 1980: Chapters 3–7; Meyer and Whittier 1994), while others were the heirs of older women's lobbies (Rupp and Taylor 1987). When the new women's movement appeared on the scene in the mid-1960s, many observers, write Anne and Doug Costain, regarded it as "a transitory phenomenon, imitating the black civil rights movement, but without that movement's capacity to endure" (1987: 1).

But the new women's movement *did* endure. In its first two decades, it was at least in part responsible for the following:

---

[10] Jacques F. Fomerand's "Policy Formulation and Change in Gaullist France. The 1968 Orientation Act of Higher Education" (1975) is the best source in English on the orientation act and its politics.

- Campaigns such as the campaign for an Equal Rights Amendment to the U.S. constitution, which occupied the energies of vast numbers of women (Mansbridge 1986)
- A new women's self-representation through changing forms of dress, language, manners, and collective activities
- The spread of feminist ideas – if not actual feminist organizations – into institutions such as the Catholic church and the armed forces (Katzenstein 1998)
- The creation of a wide variety of organizational forms, from the highly bureaucratic National Organization for Women (NOW) to the puckishly named Women's International Terrorist Conspiracy from Hell (WITCH) to growing female activism in the union movement

In addition, writes Nancy Whittier, women "established organizations, such as rape crisis centers, battered women's shelters, feminist bookstores, and women's studies programs, that aimed both to improve women's lives in the present and to lay the groundwork for more sweeping social transformations in the future (1995: 1).

The signs of growth were both attitudinal – as more and more women declared themselves sympathetic to feminism – and organizational – with membership in major feminist organizations growing to about 250,000 by the 1980s (Minkoff 1995; Mueller 1987). Even as the American activist culture declined, the women's movement afforded women "a vehicle to sustain their activism as well as a community to support a more general feminist lifestyle" (McAdam 1988: 202). Results included growth in the number of women elected to office and a wave of laws of interest to women passed by Congress (Mueller 1987: 96–97; Costain 1992: 10–11). Another result was increased "standing" by women as spokespersons on issues such as abortion (Ferree et al. 2002: 133–134).

From the first, the movement embedded itself in institutions (Katzenstein and Mueller eds. 1987). The first turning point came with President Kennedy's Commission on the Status of Women in 1961 and the inclusion of women's rights in the Civil Rights Act of 1964 (Beckwith 2003). Then came a series of executive orders that monitored wage equality and discrimination in hiring (Katzenstein 2003). Figure 11.1, drawing on Costain's book, *Inviting Women's Rebellion* (1992), tracks the temporal relationship between women's movement activities, as reflected in news coverage, and congressional bills of interest to women as a percentage of all bills introduced in Congress between 1950 and 1986.

This correlation over time indicates a close relationship between women's public presence and the political process. Yet researchers have found little evidence of a direct effect of women's presence in protest events on congressional hearings or House and Senate roll call votes on women's issues (Soule et al. 1999). And this is no surprise: Many of its early advocates were polite middle-class women working quietly in conventional politics and interest groups; others were feminist lawyers who carried out their movement work on the sidelines

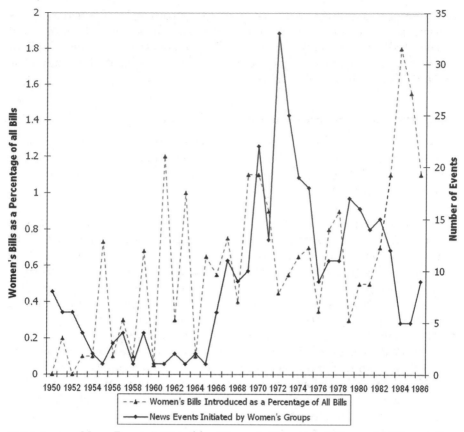

FIGURE 11.1. News Events Initiated by Women's Groups and Women's Bills as a Percentage of All Bills Introduced in Congress, 1950–1985. *Source:* Adapted with permission from Anne N. Costain, *Inviting Women's Rebellion: A Political Process, Interpretation of the Women's Movement*, pp. 108, 113. Johns Hopkins University Press, 1992.

of busy careers; most were not organizationally active at all – or worked in organizations whose primary purposes were labor, civil rights, family issues, public health, or the Church.

Moreover, the movement's progress was marked by significant defeats: the failure of the Equal Rights Amendment in 1983; the whittling down of a woman's right to choose during the Reagan and Bush Administrations; and the growing success of the Pro-Life movement in the 1980s and 1990s. But the signs of a dynamic movement were everywhere present in public space. Between 1965 and 1975, press coverage of women's events in general (Costain 1987: 9) and of their protest actions in particular (p. 19) was tremendously increased. With the appearance of a "gender gap" in the electorate, politicians began to respond to women's issues (Freeman 1987: 206–208). Between the pre-1970 period and the early 1990s, women "speakers" in American press treatments of abortion rose from only about 20% to about 40% of the total (Ferree et al. 2002: 133). Born in the shadow of civil rights and the New Left, this was a movement that began slowly, began life in institutions, but grew steadily in strength and importance.

Comparing French Students and American Women

What explains the dramatic differences between the success of the American women's movement and the failure of the French student movement? We can summarize the differences with respect to all of the four powers in movement that we examined in Part II of this study:

- *The Repertoires of Contention:* The French student movement drew on a repertoire inherited from the past – recalling for supporters and opponents the most conflictual moments of French history. In contrast, the American women's movement used a variety of forms of action – public and private – that leaned heavily toward the contained, the discursive, and the symbolic. In addition, in the interstices of American family and work groups, feminists acted out the slogan "the personal is political" (Evans 1980: Chapter 9).
- *Mobilizing Structures:* While both had in common with many contemporary movements a dedication to autonomy, decentralization, and spontaneity, the French student movement never developed strong connective structures and rapidly collapsed as students went off for their summer vacations. In contrast, the American women's movement developed a broad, varied, and growing connective structure at both the summit and the base, ranging from informal women's collectives to formal national organizations such as NOW, Women's Equity Action League (WEAL), and the National Women's Political Caucus (NWPC) (Minkoff 1995).
- *The Construction of Meaning:* The French students employed a symbolic discourse that isolated them from the language of ordinary French citizens. "Power to the imagination!" "The struggle continues!" These slogans could engage supporters and elicit enthusiasm, but they had little resonance among consumers waiting on line for gasoline, workers unable to collect their pay-checks, or peasants whose produce rotted on the way to market. In contrast, an important aspect of the American women's movement was its attention to signification: "women" rather than "girls"; "gender" rather than "sex"; "partner" rather than "girlfriend." Even the once-elite term "male chauvinist" appears to have percolated from the women's movement to the mass level of American society (Mansbridge and Flaster 2005).
- *The Balance of Opportunities and Constraints:* The French students were able to discern that the Fifth Republic had settled in, but its ruling elite was lacking in ideas. That opportunity was quickly consumed as the students' successes frightened the middle class and produced an enlarged majority for the Right. In contrast, realignments in the party system – and especially in

the Democratic Party – were crucial to the American women's movement's strategy and success (Costain, 1992; Freeman 1987). "We have gotten a lot of mileage out of this gender gap," said one lobbyist for a women's organization; "Hell, we don't want to close it... We want to widen it" (quoted in Costain and Costain 1987: 206).

RESHAPING POLITICAL CULTURE[11]

Of all the potential outcomes and impacts of social movements, the ones we know least about are cultural.[12] As Jennifer Earl writes in her thorough review of the field, "many of the numerous typologies of movement outcomes (and reviews of that literature) lack conceptual space for cultural outcomes, leaving this area of research even farther away from finding some common conceptual vocabulary" (2004: 509). Drawing on the work of Stephen Hart (1996), Earl identifies three strands of research relevant to movement influences on culture:

- Culture is social-psychological: These studies focus on changes in values, beliefs, and opinions (pp. 511–514)
- Culture as a web of signs and the signified meaning of those signs (pp. 514–517)
- Culture as the framing of the worldview and the social situation of communities or subcultures (pp. 517–519)

These different conceptions of culture have enriched the search for cultural impacts of movements, but the result is that "existing scholarship on the cultural consequences of movements has been spread broadly and thinly" (p. 511). This has led to particular ambiguity in tracing the causal mechanisms that link movement activities to cultural change. The social-psychological approach tends to specify outcomes as "well-framed arguments"; the "sign and signification" approach points to visible changes – such as the adoption of new forms of dress or music – without laying down clear guidelines about their linkage to movement activism; and the worldview and communities approach has stressed the development of collective identities and subcultures. As Earl concludes, "moving from plausible explanations to evidence of causal relations can be much harder where social movement outcomes are concerned. This is even more the case where cultural outcomes are concerned" (p. 525).

This is one reason (there are others, including the fact that the boundaries between movements are notoriously difficult to demarcate) why it may be more productive to try to understand the cultural impact of entire cycles of

---

[11] The following section draws on Jennifer Earl's excellent synthesis of research on the cultural consequences of social movements (2004) and on my "Cycles of Collective Action: Between Moments of Madness and the Repertoire of Contention" in Traugott, ed., *Repertoires and Cycles of Collective Action* (1995).

[12] In an 18-page review of the literature on movement outcomes, Giugni allocates only one page to cultural consequences (2008: 1591–1592).

contention, rather than the influence of specific social movements. Such an approach may tell us more in the long run about historical patterns of change. Here is an example:

Concerned that his conclusions about the sixties were too narrowly based on his experience interviewing former activists in the 1964 Freedom Summer experience, Doug McAdam and his collaborators administered a telephone-and-pen-and-paper questionnaire to a large sample of Americans who were born between 1943 and 1964.[13] McAdam was interested not only in the direct biological influence of New Left activism (see Table 11.1), but in the broader life-course implications of this period of activism for different age cohorts who had grown up politically during the 1960s and 1970s. McAdam speculated that departures from normative life-course choices – such as cohabitation before marriage, late marriage, not having children – that he and his collaborators identified as more typical of activists might be expected to diffuse to nonactivist segments of the same generations.

This "normalization" process, familiar from the diffusion of technical innovations from elite to mass members of a population, would logically be likely to take time to diffuse from activist to nonactivist citizens, and this would produce a greater incidence of these nontraditional life-course choices in the second (b. 1950–1956) than in the first age cohort (b. 1943–1949) and even more in the third one (b. 1957–1964). McAdam also identified a number of mediating factors that he hypothesized would be likely to assist in the adoption of nontraditional life-course choices: attendance at an "activist college"; residence in a "liberal state"; and nonattendance at weekly church services (1998: 138).

Summarizing his findings, McAdam reports that the first cohort of citizens showed no effect of the introduction of these three variables on the life-choice outcomes he had identified. For the second cohort, both New Left experience and two of the additional variables (attendance at an activist college and nonchurch attendance) had some effect on these practices. But for the third age cohort – those born between 1957 and 1964 – New Left activity was only weakly related to the life-choice variables, and the full array of mediating variables came into play. And here is the really important point: "By the time those in cohort 3 reached their formative years the alternative life-course patterns had diffused through much of society and were now being influenced by a wide range of variables," including the kind of college attended, the community of residence, and church attendance (pp. 141–142). McAdam's analysis indicated that "New Left" life-course choices diffused over these three generations to a broader public.

Of course, these findings leave unspecified and untested the mechanisms of diffusion of New Left life-course changes to the general public. But this is a lot more causally satisfying than most of the generalizations we read about the

---

[13] The larger study is reported in McAdam, Van Dyke, Munch, and Shockey (1998), but I base the following on the shorter version in McAdam (1998).

impact of "the sixties." But we can go farther in specifying the mechanisms that might generalize the cultural heritage of a cycle of contention to the society at large. In his evocative article cited earlier and in the last chapter, Aristide Zolberg (1972) concluded that "moments of madness" bring about significant transformations in three ways: first, through a "torrent of words" that involves an intensive learning experience whereby new ideas emerge as widely shared beliefs among much larger publics; second, in new networks of relationships that are rapidly constituted during periods of intense activity; and third, from the point of view of policy, through the institutionalization of claims made at the peak of the cycle (p. 206). Each of these themes implies an indirect and mediated – rather than a direct and immediate – effect of cycles of contention on political culture.

CONCLUSIONS

Few people dare to break the crust of convention. When they do, they create opportunities and provide models of thought and action for others, who conventionalize their claims in more institutionalized ways and are more effective at advancing them. What remains after the enthusiasm of the cycle is a residue of reform. Such cycles have risen and fallen periodically over the past two centuries. Each time they appear, the world seems to be turning upside down. But just as regularly, erosion of mobilization, polarization between sectors of the movement, splits between institutionalization and violence, and elites' selective use of incentives and repression combine to bring the cycle to an end. At its height, the power of movement is electric and seems irresistible; but by the end, it is integrated by the political process.

Much has changed in contentious politics in the first decade of the twenty-first century. Over a decade ago, social movement scholars thought that protest was becoming domesticated and that a contained "social movement" society was being formed (Meyer and Tarrow, eds. 1998). The violent conflagrations of the decades since 1989 have led some to suspect that we are entering a stage of history in which movements create continual disorder. And the globalization of the world economy and the financial crisis of 2008–2009 have convinced others that the national political contexts we have attended to in this study are no longer as relevant as they were in the past. These are the questions I will turn to in the next and final chapter.

12

Transnational Contention

"In January 1997," write Donatella della Porta and Manuela Caiani, Italian dairy farmers asked the Italian government to suspend collecting fines for the European Union (EU) related to "irregularities" allegedly committed by their organizations (della Porta and Caiani 2009: 37). The dairymen were accused of claiming they processed more milk products than Italy's dairy herds were capable of producing. But this was not their only reaction to the EU's fines:

- Similar to many European farmers (Bush and Simi 2001), they protested against their own government though the source of their complaint was the EU.
- Their protest campaign led them to create a new and decentralized organization.
- They framed a new identity around a broad social agenda.
- They joined an Italian farmers' protest in Brussels, bringing along a living symbol of their profession – "Caroline the Cow."
- And they came into contact with farmers from other European countries and joined them in protests against the World Trade Organization (p. 40).

Why begin a discussion of transnational contention with the story of a minor dairymen's protest against their own government's failure to defend their interests? More than a decade ago, it appeared to many that globalization and a growing movement against it were eroding the hegemony of the state system (Clark 2003; Florini 2003; Kaldor 2003; McMichael 1996). Scholars, nongovernmental advocacy organization (NGO) advocates, social movement activists, and enthusiastic young people joined worldwide protests against neoliberalism behind the hopeful slogan "Another World is Possible." To some, it even seemed that this new movement was laying the groundwork for a global civil society.[1]

---

[1] Introducing the first volume in the yearbook series by the same name in 2001, LSE Director, Anthony Giddens, declared that "the emergence of a *global civil society* is perhaps one of the most momentous developments taking place in the world today" (Giddens 2001: iii).

So sweeping a claim would be hard to support after the first decade of the twenty-first century. The advent of the unilateralist Bush Administration, its belligerent responses to the outrages of September 11th, the rise of religious-based fundamentalism, the divergent national responses to the global financial crisis: All of these quashed the hope of many that the state system was giving way in short order to global governance, or to "globalization from below" (Tarrow 2005: Chapter 11). Change, if it comes, will be slow, halting, and contradictory, and the story of the Italian milk producers may turn out to be more typical of emerging transnationalism than the dramatic claims of advocates for a global civil society.

Nevertheless, that story, and many others like it, may prove significant. In a long, slow, and halting process that I call "transnational contention," I see five processes developing:

- *Domestication:* the use of internal protest tactics to pressure national governments to defend people's interests from external threats
- *Global framing:* the framing of domestic issues in broader terms than their original claims would seem to dictate
- *Transnational diffusion:* the spread of similar forms of action and similar claims across borders
- *Externalization:* domestic actors targeting external actors in attempts to defend their interests
- *Transnational coalition formation:* the creation of transnational networks to support cooperation across borders (Bandy and Smith 2005: 3).

These are the themes that this chapter will explore. Part I lays out the kinds of contentious actors who on at least some occasions cross national borders or shift the scale of their actions to levels above their own state. In Part II, I will turn to the two broadest processes that most scholars see as the ultimate causes of transnational contention: *globalization* and *internationalization*. In Part III, I will examine the first two contentious processes that I identified from della Porta and Caiani's story – *domestication* and *global framing*. Part Four turns to *transnational diffusion* of contention across borders. Part Five discusses the two international processes that take activists outside their own countries – *externalization* and *transnational coalition formation*.

Actors Inside and Outside the Polity

Since the 1990s, an increasing number of contentious actors and actions have crossed national boundaries, united challengers from different countries, or targeted foreign and international targets. Consider the following:

- In Northern Quebec, South America, and rural India, campaigns to stop the construction of major dams were mounted by coalitions of indigenous groups with support from NGOs abroad.

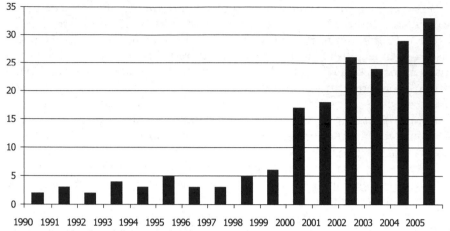

1990 1991 1992 1993 1994 1995 1996 1997 1998 1999 2000 2001 2002 2003 2004 2005

FIGURE 12.1. Growth of Transnational Civil Society Events, 1990–2005. *Source:* Adapted with permission from Mario Pianta and Raffaele Marchetti, "The Global Justice Movements: The Transnational Dimension." In Donatella Della Porta, ed., *The Global Justice Movement*, p. 41. Paradigm Press, 2007.

- In Latin America and elsewhere, similar repertoires of contention were mounted against governments implementing International Monetary Fund (IMF)-imposed austerity policies.
- In Eastern Europe, the Caucasus, and Central Asia, transnational democracy campaigners helped opposition forces defeat authoritarian leaders in "electoral revolutions."
- On the high seas, Greenpeace and other ecological groups opposed firms and governments that pollute the environment and countries that slaughter whales and baby seals.
- In the run-up to the Iraq War in 2003, millions of people around the world participated in a coordinated campaign to stop that war.

Episodes such as these have moved scholarly attention from an exclusive focus on local and national social movements to "activism beyond borders" (Keck and Sikkink 1998). This attention to transnational politics began to be visible among social movement scholarship in the middle of the 1990s, as a response to transnational events such as the United Nations (UN) conference on women, the anti-North American Free Trade Agreement (NAFTA) mobilizations, and the Rio Earth Summit.[2] Mario Pianta and his collaborators tracked two main forms of these events: NGO side-conferences and counter-summits in the context of major international organizations, and transnational civil society meetings (Pianta and Marchetti 2007: 41). Figure 12.1 charts the

[2] An earlier phase of research and theory on transnational politics occurred in the United States in the 1970s in reaction to the neo-realist models that had come to dominate American international relations theory. For the foundational document, see Keohane and Nye, eds. (1971).

numbers of such events from 1990 through 2005 from their dataset. While 5 or fewer events were reported in both categories in the period through 1997, after that year, the numbers of events rose steeply, reaching more than 30 in 2005 alone.

Although NGO side-conferences in the 1980s, including the UN women's conferences and the Rio Earth Summit, were relatively contained affairs, by the mid-1990s, more contentious meetings of anti-neo-liberal groups were proposing alternative agendas to those of the great international financial institutions. By the turn of the new century, these had evolved into more transgressive events, inventing new forms of contention and triggering a shift in police strategies toward more repressive actions (della Porta and Tarrow 2010). Although transgressive events received more attention, the more contained NGO meetings laid the groundwork for the more contentious countersummits to come.

SEATTLE AND AFTER

The key turning point in this shift to transgressive transnational events was the Seattle protest against the World Trade Organization (WTO) ministerial meeting in 1999. It was highly contentious, it aimed at the policies of a major international institution, and the protesters actually succeeded in shutting down the summit. It created unusual local coalitions among trade unionists, ecologists, and civil liberties activists (Levi and Murphy 2006) and inspired activists elsewhere to employ the combination of conventional and unconventional forms of contention employed in Seattle (Smith 2002; Lichbach and DeVries 2007).

Stimulated by the "Battle of Seattle" and by the "World Economic Fora" organized each year by economic elites in Davos, a series of global and regional "social forums" began to be organized annually, beginning in Porto Alegre, Brazil, in 2001. Social forums provide open spaces in which a variety of social actors from across the globe meet, exchange ideas, and attempt to coordinate actions in their home countries. In the decade after its initiation the World Social Forum (WSF) process brought together hundreds of thousands of individuals from well over a hundred countries. The social forum model developed rapidly in both Latin America and Western Europe, where hundreds of forums were organized at the local, national, and continental levels during the early years of the new century (della Porta 2005b). After some delay, the idea even spread to the usually parochial United States (Smith and Reese, eds. 2008).

Both the Battle of Seattle and the social forum process revealed that transnational activism is not a homogeneous phenomenon – and how could it be? Seattle, for example, drew predominantly on union members from the Northwestern United States, environmental groups, and miscellaneous radicals, with modest representatives of Canadian activists and a sprinkling of activists from other countries. In contrast, the world social forums have had greater representation from social movements and less from unions, with a substantial presence of NGOs, trade unions, and interest groups from the global South and Western Europe. Since the 1990s, a vast archipelago of groups and actors, with preferences for a wide spectrum of forms of action, have participated occasionally or consistently in such transnational events.

In the wake of Seattle and the WSF process, students of transnational politics have been impressed with the growth of what I have elsewhere called "rooted cosmopolitans" – people whose activists are based mainly in their own countries but who also engage in transnational activism on behalf of claims that go beyond the nation-state (Tarrow 2005: Chapter 2). Most activists who participate in transnational actions are domestically rooted, even when they frame their demands in global terms (Appiah 1996; Hannerz 1990). While active outside their country of origin, most of them continue to be linked to place, to the social networks that inhabit that space, and to the resources and opportunities that place provides them with (Tarrow 2005: 42ff). Some are primarily active in domestic space, while others are more deliberately transnational in their perspectives.

For example, port inspectors who monitor whether shipping companies are following the regulations set out by the International Transport Workers' Federation (ITF) are rank-and-file union members who seldom leave their own ports or think of themselves as transnational activists. Their job is to inspect the working conditions on ships flying "flags of convenience," like Liberian ones, to enforce the ITF's global strategy (Lillie 2006: Chapter 3). Similarly, the transnational trade networks that developed in the 1990s to oppose trade liberalization in the Americas were rooted in both domestic social networks and political structures (Von Bülow 2010).

Very different is the new generation of global justice activists whose protests have been gathering force since Seattle. Yet here too we find a domestic rooting. Della Porta and Caiani report that participants at the first European Social Forum were "deeply rooted in dense organizational networks that range from Catholic to Green, from voluntary social workers to labour unions, from human rights to women's organizations" (2009: 142–143 and Table 4.1). Although the weight of different types of membership varied from country to country, more than half were associated with at least one domestic social movement (p. 143).

Transnational campaigns often begin with domestic conflicts. For example, beginning with the lockout of port workers from the port of Liverpool in 1995, British, American, Canadian, Japanese, and Australian dockers began to cooperate to prevent ships loaded by "black" labor in Liverpool from unloading in their ports. This transnational coalition succeeded in slowing – if not actually stopping – shipowners from using nonunion casual labor to unload their ships (Gentile 2010; Turnbull 2004).

Dawn Wiest and Jackie Smith provide us with the best existing census of organized transnational actors, drawing on the database of the Yearbook of International Organizations. Wiest and Smith include in their analysis only those organizations whose missions are aimed at social change. Even so, their

TABLE 12.1. *Transnational Social Change Organizations, 1953–2003, by Main Issue Focus*

	1953–1977	1978–1993	1994–2003
Human Rights	27.2%	32.7%	38.8%
Environment	6.0%	13.9%	18.3%
Peace	28.9%	23.0%	23.8%
Women's rights	10.3%	13.1%	12.8%
Development	4.6%	5.9%	8.2%
Multi-issue Groups	8.6%	10.1%	14.1%
Total No. of TSMOs	349	976	1300

Note: Organizations were categorized by their predominant issue focus or foci. However, not all issues are displayed in this table, and the issue areas are not mutually exclusive.
Source: Provided courtesy of Dawn R. Wiest and Jackie Smith, *Social Movements in the World Polity: Power, Inequality and Global Change* (forthcoming, Russell Sage Foundation).

data demonstrate tremendous growth in the number of such organizations: From just over 300 in the 1950s, they identified more than 1,300 such organizations soon after the beginning of the new century. The greatest growth in transnational social change organizations came in the late 1980s and the early 1990s – a decade when the end of the Cold War provided a fertile opportunity for transnational organizing. The growth trend slowed down somewhat in the mid-1990s, but by 2003, an overall increase of almost one third was noted in the number of transnational social change organizations with respect to the 1978–1993 period. Table 12.1 reproduces Wiest and Smith's findings for transnational social change organizations in general, and their distribution among eight major sectors of transnational activity.

But can we draw so clear a line between domestic and transnational activists? Some groups do focus their activities primarily on international institutions such as the IMF, the World Bank, the UN, and the European Union. Various "watch" groups include Human Rights Watch, Bankwatch, and Transparency International. Though lodged in places such as New York, Washington, or London, their activities are truly international. The same is true of service NGOs, which, like Oxfam or Doctors Without Borders, have their administrative offices in global cities, but carry out their activities in so broad a range of countries that they have to be considered truly international.

THE WORLD OF NGOs

What is most striking about these international activists and advocates is that their organizations and repertoires of action are heavily conventional. They combine permanent secretariats with network forms of organization and regular memberships – which consist of constituent groups or individuals. Though their members can sometimes be found in demonstrations, they mainly focus on advocacy, education, lobbying, and service activities, using methods that would be familiar to their opponents in business and government. This makes it possible for them to engage these opponents in a civil manner; but it also sets them off from challengers who employ more contentious methods and generally mobilize around more radical claims.

Transnational nongovernmental organizations (TNGOs) have their most important impact in the global South, but their sources of funding are largely Northern, coming mainly from large foundations, governments, and international organizations located in New York, London, Geneva, Brussels, and Washington. In recent years, these sponsors have made determined efforts to shift the secretariats of these TNGOs to the global South, or at least to create decentralized instances of decision making there. Based on data collected up to the turn of the century, Jackie Smith found a decline in the proportion of the headquarters of transnational social change-oriented groups located in Northern "global cities," with a drop from 48 percent of the total in 1973 to 28 percent in 2000, and an increase in those headquartered in the global South from 12 percent in the former year to 21 percent at the turn of the century (Smith 2004: 273).

Although early research, such as that of Keck and Sikkink (1998), focused mainly on liberal or progressive TNGOs, scholars have found that rightwing religious and anti-Liberal TNGOs are also active internationally, and have major advantages, including the support of governments and churches (Bob 2011). Consider the area of women's rights: Although Smith and Wiest's research shows that 10 percent of the transnational social change groups operate in the loosely defined area of "women's rights," not all transnational organizations share the liberal universalism of the women's movement in the West. For example, to gain consensus on a universal HIV/AIDS declaration, the United Nations had to compromise with the Vatican and with miscellaneous Muslim groups, which worked together to prevent liberal women's groups from gaining sway (Bush 2003: Chapter 4). And in the current repression of gay rights in Africa, American religious groups are active in insisting that homosexuality is a crime (Bob 2011).

After a period of rapid growth in the 1990s, much of it financed by Northern governments and foundations, TNGOs began to suffer critiques from both Left and Right (e.g., Cooley and Ron 2002). From the Left, they were criticized for their intimacy with Western authorities and for their preference for conventional forms of action; by governments, particularly in the global South, they were criticized for their closeness to domestic insurgents who challenge these governments (Schmitz 2001). In Russia, the Putin government struck out against international NGOs and those domestic groups that cooperate with them.

In the 1990s, TNGOs had enjoyed a veil of purity from liberals and progressives who saw them as "principled issue groups" (Keck and Sikkink 1998); more recently, they have started to be seen as strategic actors. For example,

Clifford Bob sees them as actors who make policy choices according to opportunities, relative advantages, and the costs and benefits of operating in particular countries and ignoring the needs of others (Bob 2005). Of course, no contradiction is evident between acting on behalf of principle and acting strategically.

Despite these critiques, the appeal of transnational NGOs remains strong because, given the undemocratic or semi-authoritarian conditions of many parts of the world today, they provide a safer, less demanding alternative to contentious social movements and provide access for citizens of the South to sources of power, prestige, and protection from allies in the North. But this too is a double-edged sword: The most active and creative militants from the global South are often drawn into alliances with transnational NGOs that remove them from domestic struggles and cause rifts with the less fortunate compatriots they leave behind.

TRANSNATIONAL SOCIAL MOVEMENTS

A second major family of transnational actors consists of transnational social movements. By this term, I refer to *sustained contentious interactions with opponents – national or non-national – by connected networks of challengers organized across national boundaries* (Tarrow 2005). The targets of transnational movements can change from time to time; they may be transnational or national, private or public. What is important in this definition is that challengers are rooted in domestic social networks and politics, and are connected to one another across borders through common ways of seeing the world, informal or organizational ties, and contentious relationships with their targets.

This definition is restrictive, but not so restrictive that it is impossible to find real-world "outsiders" who match it. For example, Greenpeace is a sustained transnational movement organization with the properties proposed in the previous definition. It claims millions of members in a number of countries who are connected in a sustained way by a transnational organization; its members share a common worldview; and it engages in both contained and confrontational actions with governments and private firms that pollute the environment (Wapner 1996). Greenpeace has also developed an action repertoire that allows it to oppose projects and opponents outside national boundaries – for example, in its opposition to French nuclear testing in the Pacific or its stand against Shell Oil's plan to sink an oil platform in the North Sea, or against the overkill of ocean stocks by French and British trawlers (Tarrow 1998).

The most powerful transnational social movement in the world today is the loose archipelago of Islamist groups that emerged from the Middle East Safidist persuasion in the 1970s and 1980s. In addition to inspiring a number of domestic political parties in the Middle East, it has given rise to the terrorist cells that eventually congealed into the Al Queda network. Using a loose form of network organization (Sageman 2004), Al Queda has its nerve center in the group surrounding Osama Bin Laden, which was responsible for the World Trade Center bombing, but it also has multiplied into a number of autonomous groups in North Africa, in the Middle East, and even in Western Europe.

Though best known for their violent outrages against people and property, Islamist groups actually engage in a wide variety of forms of action, including a remarkably resilient ability to gain new adherents through the mass media and the Internet. With the near-miss of the "Christmas bomber" in the United States in 2009, it became apparent to Western intelligence services that "spinoff" movements from the original Bin Laden trunk had gained the ability to attract adherents and organized operations autonomously. Transnational Islamism is a polycephalous movement rooted in a number of countries with loose interpersonal links across borders (Sageman 2004).

NGOs AND SOCIAL MOVEMENT INTERACTIONS

Although transnational NGOs are analytically distinct from social movements, they intersect with movements in four ways:

- First, many of them are biologically in the debt of social movements. Many of their activists come from social movement backgrounds and continue to think of themselves as movement activists, even as they lobby in the corridors of power or offer services to underprivileged groups.
- Second, NGOs often popularize and "translate" ideas that originate with social movements in ways that make these ideas more accessible to ordinary people and more acceptable to elites and authorities.
- Third, they provide a mechanism for the diffusion of collective action to resource-poor domestic actors to help them construct their own domestic movements.
- And fourth, they sometimes collaborate with these movement activists in specific campaigns, such as the campaign against the Free Trade Area of the Americas (Korzeniewicz and Smith 2005).

The goals, repertoires of action, and cultures of TNGOs and social movements overlap somewhat but vary on a contained/transgressive axis, creating tensions and difficulties of coordination. This is so in part because of the more moderate goals of the former and the more radical goals of the latter; in part because of their different repertoires of contention; and in part because both governments and international institutions prefer to deal with NGOs that mount expertise-driven claims and shy away from those that use transgressive methods (Marks and McAdam 1999). The World Social Forum coordinators have recognized these tensions and have attempted to turn them to advantage behind the slogan, which they take from the Zapatista movement: "One world with room for many worlds within it!"[3]

[3] For a slightly more optimistic view, see Jackie Smith's extensive empirical work on the World Social Forum and other transnational instances in her *Social Movements for a Global Society* (2008) and her collaborative work with Dawn Weist (Weist and Smith 2010–2011).

But there is also a gap in the locus of activity of most of the activists involved in these two families. Although transnational TNGOs are organized internationally, with support from domestic groups in varied countries, most social movements are primarily organized at the grassroots and their activists look outward for transnational alliances and activities. In her research on the European Social Forum, Donatella della Porta found that the majority militate in domestic parties, unions and movements, and reach out through "flexible identities" to transnational allies (2005a).

Movement and NGO activists also come to transnational collective action via different processes. In her research on the Copenhagen climate change campaign, Jennifer Hadden found that transnational actors became involved in climate politics through two distinct pathways: first, through intermovement "spillover" from the global justice movement to the climate justice movement, and, second, through scale shift from domestic to transnational politics. As a result of these two different processes, these groups were able to mobilize a new constituency to engage in transgressive transnational action on climate politics largely without radicalizing the NGO constituency already involved (Hadden 2010). But as Hadden's work also shows, these two networks connected only at their outskirts and cooperation was difficult to maintain.

GLOBALIZATION AND INTERNATIONALIZATION

What accounts for the increase in transnational events and protests revealed in Figure 12.1 and for the growth in transnational social change organizations shown in Table 12.1? Scholars have pointed to two major trends that combine to produce these outcomes: globalization, and what I call "complex internationalization." Although those who studied the first wave of transnational contention against global neo-liberalism focused predominantly on the first process, I will argue that "complex internationalization" structures the relations among nonstate actors, states, and international institutions (Tarrow 2005: Chapter 2).

Globalization and Contention

The chain of causation from globalization to transnational activism goes something like this:

- The neo-liberal orthodox "Washington consensus" began to bear bitter fruit with the collapse of the Asian "tigers" and with the increasingly evident inequalities between global North and South.
- The international institutions that enshrined neo-liberalism – the IMF, World Bank, and World Trade Organization – began to take on a central role as targets of resistance to neo-liberal globalization.
- Transnational campaigns and movement organizations, such as People's Global Action and Attac (Association for the Taxation of Financial Transactions for the Aid of Citizens), grew out of this dynamic.

- New electronic technologies, cheap travel, and global culture enhanced the capacity of movement activists to organize rapidly and effectively across the planet.
- Countersummits and boycotts of large corporations added to the repertoire of protest.

These are major changes, but the picture portrayed above is far too simple. First, social movement scholars learned long ago that collective action cannot be traced directly to grievances or social cleavages. The early major opponents of global neo-liberalism come not from the global South, where the costs of neo-liberalism are greatest, but from the more prosperous regions of Europe and North America. More recently, anti-free trade groups centered in the South have gained leverage internationally (Von Bülow 2010). Second, globalization itself is not a linear trend; the recent financial crisis exposed how important the role of states remains – and not only the hegemonic United States. Finally, many of the most important forms of transnational activism cannot be traced to globalization, except by a heroic stretch in the meaning of the concept. Human rights, revolts against authoritarianism, and Islamist mobilization are all independent of economic globalization.

Part of the problem is that as many definitions of globalization are available as theorists of the phenomenon. (For a judicious synthesis, see Mittelman 2004.) Philip McMichael sees it as a process, an organizing principle, an outcome, a conjuncture, and a project (2005: 587). Peter Katzenstein sees it as a process that transcends space and time and highlights the emergence of new actors and novel relations in the world system (2005: 1). Robert Keohane defines it as the increasing volume and speed of flow of capital and goods, information and ideas, and people and forces that connect actors between countries (2002a: 194).

The definition that will be used here is the one employed by Suzanne Berger: "a set of changes in the international economy that tend to produce a single world market for goods, services, capital and labor" (2000: 44). Some scholars see globalization as primarily economic; others think it also has social and political components. Economist Axel Dreyer has put together an index of globalization that has economic, social, and political components. Figure 12.2 shows that no matter how it is measured, an increase has occurred in all three components of globalization.

When we turn to contentious politics, beyond recognizing that "something" is globalizing, there is little consensus on the nature and implications of globalization. Although some scholars see globalization creating a single world system (Ohmae 1990), others see it as no more than "an extension and deepening of patterns of internationalization and regionalization" (Hirst and Thompson 1997). While some see globalization acting directly on domestic politics in uniform ways, others see it operating through domestic coalitions and alliances that differ fundamentally (Gourevitch 1986). Finally, although some see globalization as virtually synonymous with neo-liberalism (Evans 2005), and

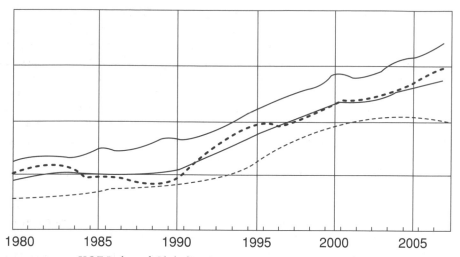

FIGURE 12.2. KOF Index of Globalization, 1980–2007. *Source:* Adapted with permission from Axel Dreher (2006). "Does Globalization Affect Growth? Evidence from a New Index of Globalization." *Applied Economics* 38:1091–1110.

therefore eroding the autonomy and authority of national governments over the political economy, others have argued that trade openness and capital mobility do not diminish governments' capacity to tax, nor its options for changing the nature of the tax system (Garrett 1998).

These differing perspectives on globalization translate into a variety of views of its effects on contentious politics. All observers have noted a growing distrust of elected politicians among the mass public; however, believers in the strong globalization thesis translate this alienation into detachment from national loyalty – a trend that empirical research has yet to verify, except perhaps among younger voters (Jung 2009). Indeed, Berger argues that "as pressures from the international economy intrude on domestic societies, citizens turn ever more urgently to their own governments for help" (2000: 58). Paradoxically, globalization may be leading not to externalization and transnational coalition formation, but to domestication. As Berger writes, "one paradoxical outcome of globalization may be to refocus political attention on the role of the state on the boundaries of national territory." At the extreme, rather than leading to growth of transnational claims and supranational loyalties, "a new political camp has emerged, organized around a program of reinforcing national controls at the frontiers" – in other words, to a revival of nationalism (Ibid.).

Complex Internationalization

If uncertainty continues about whether globalization is leading to detachment from the national state, there is an even greater ambiguity about the impact of the second major process – internationalization. By internationalization, I mean not only increased ties between states, but increased vertical links among subnational, national, and international agents, along with an increased formal and informal structure that encourages the formation of ties between nonstate, state, and international actors (Tarrow 2005: 7–9; also see Alter and Meunier, eds. 2009). Although it has produced threats to citizens, internationalization has also produced contradictions between trade, the environment, and human rights and has created opportunities for activism. Critics of neo-liberalism have tended to see only the threat side of internationalization, but internationalization is a much more complex phenomenon than the austerity policies of the IMF or the World Bank would lead us to believe (Alter and Meunier eds. 2009). It preceded the current wave of global economic integration by decades; it is by no means entirely dedicated to global neo-liberalism; and it has created opportunities and incentives for domestic actors to frame their domestic claims in global terms and to move beyond their own borders.

Since World War II, a dense network of international institutions, regimes, and intergovernmental and transnational contacts has developed, at both global and regional levels. The World Bank and the IMF, the United Nations, the World Trade Organization, international juridical bodies, and even informal standard-setting groups have knit different parts of the world together (Meyer et al. 1997; Slaughter 2004). Only with a good deal of conceptual stretching can all such international institutions be reduced to handmaidens of globalization. Some of them can be explained as attempts to find solutions to international collective action problems (Keohane 2002b); others – such as Interpol – represent attempts to control deviant or illegal behavior that crosses national boundaries; still others are intended to lessen the costs of global neo-liberalism through a process of what John Ruggie has called "embedded liberalism" (1982; 2008). These goals are frequently found in the same institutions. For example, the European Court of Justice both reinforces the EU's doctrine of free markets and protects individuals' social rights, as seen in its support for social benefits for immigrants who cross European boundaries to find work (Caporaso and Tarrow 2009).

The United Nations has developed as a kind of "coral reef" around which nonstate actors organize (Joachim and Locher 2009; O'Brien et al. 2000; Tarrow 2005).[4] NGO participation in UN activities has expanded over time. Karen Mingst writes that such participation evolved from "being marginal in the beginning to where UN bodies now talk about partnerships with NGOs – although this accessibility has become greater with those UN bodies and agencies concerned with social and humanitarian issues rather than those in the security or financial areas" (Mingst 2009: 21). The UN's working group on indigenous peoples may even have encouraged national minority groups to define themselves as "indigenous" and to identify with the goals and methods of better-organized indigenous peoples.

---

[4] Others (O'Brien et al. 2000; Joachim and Locher, eds. 2009), using somewhat different language, have made a similar point.

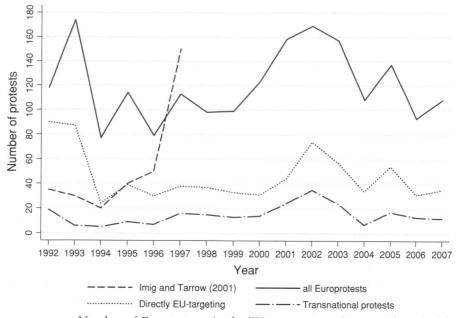

FIGURE 12.3. Number of Europrotests in the EU, 1992–2007. *Source*: Adapted with permission from Katrin Uba and Fredrik Uggla (2011), "Protest Actions Against the European Union 1992–2007." *West European Politics.*

Internationalization has gone farthest in Europe, where a succession of institutional innovations, starting with the European Coal and Steel Commission in the 1950s and extending to the European Union in the 1990s, have melded the interests and processes of European nation-states together. While scholars still debate whether these developments are *inter*national or *supra*national (Moravcsik 1996; Stone Sweet et al. 2001), what is certainly the case is that European institutions have created a new venue for nonstate actors.

What does all this have to do with transnational contention? The growth of a "contentious Europe" first began to emerge when, in the 1990s, it was found that an increasing proportion of European collective action is aimed directly or indirectly at European institutions (Imig and Tarrow, eds. 2001). In some sectors – such as the environment – "Europrotests" have continued to increase in number. When Lori Poloni-Staudinger carried out a content analysis of more than 4,000 events in which environmental groups from Britain, France, and Germany participated from 1980 to 2004, she found a net growth in European-level activities (Poloni-Staudinger 2008). On the other hand, the total number of protests targeting the EU has remained fairly steady since the 1990s, with a brief uptick around the turn of the new century. Figure 12.3, from the work of Katrin Uba and Fredrik Uggla, reflects these trends.

Although Europe has gone farthest in creating regional institutions, other areas of the globe, such as the Americas, also show how international institutions and treaty negotiations can become opportunity structures for nonstate

TABLE 12.2. *International Judicial and Quasi-Judicial Bodies as of 2010*

	International Judicial Bodies	International Quasi-Judicial Bodies
Existing	22	62
Nascent	3	5
Proposed	7	1
Total	32	68

Source: Data assembled by Sara Mitchell and kindly made available to the author from www.pict-pcti.org/publications/synoptic_chart/Synop_C4.pdf. Data are linked to the growth of human rights institutions, as seen from the data reproduced from Kim's work in Figure 12.4.

actors. When Canada, Mexico, and the United States began to create a structure to regulate North American trade through the North American Free Trade Agreement (NAFTA), the initial reaction of unions in both Canada and the United States was negative (Dreiling and Robinson 1998). It was in large part to gain labor support that the leaders of the three countries created a system for processing claims of workers from one country against firms located in one of the other two countries through the North American Agreement on Labor Cooperation (NAALC). Within the NAALC framework, each country has established a National Administrative Office that processes claims against firms in that country.

The NAALC process is cumbersome and inefficient, and has only rarely benefited claims-making unions. But it has had the unintended effect of increasing ties among once distant and mutually suspicious national unions and has helped to create some long-term ties, particularly among left-leaning American unions and some of the new independent unions that have developed in Mexico. In this respect, NAFTA has served as an incentive for transnational coalition formation among North American unions (Kay 2011 *a* and *b*).

Legalization and Human Rights

Although critics of globalization tend to see international institutions primarily as enforcers of international financial orthodoxy, many of these institutions are judicial or quasi-judicial in nature and are part of a broad trend toward legalization (Goldstein et al. 2001). Table 12.2 provides a count of existing, planned, and projected judicial and quasi-judicial international organizations in 2010 from data collected by Sara Mitchell. Although not created to support transnational collective action, many of these institutions offer venues – for example, the European Court of Human Rights – in which nongovernmental organizations can go outside their own states to advance their or their

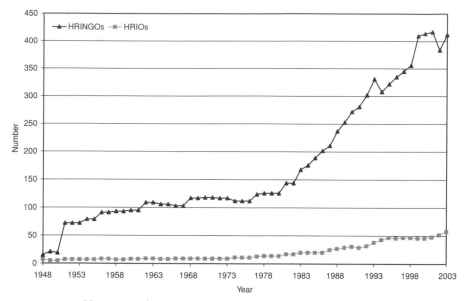

FIGURE 12.4. Human Rights International Nongovernmental and Intergovernmental Organizations Active in Each Year, 1948–2003. *Source:* Data provided courtesy of Dongwook Kim.

constituents' goals by representing them directly or by providing amicus briefs (Dolidze 2009; Cichowski 2010).

A prime area of legalization is seen in the international human rights regime. Thomas Risse and Kathryn Sikkink write, "Since World War II, human rights have been increasingly regulated and specified in international regimes" (1999: 8). This regime has brought an increase in international treaties, organizations, and nonstate human rights networks. In a quantitative analysis complementing Risse and Sikkink's institutional work, Dongwook Kim showed that growth of transnational human rights activism is directly linked to the growth of human rights institutions, as seen from his data, reproduced in Figure 12.4.

To summarize, although globalization has provided many of the threats and much of the "global framing" for transnational campaigns against neo-liberalism, internationalization has provided opportunities that structure such activism. Of course, some international organizations offer fewer incentives and more constraints than others to nonstate actors (O'Brien 2000); some regions of the world – such as Europe – are more welcoming to NGO participation than others – such as Asia (Katzenstein 2005); and some groups are better placed to take advantage of internationalization than others. Environmental groups, the organized sectors of agriculture, and, of course, business groups have been most able to gain access to international institutions, while poor peasants, workers, and the unemployed have gained the least leverage.

LOCAL/GLOBAL INTERACTIONS

Not only is transnational activism domestically rooted, but it rises and falls in response to different national rhythms. After the surge of interest in global issues triggered by the "Battle of Seattle," transnational activism was chilled by the 9/11 massacres in the United States, but not elsewhere (Pobodnick 2005). In contrast, the imminent attack on Iraq in 2002 and 2003 revitalized the peace movement both in the United States and internationally (Hadden and Tarrow 2007; Walgrave and Rucht, eds. 2010). But in the United States, that movement lost much of its drive in the effort to defeat the Bush Administration and elect Barack Obama President. Not only that: As Democratic Party-linked activists deserted the peace movement to support the Obama campaign, and as the Democratic Administration was elected in 2009, the character of the movement changed. As Michael Heaney and Fabio Rojas conclude: "The withdrawal of Democratic activists changed the character of the antiwar movement by undermining broad coalitions in the movement and encouraging the formation of smaller, more radical coalitions" (2011).

Systematic comparative evidence of the impact of domestic politics on transnational activism is difficult to collect, but some evidence can be found in the research of Lori Poloni-Staudinger on the environmental groups she studied in Britain, France, and Germany. Her research shows distinct connections between aspects of political opportunity structure in these three countries and the groups' participation in European collective action.[5] In particular, Poloni-Staudinnger found that the domestic electoral calendar has a dramatic influence on whether groups take action at the supranational level. "During election years," she writes, "the odds that groups will engage in supranational activity increases, all else being equal."

But political structure on its own does not determine outcomes; it is the strategies of activists that determine their targets and their outcomes. American activists who defected from the antiwar movement after 2003 did not do so because structure somehow obliged them to do so; the Western European activists who "chose" Europe during election years did so to put pressure on parties competing for the environmental vote. In other words, to understand the dynamics of transnational contention, we must turn from a structural analysis to the processes that link domestic actors to the international system. Two of these processes – domestication and global framing – are primarily domestic;

---

[5] Her conclusions are worth quoting in detail:

> Examining political opportunity structure explanations for activity, I find that changes in domestic elite alliances and electoral cleavages help to explain why groups choose to target activity at the supranational level. When the domestic opportunity structure is closed, supranational activity becomes more likely. The opening of the domestic political opportunity structure decreases supranational activity among groups (2008: 531).

one – diffusion – connects activists across borders; two more – externalization and transnational coalition formation – transcend the nation-state.

Two Internal Processes

Domestication. Remember how della Porta and Caiani's dairymen turned on their national government when the EU demanded that their organizations pay fines for "irregularities" in complying with milk quotas? Their dominant response was not to go beyond borders, but to begin a process of *domestication.*[6] Those Italian farmers were not alone: Imig and Tarrow found that most European contention takes place on domestic ground as social actors respond to EU directives by protesting against their own governments (Imig and Tarrow 2001). From their time-series on Europrotests, Uba and Uggla also found a dominance of domestication strategies over direct mobilization against the European Union.[7]

The last few decades have seen the domestication of international norms across the globe (Meyer et al. 1997). The most dramatic is the domestication of international human rights norms (Risse, Ropp, and Sikkink, eds., 1999). Human rights treaties and institutions have helped to spread human rights norms, even if they have not had the same effect on the *practice* of human rights (Hafner-Burton et al. 2008). Although specialists disagree about the effects of attempts to enforce human rights norms (Sikkink and Walling 2007; Snyder and Vinjimori 2003–2004), few would deny that these norms have come to be regarded as universal standards.

We can see how universal norms are domesticated in the campaign for equal rights of Koreans in Japan, as studied by Kiyoturo Tsutsui and Hwa-Ji Shin (2008). Japanese occupation of Korea had brought a large number of Koreans to Japan, and 600,000 of them stayed there, despite the fact that they were denied Japanese citizenship. To make matters worse, the war on the Korean peninsula in 1950 split them into conflicting Northern and Southern factions. But as the Cold War waned, resident Koreans began to mobilize against Japanese discrimination. They framed their campaign in four main ways: for civil rights against the practice of mandatory fingerprinting in civil rights; for the political rights of alien suffrage; for the social/economic right to participate in the national pension system in social/economic rights; and for the cultural rights of ethnic education and Korean language teaching (Tsutsui and Shin: 399–407). By domesticating international human rights norms, Koreans

---

[6] This was a process first identified in the mid-1990s in a conflict between Spanish tuna fishermen and the big industrial factory ships that were stealing their business (Tarrow 1998a). In subsequent work, Imig and I reported that a majority of Europeans' protests against EU policies up to the late 1990s were mounted against domestic targets (Imig and Tarrow 2001). Note that the term "domestication" has also been used to denote the internalization of human rights norms. Thanks to Jackie Smith for this observation.

[7] Data provided courtesy of Fredrik Uggla from a forthcoming article in *West European Politics* with Katrin Uba.

in Japan moved closer to the status of citizenship that they had been denied by generations of Japanese policymakers.

Global Framing. By global framing, I mean the framing of domestic issues in broader terms (Tarrow 2005: Chapter 4). Issues that were once interpreted in largely national terms now are often framed as global. Hans Schattle surveyed a sample of international news sources to find out how widely global thinking had spread. He found a dramatic increase in writers' use of terms such as "global citizenship" over the decade of the 1990s in a broad range of media sources (Schattle 2008). This has even caused domestic trade union movements to increasingly blame their inability to achieve wage gains for their members on "globalization" (Tarrow 2005: Chapter 4).

We can see the effects of global framing in the development of the global anti-U.S. basing movement in Asia and elsewhere. As is well known, the United States maintains more than 800 foreign military bases in 39 foreign countries (Yeo 2009: 572). The end of the Cold War "created an environment favorable for domestic mobilization and civil societal opposition against US bases" (p. 573). The onset of 9/11 and the global restructuring of American forces did not close that window of opportunity, but it did generate a new set of challenges for anti-base activists. The U.S. war in Iraq "presented activists the global frames necessary to accelerate the pace of diffusion, scale-shift, and brokerage, and hence, the consolidation of a transnational anti-base network," writes Andrew Yeo (p. 571).

These two processes – domestication and global framing – both occur primarily on domestic ground. Although they draw on international norms and policies and connect cognitively to foreign sources, both are local processes. But as the quotation above from Yeo's work on the anti-basing movement suggests, they have transnational (i.e., cross-border) implications. The most obvious implication is the increase in diffusion of transnational activism.

Transnational Diffusion

How do forms of collective action that arise in national settings spread to other countries? And, in particular, how do globalization and internationalization affect the speed and facility with which these forms diffuse? Determined activists have always been able to adapt new forms of contention across borders. But with the growth of internationalization and global communication, diffusion has both increased and accelerated. For example, although it took a half-century for antislavery agitation to spread from England to the European continent and across the Atlantic (Drescher 1987), the practice of suicide bombing diffused across Asia and the Middle East within a decade of its appearance (Tarrow 2005: Chapter 6), and the electoral model of authoritarian challenge diffused over only a few years from Central to Southeastern Europe and to the Caucasus and Central Asia (Bunce and Wolchik 2010).

As we saw in Chapter 9, scholars have identified three kinds of pathways of diffusion: *direct, indirect, and mediated*. See Givan, Roberts, and Soule (2010).

In the first pathway, *direct diffusion,* the bonds between individuals who know each other or who have something important in common (e.g., a common ethnic identity) help speed innovation from one actor to another (Rogers 1995). This is what I will call *relational diffusion:* the transfer of information along established lines of interaction through networks of trust or formed around mutual advantage (Lee and Strang 2003). It could be observed as nationalism spread among minority groups living in different Republics of the former Soviet Union in the late 1980s and early 1990s (Beissinger 2002).

In the second, *indirect diffusion,* new forms of contention or participation in existing forms can spread through *nonrelational means* among people who have few or no social ties. This can spread by word-of-mouth among strangers but today is more likely to spread through radio and television, print, and forms of electronic communication such as the Internet. We saw a dramatic example of nonrelational diffusion in the spread of information about the Chiapas Rebellion among sympathetic groups in the United States and Western Europe (Olesen 2005).

Finally, new forms of contention spread through the actions of brokers through a process I call *mediated diffusion.* In her research on the spread of the strategy of "electoral revolution" in East Central Europe and the Balkans, Tsveta Petrova points to the brokerage role of American NGOs in Slovakia:

> In late 1998, a US donor [Freedom House] encouraged several of the key OK 98 organizers to prepare a seminar in Bratislava to share their campaign experience with interested representatives from Croatia, Serbia, Ukraine, Belarus, and Russia. At the request of civic and political oppositions throughout the region, prominent Slovak civic activists subsequently led a number of additional exchanges and seminars in Slovakia and abroad (Petrova 2010: 111).

All three pathways combined in the transnational diffusion of the electoral model across the former Soviet sphere. "From 1996–2005," write Valerie Bunce and Sharon Wolchik, "eight countries in postcommunist Europe and Eurasia held elections that replaced illiberal leaders or their anointed successors with leaders of the democratic opposition" (2011: ms. p. 210). First, in Serbia, opponents to the authoritarian government of Sloboden Milosevic drew on the advice and the teaching of Western advocates of nonviolence and on the direct support of American allies. Then, in Georgia, opponents to the Shevarnadze government visited Belgrade to learn what they could from their Serbian predecessors and brought back a film made by an American democracy promotion group to train their militants in the use of similar tactics. And in a third stage, direct involvement, indirect diffusion and brokered involvement were combined in the so-called "Orange Revolution" led by Victor Yushchenko to defeat the Russian-backed campaign of Victor Yanukovych (Bunce and Wokchik 2011).

The long-term future of democracy in Serbia, Georgia, and the Ukraine is still in doubt. Nor did the "electoral model" work in less promising settings such as Belarus and Central Asia (Bunce and Wolchik 2011). But these examples show that innovations in the repertoire of contention can cross broad cultural and spatial divides, even where established lines of interaction are weak. They do so through personal ties among activists; through the press, videos, and TV reports; and through the intervention of international agencies, NGOs, and foreign governments. Emulation is an important source of diffusion, but, as Bunce and Wolchik conclude: "central to transmission was the hard work of a transnational network, co-organized by the United States, private foundations based in the West, the European Union (albeit to a lesser extent), regional democracy promoters, and local oppositions and non-governmental organizations" (2011: ms. p. 241).

The Internet, the cell phone, and cheap international transportation have helped in the diffusion of activism to people and groups who emulate what they read, hear, or see. But on their own, such indirect mechanisms cannot fully explain the diffusion of transnational activism. As Lance Bennett and Amoshaun Toft write, "narratives flow through gatekeeping nodes in networks such as planning committees or network support organizations" (2009: 246).

Two International Processes

Externalization. The converse of domestication is externalization, in which domestic actors, frustrated by their inability to gain redress from their governments, mobilize against foreign or international targets. This process is familiar from European history, in which nationalists in countries such as Italy and Greece sought the support of Western allies to help them to gain independence, respectively, from the Hapsburg and Ottoman empires. But it was only with the creation of a panoply of international and regional institutions in the twentieth century that weak domestic groups had a chance to do so effectively. Margaret Keck and Kathryn Sikkink have built a model of transnational activism based on what they call "the boomerang effect" (1998). In this process, domestic actors who are blocked from gaining redress for their claims domestically seek the assistance of international allies.

International institutions offer a framework for externalizing claims in three main ways: by monitoring the practices of states and publicizing them, by censuring their behavior, and by imposing actual sanctions. Given the state-centered nature of the international system, the first is more widespread than the second, and the second more common than the third. Only in the European Union do mechanisms regularly function to constrain states to conform to international norms. For example, della Porta and Caiani's research on 387 European organizations found externalization as the dominant process in 38% of the European claims they studied (2007: 54).

From the 1970s on, European women's groups have been claiming equal employment rights by externalizing their claims to the institutions of the European Union. The European Court of Justice (ECJ) and the European Court of Human Rights (ECHR) are two of the most interesting channels for nonstate public actors to engage in external activism. Over the years, and with the help of the European Commission, the ECJ has transformed the European legal

order in a supranational direction, and this has allowed weak social actors –
such as women – to significantly improve their positions in the labor market.
From 1970 to the late 1990s, 177 cases involving gender equality laws came
before the Court (Cichowski 2001: 122).

In this effort, internal actors such as the UK Equal Opportunity Commission
and the trade unions, with an external assist from the European Commission,
pushed to develop the cases that led the Court to hold that British gender
practices undermined the European Treaties (Alter and Vargas 2000: 458–459).
The key decision came in 1982, when the Court found the United Kingdom
to be in violation of the EU's Equal Pay Directive. To this decision, the UK
government offered stiff resistance, but the ultimate results were dramatic, both
in terms of the government's compliance with the Court's decisions (Chicowski
2001: 130) and in compromising the long-held principle of the sovereignty of
the UK Parliament (Caporaso and Jupille 2001: 40–41). Through resistance
to a government that was not responsive to their demands, British women's
groups used a process of externalization to put forward their claims.

Transnational Coalition Formation. Though more difficult to accomplish and
harder to sustain than externalization, transnational coalition formation is the
major route to the construction of transnational social movements (Bandy and
Smith, ed. 2005; Tarrow 2005). Many coalitions are temporary and loosely
coupled, and dissolve soon afterward. These are what I elsewhere have called
"event-based" coalitions (Tarrow 2005: 168). For example, the "Battle of
Seattle" was mounted by a heterodox coalition of trade unionists, environ-
mentalists, and anarcho-syndicalist radicals that disappeared soon afterward
(Levi and Murphy 2006). Similarly, in Mexico and Central America, American trade unionists and NGOs have formed temporary coalitions with apparel
workers seeking the right to organize and obtain higher labor standards (Anner
2000).

Obstacles to the formation of longer-term transnational coalitions are
formidable. However, in her research, Jackie Smith has found that the coalition
form has been increasing vis-à-vis more traditional federal forms of organization among the TNGOs she studied. Between 1973 and 2000, the proportion
of coalitions in the population of these organizations increased from 25 percent of the total to 60 percent at the turn of the century (Smith 2004b: 278).
Using a different measure, Bruce Podobnik found that transnational protest
cooperation increased in the course of the 1990s and grew through the turn of
the century until at least 2003–2004 (Podobnik 2009).

These coalitions take two different forms: *insider/outsider coalitions* between domestic actors and international allies, and *coalitions among domestic
actors across borders*. By the term "insider/outsider" coalition, I mean, with
Kathryn Sikkink, the involvement of external NGOs in the claims making
of internal activists (Sikkink 2005). In authoritarian regimes, internal opponents are often blocked from participation by the threat of repression (Keck
and Sikkink 1998). But even in regimes that have opened up to internal

participation, domestic actors may continue to draw on these allies for the access they can offer to influential states or international institutions (Sikkink 2005). Sikkink offers the example of Argentine human rights activists who had drawn on foreign support during Argentina's period of military dictatorship (Sikkink 2005). When that regime fell and politics opened up, they continued to cooperate with external human rights allies to force their government to investigate the abuses of their military predecessors.

Coalitions between similar domestic actors, in contrast, are more difficult to organize because they oblige such actors to balance between the claims of their own supporters, the constraints of their governments, and the goals of external coalition partners. It is no wonder that most horizontal coalitions are generally short-lived and hard to sustain. But two such coalitions have been resounding successes: the World Social Forum process, and the international landmine campaign.

The WSF Process: This process represents a sustained collaboration among a loosely connected set of very diverse groups meeting periodically in different parts of the world (Escobar 2003; Juris 2008). Although it was originally a reaction to the World Economic Forum, the WSF process took on a life of its own and has endured for almost a decade because of the learning, the relationships formed, and the shifts in frames/discourses made possible through earlier organizing efforts (Weist and Smith 2010–2011). The WSF process has also spurred the formation of local, national, and regional social forums, such as the European Social Forum, which began in Florence in 2001 (della Porta 2005a), and the Latin American Social Forum.

The International Campaign to Ban Landmines: As in many areas of transnational activism, it was interstate politics that provided the opponents of anti-personnel landmines with the basic opportunity structure around which to mobilize in the 1990s. Efforts to limit the use of landmines first surfaced in 1980 in a United Nations conference to ban weapons with indiscriminate effects (the CCW), but enough gaps in landmine controls were left to permit increasing carnage on the battlefield. After wars in Afghanistan, Angola, Mozambique, and Cambodia left thousands maimed and killed, an NGO coalition of humanitarian and public health groups emerged to try to replace the CCW with a more robust international agreement (Price 1998; Williams and Goose 1998).

A coalition of international religious, humanitarian, and de-mining NGOs working in postwar Cambodia in the 1980s was especially significant in launching this coalition.[8] But permanent NGOs in France, Canada, and the United States were also influential in the campaign as it got under way. These groups might have made scant headway had it not been for the convergence of their efforts with international institutions such as the International Committee of

---

[8] They included the religious-based Coalition for Peace and Reconciliation; the humanitarian Handicap International, and the British de-mining group, Mines Advisory Group.

the Red Cross and the UN, and with three medium-sized states – Canada, France, and Norway – which gave the movement legitimacy, provided sites for its meetings, and formed the core of a bloc of interested governments (Maslen 1998; Lawson, et al. 1998).

At first, progress in convincing states to sign a convention to ban landmines was slow and uneven, and the most important state, the United States, never did sign it (Wareham 1998). But after the core states took ownership of the campaign and landmine activist Jody Williams won the Nobel Peace Prize in 1997, the pace of adhesion to the convention picked up rapidly. Ultimately, with the lead taken by Canada and its Foreign Minister, Lloyd Axworthy, 112 countries signed the convention against anti-personnel mines in Ottawa in 1998 (Cameron, et al. 1998: pp. 26–27).

Coalitions similar to these two can be found throughout the world and in many sectors of transnational activism. The loose coalition among environmental, consumer, and public health organizations that launched the anti-genetic seed campaign in Western Europe was such a coalition (Kettnaker 2001). Another was the coalition that organized the global anti-Iraq War demonstration on February 15, 2003 (Walgrave and Rucht eds. 2010). Such efforts to construct transnational coalitions should not lead us to believe that a global civil society, detached from domestic social networks and political opportunities and constraints, is around the corner. They often founder on the different priorities and constraints of national members. As Joe Bandy and Jackie Smith concluded from their study of transnational coalitions: "If transnational movements are to emerge and develop, they must rely on well-established national or local movements" (2005: 293).

CONCLUSIONS

The processes sketched in this chapter – domestication, global framing, diffusion, externalization, and transnational coalition formation – are far from bringing to an end the state system that has endured since the Treaty of Westphalia. Since September 11, 2001, it has become clear – if it was ever *un*clear – that the power of states is not going to disappear in short order. The process of globalization that been the source of the framing of many transnational mobilizations is reversible and has in some ways increased the power of states – especially hegemonic states. The internationalization that shapes transnational mobilization takes a number of forms that have impinged upon but not destroyed state power. Partial and regional arrangements such as the "multilevel governance" structures in the European Union (Hooghe and Marks 2002); the "complex multilateralism" described by O'Brien and his collaborators (2000); the "international regime complexity" described by Alter and Meunier and their collaborators (2009); and the weaker mechanisms of regionalism within NAFTA (Kay 2011 *a* and *b*) are nibbling away at the autonomy of the national state but not at its sovereignty.

Why not? Globalization and internationalization are not inexorable forces working against the state, but a loose framework of institutions, regimes, practices, and processes that relate states and international institutions with non-state actors and both penetrate and depend upon domestic politics. Contentious politics in the twenty-first century is, predictably, a combination of the very old and the very new, the very transgressive and the highly contained, and the transnational and the domestic, as I will argue in the final chapter of this book.

Conclusions

The Future of Social Movements

The month of May 2010 was an active one for contentious politics in Europe:

- In Athens, on the 5th, three people were killed as protesters set fire to a bank during a general strike over planned austerity measures.
- On the same day, Chancellor Angela Merkel was heckled in the German Parliament as she urged MPs to back the country's €22.4bn bailout for Greece.
- In Madrid the main union federation called a strike of public sector workers over the Socialist government's tough new austerity program.

These events – and many more – were the direct or indirect results of the global financial crisis that began in the American housing market in 2008 and ultimately diffused around the world. Not that there were no domestic effects: The so-called "Tea Party movement" that we discussed in Chapter 5 was a direct effect of the collapse of the American housing market and the bailout of Wall Street banks. But other effects occurred around the planet:

- In January 28, in financially beleaguered Iceland, following the collapse of the country's currency, large outbursts of public protest forced the cabinet to resign.
- On February 20, Latvia's center-right government also collapsed, a victim of the country's economic and political turmoil.
- In Hungary, the economic crisis offered an opportunity for the comeback of Victor Orban, the leader of Hungary's conservative opposition.
- Ukraine and Georgia moved into a period of political uncertainty.

Public discontent over the fallout from the economic crisis was also coming to a head in places as diverse as Japan, Thailand, Haiti, and China. But it was in the European Union (EU) that the crisis hit the hardest (CRS 2009: 8). Since the turn of the century, Greece had been running large budget and current account deficits and borrowing heavily in European capital markets. The low interest rates that followed its entry into the Eurozone – the club of countries that had adopted the European common currency – enabled the government to borrow cheaply and spend wildly, even as wage costs were rising and its international trade balance was declining. When Prime Minister Papandreou announced, in effect, that the last government had been cooking its books to fool the EU, already-nervous investors panicked and financial speculators began to bet against the Euro.

Papandreou responded with a series of austerity measures, culminating in a package that included a rise in value-added tax (VAT), personal and corporate taxes, a civil service hiring freeze, a 10% cut in civil service salary bonuses, and liquidation of civil servants' "fourteenth" month pay supplement (CRS 2010: 7). But none of these measures reduced the pressure on Greece, and as March gave way to April, a sovereign debt default seemed increasingly in the cards. It was at this point that EU leaders became alarmed. For if Greece defaulted, not only would the default affect the French and German bankers, who held the largest part of its debt; the entire monetary structure of the Eurozone and its carefully crafted unity might crumble.

As speculative pressure mounted on Greece, the Euro's exchange rate began to slide, and observers feared contagion to Portugal, Italy, Ireland, and Spain (a group of nations that, with the inclusion of Greece, soon gained the unflattering label of "PIIGS"; CRS 2010: 11–12). In response, France and Germany, in cooperation with the IMF, began to consider offering financial guarantees to staunch the contagion that was threatening to bring down the Euro (pp. 9–12).

At this point, the vaunted monetary unity of the EU began to crumble. Although Greece's leaders were anxious for an EU/International Monetary Fund (IMF) rescue, Greek civil servants, students, and a small but volatile anarchist fringe were not. A series of violent protests targeting both the government and the EU began in April and culminated in the burning of a bank and the deaths of the trapped bank employees on May 5th. Other vulnerable EU members, such as Spain, also suffered widespread strikes. On May 15, following a reputed phone call from Barack Obama, Prime Minister Zapatero announced a sharp reduction in civil service salaries. In France, although President Sarkozy was determined to support the bailout, his austerity program was greeted by strikes and demonstrations, not only from civil servants but from teachers, students, railway men, and even representatives of the homeless movement. As for Britain, which had stayed out of the Eurozone, its incoming Chancellor of the Exchequer, George Osborne, made it clear that Greece's problems were no concern of his.

Germany, as the largest EU economy, had the most to lose. But the German public was outraged that the prudent Germans were expected to bail out the improvident Greeks. Chancellor Merkel, facing crucial regional elections in mid-May, held off supporting the bailout until Athens showed "proof" of its fiscal seriousness. While Merkel dawdled, the cost of the bailout mushroomed from an estimated commitment of €22 billion to €750 billion. In the event, her party lost the regional election, and she emerged from the crisis politically weakened.

What Is Happening Here?

Why begin the final chapter of a book that has been largely occupied with social movements with the diffusion of the 2008 financial crisis to Europe? The short answer is that this book has been not *only* about social movements, it has been about the broader spectrum of conflicts we call "contentious politics." Had we limited our attention to the kind of social movement organizations that have dominated scholars' attention in the United States, we would have no purchase on the tangled skein of contentious events following the financial crisis in Europe. The first lesson of the story is that it is not possible today – if it ever was – to separate politics in the streets from elite and institutional politics.

The second lesson has to do with the nature of the capitalist crisis that triggered the events sketched above. In the 1920s, an international financial crisis was touched off by the excesses on Wall Street. But when it came down to it, the decision makers of the major capitalist systems had not the will nor the wisdom to overcome their national interests. As Karl Polanyi pointed out in his *The Great Transformation,* a contradiction was evident between the international and the domestic facets of the international capitalist economy (2001 [1944]). Both the transnational spread of contention from the United States to Europe in 2008–2010 and the international efforts to resolve the crisis tell us that we live in a far more integrated international political economy than our predecessors did. The lesson is that it is not possible to quarantine what happens in one political economy from what goes on in others, and this goes for both political economy and contentious politics.

The third lesson is that – despite globalization – societies do not respond in lock step to the same stimuli. The countries surveyed above responded to the Wall Street crisis with different combinations of transgressive and conventional contention: As Greek anarchists torched the center of Athens, the French used the austerity crisis as a pretext to demonstrate for broader social issues, the Spanish unions struck around narrower issues, the Germans heckled their Chancellor, the American Tea Party was industriously backing rightwing candidates in the 2010 congressional elections, and the British turned away in distaste.

That raises a question. When the first edition of *Power in Movement* was published in the 1990s, it seemed to many that a "movement society" was developing. It was widely suggested that unconventional forms of participation were becoming so widespread that these forms of action were themselves becoming conventionalized (Meyer and Tarrow, eds. 1998). Those trends are still evident in the more contained aspects of citizen politics that we see today (Dalton 2007), but there are contrary signs as well – in the violence in the streets of Athens; in the appearance of violent demonstrators at international summits; in the return of the police to aggressive protest policing (della Porta, Petersen and Rieter, eds. 2006); and in the surge of Islamist terrorism around the world. The world may indeed be becoming "a movement society," but because of changes in states, capitalism, and the international system, that society is increasingly turbulent.

To assess what has changed in the world of contentious politics and what remains constant, I will begin this chapter with a return to history – with what it has taught us and with what it fails to teach. I will then turn to the new social and political actors who have appeared prominently in contentious politics in the last decade. I will close the chapter, and this book, with some reflections on current issues in the study of contentious politics.

WHAT HISTORY TEACHES – AND DOES NOT

The transnational spread of the financial crisis of 2008–2009 and the contentious responses to it were presaged by many of the historical episodes we have touched on in this book: In 1789, as word of France's Revolution reached England, abolitionist Thomas Clarkson crossed the Channel to urge his French colleagues to join his country's antislavery movement. Clarkson took the same route again in 1814, following a second wave of British agitation. But "twice," writes the leading American student of antislavery, "he failed utterly" (Drescher 1991).

As we have seen repeatedly in this book, the diffusion of claims, repertoires, and outcomes of contentious politics is often indirect and contradictory. Consider two of the outcomes of the French Revolution: on the one hand, the Terror that consumed the lives of thousands of citizens presaged the future of totalitarian democracy; on the other, the Declaration of the Rights of Man and the Citizen was adopted by the National Assembly six weeks after frenzied Parisians carried the heads of their victims around the streets of Paris on pikes. In the face of the violence and chaos that shocked all of Europe, the Assembly adopted a far-reaching declaration of rights.

The years that followed made a mockery of the liberal sentiments of the Assembly, but the rights embedded in the revolutionary Declaration echoed across the planet. Figure C.1, from the research of Zachary Elkins and Tom Ginsburg, is illustrative of this influence. It measures the degree of similarity in the language regarding 74 different rights between the French Declaration and the language about rights in each of 583 constitutions written after 1789. The graph reveals a stunning diffusion of the language about rights from the Revolutionary Declaration into other constitutions. The French revolutionaries massacred their enemies and invented the guillotine, but they also invented and diffused the idea of universal rights.

The diffusion of contentious claims became more rapid with the spread of modern means of communication and the modularity of repertoires of contention. As we saw in Chapter 10, in 1848, revolutionary movements rolled across Europe, even reaching Latin America (Weyland 2009). The same was true in the 1960s, when activism spread from the United States to Western Europe (McAdam and Rucht 1993). This was also true of the fall of communism in 1989 and of the so-called "color revolutions" that spread across the

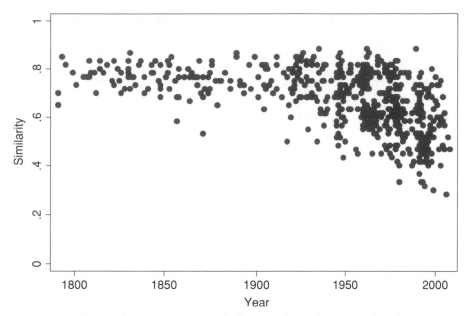

FIGURE C.I. National Constitutions and the French Declaration of Rights. *Source:* Data provided courtesy of Zachary Elkins and Tom Ginsburg, "Constitutional Convergence in Human Rights? The Reciprocal Relationship between Human Rights Treaties and National Constitutions," from their unpublished paper. Available at www.comparativeconstitutionsproject.org (2009).

same region around the turn of the century (Bunce 1999; Bunce and Wolchik 2006). History teaches that social movement claims have long diffused across territory (Givan, Roberts, and Soule, eds. 2010).

Not only contentious claims but also repertoires and forms of contention have spread rapidly around the world. As Chapters 5 and 6 showed, there has been a "modularization" of the practice and organization of contentious politics: People across the globe have been rapidly imitating practices and forms of organization that originate elsewhere. Diffusion by personal contacts and the press have been joined by radio and TV and, more recently, by the cell phone and the Internet. As we saw in the last chapter, globalization has provided a frame and a set of highly visible targets for protesters, while internationalization has offered them institutional frameworks as both targets and forums for contention. In 1789, antislavery advocates had difficulty bringing their movement across thirty miles of water, but in 2008–2009, the financial crisis diffused rapidly from America to Iceland, Ireland, and Greece, bringing contention in its wake.

But we should be cautious before deciding that globalization and the Internet have changed everything. As argued in Chapter 6, while "indirect diffusion" by the Internet spreads word of contention quickly and widely, it cannot substitute for the interpersonal trust that comes from personal ties. Remember

Tan Guocheng, whom we met in Chapter 6? He triggered a strike against a powerful corporation in the heart of an authoritarian state by building on his personal ties with other workers, especially those from his native Hunan. As for globalization, as we saw earlier in the case of the 2010 austerity protests in Europe and America, national reactions to it are very different and may be producing a recrudescence of nationalism. This takes us to how different political contexts affect the forms of contention.

Varieties of Opportunity and Constraint

The rage of both American Tea Partiers and Greek anarchists may have been triggered by the same economic crisis, but their responses were filtered through fundamentally national contexts. Enough has been said about political opportunities and constraints in this study to make it necessary to repeat only that while they do not on their own "explain" social movements, these opportunities and constraints play a major role in shaping how episodes of contention progress. They do so as the vulnerability of elites is revealed, new social actors and new forms of conflict appear, new alliances are struck, and repression becomes more ruthless, more sluggish, or more inconsistent. Some societies and some sectors of society respond more rapidly to changes in opportunity than others, but this is no more than saying that grievances, capacities, and threats vary and combine in manifold ways.

How much "punch" do political opportunities have in explaining the advent of contentious episodes? If we had elevated the concept into a general covering law, we would always find movements that it cannot "explain" and those that arise only as opportunities are closing. But finding a single explanatory factor for contention has not been the aim of this study. Instead, I have tried to show how movements develop in interaction with other actors and within general contexts of contention, depending on the "powers in movement" – the forms of mobilization they employ, their meanings and identities, and the social networks and connective structures on which they build.

I made this argument first historically – through the structural and cultural changes of the last two centuries – and then analytically – by employing the concepts of contentious repertoires, mobilizing organizations and networks, and construction of frames and meanings, as well as opportunities and constraints. A brief review of what these chapters have argued will take us to some current problems in the study of contentious politics.

Old and New Repertoires

Long before the appearance of the modern social movement, contention took manifold forms, including uprisings, revolts, revolutions, and civil and religious wars. The structure of early modern society made it possible to make war over religion or dynastic succession, but it inhibited seekers of bread, belief, land, and freedom from oppression from aggregating their interests. These inhibitions were reflected in the nature of claim making, which remained for the most part direct, parochial, and segmented.

The societies that formed around consolidating states in the last two centuries provided broader connections, more rapid communications, denser associational networks, and – especially – targets and arenas for people who felt their interests were impaired. Print and association not only provided instruments for the communication of contention to others; they also provided means through which contention was constructed.

But these processes did not stop with the availability of opportunities offered by print and association. The social movement was an outcome of capitalist modes of production and the result of long, tormented, interactive processes of state formation and citizenship and the diffusion of these forms of interaction over time and across territory. Capitalism produced the major conflicts that threatened people's interests and values; states developed the structure of constraints and opportunities that they used to do so. This takes us to the arguments made in the central core of the book.

Repertoires, Mobilizing Structures, and Framing

Once opportunities open and constraints contract, the main powers that organizers turn to are three:

- The forms of contention that arise out of – and innovate upon – culturally familiar repertoires
- The informal networks and connective structures that people live within and build
- And the cultural frames they find in their societies and create in struggle

Singly and in combination, movements use different forms of collective action to link people to one another and to opponents, supporters, and third parties. They take advantage of the cultural familiarity of these forms of action and innovate around their edges to inspire the imagination of supporters and create fear among opponents. Collective action is best seen not as a simple cost, but as both a cost and a benefit for contentious actors, for it is a means of communication and mobilization, as well as a message and a challenge to opponents.

The balance between the costs and benefits of collective action helps to determine the dynamics of the movement. As the benefits of a particular performance wane and people weary of contention, organizers have incentives to develop new forms, appeal to new participants, or radicalize their interaction with opponents. The conflicts and defections we often see within movements, as well as their increased confrontations with the state, in part are the result of the attempt to maintain their momentum through the use of new and more daring forms of collective action, and in part are caused by the changing balance of moderates and radicals within their circle of activists.

In the formation of a social movement, more than a "pull" toward particular forms of collective action and targets is needed; the "push" of solidarity and collective identity is also required. Solidarity has much to do with interest, but it produces a sustained social movement only when consensus can be built around common meanings and identities. These meanings and identities are partly inherited and partly constructed in the act of confronting opponents. They are also constituted by the interactions within movements. One of the main factors distinguishing successful movements from failed ones is their capacity to link inherited understandings to the imperative for activism.

Collective action is often led by organizations, but these are sometimes beneficiaries, sometimes initiators, and at other times inhibitors of popular politics. It is less formal organizations that mobilize people than the social networks at the base of society and the connective structures that link them to one another. Sustaining a movement is the result of a delicate balance between throttling the power in movement by providing too much organization and leaving followers to spin off into the tyranny of decentralization.

Opportunities, Cycles, and the Ends of Movements

Collective action repertoires, cultural frames, and mobilizing structures are only potential sources of the power in movements; they can be employed just as easily for social control as for insurgency. The recurring cycles of contention that were described in Chapter 10 are the products of a wider diffusion of political opportunities, which transform the potential for mobilization into action. In these crucibles of conflict and innovation, challengers and their opponents not only take advantage of available opportunities; they create them for others by producing new forms of action, hammering out new "master frames," and making coalitions that force the state to respond to the disorder around it.

The response to a cycle of contention is often repressive, but even repression is often mixed with facilitation and reform, leading to very different outcomes for similar forms of political opposition. Particularly when groups within the system see the opportunity to aggrandize themselves in alliance with a slice of challengers, rulers are placed in a vulnerable position, to which reformism is a frequent response. As conflict collapses and militants retire to lick their wounds, many of their advances are reversed, but they often leave behind incremental expansions in participation, changes in popular culture, and residual movement networks. Cycles of contention are a season for sowing, but reaping is often done during the periods of demobilization that follow, by late-comers to the cause, by elites, and by authorities.

If cycles are opened by expanding opportunities, how do they decline, as they inevitably do? Is it simply because people tire of agitation, because enervating factional struggles develop, because organizations become oppressive, or because elites repress and placate challengers? All these are contributory causes of cyclical decline, but there is a more systemic cause as well: Since the power in movement depends on the mobilization of external opportunities, when opportunities expand from initial challengers to others – some of whom are elites and authorities – movements lose their primary source of power. For brief periods, the power in movement seems irresistible, but it disperses rapidly and passes inexorably into more institutional forms. Clever power holders exploit these opportunities by selectively facilitating some movements and repressing or ignoring others.

NEW MOVEMENTS; CHANGING PROBLEMS

Contentious politics since the turn of the new century have consolidated many of the findings summarized previously. But they also brought a wave of new challenges – not only to states but to how movements have been studied since the 1960s and 1970s. Some of these challenges to movement theory – like the cultural turn described in Chapter 7 – were put forward as challenges but have been creatively absorbed into social movement studies. Others, such as the postmodern turn that briefly flew in the social movement world, fell to the ground as its essential nihilism revealed itself. But three other challenges remain on the agenda of both international politics and social movement theory. The most disturbing are the violent movements of the 1990s and 2000s; less threatening, but equally important are the trends to the "normalization" of contention in Western democracies. A third has to do with the threats of suppression of contentious politics.

Warring Movements

Are the ethnic and religious conflicts and the guerilla and civil wars that we discussed in Chapter 5 no more than a peripheral reflex of the crises of liberal capitalism and the end of state socialism, or do they represent something fundamentally new? Disturbing signs suggest that the postwar synthesis of economic expansion and liberal politics that brought social peace to the North and a *pax Americana* to the South is ending. In Western Europe, the running sore of Catholic nationalism in Northern Ireland was staunched only in the late 1990s (Tilly and Tarrow 2007: 145–51). Rightwing parties such as the French *Front National*, the *Flemish Vlaams Belang*, and the Austrian Freedom party, as well as skinhead violence, have gained support from those suffering from rising unemployment and anti-immigrant phobia. And from the Middle East and South Asia, Islamist violence has spread into the capitalist core, often drawing on the alienation of second-generation immigrants from South Asia and the Middle East.

The United States has not been bereft of such "ugly movements." Although peace, women's, and ecology movements of previous decades have increasingly become part of contained "advocacy organizations" (Andrews and Edwards 2004), less pacific movements were also mobilizing. In the American West and Southwest, militant antigovernmental movements and armed militias have defied the federal government, attacking both churches and Jewish institutions. In Waco, Texas, the members of a religious sect were incinerated when federal officials tried to eject them from a ranch complex. In Oklahoma City, a pair of rightwing militants destroyed a federal building and took the lives of hundreds of citizens with a bomb intended to strike a blow against the state (Wright 2007).

The spread of violent, sectarian, and self-enclosed identity movements reflects the powers of movement that I have described in this book. But it also raises troubling questions for social movement theory: about the increase in hatred, the recrudescence of ethnic conflict, the decline of civility, and the internationalization of conflict. To the extent to which we have allowed the examples of civil Western movements from the 1960s to shape our models, we will not be able to understand them. Some students of nationalism, ethnic conflict, and terrorism have concluded that these models are simply irrelevant in the post-1989 world. Others have argued that these models can serve us well, but only if the static categories of the traditional canon are put into motion (McAdam et al. 2001). We need to develop a general but nondeterministic approach to contentious politics that includes, but is not dominated by, the experience of the reformist movements of the United States and Western Europe in the 1960s and 1970s, if we are to understand the warring movements both there and further afield.

The Containment of Contention

As the world approaches a new century, trends are moving in a very different direction. In his fine textbook on citizen politics, Russell Dalton has analyzed protest participation in four liberal democracies of the West (the United States, Britain, Germany, and France). His analysis shows that participation in protest and related activities was more common at the end of the period he studied (1974–1999) than at the beginning (2006: 68). These changes were not linear or equal for all countries. But in places as different as peaceful Switzerland and turbulent Italy, the end of the protest cycle of the late 1960s left a larger constituency for contention than at its beginning. Similarly, when Hanspeter Kriesi and his collaborators examined the trend of "new" social movements of the 1970s and 1980s in four western European countries, three of these countries described protest cycles similar in shape to what we saw in the 1960s (the fourth was France.) At the end of the 1980s, Germany, Holland, and Switzerland hosted a larger number of protests by new social movements than in the mid-1970s (Kriesi et al. 1995: 74).

In addition to being more frequent, relatively contained forms of contentious politics appear to be employed by a wider variety of organizations and a broader range of social groups than was the case thirty years ago. Particularly in the United States, but also in Western Europe, a dramatic increase in the establishment of interest organizations has occurred on the basis of conscience constituencies who claim to support distant constituencies, marginal social groups, or "the public interest." Such organizations often combine institutional advocacy with more contentious activities (Minkoff 1994; Walker 1991). Even older ones – such as staid conservation groups in the United States or the once-compliant unions in Germany – have experienced an increase in protest activity.

But as participation in unconventional political action has become more widespread, it has also become more complicated. This is so not only because of the presence of a larger number of sophisticated organizations in the movement field, but also because the technical threshold for participation has risen. Activism is no longer a matter of going down to the pub to a meeting or joining friends or neighbors for a march or demonstration; it increasingly requires Internet skills, the ability to form coalitions with like-minded groups, and the courage to get up in public (either virtually or "offline") to speak one's mind (Dalton 2006: 74). Moreover, as one-shot protest events have given way to extended campaigns (see Chapter 9), ordinary people with work or family requirements may not be able to sustain their participation. The "movement society" that David Meyer and this author wrote of in the 1990s may actually be increasing the participation gap between rich and poor, the well-networked and the relatively isolated, and those with full-time occupations and those with disposable income and free time.

New social actors have been increasingly visible in protest activities since the 1960s. Middle-class Britons protesting against new highways or the barbarism of the hunt; truck drivers blocking roads against pension reform in France; Catholic priests and Protestant ministers demonstrating for peace in the Netherlands; shopkeepers protesting against stricter tax collection in Italy, alongside traditional protesting groups of students, peasants, and workers – these have become familiar figures in the contentious politics of the 1990s and 2000s (Jiménez 2006).

The most striking shift has been the increasing presence of women in contentious politics. Although men still protest more often than women, writes Dalton, "there is evidence that this pattern is changing with a narrowing of gender roles" (2006: 70). Consider the most dramatic protest movements in the United States over the past two decades: From Phyllis Schlafly's Anti-ERA campaign and Mothers Against Drunk Driving in the 1980s to the antiabortion blockades and the Gay and Lesbian March on Washington in 1994, and the Tea Party movement after 2008 – women have been found increasingly in leadership roles. This trend is not limited to the United States. In Latin America, some of the most visible protests against military rule, torture, and disappearances were mounted by groups of mothers and even grandmothers.

But does the extension of the use of contentious forms of behavior to new groups of citizens expand conflict outside the confines of routine politics? Or does it mean that these confines themselves are expanding? If the former is the case, then we may be witnessing growth of more transgressive politics vis-à-vis elections and interest groups; if the latter, then we may be seeing conventionalization of protest, removing its sting and adding protest to the contained repertoire of contention. In countries in which marches and demonstrations are frequent, signs of the conventionalization of protest are already apparent.

The evidence is not yet in: On the one hand, we are seeing growth in contentious politics in general; on the other, it is the least transgressive forms of contention – for example, participation in peaceful demonstrations, and signing online petitions – that are increasing, while participation in more disruptive forms of contention has decreased. In the United States, the use of political violence fell dramatically between the early 1970s and the late 1980s (Gurr 1989), making the occasional dramatic incident, such as the Oklahoma City bombing, all the more shocking.

A third possibility is that we are witnessing growth of both contained and violent forms of contention. With Charles Tilly (Tilly and Tarrow 2007: Chapter 8), I examined an extreme form of such a co-occurrence in Israel/Palestine, where conventional social movement activity exists side by side with bombings, assassinations, and military repression. After dedicating a chapter to social movements and their relatively contained forms of contention and another to "lethal conflicts" marked by organized violence (Tilly and Tarrow 2007: Chapters 6 and 7), we realized the many ways in which more conventional and more contentious forms of collective action can combine:

- They combine in the sustained campaigns of broad coalitions of actors who employ combinations of contained and transgressive forms of action.
- They combine in what we called "composite systems," in which different actors engaged in these polar forms of contention and affected one another's strategies and outcomes (Chapter 8).
- And they combine in forms of action that cross the boundary of the polity.

One area that is rich with intersections between routine and contentious processes is the study of elections. For many years, political scientists and sociologists have divided up the study of participatory politics along the contained/transgressive frontier, with political scientists using ever more sophisticated tools to study elections and sociologists specializing in social movements. Neither group of scholars gave particular attention to the interactions and exchanges between movements and elections (McAdam and Tarrow 2010). But with growing connections among sociologists and political scientists, efforts to specify the connections between social movements and elections are increasing.

In an exemplary effort, Michael Heaney and Fabio Rojas have shown how the anti-Iraq War movement affected the election campaigns of 2006 and 2008, and how this movement was reshaped by the election of Barack Obama. The 2006 and 2008 elections moved a large proportion of partisan activists from the antiwar movement into electoral politics, leaving the movement more under the control of "the party in the street" (Heaney and Rojas 2007). In a very different setting, Carew Boulding has studied the interaction between protest and voter turnout in Bolivia (2009). And of course, the studies that have recently appeared on the "electoral revolutions" in the former Soviet sphere all concern the intersection of social movements and elections (Beissinger 2007). This is an area ripe with possibilities for research.

The Suppression of Contention

In Chapter 8, we saw that physical repression is only one method that states and elites use to counter opponents. States can cut off their funding, pass onerous tax laws and permitting requirements, and impose restrictions on people who have been booked at demonstrations, and elites can limit patronage to moderate groups and regulate behavior in their firms similar to company towns. In addition, states have substantial influence on how the media treat protest and control the content of the Internet. We saw the effects of such control in China in 2010, when Google chose to pull out of the country because of authorities' tight hand on content.

Authoritarian states have always striven to control protest and protesters, but in the new century, a more serious issue is whether such control is also increasing in liberal democratic states. In terms of direct coercion of protesters, constitutional states forbid only violent forms of protest; they tolerate a wide range of behaviors; and they encourage and, in some cases, require people to vote. But in the wake of September 11, 2001, and other outrages, there have been changes that have raised concerns about growing suppression of the preconditions of protest.

In the United States, the swift passage of the U.S. Patriot Act soon after 9/11 left little room for advocates of civil liberties to have their say; in the United Kingdom, even before the subway bombings of 2007, a steady increase in surveillance was provided by thousands of surveillance cameras in public places. In both countries, preventive detention has increased, and, in the case of terrorism suspects, there has been use of torture and detention without trial. In June 2010, the U.S. Supreme Court, with the enthusiastic support of the Obama Administration, interpreted the Patriot Act to ban domestic groups from providing advice – even advice on how to engage in peaceful negotiations – to groups that had been labeled terrorist by the government.

How have citizens responded to these threats to civil liberties? In protesting against the U.S. Patriot Act and other threats, both lawyers and other groups have employed a variety of strategies, such as cause lawyers using the courts, private associations defending civil liberties, and grassroots organizations mobilizing citizens on behalf of rights.

Using the Courts to Defend Rights: Since the Civil Rights and women's movements, scholars of law and social movements have been aware of the many ways in which movements use the courts. But only with the aggressive expansion of executive powers under the second Bush Administration has the role of cause lawyers become prominent. In conflicts over the *habeas corpus* rights of Guantanamo detainees; in the protection of privacy rights; and in the growing issue of undocumented immigrants, lawyers have been organizing in ways that strikingly resemble how social movements form networks, frame their claims, and interact with authorities (Center for Constitutional Rights 2006; Margulies 2006; McCann and Dudas 2006; Sidel 2004).

Librarians to the Rescue: Private associations, such as the American Bar Association, have also been important in defending citizens' rights against government intrusion. An unusual example was the campaign launched by the American Librarians' Association denouncing an article of the U.S. Patriot Act that allowed the FBI access to the records of library loans of individuals. Working with more typical defenders of civil liberties, such as the ACLU (American Civil Liberties Union), the librarians exposed not only the threats, but the absurdities of the U.S. Patriot Act (Blanc 2010; Sidel 2004).

Back to the Grassroots: More typical of traditional social movement activity was the grassroots movement created to protect First Amendment rights soon after passage of the U.S. Patriot Act. Beginning in New England, where the institution of the town meeting had its start, and based at first on established civil liberties groups, a national network of supporters of first amendment rights was formed (Blanc 2010; Vasi and Strang 2009). What was most interesting about this network was that, as it diffused, the range of its participants broadened, from the "usual suspects" on the progressive and liberal left to more mainstream groups and associations. This was similar to the trajectory of the 1980s peace movement, which began in the grassroots of New England but shifted in scale to Washington, and thence to traditional sectors of the Democratic Party (Meyer 1990).

My inclusion of lawyers, librarians, and local civil liberties groups in contentious politics may surprise some students of social movements. After all, such groups do not employ the traditional disruptive performances that movements typically use; they have not created sustained movement organizations; and they frame their claims around traditional values of American political culture, such as civil liberties. But if we are interested in the broader range of contentious politics, and not simply in traditional social movements, we will see that these examples provide evidence that contention against state expansion is still alive. All these groups used a variety of forms of contention, both transgressive and contained, to make their claims, shifting sometimes toward one and sometimes toward the other, depending on the seriousness of the threat and the opportunities for each.

Figure 1.1 back in Chapter 1 made that point graphically. Just as social movements routinely cross the boundary of the polity into the interstices of routine politics, mainstream actors in American society occasionally venture into the less familiar precincts of transgressive politics. If there is a change – and it is not one that we can quantify at this writing – it would be in the density and the multiplicity of hybrid forms of interaction that bridge convention and contention across the boundaries of the polity.

EMERGING CHALLENGES

The growth of democratic states' capacity for suppression and its relationship to changes in protest behavior is an important emerging area of research (e.g., see della Porta et al. 2006). But as in any dynamic field of study, the next generation of scholars should attend to many such issues. Here are some of the issues that seem most pressing to this author.

What about social movements that do not target the state? Do they fall outside the range of "contentious politics"? In recent years, a number of "stockholder revolts" have occurred. These do not look much like traditional social movements, but they certainly qualify for what this book has regarded as part of contentious politics (Soule 2009). The next generation of scholars of contention will have to take these protests more seriously.

Do new forms of collective action – particularly Internet-based campaigns – challenge existing approaches to contentious politics, or will they eventually be absorbed into the repertoire of contention, much as the newspaper and television were in previous epochs? A number of scholars argue forcefully that the Internet has transformed not only ways of communicating but also the basic organization of social movements (Bennett et al. 2008). Others, such as Tilly and Wood (2009), have been more cautious. These issues are already producing interesting research and will produce more in the years to come.

What of globalization? Does it shift the targets of contention from national states to something beyond the state, or does it simply add the possibility of transnational "forum shopping" to the strategies of claim makers? If the former, there is some support for the more optimistic calls for a "global civil society"; if the latter, then the relationships characteristic of political contention within the nation-state may simply be extended farther.

And what of the "warring movements" discussed previously and in Chapter 5? Are they likely to continue to attack secular, Western societies with the same ferocity they exhibited in the attacks of 2001 in the United States and in 2007 in Great Britain? Or will they, similar to previous waves of violent movements, eventually become institutionalized? Let me close with a reflection on this impossible question.

The citizens of modern states have lived through such "moments of madness" before. It is enough to remember that severed heads were paraded around Paris on pikes during the great French Revolution. That revolution produced the Terror and the first modern dictatorship under Napoleon, but it also produced the citizen army, the modern administrative state, the end of feudalism, and the career open to talents, as well as a highly influential beacon of modern constitutional politics, the Declaration of the Rights of Man and the Citizen (see Figure C1 above). The same has been true of the mixed messages of many cycles of contention in the past.

Of course, the concern raised by recent outbreaks of violence is that movements are better armed, have a broader cultural valence, and have greater diffusion than movements that broke out in Paris in 1789. Does this mean that the "New World Order" that was supposed to result from the liberation movements of 1989 is turning instead into a permanent state of violence and disorder? Have the resources for violent collective action become so widely accessible, integralist identities so widespread, and militants so free of the national state that a violent movement society is resulting? Or will the current wave of ethnic and religious movements be partially outgrown, partially domesticated, and partially mediated by the political process, as in previous cycles of contention?

The violence and intolerance that we have seen during the first decade of the new century constitute a frightening trend. But this is not the first great wave of movement in history, nor will it be the last. If its dynamic comes to resemble the social movements that we have encountered in this book, then its power will at first be ferocious, uncontrolled, and widely diffused, but ultimately ephemeral and institutionalized. If so, as Aristide Zolberg wrote of the 1960s movements, it will disperse "like a flood tide which loosens up much of the soil but leaves alluvial deposits in its wake" (Zolberg 1972: 206). Or so we may hope.

Sources

Ackerman, Bruce. 1994. "Rooted Cosmopolitanism." *Ethics* 104:516–535.
Aghulon, Maurice. 1979. *Marianne au combat: L'imagerie et la symbolique républicaines de 1789 a 1880*. Paris: Flammarion.
———. 1982. *The Republic in the Village: The People of the Var from the French Revolution to the Second Republic*. Cambridge: Cambridge University Press.
Agnew, John. 1997. *Political Geography: A Reader*. London: Arnold.
Alimi, Eitan. 2006. "Constructing Political Opportunity: 1987 – The Palestinian Year of Discontent." *Mobilization* 11:67–80.
———. 2007. *Israeli Politics and the First Palestinian Intifada*, London and New York: Routledge.
———. 2009. "Mobilizing Under the Gun: Theorizing Political Opportunity Structure in a Highly Repressive Setting." *Mobilization* 14:219–237.
———. Forthcoming. "The Relational Context of Radicalization: The Case of Jewish Settlers' Contention Before and After the Gaza Pullout."
Alinsky, Saul. 1971. *Rules for Radicals*. New York: Vintage.
Alter, Karen and Jeannette Vargas. 2000. "Explaining Variation in the Use of European Litigation Strategies: EC Law and UK Gender Equality Policy." *Comparative Political Studies* 33:452–482.
Alter, Karen J. and Sophie Meunier, eds. 2009. "Symposium: The Politics of International Regime Complexity." *Perspectives on Politics* 7:13–70.
Amenta, Edwin. 2006. *When Movements Matter: The Townsend Plan and the Rise of Social Security*. Princeton, NJ: Princeton University Press.
Amenta, Erwin and Neal Caren. 2004. "The Legislative, Organizational, and Beneficiary Consequences of State-Oriented Challengers," pp. 461–488 in *The Blackwell Companion to Social Movements*, edited by D. Snow, S. Soule, and H. Kriesi. Oxford: Blackwell.
Amenta, Edwin, Bruce G. Caruthers, and Yvonne Zylan. 1992. "A Hero for the Aged? The Townsend Movement, The Political Mediation Model, and the U.S. Old-Age Policy, 1934–1950." *American Journal of Sociology* 98:308–339.
Amenta, Edwin, Drew Halfmann, and Michael P. Young. 1999. "The Strategies and Contexts of Social Protest: Political Mediation and the Impact of the Townsend Movement in California." *Mobilization* 4:1–24.

Aminzade, Ronald R. 1981. *Class, Politics, and Early Industrial Capitalism: A Study of Mid-Nineteenth-Century Toulouse, France*. Albany: State University of New York.

Aminzade, Ronald R. and Doug McAdam. 2001. "Emotions and Contentious Politics." Chap. 2 in *Silence and Voice in the Study of Contentious Politics*, in R. R. Aminzade, et al. New York and Cambridge: Cambridge University Press.

Aminzade, Ronald R. and Elizabeth J. Perry. 2001. "The Sacred, Religious and Secular in Contentious Politics: Blurring the Boundaries." Chap. 6 in *Silence and Voice in the Study of Contentious Politics*, In R. R. Aminzade, et al. New York and Cambridge: Cambridge University Press.

Aminzade, Ronald R., Jack Goldstone, Doug McAdam, Elizabeth Perry, William H. Sewell, Jr., Sidney Tarrow, and Charles Tilly. 2001. *Silence and Voice in the Study of Contentious Politics*. New York and Cambridge: Cambridge University Press.

Anderson, Benedict. 1990. "Language, Fantasy, Revolution: Java, 1900–1945." *Prisma* 50:25–39.

———. 1991. *Imagined Communities. Reflections on the Origin and Spread of Nationalism*. London: Verso.

Andrews, Kenneth T. and Michael Biggs. 2006. "The Dynamics of Protest Diffusion: Movement Organizations, Social Networks, and News Media in the 1960 Sit-Ins." *American Sociological Review* 71:752–777.

Andrews, Kenneth T. and Bob Edwards. 2004. "Advocacy Organizations in the U.S. Political Process." *Annual Review of Sociology* 30:479–506.

Anner, Mark. 2000. "Local and Transnational Campaigns to End Sweatshop Practices." Chap. 12 in *Transnational Cooperation Among Trade Unions*, edited by M. Gordon and L. Turner. Ithaca: Cornell University Press.

Appiah, Kwame Anthony. 1996. "Cosmopolitan Patriots." pp. 21–29 in *For Love of Country*, edited by J. Cohen. Boston, MA: Beacon Press.

Apter, David E., ed. 1964. *Ideology and Discontent*. London: The Free Press.

Aptheker, Herbert. 1989. *Abolitionism: A Revolutionary Movement*. Boston, MA: Twayne Publishers.

Ardant, Gabriel. 1975. "Financial Policy and Economic Infrastructure of Modern States and Nations." Chap. 3 in *The Formation of National States in Western Europe*, edited by C. Tilly. Princeton, NJ: Princeton University Press.

Armstrong, Elisabeth A. 2005. "From Struggle to Settlement: The Crystallization of a Field of Lesbian/Gay Organizations in San Francisco, 1969–1973." Chap. 6 in *Social Movements and Organizational Theory*, edited by G. F. Davis, D. McAdam, W. R. Scott, and M. N. Zald. New York and Cambridge: Cambridge University Press.

Auyero, Javier. 2007. *Routine Politics and Violence in Argentina. The Gray Zone of State Power*. New York and Cambridge: Cambridge University Press.

Bailin, Bernard. 1967. *The Ideological Origins of the American Revolution*. Cambridge, MA: Harvard University Press.

Baker, Keith Michael. 1994. "Introduction." In *The French Revolution and the Creation of Modern Political Culture*, vol. 4: The Terror, edited by K. M. Baker. Oxford and New York: Pergamon.

Baldassari, Delia and Mario Diani. 2007. "The Integrative Power of Civil Networks." *American Journal of Sociology* 113:735–780.

Banaszak, Lee Ann. 1996. *Why Movements Succeed or Fail: Opportunity, Culture, and the Struggle for Woman Suffrage*. Princeton, NJ: Princeton University Press.

Bandy, Joe and Jackie Smith, eds. 2004. *Coalitions Across Borders: Transnational Protest and the Neoliberal Order*. Lanham, MD: Rowman and Littlefield.

Barkan, Steven E. 1984. "Legal Control of the Southern Civil Rights Movement." *American Sociological Review* 49:552–565.

Barnes, Samuel and Max Kaase, et al. 1979. *Political Action: Mass Participation in Five Western Democracies*. Thousand Oaks, CA: Sage Publications.

Bartolini, Stefano and Peter Mair. 2008. *Identity, Competition and Electoral Availability: The Stabilization of European Electorates, 1885–1985*. Cambridge and New York: Cambridge University Press.

Beckwith, Karen. 2003. "The Gendering Ways of States: Women's Representation and State Reconfiguration in France, Great Britain, and the United States." Chap. 8 in *Women's Movements Facing the Reconfigured State*, edited by L. A. Banaszak, K. Beckwith, and D. Rucht. New York: Cambridge University Press.

Beissinger, Mark R. 2002. *Nationalist Mobilization and the Collapse of the Soviet Union*. New York and Cambridge: Cambridge University Press.

———. 2007. "Structure and Example in Modular Political Phenomena: The Diffusion of Bulldozer/Rose/Orange/Tulip Revolutions." *Perspectives on Politics* 5:259–276.

———. 2011. "Mechanisms of Maidan: The Structure of Contingency in the Making of Colored Revolution." *Mobilization* 16.

Benford, Robert D. 1993. "Frame Disputes within the Disarmament Movement." *Social Forces* 71:677–701.

Benford, Robert D. and Scott A. Hunt. 1992. "Dramaturgy and Social Movements: The Social Construction and Communication of Power." *Sociological Inquiry* 62: 36–55.

Bennett, W. Lance. 2003. "Communicating Global Activism: Some Strengths and Vulnerabilities of Networked Politics." pp. 123–146 in *Cyberprotest: New Media, Citizens and Social Movements*, edited by W. Donk, P. Nixon, and D. Rucht. London: Routledge.

Bennett, W. Lance, Christian Breunig, and Terri Givens. 2008. "Communication and Political Mobilization: Digital Media and the Organization of Anti-Iraq War Demonstrations in the U.S." *Political Communication* 25:269–289.

Bennett, W. Lance, Terri E. Givens, and Lars Willnat. 2004. "Crossing Political Divides: Internet Use and Political Identifications in Transnational Anti-War and Social Justice Activists in Eight Nations." Uppsala, Sweden: European Consortium for Political Research.

Bensel, Richard F. 1990. *Yankee Leviathan. The Origins of Central Authority in America, 1859–1877*. New York and Cambridge: Cambridge University Press.

Bercé, Yves-Marie. 1990. *History of Peasant Revolts: The Social Origins of Rebellion in Early Modern France*. Ithaca, NY: Cornell University Press.

Berejikian, Jeffrey. 1992. "Revolutionary Collective Action and the Agent-Structure Problem." *American Political Science Review* 86:649–657.

Berezin, Mabel. 1997. *Making the Fascist Self: The Political Culture of Interwar Italy*. Ithaca and London: Cornell University Press.

Berger, Suzanne. 2000. "Globalization and Politics." *Annual Review of Political Science* 3:43–62.

Bergeson, Albert. 2007. "A Three-Step Model of Terrorist Violence." *Mobilization* 12:109–118.

Berman, Eli and David Laitin. 2008. "Religion, Terrorism and Public Goods: Testing the Club Model." *Journal of Public Economics* 92:1942–1967.

Bermeo, Nancy. 1997. "Myths of Moderation. Confrontation and Conflict during Democratic Transitions." *Comparative Politics* 27:305–322.

Birnbaum, Pierre. 1988. *States and Collective Action: The European Experience.* Cambridge and New York: Cambridge University Press.

Blake, Donald. 1960. "Swedish Trade Unions and the Social Democratic Party: The Formative Years." *Scandinavian Economic History Review* 8:19–44.

Blanc, Florent. 2010. "Mobilization of Librarians, ACLU, Cities and Lawyers." Unpublished PhD Dissertation Thesis. Evanston, IL: Department of Political Science, Northwestern University.

Bloch, Marc. 1931. *Les caractères originaux de l'histoire rurale francaise.* Paris: Armand Colin.

Block, Fred. 2003. "Karl Polanyi and the Writing of *The Great Transformation.*" *Theory and Society* 36:1–32.

Block, Jack S. Jr. 1989. *American Temperance Movements: Cycles of Reform.* Boston, MA: Twayne Publishers.

Bob, Clifford. 2005. *The Marketing of Rebellion: Insurgents, Media and International Activism.* New York and Cambridge: Cambridge University Press.

———. 2011. *Globalizing the Right: Conservative Activism and World Politics.* Cambridge, MA: Cambridge University Press.

Bonnell, Victoria, Ann Cooper, and Gregory Freidin. *Russia and the Barricades: Eye Witness Accounts of the Moscow Coup.* New York: M.E. Sharpe.

Bosi, Lorenzo. 2006. "The Dynamics of Social Movement Development: Northern Ireland's Civil Rights Movement in the 1960's." *Mobilization* 81–100.

Bosi, Lorenzo and Katrin Uba. 2009. "Special Focus Issue on Social Movement Outcomes." *Mobilization* 14:409–504.

Boudreau, Vincent. 1996. "Northern Theory, Southern Protest: Opportunity Structure Analysis in a Cross-National Perspective." *Mobilization* 1:175–189.

Boulding, Carew Elizabeth. 2010. "NGOs and Political Participation in Weak Democracies: Sub-national Evidence on Protest and Voter Turnout from Bolivia." *Journal of Politics* 72:456–468.

Boykoff, Jules. 2007. *Beyond Bullets: The Suppression of Dissent in the United States.* Oakland, CA: AK Press.

Boyte, Harry C. 1980. *The Backyard Revolution.* Philadelphia, PA: Temple University Press.

Brand, Karl-Werner. 1990. "Cyclical Aspects of New Social Movements: Waves of Cultural Criticism and Mobilization Cycles of New Middle-class Radicalism." pp. 23–42 in *Challenging the Political Order*, edited by R. Dalton and M. Kuechler. Oxford, UK: Oxford University Press.

Brass, Paul. 1974. *Language, Religion and Politics in North India.* New York and Cambridge. Cambridge University Press.

———. 2003. *The Production of Hindu-Muslim Violence in Contemporary India.* Seattle and London: University of Washington Press.

Brewer, John. 1976. *Party Ideology and Popular Politics at the Accession of George III.* Cambridge, MA: Cambridge University Press.

Brewer, John. 1990. *The Sinews of Power: War, Money and the English State, 1688–1783.* Cambridge MA, Harvard University Press.

Bridges, Amy. 1986. "Becoming American: The Working Classes in the United States before the Civil War." Chap. 5 in *Working Class Formation: Nineteenth Century Patterns in Western Europe and the United States*, edited by I. Katznelson and A. R. Zolberg. Princeton, NJ: Princeton University Press.

Bridgford, Jeff. 1989. "The Events of May: Consequences for Industrial Relations in France," pp. 100–116 in *Statemaking and Social Movements: Essays in History and*

Theory, edited by C. Bright and S. Harding. Ann Arbor, MI: University of Michigan Press.

Bright, Charles C. 1984. "The State in the United States during the Nineteenth Century." pp. 121–122 in *Statemaking and Social Movements: Essays in History and Theory*, edited by C. Bright and S. Harding. Ann Arbor, MI: University of Michigan Press.

Brockett, Charles D. 1991. "The Structure of Political Opportunities and Peasant Mobilization in Central America." *Comparative Politics* 23:253–274.

Brockett, Charles D. 1995. "A Protest-Cycle Resolution of the Repression/Popular Protest Paradox." pp. 117–144 in *Repertoires and Cycles of Collective Action*, edited by M. Traugott. Durham, NC: Duke University Press.

Broer, Christian and Jan Willem Duyvendak. 2009. "Discursive Opportunities, Feeling Rules, and the Rise of Protest Against Aircraft Noise." *Mobilization* 14:337–356.

Brown, Richard D. 1970. *Revolutionary Politics in Massachusetts: The Boston Committee of Correspondence and the Towns, 1772–1774*. Cambridge, MA: Harvard University Press.

———. 1989. *Knowledge Is Power: The Diffusion of Information in Early America*. New York: Oxford.

Browning, Rufus, Dale Rogers Marshall and David H. Tabb. 1984. *Protest is Not Enough. The Struggle of Blacks and Hispanics for Equality in Urban Politics*. Berkeley and Los Angeles: University of California Press.

Brulle, Robert, Liesel Hall Turner, Jason Carmichael, and J. Craig Jenkins. 2007. "Measuring Social Movement Organization Populations: A Comprehensive Census of U.S. Environmental Movement Organizations." *Mobilization* 12:255–270.

Bruneteaux, Patrick. 1996. *Maintenir l'ordre. Les transformations de la violence d'Etat en régime democratique*. Paris: Presse de la Fondation Nationale des Sciences Politques.

Bruszt, László, Nauro F. Campos, Jan Fidrmuc, and Gérard Roland. 2010. "Civil Society, Institutional Change and the Politics of Reform: The Great Transition." *UNU-Wider Working Paper* 38.

Buechler, Steven M. 1986. *The Transformation of the Woman Suffrage Movement: The Case of Illinois, 1850–1920*. New Brunswick, NJ: Rutgers University Press.

———. 2004. "The Strange Career of Strain and Breakdown Theories of Collective Action." Chap. 3 in *The Blackwell Companion to Social Movements*, edited by D. Snow, S. Soule, and H. Kriesi. Malden, MA and Oxford: Blackwell.

Bunce, Valerie. 1984–1985. "The Empire Strikes Back: The Transformation of Eastern Europe from a Soviet Asset to a Soviet Liability." *International Organization* 39:1–46.

———. 1999. *Subversive Institutions: The Design and the Destruction of Socialism and the State*. New York and Cambridge: Cambridge University Press.

Bunce, Valerie and Sharon Wolchik. 2006. "International Diffusion and Postcommunist Electoral Revolutions." *Communist and Postcommunist Studies* 39:283–304.

———. 2010. "Transnational Networks, Diffusion Dynamics, and Electoral Change in the Postcommunist World." Chap. 8 in *The Diffusion of Social Movements; Actors, Mechanisms and Political Effects* edited by R. K.Givan, K.M. Roberts, and S.A. Soule. New York and Cambridge: Cambridge University Press.

———. 2011. *Defeating Authoritarian Leaders in Mixed Regimes: Electoral Struggles, U.S. Democracy Assistance, and International Diffusion in Post-Communist Europe and Eurasia*. New York and Cambridge: Cambridge University Press. To be published.

Burstein, Paul. 1985. *Discrimination, Jobs, and Politics: The Struggle for Equal Opportunity in the United States*. Chicago, IL: University of Chicago Press.

————. 1998. "Interest Organizations, Political Parties, and the Study of Democratic Politics." pp. 39–56 in *Social Movements and American Political Institutions*, edited by A. Costain and A. McFarland. Lanham, MD: Rowman and Littlefield.

Burstein, Paul, Rachel L. Einwohner, and Jocelyn A. Hollander. 1991. "The Success of Political Movements: A Bargaining Perspective." Seattle, WA: University of Washington, Department of Sociology.

Burstein, Paul and April Linton. 2002. "The Impact of Political Parties, Interest Groups and Social Movements on Public Policy: Some Recent Evidence and Theoretical Concerns." *Social Forces* 81:380–408.

Burt, Ronald S. 1997. "The Contingent Value of Social Capital." *Administrative Science Quarterly* 42:339–365.

Bush, Evelyn L. 2004. "Transnational Religion and Secular Institutions: Structure, Framing and Influence in Human Rights." Unpublished PhD Thesis. Ithaca, NY: Department of Sociology, Cornell University.

Bush, Evelyn L. and Pete Simi. 2001. "European Farmers and their Protests." Chap. 5 in *Contentious Europeans: Protest and Politics in an Emerging Polity*, edited by D. Imig and S. Tarrow. Lanham, MD: Rowman and Littlefield.

Bushnell, John. 1990. *Moscow Graffiti: Language and Subculture*. Boston, MA: Unwin Hyman.

Cain, Bruce, Russell J. Dalton, and Susan Scarrow, eds. 2003. *Democracy Transformed? Expanding Political Opportunities in Advanced Industrial Democracies*. Oxford, UK: Oxford University Press.

Calhoun, Craig. 1982. *The Question of Class Struggle: Social Foundations of Popular Radicalism during the Industrial Revolution*. Chicago, IL: University of Chicago Press.

————. 1994a. *Neither Gods Nor Emperors: Students and the Struggle for Democracy in China*. Berkeley and Los Angeles: University of California Press.

————. 1994b. *Social Theory and the Politics of Identity*. Oxford, UK: Blackwell.

————. 1995. "New Social Movements of the Early Nineteenth Century." pp. 173–216 in *Repertoires and Cycles of Collective Action*, edited by M. Traugott. Durham and London: Duke University Press.

Cameron, Maxwell A., Robert J. Lawson, and Brian W. Tomlin. 1998. *To Walk Without Fear. The Global Movement to Ban Landmines*. Toronto, Oxford, and New York: Oxford University Press.

Campbell, John L. 2005. "Where Do We Stand? Common Mechanisms in Organizations and Social Movements Research." Chap. 2 in *Social Movements and Organization Theory*, edited by G. F. Davis, D. McAdam, W. R. Scott, and M. N. Zald. New York and Cambridge: Cambridge University Press.

Caporaso, James A. and Joseph Jupille. 2001. "The Europeanization of Gender Equality Policy and Domestic Structural Change." pp. 21–43 in *Transforming Europe: Europeanization and Domestic Change*, edited by M. G. Cowles, J. A. Caporaso, and T. Risse. Ithaca, NY: Cornell University Press.

Caporaso, James A. and Sidney Tarrow. 2009. "Polanyi in Brussels: Supernational Institutions and the Transnational Embedding of Markets." *International Organization* 3:593–620.

Cardon, Dominique and Jean-Philippe Huertin. 1991. "'Tenir les rangs.' Les services d'encadrement des manifestations ouvrières (1909–1936)." pp. 123–155 in *La manifestation*, edited by P. Favre. Paris: Presses de la Fondation Nationale des Sciences Politiques.

Caren, Neal, Raj Ghoshal, and Vanessa Ribas. 2009. "A Social Movement Generation: Trends in Protesting and Petition Signing, 1973–2006." Unpublished paper. Chapel Hill, NC: University of North Carolina.

Censer, Jack R. and Jeremy D. Popkin. 1987. *Press and Politics in Pre-Revolutionary France*. Berkeley, CA: University of California Press.

Center for Constitutional Rights. 2006. *Articles of Impeachment Against George W. Bush*. Hoboken, NJ: Melville House Publishing.

Chabanet, Didier. 2002. "Les marches européennes contre le chômage, la précarité et les exclusions." Chap. 12 in *L'action collective en Europe*, edited by R. Balme, D. Chabanet, and V. Wright. Paris: Presses de Sciences Po.

Chabot, Sean. 2002. "Transnational Diffusion and the African-American Reinvention of the Gandhian Repertoire." Chap. 6 in *Globalization and Resistance: Transnational Dimensions of Social Movements*, edited by J. Smith and H. Johnston. Lanham, MD: Rowman and Littlefield.

Chamberlin, John. 1974. "Provision of Collective Goods as a Function of Group Size." *American Political Science Review* 68:707–716.

Champagne, Patrick. 1996. *Maintenir l'ordre: Les transformations de la violence d'Etat en régime démocratique*. Paris: Presses de la Fondation Nationale des Sciences Politiques.

Chandra, Kanchan. 2004. *Why Ethnic Parties Succeed: Patronage and Head Counts in India*. New York and Cambridge: Cambridge University Press.

Charlesworth, Andrew. 1983. *An Atlas of Rural Protest in Britain, 1548–1900*. Philadelphia, PA: University of Pennsylvania Press.

Chartier, Roger. 1987. *The Cultural Uses of Print in Early Modern France*. Princeton, NJ: Princeton University Press.

———. 1991. *The Cultural Origins of the French Revolution*. Durham, NC: Duke University Press.

Chhibber, P. K. and S. Misra. 1993. "Hindus and the Babri Masjid: The Sectional Bias of Communal Attitudes." *Asian Survey* 33:665–672.

Christie, Ian. 1982. *Wilkes, Wyvill and Reform: The Parliamentary Reform Movement in British Politics, 1760–1785*. London, UK: Macmillan.

Cichowski, Rachel A. 2001. "Judicial Rulemaking and the Institutionalization of the European Union Sex Policy." Chap. 6 in *The Institutionalization of Europe*, edited by A. Stone Sweet, N. Fligstein, and W. Sandholtz. Oxford, UK: Oxford University Press.

———. 2010. "Civic Society and the European Court of Human Rights." Unpublished paper presented at the annual meeting of the American Political Science Association, Washington, D.C., September 3–6.

Clark, John D. 2003. *Globalizing Civic Engagement: Civil Society and Transnational Action*. London, UK: Earthscan.

Clemens, Elisabeth S. and Debra C. Minkoff. 2004. "Beyond the Iron Law: Rethinking the Place of Organizations in Social Movement Research." Chap. 7 in *Blackwell Companion to Social Movements*, edited by D. Snow, S. Soule, and H. Kriesi. Malden MA and Oxford: Blackwell.

Cloward, Richard and Frances Fox Piven. 1977. *Poor People's Movements: Why They Succeed, How They Fail*. New York: Vintage Books.

Collier, David and Ruth Collier. 1991. *Shaping the Political Arena: Critical Junctures, the Labor Movement, and Regime Dynamics in Latin America*. Princeton, NJ: Princeton University Press.

Collier, Paul and Anke Hoeffler. 2004. "Greed and Grievance in Civil War." *Oxford Economic Papers* 56:563–595.

Collier, Paul and Nicholas Sambanis, eds. 2005. *Understanding Civil War: Evidence and Analysis*. Washington, DC: World Bank. 2 vols.

Conell, Carol. 1978. "Was Holding Out the Key to Winning Strikes? Massachusetts, 1881–1894." Ann Arbor, MI: Center for Research on Social Organization Working Paper No. 187.

Cooley, Alexander and James Ron. 2002. "The NGO Scramble: Organizational Insecurity and the Political Economy of Transnational Action." *International Security* 27:5–39.

Corbin, Alain. 1994. "L'impossible présence du roi: Fêtes politiques et mises en scene du pouvoir sous la Monarchie de Julliet." pp.77–160 in *Les usages politiques des fêtes au XIX-XX siecles*, edited by A. Corbin, N. Gérôme, and D. Tartakowsky. Paris: Publications de la Sorbonne.

Cornwall, Marie, Brayden G. King, Elizabeth M. Legerski, Eric C. Dahlin, and Kendra S. Schiffman. 2007. "Signals or Mixed Signals: Why Opportunities for Mobilization Are Not Opportunities for Policy Reform." *Mobilization* 12:239–254.

Cortright, David. 2009. *Gandhi and Beyond: Nonviolence for a New Political Age*. Boulder CO: Paradigm Press.

Costain, Anne. 1992. *Inviting Women's Rebellion: A Political Process Interpretation of the Women's Movement*. Baltimore, MD: Johns Hopkins University Press.

Costain, Anne and W. Douglas Costain. 1987. "Strategy and Tactics of the Women's Movement in the United States: The Role of Political Parties." pp. 196–214 in *The Women's Movements of the United States and Western Europe: Consciousness, Political Opportunity and Public Policy*, edited by M. F. Katzenstein and C. M. Mueller. Philadelphia, PA: Temple University Press.

Cott, Nancy. 1977. *The Bonds of Womanhood*. New Haven, CT: Yale University Press.

Countryman, Edward. 1981. *A People in Revolution: The American Revolution and Political Society in New York, 1760–1790*. Baltimore, MD: Johns Hopkins University Press.

Courty, Guillaume. 1993. "Barrer, filtrer, encombrer: Les routiers et l'art de retenir ses semblables." *Project* 235 (fall):143–168.

Cowie, Jefferson. 2010. *Stayin' Alive: The 1970s and the Last Days of the Working Class New York*, New York: The New Press.

————. CRS (Congressional Research Service). 2009. "The Global Financial Crisis: Foreign and Trade Policy Effects." Washington, DC.

————. 2010. "Greece's Debt Crisis: Overview, Policy Responses, and Implications." Washington, DC.

d'Anieri, Paul, Claire Ernest, and Elizabeth Kier. 1990. "New Social Movements in Historical Perspective." *Comparative Politics* 22:445–458.

d'Anjou, Leo. 1996. *Social Movements and Cultural Change: The First Abolition Campaign Revisited*. New York: Aldine de Gruyter.

d'Emilio, John. 1992. *Making Trouble: Essays on Gay History, Politics and the University*. New York: Routledge.

Dalton, Russell J. 2007. *Citizen Politics: Public Opinion and Political Parties in Advanced Industrial Democracies*. Washington, DC: CQ Press.

Dalton, Russell J., Bruce Cain, and Susan E. Scarrow. 2003. "Democratic Publics and Democratic Institutions." pp. 1–20 in *Democracy Transformed? Expanding Political*

Opportunities in Advanced Industrial Democracies, edited by B. Cain, R. J. Dalton, and S. Scarrow. Oxford, UK: Oxford University Press.

Darnton, Robert. 1979. *The Business of Enlightenment: A Publishing History of the Encyclopédie, 1775–1800*. Cambridge, MA: Harvard University Press.

———. 1982. *The Literary Underground of the Old Regime*. Cambridge, MA: Harvard University Press.

———. 1989. "Philosophy under the Cloak." pp. 27–49 in *Revolution in Print: The Press in France, 1775–1800*, edited by R. Darnton and D. Roche. Berkeley, CA: University of California Press.

Davis, Natalie. 1973. "The Rites of Violence: Religious Riot in Sixteenth-Century France." *Past and Present* 59:51–91.

Dawes, Robyn, Alphons J.C. Van de Kragt and John M. Orbell. 1988. "Not Me or Thee but We." *Acta Psychologica* 68:83–97.

de Baecque, Antoine 1989. "Pamphlets: Libel and Political Mythology." pp. 165–176 in *A Revolution in Print. The Press in France, 1775–1800*, edited by R. Darnton and D. Roche. Berkeley and Los Angeles: University of California Press.

della Porta, Donatella. 1990. *Il terrorismo di sinistra*. Bologna: Il Mulino.

———. 1995. *Social Movements, Political Violence and the State: A Comparative Analysis of Italy and Germany*. New York: Cambridge University Press.

———. 1996. "Social Movements and the State: Thoughts on the Policing of Protests." pp. 62–92 in *Comparative Perspectives on Social Movements: Political Opportunitie, Mobilizing Structures, and Cultural Framings*, edited by D. McAdam, J. McCarthy, and M. Zald. Cambridge, MA: Cambridge University Press.

———. 2005a. "Making the Polis: Social Forums and Democracy in the Global Justice Movement." *Mobilization* 10:73–94.

———. 2005b. "Multiple Belongings, Flexible Identities, and the Construction of 'Another Politics': Between the European Social Forum and Local Social Fora." pp. 175–202 in *Transnational Protest and Global Activism*, edited by D. della Porta and S. Tarrow. Lanham, MD: Rowman and Littlefield.

della Porta, Donatella and Olivier Fillieule. 2004. "Policing Social Protest." Chap. 10 in *The Blackwell Companion to Social Movements*, edited by D. A. Snow, S. A. Soule, and H. Kriesi. Malden, MA and Oxford: Blackwell.

della Porta, Donatella, Olivier Fillieule, and Herbert Reiter. 1998. "Policing Protest in France and Italy: From Intimidation to Cooperation?" Chap. 5 in *The Social Movement Society*, edited by D. S. Meyer and S. Tarrow. Lanham, MD: Rowman and Littlefield.

della Porta, Donatella, Abby Peterson, and Herbert Reiter, eds. 2006. *The Policing of Transnational Protest*. Aldershot, UK: Ashgate Publishing.

della Porta, Donatella and Herbert Rieter. 1997. *Policing Protest: The Control of Mass Demonstrations in Contemporary Democracies*. Minneapolis, MN: University of Minnesota Press.

della Porta, Donatella and Sidney Tarrow. 1986. "Unwanted Children: Political Violence and the Cycle of Protest in Italy." *European Journal of Political Research* 14:607–632.

———. 2010. "Double Diffusion: The Co-Evolution of Police and Protests in Transnational Contention." Unpublished paper.

DeNardo, James. 1985. *Power in Numbers*. Princeton, NJ: Princeton University Press.

Des Forges, Alison L. 1999. *"Leave none to tell the story": Genocide in Rwanda.* New York and Paris: Human Rights Watch.

Diani, Mario. 1995. *Green Networks: A Structural Analysis of the Italian Environmental Movement.* Edinburgh, UK: Edinburgh University Press.

———. 2004a. "Cities in the World: Local Civil Society and Global Issues in Britain." Chap. 3 in *Transnational Protest and Global Activism*, edited by D. della Porta and S. Tarrow. Lanham, MD: Rowman and Littlefield.

———. 2004b. "Networks and Participation." Chap. 15 in *Blackwell Companion to Social Movements*, edited by D. A. Snow, S. A. Soule, and H. Kriesi. Malden MA and Oxford: Blackwell.

———. 2009. "The Structural Bases of Protest Events: Multiple Memberships and Civil Society Networks in the February 15, 2003 Anti-War Demonstrations." *Acta Sociologica* 52:63–83.

Diani, Mario and Doug McAdam, eds. 2003. *Social Movements and Networks: Relational Approaches to Collective Action.* Oxford and New York: Oxford University.

Dolidze, Anna. 2009. "Looking at the Backseat Driver: NGOs and the European Court of Human Rights." Unpublished paper, Ithaca, NY: Cornell University Law School.

Dreher, Axel. 2006. "Does Globalization Affect Growth? Evidence from a New Index of Globalization." *Applied Economics* 38:109–110.

Dreiling, Michael and Ian Robinson. 1998. "Union Responses to NAFTA in the US and Canada: Explaining Intra- and International Variation." *Mobilization* 3:163–184.

Drescher, Seymour. 1982. "Public Opinion and the Destruction of British Colonial Slavery." pp. 22–48 in *Slavery and British Society, 1776–1846*, edited by J. Walvin. Baton Rouge, LA: Louisiana State University Press.

———. 1987. *Capitalism and Antislavery: British Mobilization in Comparative Perspective.* New York: Oxford University Press.

———. 1991. "British Way, French Way: Opinion Building and Revolution in the Second French Slave Emancipation." *American Historical Review* 96:709–734.

Durkheim, Emile. 1951. *Suicide: A Study in Sociological Interpretation.* Glencoe, IL: Free Press.

Earl, Jennifer. 2003. "Tanks, Tear Gas, and Taxes: Toward a Theory of Movement Repression." *Sociological Theory* 21:44–68.

———. 2004. "The Cultural Consequences of Social Movements." pp. 508–50 in *The Blackwell Companion to Social Movements*, edited by D. Snow, S. Soule, and H. Kriesi. Oxford, UK: Blackwell.

———. 2005. "You Can Beat the Rap, but You Can't Beat the Ride." *Research in Social Movements, Conflict and Change* 26:101–139.

———. 2006. "Repression and the Social Control of Protest. Introduction to the Special Focus Issue on Repression and the Social Control of Protest." *Mobilization* 11:129–144.

Earl, Jennifer and Sarah A. Soule. 2006. "Seeing Blue: A Police-Centered Explanation of Protest Policing." *Mobilization* 11:145–164.

———. 2010. "The Impacts of Repression: The Effect of Police Presence and Action on Subsequent Protest Rates." *Research in Social Movements, Conflict and Change* 30:75–113.

Edwards, Bob and Michael Foley. 2003. "Social Movements Organizations Beyond the Beltway: Understanding the Diversity of One Social Movement Industry." *Mobilization* 8:85–107.

Edwards, Bob and John D. McCarthy. 2004. "Strategy Matters: The Contingent Value of Social Capital in the Survival of Local Social Movement Organizations." *Social Forces* 83:62–651.

———. 2004. "Resources and Social Movement Mobilization." Chap. 6 in *Blackwell Companion to Social Movements,* edited by D. A. Snow, S. A. Soule, and H. Kriesi. Malden MA and Oxford: Blackwell.

Egret, Jean. 1977. *The French Pre-revolution, 1787–88.* Chicago, IL: University of Chicago Press.

Eisenstein, Elizabeth. 1986. "Revolution and the Printed Word." pp. 186–205 in *Revolution in History,* edited by R. Porter and M. Teich. Cambridge, MA: Cambridge University Press.

Eisenstein, Zillah. 1996. *Hatreds: Radicalized and Sexualized Conflicts in the 21st Century.* New York: Routledge.

Eisinger, Peter K. 1973. "The Conditions of Protest Behavior in American Cities." *American Political Science Review* 67:11–28.

Elias, Norbert. 1994. *The Civilizing Process,* vol. 2. Oxford, UK: Blackwell.

Elkins, Stanley and Eric Mckitrick. 1993. *The Age of Federalism.* New York and Oxford: Oxford University Press.

Eriksson, Mikael and Peter Wallensteen. 2004. "Armed Conflict, 1989–2003." *Journal of Peace Research* 41:625–636.

Ernst, Claire 1997. "Americans in Paris. Act Up–Paris and Identity Politics." *French Politics and Society.*

Escobar, Arturo. 2003. "Displacement, Development and Modernity in the Colombian Pacific." *International Social Science Journal* 175:157–167.

Esherick, Joseph W. and Jeffrey N. Wasserstrom. 1990. "Acting Out Democracy." *Journal of Asian Studies* 49:835–865.

Esping-Anderson, Gösta. 1990. *Three Worlds of Welfare Capitalism.* Princeton, NJ: Princeton University Press.

Evans, Peter. 2005. "Counter-Hegemonic Globalization: Transnational Social Movements in the Contemporary Global Political Economy." Chap. 32 in *Handbook of Political Sociology,* edited by T. Janoski, A. Hicks, and M. Schwartz. New York: Cambridge University Press.

Evans, Peter, Deitrich Rueschemeyer, and Theda Skocpol, eds. 1985. *Bringing the State Back In.* New York and Cambridge: Cambridge University Press.

Evans, Sara M. 1980. *Personal Politics: The Roots of Women's Liberation in the Civil Rights Movement and the New Left.* New York: Vintage Books.

Eyerman, Ron and Andrew Jamison. 1991. *Social Movements: A Cognitive Approach.* University Park, PA: The Pennsylvania State University Press.

Fantasia, Rick. 1988. *Cultures of Solidarity: Consciousness, Action and Contemporary American Workers.* Berkeley, CA: University of California Press.

Favre, Pierre. 1990. *La Manifestation.* Paris: Presses de la Fondation Nationale des Sciences Politiques.

Fearon, James D. and David Laitin. 2003. "Ethnicity, Insurgency, and Civil War." *American Political Science Review* 97:75–90.

Fendrich, James M and Ellis S Krauss. 1978. "Student Activism and Adult Left-wing Politics: A Causal Model of Political Socialization for Black, White and Japanese Students of the 1960s Generation." pp. 231–255 in *Research in Social Movements, Conflicts and Change,* vol. 1, edited by L. Kriesberg. Greenwich, CT: JAI.

Ferree, Myra Marx, William A. Gamson, Jürgen Gerhards, and Dieter Rucht. 2002. *Shaping Abortion Discourse: Democracy and the Public Sphere in Germany and the United States*. Cambridge and New York: Cambridge University Press.

Ferree, Myra Marx and Patricia Yancey Martin. 1995. *Feminist Organization: Harvest of the New Women's Movement*. Philadelphia, PA: Temple University Press.

Fillieule, Olivier. 1997. *Stratégies de la rue. Les manifestations en France*. Paris: Presses de la Fondation Nationale des Sciences Politiques.

Fillieule, Olivier and Danielle Tartakowsky. 2008. *La Manifestation*. Paris: Presses de Sciences Po.

Finer, Samuel E. 1975. "State-and Nation-Building in Europe: The Role of the Military." pp. 84–163 in *The Formation of National States in Western Europe*, edited by C. Tilly. Princeton, NJ: Princeton University Press.

Finnemore, Martha and Kathryn Sikkink. 1998. "International Norm Dynamics and Political Change." *International Organization* 52:887–917.

Fischer, David Hackett. 1994. *Paul Revere's Ride*. New York and Oxford: Oxford University Press.

Fish, Steven. 1995. *Democracy from Scratch: Opposition and Regime in the New Russian Revolution*. Princeton, NJ: Princeton University Press.

Fisher, Dana R., Kevin Stanley, David Berman, and Gina Neff. 2005. "How Do Organizations Matter? Mobilization and Support for Participants at Five Globalization Protests." *Social Problems* 52:102–121.

Florini, Ann M. 2003. *The Coming Democracy: New Rules for Running a New World*. Washington, DC: Island Press.

Fomerand, Jacques 1975. "Policy Formulation and Change in Gaullist France. The 1968 Orientation Act of Higher Education." *Comparative Politics* 8:59–89.

Foran, John. 1993. *Fragile Resistance: Social Transformation in Iran from 1500 to the Revolution*. Boulder, CO: Westview.

Foucault, Michel. 2000. "The Subject and Power." pp. 8–26 in *Readings in Contemporary Political Sociology*, edited by K. Nash. Malden, MA: Blackwell Publishers.

Francisco, Ronald A. 1996. "Coercion and Protest in Three Coercive States." *Journal of Conflict Resolution* 39:263–282.

Francisco, Ronald A. 2004. "After the Massacre: Mobilization in the Wake of Harsh Repression." *Mobilization* 9:107–126.

Franklin, James C. 2009. "Contentious Challenges and Government Responses in Latin America." *Political Research Quarterly* 62:700–714.

Fraser, Antonia. 1996. *The Gunpowder Plot: Terror and Faith in 1605*. London, UK: Weidenfeld and Nicolson.

Freeman, Jo. 1987. "Whom You Know versus Whom You Represent: Feminist Politics in the United States." pp. 215–44 in *The Women's Movements of the United States and Western Europe: Consciousness, Political Opportunity and Public Policy*, edited by M. F. Katzenstein and C. M. Mueller. Philadelphia, PA: Temple University Press.

Friedberg, Aaron L. 2000. *In the Shadow of the Garrison State. America's Anti-Statism and Its Cold War Grand Strategy*. Princeton, NJ: Princeton University Press.

Furet, François. 1981. *Interpreting the French Revolution*. London, UK: Cambridge University Press.

Furuyama, Katie and David S. Meyer. 2011. "Sources of Certification and Civil Rights Advocacy Organizations: The JACL and NAACP and Crisis of Legitimacy." *Mobilization* 16: in press.

Gamson, William A. 1988. "Political Discourse and Collective Action." pp. 219–44 in *From Structure to Action: Comparing Social Movement Research Across Cultures. International Social Movement Research I*, edited by B. Klandermans, H. Kriesi, and S. Tarrow. Greenwich, CT: JAI Press.

———. 1990. *The Strategy of Social Protest*. Belmont, CA: Wadsworth Publishing Co.

———. 1992a. "The Social Psychology of Collective Action." pp. 53–76 in *Frontiers in Social Movement Theory*, edited by A. Morris and C. McClurg Mueller. New Haven, CT: Yale University Press.

———. 1992b. *Talking Politics*. Cambridge, MA: Cambridge University Press.

———. 2004. "Bystanders, Public Opinion, and the Media." Chap. 11 in *The Blackwell Companion to Social Movements*, edited by D. A. Snow, S. A. Soule, and H. Kriesi. Malden MA and Oxford: Blackwell.

Gamson, William A., Bruce Fireman, and Steven Rytina. 1982. *Encounters with Unjust Authority*. Homewood, IL: Dorsey Press.

Gamson, William A. and David S. Meyer. 1996. "Framing Political Opportunity." pp. 275–290 in *Comparative Perspectives on Social Movements: Political Opportunities, Mobilizing Structures, and Cultural Framings*, edited by D. McAdam, J. McCarthy, and M. N. Zald. Cambridge, MA: Cambridge University Press.

Gans, Herbert. 1979. *Deciding What's News: A Study of the CBS Evening News, NBC Nightly News, Newsweek and Time*. New York: Pantheon.

Garner, Roberta Ash and Mayer N. Zald. 1985. "The Political Economy of Social Movement Sectors." pp. 119–145 in *The Challenge of Social Control: Citizenship and Institution Building in Modern Society. Essays in Honor or Morris Janowitz*, edited by G. Suttlers and M. N. Zald. Norwood, NJ: Ablex.

Garrett, Geoffrey. 1998. *Partisan Politics in the Global Economy*. New York and Cambridge, MA: Cambridge University Press.

Geary, Roger. 1985. *Policing Industrial Disputes: 1893–1895*. Cambridge, MA: Cambridge University Press.

Gelb, Joyce. 1987. "Social Movement Success: A Comparative Analysis of Feminism in the United States and the United Kingdom." pp. 267–289 in *The Women's Movements of the United States and the Western Europe: Consciousness, Political Opportunity and Public Policy*, edited by M. F. Katzenstein and C. M. Mueller. Philadelphia, PA: Temple University Press.

Gentile, Antonina. 2010. "Historical Varieties of Labor Contention and Hegemony in Transnational Docker Campaigns." Baltimore, MD: Political Science Johns Hopkins University.

George, Alex L. and Andrew Bennett. 2004. *Case Studies and Theory Development in the Social Sciences*. Cambridge MA and London: MIT Press.

Gerhards, Jürgen and Dieter Rucht. 1992. "Mesomobilization: Organizing and Framing in Two Protest Campaigns in West Germany." *American Journal of Sociology* 98:555–596.

Giddens, Anthony 2001. "Forward." in *Global Civil Society 2001*, edited by H. Anheier, M. Glasius, and M. Kaldor. Oxford, UK: Oxford University Press.

Gillham, Patrick F. and John A. Noakes. 2007. "More than a March in a Circle: Protests and the Limits of Negotiated Management." *Mobilization* 12:341–357.

Gitlin, Todd. 1980. *The Whole World is Watching: Mass Media in the Making & Unmaking of the New Left*. Berkeley, CA: University of California Press.

_____. 1995. *Twilight of Common Dreams: Why America is Wracked by Cultural Wars*. New York: Metropolitan Books.

Giugni, Marco. 1999. "How Social Movements Matter." Introduction to *How Movements Matter*. Edited by Marco Giugni, Doug McAdam and Charles Tilly, Minneapolis and St. Paul: University of Minnesota Press.

_____. 2008. "Welfare States, Political Opportunities, and the Mobilization of the Unemployed: A Cross National Analysis." *Mobilization* 13:297–310.

Giugni, Marco and Sakura Yamasaki. 2009. "The Policy Impact of Social Movements: A Replication through Qualitative Comparative Analysis." *Mobilization* 14:467–484.

Givan, Rebecca K, Kenneth Roberts, and Sarah A Soule. 2010. *The Diffusion of Social Movements: Actors, Mechanisms, and Political Effects*. New York and Cambridge: Cambridge University Press.

Gladwell, Malcolm. 2002. *The Tipping Point. How Little Things Can Make a Big Difference*. Boston, MA: Little, Brown.

Glenn, John K. III. 1997. "Citizens in Theatres: Framing Competition and the Velvet Revolution in Czechslovakia, 1989." Cambridge, MA: Harvard University, Department of Sociology.

Godechot, Jacques. 1966. *La presse ouvrière, 1819–1850*. Paris: Bibliothèque de la Révolution de 1848.

Godechot, Jaques. 1971. *Les révolutions de 1848*. Paris: Albin Michel.

Goffman, Erving. 1974. *Frame Analysis: An Essay on the Organization of Experience*. New York: Harper Colophon.

Goldstein, Judith, Miles Kahler, Robert O. Keohane, and Anne-Marie Slaughter. 2001. *Legalization and World Politics*. Cambridge, MA: MIT Press.

Goldstone, Jack A. 1980. "The Weakness of Organization: A New Look at Gamson's 'The Strategy of Social Protest.'" *American Journal of Sociology* 85:1017–1042.

_____. 1999. "Social Movements or Revolutions? On the Evolution and Outcomes of Collective Action." Chap. 6 in *From Contention to Democracy*, edited by M. Giugni, D. McAdam, and C. Tilly. Lanham, MD: Rowman and Littlefield.

Goldstone, Jack A. and Charles Tilly. 2001. "Threat (and Opportunity): Popular Action and State Response in the Dynamics of Contentious Action." Chap. 7 in *Silence and Voice in the Study of Contentious Politics*, edited by R. R. Aminzade et al. New York: Cambridge University Press.

Goodwin, Albert. 1979. *The Friends of Liberty: The English Democratic Movement in the Age of the French Revolution*. Cambridge, MA: Harvard University Press.

Goodwin, Jeff. 2001. *No Other Way Out: States and Revolutionary Movements, 1945–1991*. Cambridge and New York: Cambridge University Press.

Goodwin, Jeff and James M. Jasper, eds. 2004. *Rethinking Social Movements: Structure, Meaning, and Emotion*. Lanham, MD: Rowman and Littlefield.

Goodwin, Jeff, James M. Jasper, and Francesca Polletta. 2001. *Passionate Politics: Emotions and Social Movements*. Chicago, IL: University of Chicago Press.

Goody, Jack. 1968. "Literacy in Traditional Societies." Cambridge, MA: Cambridge University Press.

Gould, Deborah. 2009. *Moving Politics: Emotion and ACT UP's Fight against AIDS*. Chicago, IL: University of Chicago Press.

Gould, Roger. 1995. *Insurgent Identities: Class, Community, and Protest in Paris from 1848 to the Commune*. Chicago, IL: University of Chicago Press.

_____. 1998. "Political Networks and the Local/ National Boundary in the Whiskey Rebellion." Chap. 3 in *Challenging Authority: The Historical Study of Contentious*

Politics, edited by M. P. Hanagan, L. P. Moch, and W. T. Brake. Minneapolis and St. Paul: University of Minnesota Press.

———. 2005. "Historical Sociology and Collective Action." pp. 286–299 in *Remaking Modernity: Politics, History and Society*, edited by J. Adams, E. S. Clemens and A. S. Orloff. Durham, NC: Duke University Press.

Gouldner, Alvin W. 1975–1976. "Prologue to a Theory of Revolutionary Intellectuals." *Telos* 23:3–36.

Gourevitch, Peter Alexis. 1986. *Politics in Hard Times: Comparative Responses to International Crisis*. Ithaca and London: Cornell University Press.

Graeber, David. 2009. *Direct Action: An Ethnography*. Oakland, CA: AK Press.

Gramsci, Antonio. 1971. *Selections from the Prison Notebooks of Antonio Gramsci*, edited by Q. Hoare and G. Nowell-Smith. New York: International Publishers.

Granovetter, Mark. 1973. "The Strength of Weak Ties." *American Journal of Sociology* 78:1360–1380.

Grew, Raymond. 1984. "The Nineteenth-Century European State." pp. 83–120 in *Statemaking and Social Movements: Essays in History and Theory*, edited by C. Bright and S. Harding. Ann Arbor, MI: University of Michigan Press.

Griffin, Clifford S. 1960. *Their Brothers' Keepers: Moral Stewardship in the United States, 1800–1865*. New Brunswick, NJ: Rutgers University Press.

Grimsted, David. 1998. *American Mobbing, 1828–1861. Toward Civil War*. New York: Oxford University Press.

Guérin, Daniel. 1970. *Anarchism: From Theory to Practice*. New York: Monthly Review Press.

Guiraudon, Virginie. 2001. "Weak Weapons of the Weak: Transnational Mobilization Around Migration." Chap. 8 in *Contentious Europeans: Protest and Politics in an Emerging Polity*, edited by D. Imig and S. Tarrow. Lanham, MD: Rowman and Littlefield.

Gurr, Ted Robert. 1971. *Why Men Rebel*. Princeton, NJ: Center for International Studies, Princeton University.

Habermas, Jürgen. 1981. "New Social Movements." *Telos* 49:33–37.

———. 1989. *The Structural Transformation of the Public Sphere: An Inquiry into a Category of Bourgeois Society*. Translated by T. Burger and F. Lawerence. Cambridge MA: MIT Press.

Hadden, Jennifer. 2010. "Beyond Transnational Advocacy Networks: Conflict and Competition in Global Climate Change Politics." Unpublished paper, Ithaca, NY: Cornell University Government Department.

Hadden, Jennifer and Sidney Tarrow. 2007. "Spillover or Spillout: The Global Justice Movement in the United States after 9/11." *Mobilization* 12:359–376.

Hafner-Burton, Emilie, Kiyoteo Tsutsui, and John Meyer. 2008. "International Human Rights Law and the Politics of Legitimacy: Repressive States and Human Rights Treaties." *International Sociology* 23:115–141.

Hamilton, Charles. 1986. "Social Policy and the Welfare of Black Americans: From Rights to Resources." *Political Science and Quarterly* 101:239–255.

Han, Shin-Kap. 2008. "The Other Ride of Paul Revere." *Mobilization* 4:155.

Hannan, Michael and John Freeman. 1989. *Organizational Ecology*. Cambridge, MA: Harvard University Press.

Hannerz, Ulf. 1990. "Cosmopolitans and Locals in World Culture." *Theory, Culture and Society* 7:237–251.

Harbom, Lotta and Peter Wallensteen. 2010. "Armed Conflicts, 1946–2009." *Journal of Peace Research* 47:501–509.

Hardin, Russell. 1982. *Collective Action*. Baltimore, MD: Johns Hopkins University Press.

————. 1995. *One for All: The Logic of Group Conflict*. Princeton, NJ: Princeton University Press.

Harrison, Carol. 1996. "The Unsociable Frenchmen: Associations and Democracy in Historical Perspective." *Tocqueville Review* 17:37–56.

Hartz, Louis. 1955. *The Liberal Tradition in America: An Interpretation of American Political Thought since the Revolution*. New York: Harcourt, Brace.

Harvey, Donald 2006. *The Limits to Capital*. London, UK: Verso.

Hathaway, Will and David S. Meyer. 1997. "Competition and Cooperation in Movement Coalitions: Lobbying for Peace in the 1980s." pp. 61–79 in *Coalitions and Political Movements: The Lessons of the Nuclear Freeze*, edited by T. R. Rochon and D. S. Meyer. Boulder, CO: Lynne Rienner Publishers.

Heaney, Michael T. and Fabio Rojas. 2007. "Partisans, Nonpartisans and the Antiwar Movement in the United States." *American Politics Research* 35:431–464.

————. 2011. "The Partisan Dynamics of Contention: Demobilization of the Antiwar Movement in the United States, 2007–2009." *Mobilization* 16: forthcoming.

Heberle, Rudolf. 1951. *Social Movements: An Introduction to Political Sociology*. New York: Appleton-Century-Crofts.

Hedman, Eva Lotta. 2006. *In the Name of Civil Society*. Honolulu, HI: University of Hawaii Press.

Hellman, Judith Adler. 1987. *Journeys Among Women: Feminism in Five Italian Cities*. New York: Oxford University Press.

Hellman, Stephen. 1975. "The PCI's Alliance Strategy and the Case of the Middle Classes." pp. 372–419 in *Communism in Italy and France*, edited by D. L. M. Blackmer and S. Tarrow. Princeton, NJ: Princeton University Press.

Hill, Stuart and Donald Rothchild. 1992. "The Impact of Regime on the Diffusion of Political Conflict." pp. 189–206 in *The Internationalization of Communal Strife*, edited by M. Midlarsky. London, UK: Routledge.

Hirschman, Albert O. 1982. *Shifting Involvements, Private Interest and Public Action*. Princeton, NJ: Princeton University Press.

Hirst, Paul and Grahame Thompson. 1997. "Globalization in Question." Chap. 11 in *Contemporary Capitalism: The Embeddedness of Institutions*, edited by R. Boyer and J. R. Hollingsworth. Cambridge, MA: Cambridge University Press.

Hobsbawm, Eric J. 1959. *Primitive Rebels: Studies in Archaic Forms of Social Movement in the 19th and 20th Centuries*. Manchester: Manchester University Press.

————. 1962. *The Age of Revolution: 1789–1848*. London, UK: Weidenfeld and Nicolson.

————. 1964. *Labouring Men: Studies in the History of Labour*. London, UK: Weidenfeld and Nicolson.

————. 1974. "Peasant Land Occupations." *Past and Present* 62:120–152.

Hobsbawm, Eric J. and George Rudé. 1975. *Captain Swing*. New York: Norton.

Hochschild, Arlie. 1990. "Ideology and Emotion Management: A Perspective and Path for Future Research." pp. 117–132 in *Research Agendas in the Sociology of Emotions*, edited by T. D. Kemper. Albany, NY: State University of New York Press.

Hoffer, Eric. 1951. *The True Believer*. New York: Harper and Row.

Hooghe, Liesbet and Gary Marks. 2002. *Multi-Level Governance in European Politics*. Lanham, MD: Rowman and Littlefield.

Hooghe, Marc and Gita Deneckere. 2003. "La Marche blanche de Belgique (Octobre 1996): Un mouvement de masse spectaculaire mais éphémère." *Le Mouvement Social* 202:153–164.

Hubert, Don. 2000. *The Landmine Ban: A Case Study in Humanitarian Advocacy*. Providence, RI: The Thomas J. Watson Jr. Institute for International Studies.

Hubrecht, Hubert G. 1990. "Le droit français de la manifestation." pp. 181–206 in *La manifestation*, edited by P. Favre. Paris: Presses de la Fondation Nationale des Sciences Politiques.

Hunt, Lynn. 1984. *Politics, Culture and Class in the French Revolution*. Berkeley: University of California Press.

———. 1992. *The Family Romance of the French Revolution*. Berkeley: University of California Press.

Hunt, Scott A. and Robert D. Benford. 2004. "Collective Identity, Solidarity, and Commitment." Chap. 19 in *The Blackwell Companion to Social Movements*, edited by D. A. Snow, S. A. Soule, and H. Kriesi. Malden, MA and Oxford: Blackwell.

Imig, Doug and Sidney Tarrow. 2001. "Mapping the Europeanization of Contention: Evidence from a Quantitative Data Analysis." Chap. 2 in *Contentious Europeans: Protest and Politics in an Emerging Polity*, edited by D. Imig and S. Tarrow. Lanham, MD: Rowman and Littlefield.

Imig, Doug and Sidney Tarrow, eds. 2001. *Contentious Europeans: Protest and Politics in an Emerging Polity*. Lanham, MD: Rowman and Littlefield.

Incan, Maria. 2009. "Sliding Doors of Opportunity: Zapatistas and their Cycle of Protest." *Mobilization* 14:85–106.

Inglehart, Ronald. 1990. *Culture Shift in Advanced Industrial Societies*. Princeton, NJ: Princeton University Press.

Jaffrelot, Christophe. 1996. *The Hindu Nationalist Movement and Indian Politics. 1925 to the 1990s*. New Delhi and New York: Penguin.

Jasper, James. 1998. "The Emotions of Protest: Affective and Reactive Emotions in and around Social Movements." *Sociological Forum* 13:397–424.

Jenkins, J. Craig and Craig Eckert. 1986. "Channeling Black Insurgency: Elite Patronage and the Development of the Civil Rights Movement." *American Sociological Review* 51:812–830.

Jenkins, J. Craig and Charles Perrow. 1977. "Insurgency of the Powerless: Farm Worker Movements (1946–1972)." *American Sociological Review* 42:249–268.

Jenkins, J. Craig and Bert Klandermans, eds. 1995. *The Politics of Social Protest: Comparative Perspectives on States and Social Movements*. Minneapolis, MN: University of Minnesota Press.

Jiménez, Manuel. 2006. "Cuando la protesta importa electoralmente. El perfil socio-demográfico y politico de los manifestantes contra la Guerra de Irak." *Papers* 81:89–116.

Joachim, Jutta and Birgit Locher, eds. 2009. *Transnational Activism in the UN and the EU*. London and New York: Routledge.

Johnson, Chalmers A. 1962. *Peasant Nationalism and Communist Power*. Stanford CA: Stanford University Press.

Johnson, Paul E. 1978. *A Shopkeeper's Millennium: Society and Revivals in Rochester, New York, 1815–1837*. New York: Hill and Wang.

Johnston, Hank. 2006. "'Let's Get Small': The Dynamics of (Small) Contention in Repressive States." *Mobilization* 11:195–212.

Johnston, Hank and Bert Klandermans. 1995. *Social Movements and Culture*. Minneapolis and St. Paul: University of Minnesota Press.

Jossin, Ariane. 2010. "How Do Activists Experience Transnational Protest Events? The Case of Young Global Justice Activists from Germany and France." in *The Transnational Condition: Protest Dynamics in an Entangled Europe*, edited by S. Teune. Berlin: Campus.

Judt, Tony. 2010. "Revolutionaries." *The New York Review of Books* 57.3:18–19.

Jung, Jai Kwan. 2009. "Growing Supranational Identities in a Globalizing World? A Multi-level Analysis of the World Values Surveys." *European Journal of Political Research* 47:578–609.

_____. 2010. "Disentangling Protest Cycles: An Event-History Analysis of New Social Movements in Western Europe." *Mobilization* 15:25–44.

Juris, Jeffrey. 2008. *Networking Futures*. Durham, NC: Duke University Press.

Kafka, Franz. 1937. *Parables and Paradoxes*. New York: Schocken.

Kaldor, Mary. 2003. *Global Civil Society: An Answer to War*. Cambridge, MA: Polity Press.

Kalyvas, Stathis N. 2003. "The Ontology of 'Political Violence': Action and Identity in Civil Wars." *Perspectives on Politics* 1:275–294.

_____. 2006. *The Logic of Violence in Civil War*. New York and Cambridge: Cambridge University Press.

Kalyvas, Stathis N. 2007. "Civil Wars." Chap. 18 in *Oxford Handbook of Comparative Politics*, edited by C. Boix and S. Stokes. New York and Oxford: Oxford University Press.

Kaplan, Steven L. 1982. "The Famine Plot Persuasion." *The American Philosophical Society*.

_____. 1984. *Provisioning Paris. Merchants and Millers in the Grain and Flour Trade During the Eighteenth Century*. Ithaca and London: Cornell University Press.

Kaplan, Temma. 1982. "Female Consciousness and Collective Action: The Case of Barcelona, 1910–1918." *Signs* 7:545–566.

Karapin, Roger. 2011. "Opportunity/Threat Spirals in Social Movements: A Neglected Process in their Expansion." *Mobilization* 16: forthcoming.

Karpf, David. 2009a. "All the Dogs that Didn't Bark: Understanding the Dearth of Online Conservative Infrastructure." Presented at the Annual Meeting of the American Political Science Association.

_____. 2009b. "The MoveOn Effect: Disruptive Innovation and the New Generation of American Political Associations." Providence, RI: Taubman Center, Brown University.

Katzenstein, Mary F. 1979. *Equality and Ethnicity. The Shiv and Sena Party and Preferential Politics in Bombay*. Ithaca and London: Cornell University Press.

_____. 1995. "Discursive Politics and Feminist Activism in the Catholic Church." pp. 35–52 in *Feminist Organization: Harvest of the New Women's Movement*, Edited by M. M. Ferree and P. Y. Martin. Philadelphia, PA: Temple University Press.

_____. 1998. *Faithful and Fearless: Moving Feminist Protest Inside the Church and Military*. Princeton, NJ: Princeton University Press.

_____. 2003. "Re-Dividing Citizens – Divided Feminisms: The Reconfigured U.S. State and Women's Citizenship." Chap. 9 in *Women's Movements Facing the Reconfigured State*, edited by L. A. Banaszak, K. Beckwith, and D. Rucht. New York: Cambridge University Press.

Katzenstein, Mary F., Uday Singh Mehta and Usha Thakkar. 1997, "The Rebirth of Shiv Sena; The Symbiosis of Discursive and Organizational Power," *Journal of Asian Studies,* Spring, pp. 371–91,

Katzenstein, Mary F. and Carol McClurg Mueller, eds. 1987. *The Women's Movements of the United States and Western Europe : Consciousness, Political Opportunity, and Public Policy.* Philadelphia, PA: Temple University Press.

Katzenstein, Peter J. 2005. *A World of Regions: Asia and Europe in the American Imperium.* Ithaca and London: Cornell University Press.

Katznelson, Ira. 1981. *City Trenches: Urban Politics and the Patterning of Class in the United States.* New York: Pantheon Books.

_____. 2002. "Flexible Capacity: The Military and Early American Statebuilding." Chap. 4 in *Shaped by War and Trade. International Influences on American Political Development,* edited by I. Katznelson and M. Shefter. Princeton, NJ: Princeton University Press.

Kay, Tamara. 2011 *a.* "Legal Transnationalism: The Relationship between Transnational Social Movement Building and International Law." *Law and Social Inquiry* 36.

_____. 2011 *b. NAFTA and the Politics of Labor Transnationalism.* New York and Cambridge: Cambridge University Press.

Keck, Margaret and Kathryn Sikkink. 1998. *Activists Beyond Borders: Transnational Activist Networks in International Politics.* Ithaca and London: Cornell University Press.

_____. 1998. "Transnational Advocacy Networks in the Global Society." Chap. 10 in *The Social Movement Society,* edited by D. S. Meyer and S. Tarrow. Lanham, MD: Rowman and Littlefield.

Keniston, Kenneth. 1968. *Young Radicals.* New York: Harcourt, Brace Jovanovich.

Kennan, John. 1986. "The Economics of Strikes." pp. 1091–1137 in *Handbook of Labor Economics,* vol 2, edited by O. Ashenfelter and R. Layard. Amsterdam: Elsevier Science Publishers.

Keohane, Robert O. 2002. *Power and Governance in a Partially Globalized World.* New York: Routledge.

_____. 2002a. "The Globalization of Informal Violence, Theories of World Politics, and the 'Liberalism of Fear.'" *Dialog-IO* Spring 2002:29–43.

Keohane, Robert O. and Joseph S. Nye, eds. 1971. *Transnational Relations and World Politics.* Cambridge, MA: Harvard University Press.

Kertzer, David. 1988. *Ritual, Politics and Power.* New Haven, CT: Yale University Press.

Kettnaker, Vera. 2001. "The European Conflict over Genetically-engineered Crops, 1995–1997." Chap. 10 in *Contentious Europeans: Protest and Politics in an Emerging Polity,* edited by D. Imig and S. Tarrow. Lanham, MD: Rowman and Littlefield.

Kielbowicz, Richard B. and Clifford Scherer. 1986. "The Role of the Press in the Dynamics of Social Movements." pp. 71–96 in *Research in Social Movements, Conflict and Change,* edited by L. Kriesberg. Greenwich, CT: JAI.

Kier, Elizabeth and Ronald R. Krebs, eds. 2010. *In War's Wake: International Conflict and the Fate of Liberal Democracy.* New York and Cambridge: Cambridge University Press.

Kinealy, Christine. 2003. "Les marches orangistes en Irlande du Nord. Histoire d'un droit." *Le Mouvement Social* 165–182.

Kitschelt, Herbert. 1986. "Political Opportunity Structures and Political Protest: Anti-Nuclear Movements in Four Democracies." *British Journal of Political Science* 16:57–85.

Klandermans, Bert. 1988. "The Formation and Mobilization of Consensus." pp. 173–196 in *From Structure to Action: Comparing Social Movement Research Across Cultures,* edited by B. Klandermans, H. Kriesi, and S. Tarrow. Greenwich, CT: JAI Press.

———. 1997. *The Social Psychology of Protest.* Oxford, UK: Blackwell Publishers.

———. 2004. "The Demand and Supply of Participation: Social-Psychological Correlates of Participation in Social Movements." Chap. 16 in *The Blackwell Companion to Social Movements,* edited by D. A. Snow, S. A. Soule, and H. Kriesi. Malden, MA and Oxford: Blackwell.

Klandermans, Bert, Hanspeter Kriesi, and Sidney Tarrow, eds. 1988. *From Structure to Action: Comparing Social Movement Participation Across Cultures.* Greenwich, CT: JAI Press.

Klandermans, Bert, Marlene Roefs, and Johan Olivier. 1998. "A Movement Takes Office." Chap. 8 in *The Social Movement Society: Contentious Politics for a New Century,* edited by D. Meyer and S. Tarrow. Boulder, CO: Rowman and Littlefield.

Klandermans, Bert and Sidney Tarrow. 1988. "Mobilization into Social Movements: Synthesizing European and American Approaches." pp. 1–38 in *From Structure to Action: Comparing Social Movement Research Across Cultures,* edited by B. Klandermans, H. Kriesi, and S. Tarrow. Greenwich, CT: JAI Press.

Kleidman, Robert. 1992. "Organizations and Coalitions in the Cycles of the American Peace Movement." Cleveland, Ohio: Cleveland State University.

Knapp, Vincent. 1980. *Austrian Social Democracy, 1889–1914.* Washington, DC: University Press of America.

Kolb, Felix. 2007. *Protest and Opportunities: The Political Outcomes of Social Movements.* Frankfurt and New York: Campus.

Koopmans, Ruud. 1993. "The Dynamics of Protest Waves: West Germany, 1965–1989." *American Sociological Review* 58:637–658.

———. 2004. "Protest in Time and Space: The Evolution of Waves of Contention." Chap. 2 in *The Blackwell Companion to Social Movements,* edited by D. A. Snow, S. A. Soule, and H. Kriesi. Malden and Oxford: Blackwell.

Koopmans, Ruud and Susan Olzak. 2004. "Discursive Opportunities and the Evolution of Right-Wing Violence in Germany." *American Journal of Sociology* 110:198–230.

Kornhauser, William. 1959. *The Politics of Mass Society.* New York: Free Press.

Korzeniewicz, Patricio R. and William S. Smith. 2005. "Transnational Civil Society Actors and Regional Governance in the Americas: Elite Projects and Action from Below." pp. 135–157 in *Regionalism and Governance in the Americas: Continental Drift,* edited by L. Fawcett and M. Serrano. London, UK: Palgrave.

Kramnick, Isaac. 1990. *Republicanism and Bourgeois Radicalism.* Ithaca, NY: Cornell University Press.

Kriesi, Hanspeter. 1995. "The Political Opportunity Structure of the New Social Movements: Its Impact on Their Mobilization." Chap. 7 in *The Politics of Social Protest,* edited by J. C. Jenkins and B. Klandermans. Minneapolis and St. Paul: University of Minnesota Press.

———. 1996. "The Organizational Structure of New Social Movements in a Political Context." pp. 152–184 in *Comparative Perspectives on Social Movements,* edited by D. McAdam, J. McCarthy, and M. N. Zald. Cambridge, MA: Cambridge University Press.

———. 2004. "Political Context and Opportunity." pp. 67–90 in *The Blackwell Companion to Social Movements*, edited by D. A. Snow, S. A. Soule, and H. Kriesi. Malden, MA: Blackwell Publishing.

Kriesi, Hanspeter, Ruud Koopmans, Jan Willem Duyvendak, and Marco Giugni, 1995. *The Politics of New Social Movements in Western Europe*. Minneapolis and St. Paul: University of Minnesota Press.

Kryder, Daniel. 2000. *Divided Arsenal: Race and the American State During World War Two*. New York and Cambridge: Cambridge University Press.

Kubik, Jan. 1994. *The Power of Symbols Against the Symbols of Power: The Rise of Solidarity and the Fall of State Socialism in Poland*. University Park, PA: Pennsylvania State University Press.

———. 2009. "Solidarity." pp. 3072–3080 in *International Encyclopedia of Revolution and Protest 1500–Present*, edited by I. Ness. Oxford, UK: Blackwell Publishing.

Kuran, Timur. 1991. "Now Out of Never: The Element of Surprise in the East European Revolution of 1989." pp. 7–48 in *Liberalization and Democratization: Change in the Soviet Union and Eastern Europe,* edited by N. Bermeo. Baltimore, MD: Johns Hopkins University Press.

Kurzman, Charles. 1996. "Structural Opportunities and Perceived Opportunities in Social-Movement Theory: Evidence from the Iranian Revolution of 1798." *American Sociological Review* 61:153–170.

———. 1998. "Organizational Opportunity and Social Movement Mobilization: A Comparative Analysis of Four Religious Movements." *Mobilization* 3:23–50.

Lahusan, Christian. 1996. *The Rhetoric of Moral Protest: Public Campaigns, Celebrity Endorsement, and Political Mobilization*. New York: De Gruyter.

Laitin, David. 1988. "Political Culture and Political Preferences." *American Political Science Review* 82:589–597.

Lange, Peter, Sidney Tarrow, and Cynthia Irvin. 1989. "Mobilization, Social Movements and Party Recruitment: The Italian Communist Party since the 1960s." *British Journal of Political Science* 20:15–42.

Laraña, Enrique, Hank Johnston, and Joseph Gusfield, eds. 1994. *New Social Movements: From Ideology to Identity*. Philadelphia, PA: Temple University Press.

Larson, Jeff A. and Sarah Soule. 2009. "Sector-Level Dynamics and Collective Action in the United States, 1965–1975." *Mobilization* 14:293–314.

Lawson, Robert J., Mark Gwozdecky, Jill Sinclair, and Ralph Lysyshyn. 1998. "The Ottawa Process and the International Movement to Ban Landmines." Chap. 10 in *To Walk Without Fear. The Global Movement to Ban Landmines*, edited by M. A. Cameron, R. J. Lawson, and B. W. Tomlin. Toronto, Oxford, and New York: Oxford University Press.

Le Bon, Gustave 1977. *The Crowd: A Study of the Popular Mind*. New York: Penguin.

Le Roy Ladourie, Emmanuel 1980. *Carnival in Romans*. New York: Brazilier.

Lee, C. K. and D. Strang. 2003. "The International Diffusion of Public Sector Downsizing Network Emulation and Theory-Driven Learning." *International Organization* 60:883–909.

Lefebvre, Georges. 1967. *The Coming of the French Revolution*. Princeton, NJ: Princeton University Press.

Lenin, V. I. 1929. *What is to Be Done? Burning Questions of Our Movement*. New York: International Publishers.

Levi, Margaret and Gillian Murphy. 2006. "Coalitions of Contention." *Political Studies* 54:651–667.

Levine, Daniel H. 1990. "Popular Groups, Popular Culture, and Popular Religion." *Comparative Studies in Society and History* 32:718–764.

Lichbach, Mark I. 1995. *The Rebel's Dilemma*. Ann Arbor, MI: University of Michigan Press.

Lichbach, Mark I. and Helma DeVries. 2007. "Mechanisms of Globalized Protest Movements." pp. 461–496 in *The Oxford Handbook of Comparative Politics*, edited by C. Boix and S. C. Stokes. New York and Oxford: Oxford University Press.

Lichbach, Mark I. and Ted R. Gurr. 1981. "The Conflict Process: A Formal Model." *Journal of Conflict Resolution* 25:3–29.

Lichterman, Paul. 1996. *The Search for Political Community: American Activists Reinventing Commitment*. New York: Cambridge University Press.

Lillie, Nathan. 2006. *A Global Union for Global Workers: Collective Bargaining and Regulatory Politics in Maritime Shipping*. New York and London: Routledge.

Lindkilde, Lasse. 2008. "In the Name of the Prophet? Danish Muslim Mobilization During the Muhammad Caricatures Controversy." *Mobilization* 13:219–238.

Linebaugh, Peter and Marcus Rediker. 1990. "The Many-Headed Hydra: Sailors, Slaves, and the Atlantic Working Class in the Eighteenth Century." *Journal of Historical Sociology* 3:225–252.

Lipsky, Michael. 1968. "Protest as a Resource." *American Political Science Review* 62:1144–1158.

Lipsky, Michael and David Olson. 1976. "The Processing of Racial Crisis in America." *Politics and Society* 6:79–103.

Lockridge, Kenneth. 1974. *Literacy in Colonial New England: An Enquiry into the Social Context of Literacy in the Early Modern West*. New York: Norton.

Lohmann, Susanne. 1994. "The Dynamics of Information Cascades: The Monday Demonstrations in Leizpzig, East Germany, 1989–1991." *World Politics* 47:42–101.

Lounsbury, Michael. 2005. "Institutional Variation in the Evolution of Social Movements: Competing Logics and the Spread of Recycling Advocacy Groups." Chap. 3 in *Social Movements and Organization Theory*, edited by G. F. Davis, D. McAdam, W. R. Scott, and M. N. Zald. New York and Cambridge: Cambridge University Press.

Luders, Joseph E. 2010. *The Civil Rights Movement and the Logic of Social Change*. New York and Cambridge: Cambridge University Press.

Luker, Kristin. 1985. *Abortion and the Politics of Motherhood*. Berkeley and Los Angeles; University of California Press.

Lumley, Robert. 1990. *States of Emergency: Cultures of Revolt in Italy from 1968 to 1978*. London, UK: Verso.

Lusebrink, Hans-Jürgen. 1983. "L'imaginaire social et ses focalisations en France et Allemagne à la fin du siècle." *Revue Roumaine d'Histoire* 22:371–383.

Maguire, Diarmuid. 1990. "New Social Movements and Old Political Institutions: The Campaign for Nuclear Disarmament, 1979–1989." Unpublished PhD dissertation. Ithaca, NY: Cornell University.

Mahoney, James. 2000. "Path Dependence in Historical Sociology." *Theory and Society* 24:507–548.

Maier, Pauline. 1972. *From Resistance to Revolution: Colonial Radicals and the Development of American Opposition to Britain, 1765–1776*. New York: Knopf.

Mair, Peter. 1997. *Party System Change: Approaches and Interpretations*. Oxford and New York: Oxford University Press.

Maney, Gregory M., Lynne M. Woehrle, and Patrick G. Coy. 2009. "Ideological Consistency and Contextual Adaptation: U.S. Peace Movement Emotional Work Before and After 9/11." *American Behavioral Scientist* 53:114–132.

Mansbridge, Jane. 1986. *Why We Lost the ERA*. Chicago, IL: University of Chicago Press.

Mansbridge, Jane and Katherine Flaster. 2005. "'Male chauvinist,' 'feminist,' 'sexist,' and 'sexual harassment': Divergent trajectories in feminist linguistic innovation." *American Speech* 80:56–279.

Margadant, Ted W. 1979. *French Peasants in Revolt: The Insurrection of 1851*. Princeton, NJ: Princeton University Press.

Margulies, Joseph. 2006. *Guantanamo and the Abuse of Presidential Power*. New York: Simon and Schuster Paperbacks.

———. in preparation. *Like a Single Mind*: Forthcoming.

Markoff, John. 1986. "Literacy and Revolt." *American Journal of Sociology* 92:323–349.

———. 1997. *The Abolition of Feudalism: Peasants, Lords, and Legislators in the French Revolution*. University Park: Pennsylvania State University Press.

Marks, Gary and Doug McAdam. 1996. "Social Movements and the Changing Structure of Political Opportunity in the European Union." pp. 95–120 in *Governance in the European Union*, edited by G. Marks, F. W. Scharpf, P. C. Schmitter and W. Streek. Thousand Oaks, CA: Sage Publications.

———. 1999. "On the Relationship of Political Opportunities to the Form of Collective Action: The Case of the European Union." pp. 97–111 in *Social Movements in a Globalizing World*, edited by D. della Porta, H. Kriesi, and D. Rucht. New York: St. Martin's Press.

Marseille, Jacques and Dominique Margairez. 1989. *1790. Au jour le jour*. Paris: Albin Michel.

Marwell, Gerald and Pamela E. Oliver. 1993. *The Critical Mass in Collective Action: A Micro-social Theory*. Cambridge, MA: Cambridge University Press.

Marx, Gary T. and Michael Useem. 1971. "Majority Participation in Minority Movements: Civil Rights, Abolition, Untouchability." *Journal of Social Issues* 27:81–104.

Marx, Gary T. and James L. Wood. 1975. "Strands of Theory and Research in Collective Behavior." *Annual Review of Sociology* 1:363–428.

Marx, Karl. 1963. *The Poverty of Philosophy*. New York: International Publishers.

———. 1978. "The Eighteenth Brumaire of Louis Bonaparte." pp. 41–49 in *The Marx-Engels Reader*, edited by R. C. Tucker. New York and London: Norton.

Maslen, Stuart. 1998. "The Role of the International Committee of the Red Cross." Chap. 6 in *To Walk Without Fear. The Global Movement to Ban Landmines*, edited by M. A. Cameron, R. J. Lawson, and B. W. Tomlin. Toronto, Oxford, and New York: Oxford University Press.

Mathews, Donald G. 1969. "The Second Great Awakening as an Organizing Process, 1780–1830." *American Quarterly* 21:23–43.

McAdam, Doug. 1983. "Tactical Innovation and the Pace of Insurgency." *American Sociological Review* 48:735–754.

———. 1986. "Recruitment to High-Risk Activism: The Case of Freedom Summer." *American Journal of Sociology* 92:64–90.

———. 1988. *Freedom Summer*. New York: Oxford University Press.

_____. 1995. "'Initiator' and 'Spin-Off' Movements: Diffusion Processes in Protest Cycles." pp. 217–240 in *Repertoires and Cycles of Collective Action*, edited by M. Traugott. Durham, NC: Duke University Press.

_____. 1999. "The Biographical Impact of Activism." Chap. 6 in *How Social Movements Matter*, edited by M. Giugni, D. McAdam, and C. Tilly. Minneapolis and St. Paul: University of Minnesota.

_____. 1999[1982]. *The Political Process and the Development of Black Insurgency, 1930–1970*. Chicago, IL: University of Chicago Press.

McAdam, Doug, N. Van Dyke, A. Munch, and J. Shockey. 1998. *"Social Movements and the Life-Course."* Tucson, AZ: Department of Sociology, University of Arizona.

McAdam, Doug, John McCarthy, and Mayer N. Zald. 1988. "Social Movements." pp. 695–737 in *Handbook of Sociology*, edited by N. J. Smelser. Newbury Park, CA: Sage Publications.

McAdam, Doug, John McCarthy, and Mayer N. Zald, eds. 1996. *Comparative Perspectives on Social Movements: Political Opportunities, Mobilizing Structures and Cultural Framings*. Cambridge, MA: Cambridge University Press.

McAdam, Doug and Dieter Rucht. 1993. "The Cross-National Diffusion of Movement Ideas." *The Annals of the American Academy of the Political and Social Sciences* 528:56–74.

McAdam, Doug and Sidney Tarrow. 2005. "Scale Shift in Transnational Contention." Chap. 6 in *Transnational Protest & Global Activism*, edited by D. della Porta and S. Tarrow. Lanham, MD: Rowman and Littlefield Publishers Inc.

_____. 2010. "Ballots and Barricades: On the Reciprocal Relations between Elections and Social Movements." *Perspectives on Politics* 8:529–542.

McAdam, Doug, Sidney Tarrow, and Charles Tilly. 2001. *Dynamics of Contention*. New York and Cambridge: Cambridge University Press.

McCammon, Holly J., Karen E. Campbell, Ellen M. Granberg, and Christine Mowery. 2001. "How Movements Win: Gendered Opportunity Structures and the State Women's Suffrage Movements, 1866–1919." *American Sociological Review* 66:49–70.

McCammon, Holly J. and Karen E. Campbell. 2002. "Allies on the Road to Victory: Coalition Formation Between the Suffragists and the Woman's Christian Temperance Union." *Mobilization* 7:231–251.

McCann, David and Jeffrey Dudas. 2006. "Retrenchment . . . and Resurgence? Mapping the Changing Context of Cause Lawyering." pp. 37–59 in *Cause Lawyering and Social Movements*, edited by A. Sarat and S. A. Scheingold. Stanford, CA: Stanford Law and Politics.

McCarthy, John. 1987. "Pro-Life and Pro-Choice Mobilization: Infrastructure Deficits and New Technologies." pp. 49–66 in *Social Movements in an Organizations Society*, edited by M. N. Zald and J. McCarthy. New Brunswick, NJ: Transaction Books.

McCarthy, John 2005. "Persistence and Change Among Nationally Federated Social Movements." Chap. 7 in *Social Movements and Organization Theory*, edited by G. F. Davis, D. McAdam, W. R. Scott, and M. N. Zald. New York and Cambridge: Cambridge University Press.

McCarthy, John and Clark McPhail. 1998. "The Institutionalization of Protest in the United States." pp. 83–110 in *The Social Movement Society: Contentious Politics for a New Century*, edited by D. S. Meyer and S. Tarrow. Lanham, MD: Rowman and Littlefield.

McCarthy, John and Mark Wolfson. 1992. "Consensus Movements, Conflict Movements and the Cooperation of Civic and State Infrastructures." pp. 273–297 in *Frontiers in Social Movement Theory*, edited by A. Morris and C. M. Mueller. New Haven, CT: Yale University Press.

McCarthy, John and Mayer N. Zald. 1973. *The Trend of Social Movements in America: Professionalization and Resource Mobilization*. Morristown, NJ: General Learning Press.

———. 1977. "Resource Mobilization and Social Movements: A Partial Theory." *American Journal of Sociology* 82:1212–1241.

McGrath, Ben. 2010. "The Movement: The Rise of Tea Party Activism." *The New Yorker* Feb. 1:40–49.

McMichael, Philip. 1996. *Development and Global Change: A Global Perspective*. Thousand Oaks, CA: Pine Forge Press.

———. 2005. "Globalization." pp. 587–606 in *Handbook of Political Sociology*, edited by T. Janoski, R. Alford, A. M. Hicks, and M. Schwartz. New York and Cambridge: Cambridge University Press.

McPhail, Clark. 1991. *The Myth of the Madding Crowd*. New York: Aldine De Gruyter.

Mehta, Ved. 1993. "The Mosque and the Temple: The Rise of Fundamentalism." *Foreign Affairs* 72:16–21.

Melucci, Alberto. 1988. "Getting Involved: Identity and Mobilization in Social Movements." pp. 329–48 in *From Structure to Action: Comparing Social Movements Across Cultures*, vol. 1, *International Social Movement Research*, edited by B. Klandermans, H. Kriesi, and S. Tarrow. Greenwich, CT: JAI Press.

———. 1989. *Nomads of the Present: Social Movements and Individual Needs in Contemporary Society*. Philadelphia, PA: Temple University Press.

———. 1996. *Challenging Codes: Collective Action in the Information Age*. New York and Cambridge: Cambridge University Press.

Mendelson, Sarah E. and Theodore P. Gerber. 2007. "Local Activist Culture and Transnational Diffusion: An Experiment in Social Marketing Among Human Rights Groups in Russia." *Post Soviet Affairs* 23:50–75.

Merry, Sally Engle. 2006. *Human Rights and Gender Violence: Translating International Law into Local Justice*. Chicago, IL: University of Chicago Press.

Mershon, Carol A. 1990. "Generazioni di leader sindicali in fabbrica. L'eredità dell'autunno caldo." *Polis* 2:277–323.

Meyer, David S. 1990. *A Winter of Discontent: The Nuclear Freeze and American Politics*. New York: Praeger.

———. 1993. "Institutionalizing Dissent: The United States Political Opportunity Structure and the End of the Nuclear Freeze Movement." *Sociological Forum* 8:157–179.

———. 2004. "Protest and Political Opportunities." *Annual Review of Sociology* 30:125–145.

———. 2005. "Social Movements and Public Policy: Eggs, Chicken, and Theory." in Introduction to *Routing the Opposition: Social Movements, Public Policy and Democracy*, edited by H. Ingram, V. Jenness, and D. Meyer. Minneapolis and St. Paul: University of Minnesota Press.

———. 2006. "Claiming Credit: Stories of Movement Influence as Outcomes." *Mobilization* 11:201–218.

Meyer, David S. and Catherine Corrigal-Brown. 2006. "Coalitions and Political Context: U.S. Movements Against Wars in Iraq." *Mobilization* 10:327–344.

Meyer, David S. and Josh Gamson. 1995. "The Challenge of Cultural Elites: Celebrities and Social Movements." *Sociological Inquiry* 65:181–206.

Meyer, David S. and Suzanne Staggenborg. 1996. "Movements, Countermovements, and the Structure of Political Opportunity." *American Journal of Sociology* 101: 1628–1660.

———. 1998. "Countermovement Dynamics in Federal Systems: A Comparison of Abortion Politics in Canada and the United States." *Research in Political Sociology* 8:209–240.

Meyer, David S. and Sidney Tarrow, eds. 1998. *The Social Movement Society: Contentious Politics for a New Century*. Lanham, MD: Rowman and Littlefield.

Meyer, David S. and Nancy Whittier. 1994. "Social Movement Spillover." *Social Problems* 41:277–298.

Meyer, John W. and John Boli. 1997. "World Society and the Nation-State." *American Journal of Sociology* 103:144–181.

Michels, Robert. 1962. *Political Parties: A Sociological Study of the Oligarchical Tendencies of Modern Democracy*. New York: Collier Books.

Mikkelsen, Flemming. 1996. "Contention and Social Movements in Denmark in a Transnational Perspective." Presented at the Second European Conference on Social Movements. University of the Basque Country, Bilbao, July.

Miller, James. 1987. *Democracy is in the Streets: From Port Huron to the Siege of Chicago*. New York: Simon and Schuster.

Mingst, Karen. 2009. "Civil Society Organizations in the United Nations." Chap. 2 in *Transnational Activism in the UN and the EU*, edited by J. Joachim and B. Locher. New York and London: Routledge.

Minkoff, Debra C. 1994. "From Service Provision to Institutional Advocacy: The Shifting of Organizational Forms." *Social Forces* 72:943–969.

———. 1995. *Organizing for Equality: The Evolution of Women's and Racial-ethnic Organizations in America, 1955–1985*. New Brunswick, NJ: Rutgers University Press.

———. 1997. "Producing Social Capital: National Social Movements and Civil Society." *American Behavioral Scientist* 40:606–619.

Mische, Ann. 2008. *Partisan Publics: Communication and Contention Across Brazilian Youth Activist Networks*. Princeton and Oxford: Princeton University Press.

Mittelman, James H. 2004. *Whither Globalization? The Vortex of Knowledge and Ideology*. London and New York: Routledge.

Mobilization. 2011. "Dynamics of Contention, Ten Years On." *Mobilization* 16: forthcoming.

Monforte, Pierre. 2009. "Social Movements and Europeanization Process: The Case of the French Associations Mobilizing Around the Asylum Issue." *Social Movement Studies* 8:409–426.

Moore, Barrington Jr. 1966. *The Social Origins of Dictatorship and Democracy: Lord and Peasant in the Modern World*. Boston, MA: Beacon Press.

———. 1978. *Injustice: The Social Bases of Obedience and Revolt*. White Plains, NY: M.E. Sharpe.

Moore, R. Lawrence. 1994. *Selling God: American Religion in the Marketplace of Culture*. New York: Oxford University Press.

Moravcsik, Andrew. 1996. *The Choice for Europe: Social Purpose and State Power*. Cambridge, MA: Harvard University Press.

Morgan, Jane. 1987. *Conflict and Order: The Police and Labor Disputes in England and Wales, 1900–1939.* Oxford, UK: Oxford University Press.

Mouriaux, René and Jacques Capdeveille. 1988. "Approche politique de la grève en France: 1966–1988." Paris: Cahiers du CEVIPOF.

Morris, Aldon. 1984. *The Origins of the Civil Rights Movement: Black Communities Organizing for Change.* New York: Free Press.

Morris, Aldon and Carol McClurg Mueller, eds. 1992. *Frontiers of Social Movement Research.* New Haven, CT: Yale University Press.

Morris, R. J. 1983. "Voluntary Societies and British Urban Elites, 1780–1850: An Analysis." *Historical Journal* 26:95–118.

Mueller, Carol McClurg. 1987. "Collective Consciousness. Identity Transformation, and the Rise of Women in Public Office in the United States." pp. 89–108 in *The Women's Movements of the United States and Western Europe: Consciousness, Political Opportunity, and Public Policy*, edited by M. F. Katzenstein and C. M. Mueller. Philadelphia, PA: Temple University Press.

―――. 1999. "Claim 'Radicalization?' The 1989 Protest Cycle in the GDR." *Social Problems* 46:528–547.

Muir, Edward. 1997. *Ritual in Early Modern Europe.* Cambridge and New York: Cambridge University Press.

Muller, Edward N. and Erich Weede. 1990. "Cross National Variation in Political Violence." *Journal of Conflict Resolution* 34:624–651.

Myers, Daniel J. 2000. "The Diffusion of Collective Violence: Infectiousness, Susceptibility, and Mass Media Networks." *American Journal of Sociology* 106:173–208.

Nah, Seungahn, Aaron S. Veenstra, and Dhavan V. Shah. 2006. "The Internet and Anti-War Activism: A Case Study of Information, Expression, and Action." *Journal of Computer-Mediated Communication* 12:230–247.

Nam, Taehyun. 2006. "The Broken Promises of Democracy: Protest-Repression Dynamics in Korea, 1991–1994." *Mobilization* 11:427–442.

Nandy, Ahsis, Shikha Trivedy, Shail Mayaram, and Achyout Yagnik. 1998. *Creating a Nationality: The Ramjanmabhumi Movement and the Fear of the Self.* Delhi, India: Oxford University Press.

Nash, Kate, ed. 2000. *Readings in Contemporary Political Sociology.* Malden, MA: Blackwell Publishers.

Nelkin, Dorothy. 1975. "The Political Impact of Technical Expertise." *Social Studies of Science* 5:35–54.

Netti, J. P. 1968. "The State as a Conceptual Variable." *World Politics* 20:559–592.

O'Brien, Kevin J. 2006. *Rightful Resistance in Rural China.* New York: Cambridge University Press.

O'Brien, Kevin J. and Lianjiang Li. 2005. "Popular Contention and Its Impact in Rural China." *Comparative Political Studies* 38:235–259.

O'Brien, Kevin J., ed. 2008. *Popular Protest in China.* Cambridge, MA: Harvard University Press.

O'Brien, Robert, Anne Marie Goetz, Jan Aart Scholte, and Marc Williams. 2000. *Contesting Global Governance: Multilateral Economic Institutions and Global Social Movements.* Cambridge, MA: Cambridge University Press.

O'Donnell, Guillermo, Philippe Schmitter, and Lawrence Whitehead, eds. 1986. *Transitions from Authoritarian Rule: Prospects for Democracy.* Baltimore, MD: Johns Hopkins University Press.

Offe, Claus. 1990. "Reflections on the Institutional Self-Transformation of Movement Politics: A Tentative Stage Model." pp. 232–250 in *Challenging the Political Order: New Social and Political Movements in Western Democracies*, edited by R. J. Dalton and M. Kuechler. Cambridge, MA: Polity.

Ohmae, Kenichi. 1990. *The Borderless World: Power and Strategy in the Interlinked Economy*. New York: Harper Business.

Olesen, Thomas. 2005. *International Zapatismo: The Construction of Solidarity in the Age of Globalization*. London, UK: ZED Books.

———. 2007. "Contentious Cartoons: Elite and Media-Driven Mobilization." *Mobilization* 12:37–52.

Olson, Mancur. 1965. *The Logic of Collective Action*. Cambridge, MA: Harvard University Press.

Opp, Karl-Dieter and Wolfgang Roehl. 1990. "Repression, Micromobilization, and Political Protest." *Social Forces* 69:521–547.

Osa, Maryjane. 1998. "Contention and Democracy: Labor Protest in Poland, 1989–1993." *Communist and Post Communist Studies* 31:29–42.

Osa, Maryjane 2001. "Mobilizing Structures and Cycles of Protest: Post-Stalinist Contention in Poland, 1954–1959." *Mobilization* 6:211–231.

Ozouf, Mona. 1988. *Festivals and the French Revolution*. Translated by A. Sheridan. Cambridge, MA: Harvard University Press.

Paine, Thomas. 1989. *Political Writings*, edited by B. Kuklick. Cambridge, MA: Cambridge University Press.

Park, Hyung Sam. 2008. "Forming Coalitions: A Network-Theoretic Approach to the Contemporary South Korean Environmental Movement." *Mobilization* 13.

Perry, Elizabeth J. 1993. *Shanghai on Strike: the Politics of Chinese Labor*. Stanford, CA: Stanford University Press.

Petrova, Tsveta. 2010. "From Recipients to Donors: New Europe Promotes Democracy in the Neighborhood." Unpublished PhD Dissertation Thesis. Ithaca, NY: Department of Government, Cornell University.

Pianta, Mario and Raffaele Marchetti. 2007. "The Global Justice Movements: The Transnational Dimension." Chap. 2 in *The Global Justice Movement: Cross-National and Transnational Perspectives*, edited by D. Della Porta. Boulder, CO and London: Paradigm.

Pierson, Paul. 2004. *Politics in Time: History, Politics, and Social Analysis*. Princeton, NJ: Princeton University Press.

Pigenet, Michel and Danielle Tartakowsky. 2003. "Les marches." in *Le mouvement social*, vol. 202 (January-March).

Pitt-Rivers, Julian. 1971. *People of the Sierra*, 12th ed. Chicago, IL: University of Chicago Press.

Piven, Frances Fox and Richard Cloward. 1972. *Regulating the Poor*. New York: Vintage Books.

———. 1977. *Poor People's Movements: Why They Succeed, How They Fail*. New York: Vintage.

———. 1992. "Normalizing Collective Protest." Chap. 13 in *Frontiers in Social Movement Theory*, edited by A. Morris and C. McClurg Mueller. New Haven, CT: Yale University Press.

Pizzorno, Alessandro. 1978. "Political Exchange and Collective Identity in Industrial Conflict." pp. 277–298 in *The Resurgence of Class Conflict in Western Europe since 1968*, vol. 2, edited by C. Crouch and A. Pizzorno. London, UK: Macmillan Press.

Plamenatz, John. 1954. *German Marxism and Russian Communism*. London, UK: Longmans, Green.

Podobnik, Bruce. 2009. "Resistance to Globalization: Cycles and Evolutions in the Globalization Protest Movement." pp. 51–68 in *Transforming Globalization: Challenges and Opportunities in the Post 9/11 Era*, edited by B. Podobnik and T. Reifer. Chicago, IL: Haymarket Books.

Polanyi, Karl. 2001 [1944]. *The Great Transformation: The Political and Economic Origins of Our Time*. Boston, MA: Beacon Press.

Polletta, Francesca. 2006. *It Was Like a Fever: Story-telling in Protest and Politics*. Chicago, IL: University of Chicago Press.

Polletta, Francesca and Edwin Amenta. 2002. "Conclusion: Second That Emotion? Lessons from Once-Novel Concepts in Social Movement Research." pp. 303–316 in *Passionate Politics: Emotions and Social Movements*, edited by J. Goodwin, J. M. Jasper, and F. Polletta. Chicago, IL: Chicago University Press.

Poloni-Staudinger, Lori. 2008. "The Domestic Opportunity Structure and Supernational Activity: An Explanation of Environmental Group Activity at the European Union Level." *European Union Politics* 9:531–555.

———. 2009. "Why Cooperate? Cooperation Among Environmental Groups in the United Kingdom, France, and Germany." *Mobilization* 14:375–396.

Popkin, Jeremy D. 1989. "Journals: The New Faces of News." pp. 141–164 in *Revolution in Print: The Press in France, 1775–1800*, edited by R. Darnton and D. Roche. Berkeley: University of California Press.

Posner, Eric A. and Adrian Vermeule. 2007. *Terror in the Balance: Security, Liberty and the Courts*. Oxford, UK: Oxford University Press.

Postgate, Raymond. 1955. *The Story of a Year: 1848*. London, UK: Cassell.

Price, Richard. 1998. "Reversing the Gun Sights: Transnational Civil Society Targets Land Mines." *International Organization* 52:613–644.

Price, Roger. 1989. *The Revolutions of 1848*. Atlantic Highlands, NJ: Humanities Press International.

Przeworski, Adam and John Sprague. 1986. *Paper Stones: A History of Electoral Socialism*. Chicago and London: University of Chicago Press.

Putnam, Robert D. 2000. *Bowling Alone. The Collapse and Revival of American Community*. New York: Simon and Schuster.

Quattrone, George A. and Amos Tversky. 1988. "Contrasting Rational and Psychological Analysis of Political Choice." *American Political Science Review* 82:719–736.

Rao, Hayagreeva. 1998. "Caveat Emptor: the Construction of Nonprofit Consumer Watchdog Organizations." *American Journal of Sociology* 103:912–961.

Rasler, Karen. 1996. "Concessions, Repression and Political Protest." *American Sociological Review* 61:132–152.

———. 2004. "Causal Explanations for the Expansion and Contraction of a Protest Wave: An Illustration from the Intifada, 1987–1991." Unpublished paper, International Studies Association, Honolulu, Hawaii, March.

Read, Donald. 1964. *The English Provinces, c. 1760–1960: A Study in Influence*. New York: St. Martin's.

Regalia, Ida. 1984. *Eletti e abbandonati*. Bologna: Il Mulino.

Reger, Jo, Daniel J. Myers, and Rachel L. Einwoher, eds. 2008. *Identity Work in Social Movements*. Minneapolis and St. Paul: University of Minneapolis.

Reid, Edna and Hsinchen Chen. 2007. "Internet-Savvy U.S. and Eastern Extremist Groups." *Mobilization* 12:177–192.

Reitan, Ruth. 2010. "Coordinated Power in Contemporary Leftist Activism." Chap. 4 in *Power and Global Activism*, edited by T. Olesen. London, UK: Routledge.

Rheingold, Howard. 2002. *Smart Mobs: The Next Social Revolution.* Cambridge, MA: Perseus Publishing.

Risse, Thomas, Stephen C. Ropp, and Kathryn Sikkink, eds. 1999. *The Power of Human Rights: International Norms and Domestic Change.* Cambridge and New York: Cambridge University Press.

Risse, Thomas and Kathryn Sikkink. 1999. "The Socialization of International Human Rights Norms into Domestic Practices: Introduction." Chap. 1 in *The Power of Human Rights: International Norms and Domestic Change*, edited by T. Risse, S. C. Ropp, and K. Sikkink. New York: Cambridge University Press.

Rochon, Thomas R. 1988. *Mobilizing for Peace. The Antinuclear Movements in Western Europe.* Princeton, NJ: Princeton University Press.

———. 1998. *Culture Moves: Ideas, Activism, and Changing Values.* Princeton, NJ: Princeton University Press.

Rochon, Thomas R. and Daniel Mazmanian. 1993. "Social Movements and the Policy Process." *Annals of the American Academy of Political and Social Sciences* 528:75–87.

Rochon, Thomas R. and David S. Meyer, eds. 1997. *Coalitions and Political Movements: The Lessons of the Nuclear Freeze.* Boulder, CO: Lynne Rienner Publishers.

Rogers, Everett. 1995. *The Diffusion of Innovation.* New York: The Free Press.

Rogers, Kim Lacy. 1993. *Righteous Lives: Narratives of the New Orleans Civil Rights Movement.* New York: New York University Press.

Rohlinger, Deana A. and Jordan Brown. 2009. "Democracy, Action, and the Internet After 9/11." *American Behavioral Scientist* 53:133–150.

Rosanvallon, Pierre. 2005. *The Demands of Liberty: Civil Society in France since the Revolution.* Cambridge and London: Harvard University Press.

Rosenthal, Naomi B. and Michael Schwartz. 1989. "Spontaneity and Democracy in Social Movements." pp. 33–60 in *Organizing for Change: Social Movement Organization in Europe and the United States*, edited by B. Klandermans. Greenwich, CT: JAI Press.

Ross, Marc Howard. 1997. "Culture and Identity in Comparative Political Analysis." Chap. 4 in *Comparative Politics: Rationality, Culture and Structure*, edited by M. I. Lichbach and A. S. Zuckerman. Cambridge, MA: Cambridge University Press.

Roth, Guenther. 1963. *The Social Democrats in Imperial Germany: A Study on Working Class Isolation and National Integration.* Totowa, NJ: Bedminster.

Rotondi, Clementia. 1951. *Bibliografia dei periodici toscani. 1847–1852.* Florence, Italy: L.S. Olschki.

Rucht, Dieter. 1990. "Campaigns, Skirmishes and Battles: Anti-Nuclear Movements in the USA, France and West Germany." *Industrial Crisis Quarterly* 4:193–222.

———. 1998. "The Structure and Culture of Collective Protest in Germany since 1950." Chap. 2 in *The Social Movement Society: Contentious Politics for a New Century*, edited by D. Meyer and S. Tarrow. Boulder, CO: Rowman and Littlefield.

———. 1999. "Linking Organization and Mobilization: Michaels's Iron Law of Oligarchy Reconsidered." *Mobilization* 4:151–169.

Rudolf, Lloyd I. 1992. "The Media and Cultural Politics." *Economic and Political Weekly* 27:1489–1496.

Ruggie, John G. 1982. "International Regimes, Transaction Costs and Change: Embedded Liberalism in the Post-War Economic Order." *International Organization* 47:379–415.

_____. 2008. "Introduction: Embedding Global Markets." pp. 1–12 in *Embedding Global Markets: An Enduring Challenge*. Aldershot and Burlington: Ashgate.

Rupp, Leila J. 1980. "Imagine My Surprise: Women's Relationships in Historical Perspective." *Frontiers* 5:61–70.

Rupp, Leila J. and Verta Taylor. 1987. *Survival in the Doldrums: The American Women's Rights Movement, 1945 to the 1960s*. New York: Oxford University Press.

Ryan, Barbara. 1992. *Feminism and the Women's Movement*. New York: Routledge.

Ryerson, Richard A 1978. *The Revolution Is Now Begun: The Radical Committees of Philadelphia, 1765–1776*. Philadelphia, PA: University of Pennsylvania Press.

Sageman, Mark. 2004. *Understanding Terror Networks*. Philadelphia, PA: University of Pennsylvania Press.

Salvati, Michele. 1981. "May 1968 and the Hot Autumn of 1969: The Responses of Two Ruling Classes." pp. 329–363 in *Organizing Interests in Western Europe*, edited by S. Berger. Cambridge, MA: Cambridge University Press.

Sambanis, Nicholas. 2004. "What Is Civil War? Conceptual and Empirical Complexities of an Operational Definition." *Journal of Conflict Resolution* 48:814–858.

Samuels, Richard J. 2003. *Machiavelli's Children: Leaders and their Legacies in Italy and Japan*. Ithaca and London: Cornell University Press.

Schama, Simon. 1989. *Citizens: A Chronicle of the French Revolution*. New York: Knopf.

Schattle, Hans. 2007. *The Practices of Global Citizenship*. Lanham, MD: Rowman and Littlefield.

Schelling, Thomas C. 1960. *The Strategy of Conflict*. Cambridge, MA: Harvard University Press.

Schlesinger, Arthur M, Jr. 1986. *The Cycles of American History*. Boston, MA: Houghton Mifflin.

Schmitz, Hans Peter. 2001. "When Networks Blind: Human Rights and Politics in Kenya." pp. 149–172 in *Intervention and Transnationalism in Africa: Global-Local Networks of Power*, edited by T. Callaghy, R. Kassimir, and R. Latham. New York: Cambridge University Press.

Schnapp, Alain and Pierre Vidal-Naquet. 1988. *Journal de la commune étudiante: Textes et documents, novembre 1967-juin 1968*. Paris: Seuil.

Schneider, Cathy. 1995. *Shantytown Protest in Pinochet's Chile*. Philadelphia, PA: Temple University Press.

Schumaker, Paul D. 1975. "Policy Responsiveness to Protest-Group Demands." *Journal of Politics* 37:488–521.

Scott, James C. 1976. *The Moral Economy of the Peasant: Rebellion and Subsistence in Southeast Asia*. New Haven and London: Yale University Press.

_____. 1985. *Weapons of the Weak: Everyday Forms of Resistance*. New Haven, CT: Yale University Press.

_____. 1990. *Domination and the Arts of Resistance: Hidden Transcripts*. New Haven, CT: Yale University Press.

Scott, James C. and Ben Kerkvliet, eds. 1986. *Everyday Forms of Resistance in Southeast Asia*. London, UK: Frank Cass.

Seidman, Gay. 2001. "Guerillas in their Midst: Armed Struggle in the South African Anti-Apartheid Movement." *Mobilization* 6:111–127.

Selb, Peter, Hanspeter Kriesi, Regla Hanggli, and Mirko Marr. 2009. "Partisan Choices in a Direct-Democratic Campaign." *European Political Science Review* 1:155–172.

Selbin, Eric. 1993. *Modern Latin American Revolutions*. Boulder, CO: Westview Press.

———. 2010. *Revolution, Rebellion, Resistance: The Power of Story*. London and New York: Zed Books.

Sewell, William Jr. 1986. "Artisans, Factory Workers, and the Formation of the French Working Class, 1789–1848." pp. 45–70 in *Working Class Formation: Nineteenth Century Patterns in Western Europe and the United States*, edited by I. Katznelson and A. R. Zolberg. Princeton, NJ: Princeton University Press.

———. 1990. "Collective Violence and Collective Loyalties in France: Why the French Revolution made a Difference." *Politics and Society* 18:527–552.

———. 1996. "Historical Events as Transformations of Structures: Inventing Revolution at the Bastille." *Theory and Society* 25:841–881.

Sharp, Gene. 1973. *The Politics of Nonviolent Action*. Boston, MA: Porter Sargent Publishers.

Sherman, Daniel. 2011. "Critical Mechanisms for Critical Masses; Exploring Variation in Active Opposition to Low-level Radioactive Waste Site Proposals." *Mobilization* 16: forthcoming.

Shorter, Edward and Charles Tilly. 1974. *Strikes in France, 1830–1968*. Cambridge, MA: Harvard University Press.

Sidel, Mark. 2007. *More Secure, Less Free? Antiterrorism Policy and Civil Liberties after September 11*. Ann Arbor, MI: University of Michigan Press.

Sigmann, Jean. 1973. *1848: The Romantic and Democratic Revolutions in Europe*. New York: Harper and Row.

Sikkink, Kathryn and Carrie Booth Walling. 2007. "The Impact of Human Rights Trials in Latin America." *Journal of Peace Research* 44:427–445.

Simeant, Johanna. 2009. *La Grève de la faim*, Paris: Les Presses de Sciences Po.

Skocpol, Theda. 1979. *States and Social Revolutions: A Comparative Analysis of France, Russia and China*. New York and Cambridge: Cambridge University Press.

———. 1985. "Bringing the State Back In: Strategies of Analysis in Current Research." pp. 3–37 in *Bringing the State Back In*, edited by P. Evans, D. Reuschmeier, and T. Skocpol. New York and Cambridge: Cambridge University Press.

———. 1994. "Rentier State and the Shi'a Islam in the Iranian Revolution." In *Social Revolutions in the Modern World*. Cambridge, MA: Cambridge University Press.

Skocpol, Theda, Marshall Ganz, and Munson Ziad. 2000. "A Nation of Organizers: The Institutional Origins of Civil Voluntarism in the United States." *American Political Science Review* 94:527–546.

Slaughter, Anne-Marie. 2004. *A New World Order*. Princeton, NJ: Princeton University Press.

Smelser, Neil J. 1962. *The Theory of Collective Behavior*. New York: Free Press of Glencoe.

Smith, Christian. 1996. *Disrupting Religion: The Force of Faith in Social Movement Activism*. New York: Routledge

Smith, Jackie. 2001. "Globalizing Resistance: The Battle of Seattle and the Future of Social Movements." *Mobilization* 6:1–19.

———. 2002. "Bridging Global Divides: Strategic Framing and Solidarity in Transnational Social Movement Organizations." *International Sociology* 17:505–528.

———. 2004. "Exploring Connections between Global Integration and Political Mobilization." *Journal of World-Systems Research* 10:255–285.

———. 2008. *Social Movements for Global Democracy*. Baltimore, MD: Johns Hopkins University Press.

Smith, Jackie and Ellen Reese. 2009. "The World Social Forum Process." *Mobilization* 13:373–394.

Snow, David A. and Robert Benford. 2000. "Clarifying the Relationship between Framing and Ideology." *Mobilization* 5:55–60.

Snow, David A. and Robert D. Benford. 1988. "Ideology, Frame Resonance, and Participant Mobilization." pp. 197–217 in *From Structure to Action: Social Movement Participation Across Cultures*, edited by B. Klandermans, H. Kriesi, and S. Tarrow. Greenwich, CT: JAI Press.

———. 1992. "Master Frames and Cycles of Protest." pp. 133–155 in *Frontiers in Social Movement Theory*, edited by A. Morris and C. McClurg Mueller. New Haven, CT: Yale University Press.

Snow, David A., Daniel Cress, Liam Downey, and Andrew Jones. 1998. "Disrupting the 'Quotidian': Reconceptualizing the Relationship Between Breakdown and Collective Action." *Mobilization* 3:1–22.

Snow, David A., E. Burke Rochford, Jr., Steven K. Worden, and Robert D. Benford. 1986. "Frame Alignment Processes, Micromobilization and Movement Participation." *American Sociological Review* 51:464–481.

Snow, David A., Sarah A. Soule, and Hanspeter Kriesi, eds. 2004. *The Blackwell Companion to Social Movements*. Malden and Oxford: Blackwell.

Snyder, David and William R. Kelly. 1976. "Industrial Violence in Italy, 1878–1903." *American Journal of Sociology* 82:131–162.

Snyder, David and Charles Tilly. 1972. "Hardship and Collective Violence in France, 1830–1960." *American Journal of Sociology* 37:520–532.

Snyder, Jack and Leslie Vinjamuri. 2003–2004. "Trials and Errors. Principle and Pragmatism in Strategies of International Justice." *International Security* 28:5–44.

Solnick, Steven L. 1998. *Stealing the State: Control and Collapse in Soviet Institutions*. Cambridge MA: Harvard University Press.

Soskice, David. 1978. "Strike Waves and Wage Explosions, 1968–1970: An Economic Interpretation." pp. 221–246 in *The Resurgence of Class Conflict in Western Europe since 1968*, vol. 2, edited by C. Crouch and A. Pizzorno. London, UK: Macmillan.

Soule, Sarah A. 1997. "The Student Divestment Movement in the United States and Tactical Diffusion: The Shantytown Protest." *Social Forces* 75:855–882.

———. 2004. "Diffusion Processes within and across Movements." Chap. 13 in *The Blackwell Companion to Social Movements*, edited by D. A. Snow, S. A. Soule, and H. Kriesi. Malden and Oxford: Blackwell.

———. 2009. *Contention and Corporate Social Responsibility*. New York: Cambridge University Press.

Soule, Sarah A. and Christian Davenport. 2009. "Velvet Glove, Iron Fist, or Even Hand? Protest Policing in the United States, 1960–1990." *Mobilization* 14:1–22.

Soule, Sarah A. and Jennifer Earl. 2005. "A Movement Society Evaluated: Collective Protest in the United States, 1960-1986." *Mobilization* 10:345–364.

Soule, Sarah A., Doug McAdam, John McCarthy, and Yang Su. 1999. "Protest Events: Cause or Consequence of State Action? The U.S. Women's Movement and Federal Congressional Activities, 1956–1979." *Mobilization* 4:239–256.

Soule, Sarah A. and Sidney Tarrow. 1991. "The 1848 Revolutions." Presented to the Social Science History Association Annual Meeting.

Spriano, Paolo. 1975. *The Occupation of the Factories: Italy, 1920*. London, UK: Pluto.

Spruyt, Hendrik. 1994. *The Sovereign State and its Competitors: An Analysis of System Change*. Princeton, NJ: Princeton University Press.

Staggenborg, Suzanne. 1986. "Coalition Work in the Pro-Choice Movement: Organizational and Environmental Opportunities and Obstacles." *Social Problems* 33:374–390.

———. 1991. *The Pro-Choice Movement: Organization and Activism in the Abortion Conflict*. New York: Oxford University Press.

Staggenborg, Suzanne and Josée Lecomte. 2008. "Social Movement Campaigns: Mobilization and Outcomes in the Montreal Women's Movement Community." *Mobilization* 14:163–180.

Steedly, Homer R. and John W. Foley. 1979. "The Success of Protest Groups: Multivariate Analyses." *Social Science Research* 8:1–15.

Steinberg, Marc W. 1999. *Fighting Words*. Ithaca, NY: Cornell University Press.

Stinchcombe, Arthur 1987. "Review of *The Contentious French* by Charles Tilly." *American Journal of Sociology* 93:1248.

Stone, Geoffrey R. 2004. *Perilous Times: Free Speech in Wartime*. New York: Norton.

Stone, Lawrence. 1969. "Literacy and Education in England, 1640–1900." *Past and Present* 42:69–139.

Stone Sweet, Alec, Neil Fligstein, and Wayne Sandholtz. 2001. "The Institutionalization of European Space." pp. 1–28 in *The Institutionalization of Europe*, edited by A. Stone Sweet, N. Fligstein, and W. Sandholtz. Oxford, UK: Oxford University Press.

Strang, David and Sarah A. Soule. 1998. "Diffusion in Organizations and Social Movements: From Hybrid Corn to Poison Pills." *Annual Review of Sociology* 24:265–290.

Streeter, Thomas. 2007. "Introduction: Redefining the Possible." In *Mousepads, Shoe Leather, and Hope: Lessons from the Howard Dean Campaign for the Future of Internet Politics*, edited by Z. Teachout and T. Streeter. Boulder and London: Paradigm Publishers.

Swarts, Heidi. 2008. *Organizing Urban America: Secular and Faith Based Progressive Movements*. Minneapolis, MN: University of Minnesota Press.

Syzmanski, Ann-Marie. 2003. *Pathways to Prohibition. Radicals, Moderates and Social Movement Outcomes*. Durham and London: Duke University Press.

Taft, Philip and Philip Ross. 1969. "American Labor Violence: Its Causes, Character, and Outcome." pp. 281–395 in *Violence in America: Historical and Comparative Perspectives*, edited by T. R. Gurr. New York: Praeger.

Tamason, Charles. 1980. "From Mortuary to Cemetery: Funeral Riots and Funeral Demonstrations in Lille, 1779–1870." *Social Science History* 4:15–31.

Tarde, Gabriel. 1989. *L' Opinion et la foule*. Paris: Presses Universitaires de France.

Tarrow, Sidney. 1967. *Peasant Communism in Southern Italy*. New Haven, CT: Yale University Press.

———. 1989a. *Democracy and Disorder: Protest and Politics in Italy, 1965–1974*. New York: Oxford University Press.

———. 1989b. "Struggle, Politics and Reform: Collective Action, Social Movements, and Cycles of Protest." Ithaca, NY: Center for International Studies, Cornell University.

———. 1992. "Mentalities, Political Cultures and Collective Action Frames: Constructing Meanings Through Action." pp. 174–202 in *Frontiers in Social Movement Theory*, edited by A. Morris and C. McClurg Mueller. New Haven, CT: Yale University Press.

———. 1995. "Cycles of Collective Action: Between Moments of Madness and the Repertoire of Contention" in Mark Traugott, ed., *Repertoires and Cycles of Collective Action*. Durham NC: Duke University Press.

———. 1996. "States and Opportunities: The Political Structuring of Social Movements." pp. 62–92 in *Comparative Perspectives on Social Movements: Political Opportunities, Mobilizing Structures, and Cultural Framings*, edited by M. Doug, J. D. McCarthy, and M. N. Zald. New York and Cambridge: Cambridge University Press.

———. 1998a. "Fishnets, Internets and Catnets: Globalization and Transnational Collective Action." Chap. 15 in *Challenging Authority: The Historical Study of Contentious Politics*, edited by M. Hanagan, L. P. Moch, and W. te Brake. Minneapolis, MN: University of Minnesota Press.

———. 1998b. "Social Protest and Policy Reform: May 1968 and the Loi d'Orientation in France." Chap. 2 in *From Contention to Democracy*, edited by M. Giugni, D. McAdam, and C. Tilly. Lanham, MD: Rowman & Littlefield.

———. 1998c. "The Very Excess of Democracy: State Building and Contentious Politics in America." Chap. 2 in *Social Movements and American Political Institutions*, edited by A. Costain and A. McFarland. Boulder, CO: Rowman and Littlefield.

———. 2005. *The New Transnational Activism*. New York and Cambridge: Cambridge University Press.

———. 2007. "Inside Insurgencies: Politics and Violence in an Age of Civil War." *Perspectives on Politics* 5:587–600.

———. 2008. "Charles Tilly and the Practice of Continuous Politics." *Social Movement Studies* 7:225–246.

Tarrow, Sidney and Doug McAdam. 2005. "Scale Shift in Transnational Contention." Chap. 6 in *Transnational Protest and Global Activism*, edited by D. della Porta and S. Tarrow. Lanham, MD: Rowman and Littlefield.

Tartakowsky, Danielle. 1996. *Le front populaire: La vie est à nous*. Paris: Découverte/ Presses de la Sorbonne.

———. 1997. *Les Manifestations de rue en France, 1918–1968*. Paris: Publications de la Sorbonne.

———. 2004. *La manif en éclat*. Paris: LaDispute.

———. 2005. *La part du rêve: Histoire du 1er Mai en France*. Paris: Hachette Littératures.

Taylor, Verta. 1995. "Watching for Vibes: Bringing Emotions into the Study of Feminist Organizations." pp. 223–233 in *Feminist Organizations: Harvest of the New Women's Movement*, edited by M. M. Ferree and P. Y. Martin. Philadelphia, PA: Temple University Press.

Taylor, Verta and Nella Van Dyke. 2004. "'Get Up, Stand Up': Tactical Repertoires of Social Movements." Chap. 12 in *The Blackwell Companion to Social Movements*, edited by D. A. Snow, S. A. Soule, and H. Kriesi. Malden and Oxford: Blackwell.

te Brake, Wayne 1998. *Shaping History: Ordinary People in European Poltics, 1500–1700*. Berkeley and Los Angeles: University of California Press.

Thomas, Malcolm I. and Peter Holt. 1977. *Threats of Revolution in Britain, 1789–1848*. London, UK: Macmillan.

Thompson, Dorothy. 1984. *The Chartists: Popular Politics in the Industrial Revolution*. New York: Pantheon Books.

Thompson, E. P. 1966. *The Making of the English Working Class*. New York: Vintage Books.

———. 1971. "The Moral Economy of the English Crowd in the Eighteenth Century." *Past and Present* 50:76–136.

Tilly, Charles. 1964. *The Vendée*. Cambridge, MA: Harvard University Press.

———. 1975. "Food Supply and Public Order in Modern Europe." pp. 380–455 in *The Formation of National States in Western Europe*, edited by C. Tilly. Princeton, NJ: Princeton University Press.

———. 1978. *From Mobilization to Revolution*. Reading, PA: Addison-Wesley.

———. 1982. "Britain Creates the Social Movement." pp. 21–51 in *Social Conflict and Political Order in Modern Britain*, edited by J. Cronin and J. Schneer. New Brunswick, NJ: Rutgers University Press.

———. 1983. "Speaking Your Mind without Elections, Surveys, or Social Movements." *Public Opinion Quarterly* 47:461–478.

———. 1984. "Social Movements and National Politics." pp. 297–317 in *Statemaking and Social Movements*, edited by C. Bright and S. Harding. Ann Arbor, MI: University of Michigan Press.

———. 1986. *The Contentious French*. Cambridge, MA: Harvard University Press.

———. 1990. *Coercion, Capital, and European States, AD 990–1992*. Cambridge, MA: Blackwell.

———. 1993. *European Revolutions, 1492–1992*. Oxford, UK: Blackwell.

———. 1995a. "Contentious Repertoires in Great Britain, 1758–1834." pp. 15–42 in *Repertoires and Cycles of Collective Action*, edited by M. Traugott. Durham, NC: Duke University Press.

———. 1995b. *Popular Contention in Great Britain, 1758–1834*. Cambridge, MA: Harvard University Press.

———. 1998. *Durable Inequality*. Berkeley, CA: University of California Press.

———. 2003. *The Politics of Collective Violence*. New York and Cambridge: Cambridge University Press.

———. 2005. *Identities, Boundaries and Social Ties*. Boulder and London: Paradigm Publishers.

———. 2006. *Regimes and Repertoires*. Cambridge, MA: Cambridge University Press.

———. 2007. *Democracy*. Cambridge, MA: Cambridge University Press.

Tilly, Charles and Sidney Tarrow. 2007. *Contentious Politics*. Boulder, CO: Paradigm Publishers.

Tilly, Charles, Louise A. Tilly, and Richard Tilly. 1975. *The Rebellious Century, 1830–1930*. Cambridge, MA: Harvard University Press.

Tilly, Charles and Lesley Wood. 2009. *Social Movements, 1768–2008*. Boulder, CO: Paradigm Press.

Tilly, Charles, ed. 1975. *The Formation of National States in Western Europe*. Princeton, NJ: Princeton University Press.

Tocqueville, Alexis de. 1954. *Democracy in America (trans. Henry Reve, ed. Phillips Brady)*, vol. 2. New York: Vintage.

———. 1955. *The Old Regime and the French Revolution*. Garden City, NY: Doubleday.

———. 1987. *Recollections: The French Revolution of 1848*. New Brunswick, NJ: Transaction Books.

Traugott, Mark. 1990. "Neighborhoods in Insurrection: The Parisian Quartier in the February Revolution of 1848." Unpublished Paper.

_____. 1995. "Barricades as Repertoire: Continuities and Discontinuities in the History of French Contention." pp. 43–56 in *Repertoires and Cycles of Collective Action*, edited by M. Traugott. Durham, NC: Duke University Press.

_____. 2010. *The Insurgent Barricade*. Berkeley and Los Angeles: University of California press.

Tsutsui, Kiyoteru and Hwa-Ji Shin. 2008. "Global Norms, Local Activism, and Social Movement Outcomes: Global Human Rights and Resident Koreans in Japan." *Social Problems* 55:391–418.

Tucker, Robert C., ed. 1978. *The Marx-Engels Reader*. New York: Norton.

Turnbull, Peter. 2004. "The War on Europe's Warfront- Repertoires of Power in the Port Transport Industry." Unpublished paper . Cardiff, UK: Cardiff Business School.

Turner, Ralph and Lewis Killian. 1987. *Collective Action*. Englewood Cliffs, NJ: Prentice Hall.

Tyrrell, Ian R. 1979. *Sobering Up: From Temperance to Prohibition in Antebellum America 1800–1860*. Westport, CT: Greenwood Press

Uba, Katrin. 2009. "The Contextual Dependence of Movement Outcomes: A Simplified Meta-Analysis." *Mobilization* 14:433–448.

Uba, Katrin and Fredrik Uggla. 2011. "Protest Actions Against the European Union, 1992–2007." *West European Politics* 34.

Valelly, Richard M. 1993. "Party, Coercion and Inclusion: The Two Reconstructions of the South's Electoral Politics." *Politics and Society* 21:37–68.

_____. 2004. *The Two Reconstructions: The Struggle for Black Enfranchisement*. Chicago, IL: University of Chicago Press.

Valocchi, Stephen. 1999. "Riding the Crest of a Protest Wave? Collective Action Frames in the Gay Liberation Movement, 1969–1973." *Mobilization* 59–73.

_____. 2008. "The Importance of Being 'We': Collective Identity and the Mobilizing Work of Progressive Activists in Hartford, Connecticut." *Mobilization* 14:65–84.

Van Dyke, Nella. 2003. "Crossing Movement Boundaries: Factors that Facilitate Coalition Protest by American College Students." *Social Problems* 50:226–250.

Varshney, Ashutosh. 2002. *Ethnic Conflict and Civic Life: Hindus and Muslims in India*. New Haven, CT: Yale University Press.

Vasi, Ion Bogdan. 2009. "Social Movements and Industry Development: The Environmental Movement's Impact on the Wind Energy Industry." *Mobilization* 14:315–336.

_____. 2011. "Brokerage, Miscibility and the Diffusion of Contention." *Mobilization* 16: forthcoming.

Vasi, Ion Bogdan and David Strang. 2009. "Civil Liberty in America: The Diffusion of Municipal Bill of Rights Resolutions After the Passage of the USA PATRIOT Act." *American Journal of Sociology* 116:1675–1715.

Vernus, Michel. 1989. "A Provincial Prospective." pp. 124–238 in *Revolution in Print: The Press in France, 1775–1800*, edited by R. Darnton and D. Roche. Berkeley, CA: University of California Press.

Vitale, Alex S. 2007. "The Command and Control and Miami Models at the Republican National Convention: New Forms of Policing Protest." *Mobilization* 12:403–415.

Von Bülow, Marisa. 2010. *Building Transnational Networks: Civil Society and the Politics of Trade in the Americas*. New York and Cambridge: Cambridge University Press.

Wada, Takeshi. 2007. "Demonstrating Repertoires of Contention." Unpublished paper. Columbia, MO: Department of Sociology, University of Missouri.

Waismel-Manor, Israel S. 2005. "Striking Differences: Hunger Strikes in Israel and the United States." *Social Movement Studies* 4:281–300.

Walgrave, Stefaan and Jan Manssens. 2000. "The Making of the White March: The Mass Media as a Mobilizing Alternative to Movement Organizations." *Mobilization* 5:217–239.

Walgrave, Stefaan and Dieter Rucht, ed. 2011. *Protest Politics: Antiwar Mobilization in Advanced Industrial Democracies*. Minneapolis and St. Paul: University of Minnesota Press.

Walker, Jack. 1991. *Mobilizing Interest Groups in America. Patrons, Professions, and Social Movements*. Ann Arbor: University of Michigan Press.

Walsh, Richard W. 1959. *Charleston's Sons of Liberty: A Study of the Artisans, 1763–1787*. New York: Columbia University Press.

Walzer, Michael. 1971. *Revolution of the Saints. A Study in the Origins of Radical Politics*. New York: Atheneum.

Wapner, Paul. 1996. *Environmental Activism and World Civil Politics*. Albany, NY: State University of New York Press.

Wareham, M. 1998. "Rhetoric and Policy Realities in the United States." Chap. 12 in *To Walk Without Fear, The Global Movement to Ban Landmines*, edited by M. A. Cameron, R. J. Lawson, and B. W. Tomlin. Toronto, Oxford, and New York: Oxford University Press.

Weinstein, Jeremy. 2006. *Inside Rebellion. The Politics of Insurgent Violence*. New York and Cambridge, MA: Cambridge University Press.

Weyland, Kurt. 2009. "The Diffusion of Revolution." *International Organization* 63:391–423.

Whittier, Nancy. 1995. *Feminist Generation*. Philadelphia, PA: Temple University Press.

Wickham-Crowley, Timothy. 1992. *Guerillas and Revolution in Latin America: A Comparative Study of Insurgents and Regimes Since 1956*. Princeton, NJ: Princeton University Press.

Wiest, Dawn R. and Jackie Smith. Forthcoming. *Social Movements and Global Change: Transnational Organizations from Decolonization through the Neoliberal Era. [working title]*. New York: Russell Sage Foundation.

Wilentz, Sean. 1984. *Chants Democratic: New York City and the Rise of the American Working Class, 1788–1850*. New York: Oxford University Press.

Williams, Heather. 2003. "Of Labor Tragedy and Legal Farce: The Han Young Factory Struggle in Tijuana, Mexico." *Social Science History* 27:525–550.

Williams, Jody and Stephen Goose. 1998. "The International Campaign to Ban Landmines." Chap. 2 in *To Walk Without Fear. The Global Movement to Ban Landmines*, edited by M. A. Cameron, R. J. Lawson, and B. W. Tomlin. Toronto, Oxford, and New York: Oxford University Press.

Wisotski, Simone. 2009. "Negotiating Human Security at the UN: Transnational Civil Society, Arms Control and Disarmament." Chap. 6 in *Transnational Activism in the UN and EU*, edited by J. Joachim and B. Locher. London and New York: Routledge.

Wood, Elisabeth Jean. 2000. *Forging Democracy From Below: Insurgent Transitions in South Africa and El Salvador*. New York and Cambridge: Cambridge University Press.

Wood, Gordon S. 1991. *The Radicalism of the American Revolution*. New York: Vintage

———. 2009. *Empire of Liberty: The Early Republic, 1789–1815*. New York and Oxford: Oxford University Press.

Wood, Lesley J. 2003. "Breaking the Bank and Taking to the Streets; How Protesters Target Neoliberalism." *Journal of World Systems Research* 10: 69–89.

———. 2004a. "Bridging the Chasms: The Case of People's Global Action." In *Coalitions Across Borders: Transnational Protest and the Neoliberal Order*, edited by J. Bandy and J. Smith. Lanham, MD: Rowman and Littlefield.

———. 2004b. "The Diffusion of Direct Action Tactics: From Seattle to Toronto and New York." Unpublished PhD Thesis. New York: Columbia University.

———. 2007. "Breaking the Wave: Repression, Identity, and Seattle Tactics." *Mobilization* 12:377–388.

Wright, Stuart A. 2007. *Patriots, Politics and the Oklahoma City Bombing.* New York and Cambridge, MA: Cambridge University Press.

Yeo, Andrew. 2009. "Not in Anyone's Backyard: The Emergence and Identity of a Transnational Anti-Base Network." *International Studies Quarterly* 53:571–594.

Zald, Mayer N. 1970. *Organizational Change: The Political Economy of the YMCA.* Chicago, IL: University of Chicago Press.

———. 2000. "Ideologically Structured Action: An Enlarged Agenda for Social Movement Research." *Mobilization* 5:1–16.

Zald, Mayer N. and Roberta Ash. 1966. "Social Movement Organizations: Growth, Decay and Change." *Social Forces* 44:327–341.

Zald, Mayer N. and Michael A. Berger. 1978. "Social Movements in Organizations: Coup d'Etat, Insurgency, and Mass Movements." *The American Journal of Sociology* 83:823–861.

Zald, Mayer N. and John McCarthy, eds. 1987. *Social Movements in an Organizational Society: Collected Essays.* New Brunswick, NJ: Transaction Books.

Zolberg, Aristide. 1972. "Moments of Madness." *Politics and Society* 2:183–207.

Index

315